DATE DUE

DEMCO 128-5046

SOMETHING ABOUT THE AUTHOR®

Something about
the Author *was named
an "Outstanding
Reference Source,"*
*the highest honor given
by the American
Library Association
Reference and Adult
Services Division.*

ISSN 0276-816X

something
ABOUT THe
AUTHOR®

Facts and Pictures about Authors
and Illustrators of Books for Young People

EDITED BY
ALAN HEDBLAD

VOLUME 92

GALE

DETROIT · NEW YORK · TORONTO · LONDON

STAFF

Editor: Alan Hedblad
Managing Editor: Joyce Nakamura
Publisher: Hal May
ate Editors: Joanna Brod, Sheryl Ciccarelli
Assistant Editor: Marilyn O'Connell Allen

Sketchwriters/Copyeditors: Linda R. Andres, Shelly Andrews,
Ronie Garcia-Johnson, Scott Gillam, Mary Gillis, Johanna Haaxma-Jurek, Janet L. Hile, Laurie Hillstrom,
Motoko Fujishiro Huthwaite, J. Sydney Jones, Pamela Nealon-LaBreck, Thomas F. McMahon, Susan Reicha,
Gerard J. Senick, Pamela L. Shelton, Diane Telgen, Michaela Swart, and Kathleen Witman

Research Manager: Victoria B. Cariappa
Project Coordinator: Cheryl L. Warnock
Research Associates: Laura C. Bissey, Tamara C. Nott,
Tracie A. Richardson, Norma Sawaya
Research Assistant: Alfred A. Gardner

Permissions Manager: Susan M. Trosky
Permissions Specialist: Maria L. Franklin
Permissions Associates: Edna M. Hedblad, Michele M. Lonoconus
Permissions Assistant: Andrea Grady

Production Director: Mary Beth Trimper
Production Assistant: Deborah Milliken

Macintosh Artist: Sherrell Hobbs
Image Database Supervisor: Randy Bassett
Imaging Specialists: Mikal Ansari and Robert Duncan
Photography Coordinator: Pamela A. Reed

Library of Congress Catalog Card Number 72-27107

ISBN 0-8103-9949-0 ISSN 0276-816X

Printed in the United States of America

10 9 8 7 6 5 4 3 2 1

Contents

Authors in Forthcoming Volumes

Below are some of the authors and illustrators that will be featured in upcoming volumes of *SATA*. These include new entries on the swiftly rising stars of the field, as well as completely revised and updated entries (indicated with *) on some of the most notable and best-loved creators of books for children.

Michael Bedard: Canadian writer Bedard is the award-winning author of mystery and suspense novels such as *Redwork, A Darker Magic* and *Painted Devil,* and also of well-received biographies and retellings for young people. Eclectic in subject matter, his unique works blend realism, fantasy, mystery, and elements of the psychological thriller.

Christopher Paul Curtis: Curtis won a 1996 Newbery honor and a host of other awards for *The Watsons Go to Birmingham—1963,* his story of a closely knit African-American family that travels down to the racially divided South during the civil rights era.

*Mel Glenn: Teacher and writer Glenn is noted for books that address the day-to-day concerns of teenagers in a unique manner—through poetry. His *Who Killed Mr. Chippendale? A Mystery in Poems* has been named to the American Library Association's 1997 list of Top Ten Best Books for Young Adults.

Nikki Grimes: A distinguished African-American poet, novelist, and biographer, Grimes has written a variety of books for young people, including a biography of Malcolm X and works of fiction and poetry that draw on her own childhood to convey the black experience while addressing universal themes such as friendship, tolerance, family and community relationships, and children surviving adolescence.

Sonya Hartnett: The novels of Australian writer Hartnett, although classified for a young adult readership, transcend the genre due to their psychological depth and sophistication. Called intense, and often devastating, her works, which include the award-winning *Sleeping Dogs, Wilful Blue,* and *The Devil Latch,* explore human character and the differences in the way individuals perceive the world around them.

*Mingfong Ho: In her critically acclaimed novels *Sing to the Dawn, Rice without Rain,* and *The Clay Marble,* Ho profiles young people in her native southeast Asia who are confronted with difficult political and social situations, including the corruption of government and the military as well as the oppression of women and the poor.

Mary E. Lyons: The author of several award-winning historical and biographical works for children, Lyons explores the importance and value of various underrepresented sources of American culture, particularly the contributions of women and African Americans.

Carol Matas: A Canadian writer of historical novels and other fiction for young readers, including the acclaimed works *Lisa's War, Daniel's Story,* and *After the War,* Matas is known for her hard-hitting stories that thrust adolescent protagonists into life and death situations while confronting readers with the vagaries and complexities of life.

Michael Morpurgo: Morpurgo is an English writer of novels and picture books for young readers. His works, including the critically esteemed stories *Why the Whales Came, Waiting for Anya,* and *The War of Jenkins' Ear,* blend elements of adventure, fantasy, history, and moral drama while focusing on themes of loyalty, hard work and determination.

Ruth Park: New Zealand-born Australian author Park has received international recognition for her work in a variety of genres over a career spanning four decades. In addition to her popular *Muddle-Headed Wombat* books for children, Park has written a number of well-received works for young adults, including the critically acclaimed novels *Playing Beatie Bow* and *My Sister Sif.*

*Maxine Rosenberg: The author of nonfiction for young people, Rosenberg has received numerous honors for her books, which focus on children in painful or otherwise challenging emotional and physical settings. Rosenberg's recent efforts include her works *On the Mend: Getting Away from Drugs, Living with a Single Parent,* and *Hiding to Survive: Stories of Jewish Children Rescued from the Holocaust.*

Introduction

Something about the Author (SATA) is an ongoing reference series that deals with the lives and works of authors and illustrators of children's books. *SATA* includes not only well-known authors and illustrators whose books are widely read, but also less prominent individuals whose works are just coming to be recognized. This series is often the only readily available information source on emerging writers and artists. You'll find *SATA* informative and entertaining, whether you are a student, a librarian, an English teacher, a parent, or simply an adult who enjoys children's literature.

What's Inside SATA

SATA provides detailed information about authors and illustrators who span the full time range of children's literature, from early figures like John Newbery and L. Frank Baum to contemporary figures like Judy Blume and Richard Peck. Authors in the series represent primarily English-speaking countries, particularly the United States, Canada, and the United Kingdom. Also included, however, are authors from around the world whose works are available in English translation. The writings represented in *SATA* include those created intentionally for children and young adults as well as those written for a general audience and known to interest younger readers. These writings cover the entire spectrum of children's literature, including picture books, humor, folk and fairy tales, animal stories, mystery and adventure, science fiction and fantasy, historical fiction, poetry and nonsense verse, drama, biography, and nonfiction.

Obituaries are also included in *SATA* and are intended not only as death notices but also as concise overviews of people's lives and work. Additionally, each edition features newly revised and updated entries for a selection of *SATA* listees who remain of interest to today's readers and who have been active enough to require extensive revisions of their earlier biographies.

Two Convenient Indexes

In response to suggestions from librarians, *SATA* indexes no longer appear in every volume but are included in alternate (odd-numbered) volumes of the series, beginning with Volume 57.

SATA continues to include two indexes that cumulate with each alternate volume: the Illustrations Index, arranged by the name of the illustrator, gives the number of the volume and page where the illustrator's work appears in the current volume as well as all preceding volumes in the series; the Author Index gives the number of the volume in which a person's Biographical Sketch or Obituary appears in the current volume as well as all preceding volumes in the series.

These indexes also include references to authors and illustrators who appear in Gale's *Yesterday's Authors of Books for Children, Children's Literature Review,* and the *Something about the Author Autobiography Series.*

Easy-to-Use Entry Format

Whether you're already familiar with the *SATA* series or just getting acquainted, you will want to be aware of the kind of information that an entry provides. In every *SATA* entry the editors attempt to give as complete a picture of the person's life and work as possible. A typical entry in *SATA* includes the following clearly labeled information sections:

- *PERSONAL:* date and place of birth and death, parents' names and occupations, name of spouse, date of marriage, names of children, educational institutions attended, degrees received, religious and political affiliations, hobbies and other interests.

- *ADDRESSES:* complete home, office, electronic mail, and agent addresses, whenever available.

- *CAREER:* name of employer, position, and dates for each career post; art exhibitions; military service; memberships and offices held in professional and civic organizations.

- *AWARDS, HONORS:* literary and professional awards received.

- *WRITINGS:* title-by-title chronological bibliography of books written and/or illustrated, listed by genre when known; lists of other notable publications, such as plays, screenplays, and periodical contributions.

- *ADAPTATIONS:* a list of films, television programs, plays, CD-ROMs, recordings, and other media presentations that have been adapted from the author's work.

- *WORK IN PROGRESS:* description of projects in progress.

- *SIDELIGHTS:* a biographical portrait of the author or illustrator's development, either directly from the biographee—and often written specifically for the *SATA* entry—or gathered from diaries, letters, interviews, or other published sources.

- *FOR MORE INFORMATION SEE:* references for further reading.

- *EXTENSIVE ILLUSTRATIONS:* photographs, movie stills, book illustrations, and other interesting visual materials supplement the text.

How a SATA Entry Is Compiled

A *SATA* entry progresses through a series of steps. If the biographee is living, the *SATA* editors try to secure information directly from him or her through a questionnaire. From the information that the biographee supplies, the editors prepare an entry, filling in any essential missing details with research and/or telephone interviews. If possible, the author or illustrator is sent a copy of the entry to check for accuracy and completeness.

If the biographee is deceased or cannot be reached by questionnaire, the *SATA* editors examine a wide variety of published sources to gather information for an entry. Biographical and bibliographic sources are consulted, as are book reviews, feature articles, published interviews, and material sometimes obtained from the biographee's family, publishers, agent, or other associates.

Entries that have not been verified by the biographees or their representatives are marked with an asterisk (*).

Contact the Editor

We encourage our readers to examine the entire *SATA* series. Please write and tell us if we can make *SATA* even more helpful to you. Give your comments and suggestions to the editor:

BY MAIL: The Editor, *Something about the Author,* Gale Research, 835 Penobscot Bldg., 645 Griswold St., Detroit, MI 48226-4094.

BY TELEPHONE: (800) 347-GALE

BY FAX: (313) 961-6599

BY E-MAIL: CYA@Gale.com@Galesmtp

Acknowledgments

Grateful acknowledgment is made to the following publishers, authors, and artists whose works appear in this volume.

ACKERMAN, SUSAN YODER. Ackerman, Susan Yoder, photograph. Reproduced by permission of Susan Yoder Ackerman.

AMATO, CAROL A. Amato, Carol A., photograph. Reproduced by permission of Carol A. Amato.

ASPRIN, ROBERT. Ruddell, Gary, illustrator. From a cover of *Time Scout,* by Robert Asprin and Linda Evans. Baen, 1995. Copyright © 1995 by Bill Fawcett & Associates. Reproduced by permission. / Warhola, James, illustrator. From a cover of *Phule's Company,* by Robert Asprin. Ace Books, 1990. Copyright © 1990 by Robert Asprin. Reproduced by permission of The Berkley Publishing Group.

BARDELL, GRAHAM. Bardell, Graham, photograph. Reproduced by permission of Graham Bardell.

BARRETT, ROBERT. Barrett, Robert, photograph. Reproduced by permission of Robert Barrett.

BENDER, EDNA. Bender, Edna, photograph. Reproduced by permission of Edna Bender.

BIRCHMORE, DANIEL A. Birchmore, Daniel A., photograph. Reproduced by permission of Daniel A. Birchmore.

BLEGEN, DANIEL M. Blegen, Daniel M., photograph. Reproduced by permission of Daniel M. Blegen.

BOGART, JO ELLEN. Bogart, Jo Ellen, photograph. Reproduced by permission of Jo Ellen Bogart. / Illustration by Barbara Reid from *Gifts,* by Jo Ellen Bogart. North Winds Press, 1994. Text copyright © 1994 by Jo Ellen Bogart. Illustrations copyright © 1994 by Barbara Reid. Reproduced by permission.

BULLOCK, ROBERT. Bullock, Robert, photograph. Reproduced by permission of Robert Bullock.

BULPIN, VICKI. Bulpin, Vicki, photograph. Reproduced by permission of Vicki Bulpin.

BURNS, KHEPHRA. Burns, Khephra, photograph. Reproduced by permission of Khephra Burns.

CALLEY, KARIN. Calley, Karin, photograph. Reproduced by permission of Karin Calley.

CARLSTROM, NANCY WHITE. Illustration by Bruce Degan from *Let's Count It Out, Jesse Bear,* by Nancy White Carlstrom. Simon & Schuster Books for Young Readers, 1996. Text copyright © 1996 Nancy White Carlstrom. Illustrations copyright © 1996 Bruce Degan. Reproduced by permission of Simon & Schuster Books for Young Readers, a division of Simon & Schuster, Inc. / Carlstrom, Nancy White, photograph. Reproduced by permission of Nancy White Carlstrom. / Dillon, Leo, and Diane Dillon, illustrators. From a jacket of *Northern Lullaby,* by Nancy White Carlstrom. Philomel, 1992. Reproduced by permission of Philomel Books. / Illustration by Sucie Stevenson from *Baby-O,* by Nancy White Carlstrom. Little, Brown, 1992. Text copyright © 1992 by Nancy White Carlstrom. Illustrations copyright © 1992 by Sucie Stevenson. Reproduced by permission of Sucie Stevenson.

CHANDONNET, ANN. Chandonnet, Ann, photograph by Judy Ferguson. Reproduced by permission of Ann Chandonnet.

CHESS, VICTORIA. Chess, Victoria, photograph. Reproduced by permission of Victoria Chess. / Illustration by Victoria Chess from *Good Night Dinosaurs,* by Judy Sierra. Clarion Books, 1996. Illustrations copyright © 1996 by Victoria Chess. Reproduced by permission of Houghton Mifflin Company. / Illustration by Victoria Chess from *The Bigness Contest,* by Florence Parry Heide. Little, Brown, 1994. Illustrations copyright © 1994 by Victoria Chess. Reproduced by permission of Little, Brown and Company.

CLIFFORD, ETH. Apple, Margot, illustrator. From a cover of *Harvey's Mystifying Raccoon Mix-Up,* by Eth Clifford. Houghton Mifflin, 1994. Jacket art © 1994 by Margot Apple. Reproduced by permission of Houghton Mifflin Company. / Clifford, Eth, photograph. Reproduced by permission of Eth Clifford Rosenberg. / Cover of *Never Hit a Ghost with a Baseball Bat,* by Eth Clifford. Apple Paperbacks, 1993. Reproduced by permission. / Coville, Kathy, illustrator. From a cover of *The Remembering Box,* by Eth Clifford. Beech Tree Books, 1992. Cover illustration copyright © 1992 by Kathy Coville. Reproduced by permission of Beech Tree Books, a division of William Morrow and Company, Inc. / Illustration by Brian Lies from *Flatfoot Fox and the Case of the Bashful Beaver,* by Eth Clifford. Houghton Mifflin, 1995. Illustrations copyright © 1995 by Brian Lies. Reproduced by permission of Houghton Mifflin Company.

COTTONWOOD, JOE. Cover of *Quake!,* by Joe Cottonwood. Apple Paperbacks, 1995. Copyright © 1995 by Joe Cottonwood. Reproduced by permission. / Cover of *The Adventures of Boone Barnaby,* by Joe Cottonwood. Scholastic Inc., 1990. Copyright © 1990 by Joe Cottonwood. Reproduced by permission.

by permission of Sandra Scoppettone.

SHAHAN, SHERRY. Shahan, Sherry, photograph. Reproduced by permission of Sherry Shahan.

SHOWERS, PAUL. Chewning, Randy, illustrator. From a cover of *Where Does the Garbage Go?* by Paul Showers. HarperCollins Publishers, 1994. Cover art © 1994 by Randy Chewning. Reproduced by permission of HarperCollins Publishers, Inc. / Illustration by Aliki Brandenberg from *The Listening Walk,* by Paul Showers. HarperCollins Publishers, 1991. Text copyright © 1961, 1991 by Paul Showers. Illustrations copyright © 1961, 1991 by Aliki Brandenberg. Reproduced by permission of HarperCollins Publishers, Inc. / Showers, Paul C., photograph. Reproduced by permission of Paul C. Showers.

SILVERSTEIN, SHEL. Illustration by Shel Silverstein from *The Giving Tree,* by Shel Silverstein. Harper & Row, Publishers, 1964. Copyright © 1964 by Shel Silverstein. Reproduced by permission of HarperCollins Publishers, Inc. / Illustration by Shel Silverstein from *Falling Up,* by Shel Silverstein. HarperCollins Publishers, 1996. Copyright © 1996 by Shel Silverstein. Reproduced by permission of HarperCollins Publishers, Inc. / Silverstein, Shel, photograph. Reproduced by permission of Shel Silverstein.

SPOONER, MICHAEL. Cover of *A Moon in Your Lunch Box,* by Michael Spooner. Redfeather Books, 1993. Reproduced by permission of Henry Holt and Company, Inc. / Spooner, Michael, photograph by Sylvia Reed. Reproduced by permission of Michael Spooner.

STEWART, WHITNEY. Stewart, Whitney, photograph. Reproduced by permission of Whitney Stewart.

THOMAS, FRANCES. Thomas, Frances, photograph by Richard Rathbone. Reproduced by permission of Frances Thomas.

THOMASSIE, TYNIA. Thomassie, Tynia, photograph. Reproduced by permission of Tynia Thomassie.

TWINEM, NEECY. Twinem, Neecy, photograph by Cynthia Reisenauer. Reproduced by permission of Neecy Twinem.

VANSANT, RHONDA JOY EDWARDS. Vansant, Rhonda Joy Edwards, photograph. Reproduced by permission of Rhonda Joy Edwards Vansant.

WEIS, MARGARET. Weis, Margaret, photograph by Peggy A. Murphy. Austin Studio. Reproduced by permission of Margaret Weis. / Youll, Stephen, illustrator. From a jacket of *The Seventh Gate,* by Margaret Weis and Tracy Hickman. Bantam Books, 1994. Jacket illustration © 1994 Stephen Youll. Reproduced by permission of Bantam Books, a division of Bantam Doubleday Dell Publishing Group, Inc.

WOOLDRIDGE, CONNIE NORDHIELM. Wooldridge, Connie Nordhielm, photograph. Reproduced by permission of Connie Nordhielm Wooldridge.

YAMAKA, SARA. Yamaka, Sara, photograph by Wendy Sothoron. Reproduced by permission of Sara Yamaka.

YATES, PHILIP. Yates, Philip, photograph. Reproduced by permission of Philip Yates.

ZONDERMAN, JON. Zonderman, Jon, photograph by David Ottenstein. Reproduced by permission of Jon Zonderman.

SOMETHING ABOUT THE AUTHOR®

ACKERMAN, Susan Yoder 1945-

■ Personal

Born November 2, 1945, in Newport News, VA; daughter of Lauren A. (a dairy business owner) and Nina Viola (a homemaker; maiden name, Stemen) Yoder; married Robert W. Ackerman II (in business administration), July 2, 1969; children: Ilse Lieve, Hans Christian, Elsbeth Anje. *Education:* Attended Eastern Mennonite College, 1962-64; College of William and Mary, B.A., 1968; graduate study at University of Virginia, Longwood College, and Hampton University. *Religion:* Christian.

■ Addresses

Home and office—524 Marlin Dr., Newport News, VA 23602. *Electronic mail*—sackerma@pen.K12.va.us.

■ Career

Elementary school teacher, Newport News, VA, 1966-67, 1972; teacher of English as a foreign language, Lubumbashi, Zaire, 1969-70, and Kongolo, Zaire, 1979-80; high school English teacher, Dunn, NC, 1970-72; middle and high school French teacher, Newport News, 1984-86, 1989-96. Day care director, Newport News, 1989-90. Speaker on African experiences and on writing; leader of workshops on writing juvenile fiction. *Member:* Foreign Language Association of Virginia.

SUSAN YODER ACKERMAN

■ Writings

Copper Moons, Herald Press, 1990.
The Flying Pie and Other Stories, Herald Press, 1996.

Contributor of stories and articles to periodicals, including *CRICKET, On the Line, With, Instructor, Story Friends, Christian Living, Purpose, Together,* and *Live.* Also contributor to McGraw-Hill testing materials.

■ Work in Progress

"More personal experiences in Africa; further collections of children's stories; researching and compiling a book of letters, documents, drawings, and other primary sources covering one hundred years of the Mennonite community I grew up in."

■ Sidelights

Susan Yoder Ackerman told *SATA:* "I used to dream of writing fantasy. But real life kept happening in such compelling detail that so far I haven't needed to bring out the wild imagination.... A baby crow swallows the tweezers my daughter is using to feed him.... An elephant chases us out of a swimming pool.... My teasing brother tries to use a lemon meringue pie to illustrate centripetal force and something goes wrong. These stories crowd to the forefront, and I take pleasure in sharing them.

"My great-grandfather was a poet, an oxymoron in a Mennonite community where hard, practical work was encouraged and flights of fancy frowned on. His son, my grandfather, published his own memoirs at eighty-eight and left me with the house he built nearly one hundred years ago. I can place my computer on the old roll-top desk, look out the window into honeysuckle and wild roses, and by writing, make peace with the Yoder ghosts of death, birth, love, and practical jokes!

"So much for roots ... what about wings? My fiance had been working as a volunteer in the Congo when he asked me to fly out and marry him. Thus began a series of adventures that still beg to be written. *Copper Moons* describes that first year. I knew I had done something right when a man called to say he had to stay home from work the day after reading the book—the story had stirred up so many memories of his own African experience!

"A total of eight years in Africa furnished me with more material as well as more writing time than I've ever found while back in Virginia where teaching French skims the cream off my energy and time. But at least I no longer write manuscripts by hand in the heat of a glowing Aladdin lamp to the whine of mosquitoes!"

AMATO, Carol A. 1942-

■ Personal

Born April 18, 1942, in Hamden, CT; daughter of Carl and Flora (Maturo) Ardito; married Philip P. Amato (a professor), August 20, 1966; children: Maria Amato Coates, Nicole. *Education:* Emerson College, B.A., 1964; Boston University, M.Ed., 1965. *Hobbies and other interests:* Nature photography, writing and reading poetry, outdoor sports including cycling, swimming, cross country skiing, and jogging, bird watching, and nature workshops and programs.

■ Addresses

Office—c/o Barron's Educational Series, 250 Wireless Blvd., Hauppauge, NY 11788.

■ Career

Language and learning specialist in the Boston area, 1965—. Volunteer at the New England Aquarium, Massachusetts Audubon at Wellfleet Bay, the Museum of Natural History, Cape Cod, and the Cape Cod Aquarium. *Member:* Authors Guild, Authors League of America, National Science Teachers Association, American Speech, Hearing, and Language Association, National Wildlife Federation, Massachusetts Audubon, Massachusetts Marine Educators Association, Arnold Arboretum, Save the Manatee Club, Northeast Hawk Watch Association, Center for Children's Environmental Writing.

■ Awards, Honors

Award from Roger Tory Peterson Notable Nature Club, 1992; award from Massachusetts Audubon; second prize, Juried Nature Photography Contest, 1994.

■ Writings

"YOUNG READERS' SERIES"; PUBLISHED BY BARRON'S EDUCATIONAL SERIES

The Truth about Sharks, 1995.
Captain Jim and the Killer Whales, illustrated by Patrick O'Brien, 1995.
To Be a Wolf, illustrated by Patrick O'Brien and David Wenzel, 1995.
Raising Ursa, 1996.
Adios, Chi Chi: The Adventures of a Tarantula, illustrated by David Wenzel, 1996.
The Bald Eagle: Free Again!, 1996.
Penguins of the Galapagos, 1996.
On the Trail of the Grizzly, illustrated by Patrick O'Brien, 1997.
Chessie's Most Excellent Adventure, in press.

■ Work in Progress

Bianca, the story of a piglet who is carried away by a tornado; a book about armadillos; a book about horseshoe crabs.

CAROL A. AMATO

■ Sidelights

Carol A. Amato told *SATA:* "As a very young child, I was fascinated by the rhythms of language. When I was three years old, I would sit on my bed (so my mother told me) and recite poems I made up aloud ('Oh look at the pigs, how dirty they are. They all look like a candy bar') while she hid behind the door writing down my words. Then she would send them to the local newspaper to be published in the poetry column. (They must have been short of adult poets!) So, early on, I was encouraged to write and praised for my efforts, I was also read to daily, before the days of picture books. This wonderful daily ritual allowed my imagination and appetite for words to grow.

"I was an introspective child, and writing gave me a means for self-expression and provided the attention I needed but was too shy to seek. I also spent most of my time outside, discovering all the wonders of nature from wild bunnies and white-footed mice to ants and caterpillars! Although I grew up in two city suburbs of Connecticut, I managed to find green, happy places by exploring far from home by foot or my faithful blue Columbia!

"I wrote all through high school and college, most often poetry and usually just for myself. I wanted desperately to be a writer, but grew up in the days when this was considered an inappropriate career for a woman. Freelance writing is still a dream for most writers, male *or* female, except for those who have come into an inheritance or won the lottery!

"Because I was still interested in language, I studied to be a speech and language pathologist and received a Masters degree in childhood aphasia, a neurological disorder affecting receptive and expressive language. As a young adult, I continued to write primarily poetry and was published in a few journals and magazines. Busy with a career and family, I didn't have much time to pursue my writing dreams. However, I never lost my love of the natural world and the out-of-doors. Through the years I became a member of many wildlife organizations and attended as many workshops and programs that I could fit into my schedule. I also volunteered at Audubon sanctuaries and local aquariums both in Boston and on Cape Cod, where we now have a summer home. I'm an avid nature photographer and have won prizes for my wildlife and landscape photos.

"Through the years as a language-learning specialist, I developed and implemented a life-science program for children with learning difficulties. In later years, I brought this program to the Boston public schools, funded by a grant. I am now presenting this program in other schools as well. An additional workshop teaches students about nonfiction writing, using my science workshop methods.

"The objectives of both my programs and the Young Readers' series are to encourage parents and teachers to develop inquiry skills in their children that make learning non-threatening and challenging, and to enable them to help children to retain their innate sense of wonder and joy in discovery learning. I also hope to promote a love and appreciation of all living things and to convey the urgency of our role in the conservation and preservation of our fragile environment."*

*   *   *

ASPRIN, Robert L(ynn) 1946-

■ Personal

Born June 28, 1946, in St. Johns, MI; son of Daniel D. (a machinist) and Lorraine (an elementary school teacher; maiden name, Coon) Asprin; married Anne Brett (a bookkeeper), December 28, 1968; children: Annette Maria, Daniel Mather. *Education:* Attended University of Michigan, 1964-65.

■ Career

University Microfilm, Ann Arbor, MI, accounts payable clerk, 1966-69, accounts receivable correspondent, 1969-70, payroll-labor analyst, 1970-74; junior cost accountant, 1974-76, cost accountant, 1976-78; freelance writer, 1978—. *Military service:* U.S. Army, 1965-66. *Member:* Science Fiction Writers of America.

■ Writings

SCIENCE FICTION NOVELS

The Cold Cash War, St. Martin's (New York City), 1977.

The Bug Wars, St. Martin's, 1979.

The Star Stalkers, Playboy Press, 1979.

(With George Takei) *Mirror Friend, Mirror Foe,* Playboy Press, 1979.

Tambu, Ace Books (New York City), 1979.

Tambu Anthology (short fiction), Ace Books, 1980.

(With Lynn Abbey) *Act of God,* Ace Books, 1980.

(With Bill Fawcett) *Cold Cash Warrior,* Ace Books, 1989.

Phule's Company, Ace Books, 1990.

Phule's Paradise, Ace Books, 1992.

(With Lynn Abbey) *Catwoman: Tiger Hunt,* Warner (New York City), 1992.

(With Linda Evans) *Time Scout,* Baen, 1995.

Wagers of Sin, Baen, 1996.

FANTASY NOVELS

Another Fine Myth, Donning (Norfolk, VA), 1978, revised edition, illustrated by Phil Foglio, 1985.

Myth Conceptions, illustrated by Polly and Kelly Freas, Donning, 1980.

The Demon Blade, St. Martin's, 1980.

Myth Directions, illustrated by Phil Foglio, Donning, 1982.

Hit or Myth, illustrated by Foglio, Donning, 1983.

Myth Adventures (includes *Another Fine Myth, Myth Directions,* and *Hit or Myth*), Doubleday (Garden City, NY), 1984.

Myth-ing Persons, illustrated by Phil Foglio, Donning, 1984.

Little Myth Marker, illustrated by Foglio, Donning, 1985.

(With Kay Reynolds) *M.Y.T.H. Inc. Link,* illustrated by Foglio, Donning, 1986.

Myth Alliances (includes *Myth-ing Persons, Little Myth Marker,* and *M.Y.T.H. Inc. Link*), Doubleday, 1987.

Myth-Nomers and Im-Pervections, illustrated by Foglio, Donning, 1987.

M.Y.T.H. Inc. in Action, illustrated by Foglio, Donning, 1990.

Sweet Myth-tery of Life, illustrated by Foglio, Donning, 1994.

GRAPHIC NOVELS

(With Phil Foglio) *Myth Adventures One* (previously published in magazine form), art by Foglio, Starblaze Graphics (Norfolk, VA), 1985.

(With Foglio) *Myth Adventures Two* (previously published in magazine form), art by Foglio, Starblaze Graphics, 1985.

(With Mel White) *Duncan and Mallory,* Starblaze Graphics, 1986.

(With Lynn Abbey) *Thieves' World Graphics,* art by Tim Sales, 6 volumes, Starblaze Graphics, 1985-87.

(With Mel White) *Duncan and Mallory: The Bar-None Ranch,* Starblaze Graphics, 1987.

(With White) *Duncan and Mallory: The Raiders,* Starblaze Graphics, 1988.

EDITOR

Thieves' World, Ace Books, 1979.

Tales from the Vulgar Unicorn, Ace Books, 1980.

Shadows of Sanctuary, Ace Books, 1981.

Sanctuary (includes *Thieves' World, Tales from the Vulgar Unicorn,* and *Shadows of Sanctuary*), Doubleday, 1982.

Storm Season, Ace Books, 1982.

(With Lynn Abbey) *The Face of Chaos,* Ace Books, 1983.

(With Abbey) *Wings of Omen,* Ace Books, 1984.

(With Abbey) *Birds of Prey,* Ace Books, 1984.

(With Abbey) *Cross-Currents* (includes *Storm Season, The Face of Chaos,* and *Wings of Omen*), Doubleday, 1984.

(With Abbey) *The Dead of Winter,* Ace Books, 1985.

(With Abbey) *Soul of the City,* Ace Books, 1986.

(With Abbey) *Blood Ties,* Ace Books, 1986.

(With Abbey) *The Shattered Sphere* (includes *The Dead of Winter, Soul of the City,* and *Blood Ties*), Doubleday, 1986.

(With Abbey and Richard Pini) *The Blood of Ten Chiefs,* Tor (New York City), 1986.

(With Abbey) *Aftermath,* Ace Books, 1987.

(With Abbey and Pini) *Wolfsong: The Blood of Ten Chiefs,* Tor, 1988.

(With Abbey) *Uneasy Alliances,* Ace Books, 1988.

(With Abbey) *Stealers' Sky,* Ace Books, 1989.

(With Abbey) *The Price of Victory* (includes *Aftermath, Uneasy Alliances,* and *Stealers' Sky*), Doubleday, 1990.

OTHER

The Capture (script for comedy slide show), Boojums Press, 1975.

■ Adaptations

Several of Asprin's novels have been recorded on cassette tape.

■ Sidelights

With both science fiction and fantasy novels, as well as the script of several graphic novels to his credit, author Robert L. Asprin commands a loyal following of both teen and adult readers. Getting his start as an author of science fiction during the mid-1970s, Asprin quickly began a move toward the fantasy genre with such novels as *Another Fine Myth, Myth Conceptions,* and 1985's *Little Myth Marker.* As the titles alone should make clear to a reader unfamiliar with his work, Asprin liberally garnishes his writing with a full dose of farce, deliberately leaden puns, and blatant parody. Comparing his work to that of author L. Sprague de Camp, Richard A. Lupoff comments in the *St. James Guide to Science Fiction Writers* on the "typical Asprin characteristics of rapid pace, slapstick action, and broad humor."

The Cold Cash War was Asprin's first published novel. Drawing from his personal background working as a financial analyst in a large U.S. corporation, Asprin wove a futuristic tale about mega-corporations that behave like nations: they wage bloodless "warfare" on each other using war-game simulations. Ignoring the efforts of actual governments to stop them, these moneyed superpowers eventually lose control of the game when real weapons enter the picture and the hits become lethal. Calling it a "very good treatment of a SF concept popular in the 50s," a *Publishers Weekly* reviewer praised *The Cold Cash War*'s "satire, action, and character."

Asprin's second novel found him mapping terrain in a different genre: fantasy. *Another Fine Myth*, published in 1978, was inspired by such heroic characters as Kane and Conan the Barbarian, and Asprin leapt into the project with relish. Basing his two main characters—an apprentice wizard named Skeeve (who also serves as narrator) and his shifty-eyed cohort, Aahz—on the relationship between Bob Hope and Bing Crosby in their classic screwball "Road" films of the 1940s, Asprin developed a winning duo whose antics have fuelled an entire series of humorous "Myth" books, in addition to spinoff graphic novels. In 1983's *Hit or Myth* the two come up against both a gang of criminals with assorted magical powers and the avaricious Queen Hemlock; dragons, demons, and an amazing assortment of fantastic ne'er-do-wells keep Asprin's fumbling heroes on their toes throughout other "Myth" books. While the series provides little in the way of the high-tech hijinks that appeal to some sci-fi followers, its lighthearted tone and steady barrage of puns, jokes, and bumbling antics have made it an entertaining read. "Asprin isn't trying to be profound," Tom Easton noted in a review in *Analog Science Fiction/Science Fact*. "He's having fun."

In his continuing effort to keep the job of writing fun, Asprin has strived to keep his subject matter from becoming stale. As he once noted, "my first three books are intentionally dissimilar. *The Cold Cash War* is speculative near-future fiction involving corporate takeover of world government. *Another Fine Myth* is a sword-and-sorcery farce full of dragons, stranded demons, and very bad puns. *The Bug Wars* does not have a human in the entire book. It was written 'first-person alien, reptile to be specific' and has been one of my greatest writing challenges to date." In addition to novel-writing, Asprin also branched out into editing; collaborating with fellow editor and writer Lynn Abbey, to produce the popular series "Thieves' World." In addition to novel-writing, Asprin also branched out into editing, collaborating with fellow editor and writer Lynn Abbey to produce the popular series "Thieves' World." Called "the toughest, seamiest backwater in the realm of fantasy" by *Voice of Youth Advocates* reviewer Carolyn Caywood, the highly acclaimed "Thieves' World" anthology series brings together a collection of original short fiction written by a host of predominately women writers, including Abbey, Janet Morris, and C. J. Cherryh. Each book in the series centers around the ongoing struggle between the evil Queen Roxanne and her nemesis, a blood-sucking enchantress named Ischade. The continuing battle between these two powerful witches continues through such collections as *Soul of the City* and *Blood Ties,* each of which takes place in a mythic city called Sanctuary.

Asprin has characterized the overall message behind his writing as "the case for Everyman. Like all science

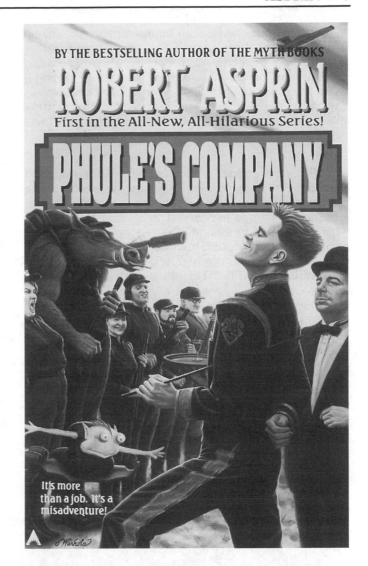

Demoted to lead a misfit company on a remote planet, Captain Willard Phule is earth's only hope to defeat a threatening enemy in Robert L. Asprin's science fiction comedy. (Cover illustration by James Warhola.)

fiction writers, I promote space travel and development. I feel, however, that we will never see it until the average guy on the street can see a place for himself in space. We will have to have the support of the common man, not just the scientists and test pilots." In 1979's *Tambu,* for example, Asprin assembles what he believes is a realistic crew for a spaceship. A renegade spaceworker who starts a kind of intra-stellar mafia, Tambu and this rough and ready crew use their collective street smarts to protect client planets from space pirates. Calling *Tambu* an "action-filled tale of how power corrupts," Claudia Morner notes in *School Library Journal* that Asprin's unusual sci-fi adventure yarn holds a great appeal for YA readers. "It is not only co-educational," the author explained of *Tambu;* "there are several racial types, ages ranging from teens to old-timers, and a wide cross-section of educational backgrounds. That is what life on Earth is all about, and that is what it is going to be like in space." Reflecting aspects of human reality within his fantasy has always been Asprin's goal; he maintains that the science fiction writer can be instrumental in changing the public's awareness of the amazing possibilities presented by travel to other worlds. "We are going to need grease monkeys as well as computer programmers," he once noted. "Few people see themselves as Superman, and as long as science fiction writers portray space travelers in that light, the taxpayers and voters could not care less about getting off the planet."

In 1990 Asprin added a new hero to his catalogue of space adventurers with *Phule's Company.* Willard Phule is a captain in the Space Legion, but his devil-may-care attitude soon finds him exiled to a remote command, where he is put in charge of a rag-tag band of fellow miscreants. Undaunted, the savvy Phule eventually shapes his troops into a highly effective—and profitable—military outfit. "This lighthearted tale is part science fiction, part spoof, part heart-warmer," noted a *Publishers Weekly* critic of the novel, which would be followed in 1992 by the sequel, *Phule's Paradise.*

Although he has retired from his unique occupation of guiding vacationers traveling through time, Kit Carson finds himself back in action when his granddaughter ventures through a dangerous gate to the past.

Another novel leaning more towards sci fi than fantasy is Asprin's *Time Scout,* which he co-wrote with Linda Evans. Taking place in the near future, the 1995 novel features a world where time travel has become a common vacation pastime. Kit Carson, a retired "time scout"—one of the daring explorers who enter new passages through time in advance of the commonfolk—must train his headstrong granddaughter to survive as the first female time scout. Calling the novel "engaging, fast moving, historically literate," and reflective of Asprin's broad knowledge of the martial arts, *Booklist* reviewer Roland Green dubbed *Time Scout* "first-class action sf."

"Philippine-Irish in ancestry, I look like a stereotyped revolutionary (which I'm not)," Asprin once commented. His offbeat "look" is reflective of several of his hobbies, which include a broad study of the martial arts. Fencing and coaching foil-, saber-, and epee-wielding, he has also served as divisional vice-chairman of the Amateur Fencing League of America. "Furthermore, I have studied the Japanese, Okinawan, and Chinese forms of armed and unarmed combat," Asprin added, "and am passable with firearms and archery. To round out the picture, I was active for several years in the Society for Creative Anachronism, which practices full-force combat with mock-ups of swords, spears, axes, and maces. As Yang the Nauseating, I organized and ran a 'household' patterned after a Mongol horde."

Fortunately, Asprin continues to take time away from his many hobbies to settle down and write. His creative side has also found other outlets: the raising and breeding of tropical fish, acting in several amateur stage productions, and playing folk guitar. But "I am first and foremost a storyteller," he will admit. Influenced by a youthful diet of action-adventure novels, Asprin has found the science fiction and fantasy genres to be another excellent outlet for both his interests and his imagination, ensuring that his novels are dependably lighthearted and entertaining. "I find long, drawn-out descriptions of explanations of mathematical theorems to be extremely boring," Asprin explains, "and therefore exclude them from my own stories. You do not have to know how to build a clock to tell time, or understand a jet engine to ride in a plane."

■ Works Cited

Caywood, Carolyn, review of *Soul of the City, Voice of Youth Advocates,* June, 1986, p. 84.

Review of *The Cold Cash War, Publishers Weekly,* July 11, 1977, p. 75.

Easton, Tom, review of *Hit or Myth, Analog Science Fiction/Science Fact,* October, 1984, p. 147.

Green, Roland, review of *Time Scout, Booklist,* January 15, 1995, p. 689.

Lupoff, Richard A., "Robert Lynn Asprin," in *St. James Guide to Science Fiction Writers,* St. James Press, 1995, pp. 35-37.

Morner, Claudia, review of *Tambu, School Library Journal,* March, 1980, p. 146.

Review of *Phule's Company, Publishers Weekly,* June 8, 1990, p. 50.

■ **For More Information See**

PERIODICALS

Analog Science Fiction-Science Fact, September, 1987, p. 163; February, 1991, p. 181.
Booklist, December 1, 1977, p. 598; January 15, 1984, p. 715; April 1, 1986, p. 1120; March 15, 1987, p. 1097; June 15, 1990, p. 1960; January 15, 1992, pp. 915, 921; December 15, 1995, p. 689.

Library Journal, November 1, 1977, p. 2279; January 15, 1980, p. 228.
Publishers Weekly, January 20, 1992, p. 60.
Voice of Youth Advocates, April 1981, p. 52; February 1987, p. 290; December 1987, p. 241.*

*   *   *

AXTON, David
See KOONTZ, Dean R(ay)

B

BALDWIN, Margaret
See WEIS, Margaret (Edith)

* * *

BARDELL, Graham

■ Personal

Born in Hamilton, Ontario, Canada. *Education:* Attended Montreal Museum of Fine Arts School of Art and Design and Ecole des Beaux-Arts, Montreal.

■ Addresses

Home and office—448 Spadina Rd., Apt. 408, Toronto, Ontario M5P 2W4, Canada.

■ Career

Illustrator/designer, Y & M Studio (advertising), Montreal, Quebec; contract illustrator, *Montreal Star* (newspaper), Montreal; freelance illustrator, *Globe & Mail* (newspaper), Toronto, Ontario; illustrator, Pronk and Associates (book designers), Toronto. Teacher of illustration and design, Montreal Museum of Fine Arts School.

■ Illustrator

Hereward Allix, *The Maladjusted Jungle,* Oxford University Press (Canada), 1991.

(And author) *Columbus's Cat,* Maxwell Macmillan (Canada), 1992.

Robynne Eagan, *Colours,* W. J. Gage (Scarborough, Canada), 1993.

Carolyn Jackson, *The Flying Ark,* W. H. Freeman (New York), 1995.

■ Work in Progress

Writing and illustrating two dog stories—*Blot* and *The Disappearing Dandy.*

GRAHAM BARDELL

■ Sidelights

Graham Bardell told *SATA:* "In Montreal, my first major projects for children were illustrations for three Christmas television specials and several stories for a weekly magazine. I enjoyed it so much that, since moving to Toronto, illustrating for children has developed into one of my main interests.

"It's difficult to say whether I've been influenced by any particular artist's style because I admire the work of so many. However, among those I respect most are the illustrators who not only bring alive the characters and action of a story but add something extra. It is well-researched details of the time and place that are not necessarily described in the story but add immeasurably to the telling.

"As an incurable animal lover, doing the illustrations for *The Flying Ark,* written by Carolyn Jackson and published by W. H. Freeman, was sheer pleasure. I read everything available on the personalities, habits, and anatomies of the animals and sketched them at the zoo. Beginning with reality, then slightly warping it, turned the animals into real characters rather than cartoons, which I felt was in keeping with a text that was both informative and amusing.

"My other interests are: cooking, reading (mysteries to historical), writing, antiques, architecture, plants, and interiors. Not surprisingly, any new interest quickly turns into research and, inevitably, becomes part of an illustration or an idea for a story.

"When writing a children's story, I'm learning to eliminate anything that can be 'said' more efficiently in a drawing. For example, 'Spot was born in a large wooden box, beside an old wood stove in Mr. Jones's bright blue country kitchen' becomes 'Spot was born in a box in Mr. Jones's kitchen,' which is more to the point and easier to read. The illustration will contain all the other elements, and I am free to use any colors that are appropriate. This switching from writer to illustrator can become confusing, but, as they say, 'it works for me.'"

■ For More Information See

PERIODICALS

Books in Canada, October, 1992, p. 50.
Canadian Materials, October, 1992, p. 261.
Quill & Quire, June, 1992, p. 34.
Scientific American, December, 1990, p. 137.

*   *   *

BARRETT, Robert T(heodore) 1949-

■ Personal

Born May 13, 1949, in Salt Lake City, UT; son of Theodore (an engineer) and Faye (a homemaker; maiden name, Walton) Barrett; married Vicki Noyce, December 13, 1972; children: Elise, Katherine, Blake, Patricia, Anne, Melissa, Brenda, David, Michael, Eric. *Education:* University of Utah, B.F.A., 1973; University of Iowa, M.A., 1975, M.F.A., 1976; attended Academy of Arts, Berlin, Germany, 1976-77. *Politics:* Republican. *Religion:* Latter-day Saint. *Hobbies and other interests:* Traveling, hiking, painting.

ROBERT T. BARRETT

■ Addresses

Home—897 East Walnut Ave., Provo, UT 84604. *Office*— Brigham Young University, 210 Brmb, Provo, UT 84602.

■ Career

Freelance illustrator. Brigham Young University, Provo, UT, assistant professor, 1982-89, associate professor, 1991-95, professor of illustration, 1995—, chairperson of Department of Design, 1991-95, associate chairperson of Department of Visual Arts, 1995—. *Member:* Society of Illustrators, Phi Kappa Phi, Church of Jesus Christ of Latter-day Saints (bishop, 1982-86).

■ Awards, Honors

German Academic Exchange Grant, 1976-77; National Endowment for the Arts/Utah Arts Council Grant, 1978-79; Utah Advertising Gold Award, 1991; Addy Award, 1991; Karl G. Maeser Teaching Award, 1995.

■ Illustrator

Pamela Kennedy, reteller, *The Other Wise Man,* by Henry Van Dyke, Ideals Children's Books (Nashville, TN), 1989.
One-Minute Stories of Great Americans, Doubleday, 1990.

Ann Warren Turner, *Dust for Dinner,* HarperCollins, 1995.

Also illustrator of cover art for numerous publishers, including Viking, Puffin, Fawcett, Thomas Nelson, Moorings, and Bookcraft.

■ Work in Progress

A limited-edition print, "Visions of Faith Market," for Mill Pond Press; Utah landscape and portrait sample work.

■ Sidelights

Robert T. Barrett told *SATA:* "As a child growing up in a small mining town in southern Utah, my exposure to the world of art was somewhat limited. My parents were, however, both artistic and loved to draw and paint. In addition, my mother was an avid reader and read all of the classics to me and my two brothers. We didn't have a television until I was in junior high school, but I loved to imagine the characters in the books I was exposed to. In addition, my parents subscribed to several magazines which at the time were lavishly illustrated and were printed in large format. I loved looking at the illustrations in those magazines, which included *Life, Post, McCall's, Redbook,* and *Ladies' Home Journal,* and at times copied some of them. I had determined before I entered high school that I would enter some kind of art-related career. I can't say I never wavered from that resolve, but I continued to come back to it over and over again. Many of my teachers in school encouraged me, and I received a variety of recognitions along the way.

"As I entered the university, I chose to study fine art instead of going in more commercial directions. This continued through graduate work and a post-graduate experience in Europe. Though many of my fellow students were intrigued by modern directions, I found myself continually drawn to traditional forms of art and narrative painting. My M.A. and M.F.A. theses involved the subject of figurative painting, and I attempted to communicate to a broader audience with a realistic approach to painting.

"Teaching through the City Colleges of Chicago (European division) in Berlin exposed me to a number of American illustrators and as I returned from Europe, I decided to go that direction with my work. I built a portfolio of figurative work and became successful at securing commissions as a freelance and, later, an in-house illustrator. I worked for a number of organizations and clients and continued to teach as well. I was invited to join the faculty at Brigham Young University as an assistant professor of illustration in 1982 and am currently a professor and associate chair of the Department of Visual Arts."

■ For More Information See

PERIODICALS

Booklist, July, 1995, p. 1885.
School Library Journal, October, 1995, p. 121.

* * *

BEIFUSS, John (Jr.) 1959-

■ Personal

Born April 8, 1959, in Chicago, IL; son of John Paul, Sr. (an English professor) and Joan (a writer; maiden name, Turner) Beifuss. *Education:* Northwestern University, B.S., 1981. *Politics:* "Inevitable." *Religion:* Catholic. *Hobbies and other interests:* Disk jockey on WEVL-FM 90, community radio station in Memphis.

■ Addresses

Home—445 Meadowcrest Cr., Memphis, TN 38117.
Office—495 Union, Memphis, TN 38103.

■ Career

Newspaper reporter, Memphis, TN, 1981—.

■ Writings

Armadillo Ray, illustrated by Peggy Turley, Chronicle Books, 1995.

■ Sidelights

John Beifuss told *SATA:* "*Armadillo Ray* chronicles the adventures of the world's most existential armadillo, and I'm pleased that readers have responded positively. Many have understood that the story is multicultural—it just happens to be about fictional animal cultures."

"My first professional writing appeared in the late, lamented magazine *Famous Monsters in Filmland.* It will be hard to top that."

■ For More Information See

PERIODICALS

Children's Book Review Service, February, 1996, p. 73.
Kirkus Reviews, November 1, 1995.
The New York Times Book Review, March 10, 1996, p. 21.*

* * *

BENDER, Edna 1941-

■ Personal

Born January 12, 1941, in Meyersdale, PA; daughter of Harvey N. and Verna (Miller) Maust; married Gordon D. Bender (a dairy farmer), 1965; children: Angela, Jencene. *Education:* Attended Baltimore School of Art, two years; Famous Artists Schools, Westport, CT, graduated, 1962; attended Frostburg State University; Garrett Community College, A.A. (three), 1989. *Religion:* Christian (Mennonite).

■ Addresses

Home—745 Fish Hatchery Rd., Accident, MD 21520.

■ Career

Freelance artist, 1963—, with hundreds of commissioned paintings in private and public collections. Art enrichment teacher for various community agencies, colleges, and private schools, 1986—. Coordinator of Annual IDEA art exhibit and competition, Accident, MD, 1991—; member of Cultural and Historical Society, Accident, 1992—.

■ Awards, Honors

Award of Merit by Excellence in Media and C. S. Lewis Award, both 1996, both for *April Bluebird.*

■ Illustrator

Esther Bender, *April Bluebird,* Herald Press, 1995.
Esther Bender, *The Crooked Tree,* Herald Press, 1996.

Contributor of art work to various publications.

EDNA BENDER

■ Work in Progress

A new picture book is being developed and research continues on Native Americans, Amish children, early settlers and native animals, as well as original methods of teaching oil painting to children.

■ Sidelights

Edna Bender told *SATA:* "I fondly remember my mother teaching me, at an early age, the first principles of shading. I have been drawing and painting ever since. My career in art began when I was a teenager, partly because I was bedfast for about five years with rheumatic fever and related complications.

"After working on commissions for several years, I decided to quit painting and begin another career. That resolution lasted for several months but I missed the thrill of creating so much that I couldn't resist doing just one more painting. Soon I was painting again with more enthusiasm than ever. I did many commissioned portraits and landscapes, but gradually I became more and more involved in teaching. I see hundreds of adults and children in my enrichment classes and I like the human contact with all age groups. I find a special satisfaction in the ability and opportunity to encourage individuals to create, in their own way, worlds that exist only in their imagination.

"Although I had done some illustrating through the years, I did not plan to get much involved with it. Now I am having such fun that I will probably continue indefinitely! Painting is certainly demanding, but I find it absorbing. I especially enjoy the research process necessary to produce a good product."

*   *   *

BERMAN, Ruth 1958-

■ Personal

Born March 19, 1958, in New York, NY; daughter of Hyman (a historian) and Betty (a librarian; maiden name, Silbering) Berman. *Education:* University of Minnesota, Minneapolis, B.A., 1986. *Hobbies and other interests:* Animals, gardening, reading, art-deco collecting, weight lifting.

■ Addresses

Home—4202 Fireside Circle, Irvine, CA 92604. *Office*—Bowtie Press, P.O. Box 6050, Mission Viejo, CA 92690.

■ Career

Lerner Publications, Minneapolis, MN, children's book editor, became senior editor, 1987-95; Bowtie Press, Irvine, CA, editor-in-chief, 1995—. Freelance children's book writer and editor. *Member:* Authors Guild, Authors League of America, National Anti-Vivisection Society.

■ Awards, Honors

Outstanding Science Trade Book, American Library Association, and Pick of the List, *American Bookseller,* both 1992, both for *American Bison.*

■ Writings

American Bison, photographs by Cheryl Walsh Bellville, Carolrhoda Books, 1992.
Sharks, photographs by Jeffrey L. Rotman, Carolrhoda Books, 1995.
Peacocks, photographs by Richard R. Hewett, Lerner Publications, 1996.
Ants, photographs by William Munoz, Lerner Publications, 1996.

■ Work in Progress

A book about dogs as pets.

■ Sidelights

The author of several science books for children, Ruth Berman told *SATA:* "I started writing children's science books as a way to instill in children a respect and love for animals and nature. I'm especially interested in pointing out the unique and fascinating qualities of the most misunderstood and least appreciated animals. All my life I've felt a strong empathy for non-human animals. Even as a young child I would go out of my way so as not to step on an ant. I had a hard time finding books about animals that were interesting, informative, and written for my level of reading and understanding. But still I spent hours poring over encyclopedias and other adult books about animals to satisfy my yearning for animal knowledge. Fortunately, children now have many ways to satisfy their curiosity about the natural world."

■ For More Information See

PERIODICALS

Booklist, August, 1996.
School Library Journal, October, 1992, p. 124; November, 1995, p. 109; May, 1996, p. 102.
Science Books & Films, October, 1992, p. 209; November, 1993, p. 251.

*   *   *

BIANCHI, Robert Steven 1943-

■ Personal

Born November 30, 1943, in New York, NY; son of Robert Vincent and Bessie (maiden name, Litrakis) Bianchi; married January 17, 1963; wife's name, Stephanie (divorced, March 17, 1978); children: Kyria Bianchi Osborne. *Education:* Institute of Fine Arts, New York University, Ph.D., 1976. *Religion:* Greek Orthodox.

■ Addresses

Home—Lenox Hill Station, P.O. Box 2129, New York, NY 10021-0053.

■ Career

Brooklyn Museum, Brooklyn, NY, curator, 1976-91; Metropolitan Museum of Art, New York City, fellow, 1992-93; Florida International Museum, St. Petersburg, FL, curator, 1994—. *Member:* Association of Hellenes from Egypt in America (board of governors), Explorers Club (fellow resident, 1979).

■ Awards, Honors

Fulbright Hayes fellow; Bert H. Hill fellow; Bourse Jacques Vandier fellow.

■ Writings

Cleopatra's Egypt, Brooklyn Museum, 1985.
The Nubians: People of the Ancient Nile, Millbrook Press, 1994.
(Editor) Anthony S. Mercatante, *Who's Who in Egyptian Mythology,* Scarecrow Press, 1995.
Splendors of Ancient Egypt, Florida International Museum, 1995.

Has written two television programs for The Learning Channel, "Who Was Cleopatra?," 1993, and "Pharaohs and Kings" (also co-host), 1996. Contributes a biannual article, "Art and Auction," to *Art and Auction Magazine.* American Research Center in Egypt, book review editor; Archaeological Institute of America, *Archaeology Magazine,* contributing editor.

■ Work in Progress

"Animating the Past," a projected video and separate interactive CD-ROM for youngsters on multicultural aspects of antiquity; research on Alexander the Great, and lives of famous ancient women as role models: Hatshepsut, Arsinoe II, Zenobia, Hypatia.

■ Sidelights

Robert Steven Bianchi told *SATA:* "Most academics are loathe to become associated with popular projects, such as writing for young audiences, because they think that stooping to such a level detracts from their status. Others, myself included, maintain that providing substantive material in a user friendly form, be it print media, video, CD-ROM, or television, is the only way for youngsters to become exposed to cutting edge theories and interpretations about our common ancient past.

"The decision to write *The Nubians* was the result of a series of lectures I delivered in Alexandria, Egypt, in

1992, to members of the expatriate Nubian community and their sons, who had to leave their ancestral homeland due to the creation of Lake Nasser behind the Aswan High Dam. The Nubian community was eager to have its past recorded in a comprehensible form for the benefit of its youngsters, and others worldwide, who could never hope to return to these lands now covered with water.

"As a father and a grandfather, I also realize that youngsters ought to be presented with the very best aspects of ancient culture so that early on they might gain an understanding for and appreciation of those ancient values which we in our own culture still hold so dear. It is for this reason that I have embarked on a joint venture, "Animating the Past," in which the team I am associated with can work toward providing fun-filled, educational animated videos and interactive CD-ROMs about different ancient cultures such as the Egyptians, the Persians, the Assyrians, the ancient Hebrews, and others. The objective is not to pontificate, but to present the cultures of these chronologically distant peoples and, in so doing, reveal the value of cultural differences.

"It is for many of these same reasons that I am interested in pursuing biographies of individuals such as Alexander the Great, and the equally significant, but virtually unknown, women of the past, such as Arsinoe II, Zenobia, and Hypatia.

"I think that my years of involvement with the ruins and artifacts of these peoples and my time spent with their modern descendants in their own lands enable me to present a window on those cultures from a very personal and academic perspective."

*   *   *

BILAL, Abdel W(ahab) 1970-

■ Personal

Born March 24, 1970, in Menoufiya, Egypt; son of Sayed (a farmer) and Tahiya Bilal. *Education:* Helwan University, Cairo, B.A. *Religion:* Muslim.

■ Addresses

Home—Toukh Dalaka, Talla, El-Menoufiya, Egypt.

■ Career

Freelance artist (including posters, book illustration, mural painting), 1993—.

■ Awards, Honors

First prize in poster design, Egyptian Film Festival, 1995; second prize for poster, Egyptian Film Festival, 1996.

■ Illustrator

Jailan Abbas, *Festivals of Egypt,* Hoopoe Books (AMIDEAST), 1995.

Books published in Arabic with illustrations by Bilal include *Strange Journey,* Atfalna, 1994; *The Hunter,* Al-Amin, 1994; and *Earthquake,* Gihad, 1995.

■ Work in Progress

Stories of the Caliphs.

■ Sidelights

With the help of translator Andy Smart of Hoopoe Books, Abdel Bilal told *SATA* that he began work as an illustrator after he finished college. "I started ... doing illustrations for articles in the Cairo weekly magazine 'Sabah el-Kheir' ('Good Morning'). My work is currently divided between book illustration and large-scale murals. My ambition is to illustrate books with as large a format as possible, and to do the biggest murals in the world! I also hope to spread an understanding of Islam through the books I illustrate."

Bilal reported that Alma-Tadema has influenced his murals. He recommends "meditation (in Arabic 'ta'amul')" for aspiring young artists.

*   *   *

BIRCHMORE, Daniel A. 1951-

■ Personal

Born September 18, 1951, in Athens, GA; son of Fred Agnew (a traveler) and Willa Deane (a teacher; maiden name, Stuckey) Birchmore. *Education:* University of Georgia, B.S., 1972; Medical College of Georgia, M.D., 1976. *Politics:* Southern. *Religion:* Methodist. *Hobbies and other interests:* Hiking, squash.

■ Addresses

Department of Ambulatory Care, U.S. Veterans Hospital, 1310 Twenty-fourth Ave. So., Nashville, TN 37212-2637.

■ Career

Vanderbilt University Hospital, residency in internal medicine, 1976-79; University of Virginia Hospital, fellowship in rheumatology, 1979-81; private practice in rheumatology, Athens, GA, 1981-90; U.S. Veterans Hospital, Elsmere, DE, chief of division of rheumatology, 1990-97; U.S. Veterans Hospital, Nashville, TN, physician, 1997—.

■ Awards, Honors

American College of Physicians fellow; Rafael Osuna Award, NCAA Tennis Coaches, 1971.

DANIEL A. BIRCHMORE

■ Writings

The Rock, illustrated by Nancy C. Willis, Cucumber Island Storytellers, 1996.
Harry, the Happy Snake of Happy Hollow, illustrated by Gail E. Lucas, Cucumber Island Storytellers, 1996.
The Reluctant Santa, or, Christmas Has Been Cancelled!, illustrated by Gail E. Lucas, Cucumber Island Storytellers, 1996.
The White Curtain, illustrated by Gail E. Lucas, Cucumber Island Storytellers, 1996.

■ Work in Progress

Pilly, Polly & Wee, illustrated by Gail E. Lucas; *Green, So Green,* a book of original poetry; researching the effects of cognition on adherence to a medications regimen in the elderly.

■ Sidelights

Daniel A. Birchmore told *SATA:* "I am a descendant of tellers of stories and writers of songs for children. My grandfather wrote the words of the children's song "Jesus Loves the Little Children." He loved nature, and he loved people, and he told simple tales. Most of my stories and songs are for my little nieces and nephews and for the good folk of Poplar Springs Methodist Campground. My goals in life are to learn how to read music so I can sing, and to someday have a family."

BLEGEN, Daniel M. 1950-

■ Personal

Born April 13, 1950, in Chicago, IL; son of M. A. (a mechanical engineer) and A. R. (a homemaker) Blegen; married Vicki Grayson (a teacher and artist), July 21, 1979; children: Tania, Erin, Kelly. *Education:* Concordia Teachers College, B.A., 1973; University of Colorado, M.A., 1988. Has also participated in the American West Institute sponsored by the National Endowment for the Humanities. *Hobbies and other interests:* Local history.

■ Addresses

Home—1624 Adkinson Avenue, Longmont, CO 80501.

■ Career

Writer. Lutheran High School, Denver, CO, teacher, 1973-75; Vikan Junior High School, Brighton, CO, teacher and chair of language arts department, 1975-83,

DANIEL M. BLEGEN

and Brighton High School, teacher, 1983—. *Member:* National Education Association.

■ Writings

(With Melvin Bacon) *Bent's Fort: Crossroads of Cultures on the Santa Fe Trail,* Millbrook Press, 1995.

Author of plays, including *In My Time,* produced in Boulder, CO; and *Faith of Our Fathers,* produced in Brighton, CO. Contributor of poetry, articles, and theatre reviews to periodicals, including *Dramatics* and *Theatreweek.*

■ Sidelights

Writer and educator Daniel Blegen leads somewhat of a double life. A published poet and the author of several plays, Blegen was briefly a costumed interpreter for Bent's Fort, a historic site located along the path of the legendary Santa Fe Trail where it crosses southeastern Colorado. Blegen has experienced what life was like in the mid-nineteenth century, even wrapping himself in buffalo robes and sleeping under the Colorado night sky. He and fellow educator/interpreter Melvin Bacon have shared their first-hand knowledge of the settlement of the American West in *Bent's Fort: Crossroads of Cultures on the Santa Fe Trail.*

With its start in Independence, Missouri, the Santa Fe Trail stretched southwest into New Mexico, providing settlers with a route to the unclaimed lands of the West. In *Bent's Fort,* Blegen and Bacon describe life in one of the trail's largest trading posts. With adobe walls fifteen feet high and three feet thick, William Bent's fort was one of the trail's few stop-off points. It provided a place where travellers and traders could exchange their goods for supplies and services until the fort was forced to close after an outbreak of cholera killed many of the Native Americans whose trade goods it relied upon. Based on actual accounts obtained from diaries of the period, including that of Susan Magoffin, the first white woman to successfully travel the trail, the book contains drawings and photographs that provide readers with a fascinating glimpse of life in the mid-1800s as well as efforts to reconstruct the fort after it was excavated by archaeologists beginning in the 1950s. In a *School Library Journal* review, Julie Halverstadt commented that there is "an amazing amount of information in this attractive volume," while *Booklist* reviewer Kay Weisman added that the first-hand descriptions plus the photographs and period drawings "offer a revealing look at life in southeastern Colorado circa 1846." Weisman also noted that the bibliography and index will be helpful to report writers, "making this a useful addition to classroom units on the westward movement or Colorado history."

■ Works Cited

Halverstadt, Julie, review of *Bent's Fort: Crossroads of Cultures on the Santa Fe Trail, School Library Journal,* November, 1995, p. 109.

Weisman, Kay, review of *Bent's Fort: Crossroads of Cultures on the Santa Fe Trail, Booklist,* January 1, 1996, p. 820.

*   *   *

BOGART, Jo Ellen 1945-

■ Personal

Born October 20, 1945, in Houston, TX; daughter of John Howard (an engineer with Bell Telephone) and Edrie May (an elementary school teacher; maiden name, House) Jenkins; married James P. Bogart (a university professor), March 11, 1967; children: Adam, Jill. *Education:* University of Texas, Austin, B.S., 1967, B.A. (cum laude), 1969. *Hobbies and other interests:* Gardening, pets, reading, writing, "spending time on the internet and corresponding with friends and family by e-mail."

■ Addresses

Home—172 Palmer St., Guelph, Ontario, Canada, N1E2R6.

■ Career

Austin Independent School District, Austin, Texas, supply teacher, 1968; Margaret Roane Center, Ruston, Louisiana, teacher of educable mentally retarded teen-

JO ELLEN BOGART

agers, 1973; Wellington County Board (Ontario), supply teacher, grades K-6, 1983-1992. *Guelph Examiner* (a small, weekly newspaper), reporter, illustrator, photographer, editorial writer, 1980. St. George's-Laurine Public School, volunteer speech therapist, 1982-83; King George Senior Public School, volunteer library assistant, 1983-84; John F. Ross CVI, Principal's Advisory Committee, 1985-87; Wellington County Board of Education, Community Relations Committee, 1986-89. *Member:* Society of Children's Book Writers and Illustrators, The Writers' Union of Canada, Canadian Society of Children's Authors Illustrators and Performers (associate editor of newsletter).

■ Awards, Honors

"Our Choice" list selection, Canadian Children's Book Centre, 1990, for *Malcolm's Runaway Soap,* 1991, for *Daniel's Dog,* 1992, for *Sarah Saw a Blue Macaw,* 1994, for *Mama's Bed,* 1995, for *Two Too Many,* and 1996, for *Gifts;* Choices List selection, Cooperative Children's Book Center, University of Wisconsin, 1990, and Children's Choice, International Reading Association/Children's Book Council (IRA/CBC), 1991, both for *Daniel's Dog;* short list, Ruth Schwartz Award, short list, Mr. Christie's Book Award, and International Board on Books for Young People (IBBY) Honour list, all for *Gifts.*

■ Writings

Dylan's Lullaby, illustrated by Cheryl Lowrey, Annick Press, 1988.
Malcolm's Runaway Soap, illustrated by Linda Hendry, North Winds Press, 1988.
10 for Dinner, illustrated by Carlos Freire, North Winds Press, 1989.
Daniel's Dog, illustrated by Janet Wilson, North Winds Press, 1990.
Sarah Saw a Blue Macaw, illustrated by Sylvie Daigneault, North Winds Press, 1991.
Mama's Bed, illustrated by Sylvie Daigneault, North Winds Press, 1993.
Two Too Many, illustrated by Yvonne Cathcart, North Winds Press, 1994.
Gifts, illustrated by Barbara Reid, North Winds Press, 1994.

Most of the author's picture books have been published in French; *Sarah Saw a Blue Macaw* was published in Spanish as *Sara Vio Una Guacamaya Azul,* Scholastic, Inc.

■ Adaptations

Cassette recordings of the author reading her stories were produced to accompany *Sarah Saw a Blue Macaw, Malcolm's Runaway Soap,* and *Daniel's Dog. 10 for Dinner* is also available on cassette.

■ Work in Progress

Jeremiah Learns to Read, expected 1997; various picture book texts and some longer works.

■ Sidelights

Jo Ellen Bogart, a citizen of both Canada and the United States, is the author of several picture books for children. Although Bogart began her career with the desire to enrich the lives of children, she did not set out to become a children's book writer. In college, she studied with the intention of working as an elementary school teacher, and she worked for a few years as a substitute teacher. It was not long, however, before Bogart realized that what she really wanted to do was write books for children. As a writer, she could educate children by providing them with books that they "could enjoy and maybe even learn something from." Bogart now hopes to help her readers "appreciate their own creativity and increase their joy in the written and spoken word. A wonderful combination of words can be as exciting as a wonderful flavor and can give a very pleasant feeling."

Bogart's first two books, *Dylan's Lullaby* and *Malcolm's Runaway Soap,* are fun books written for young children. *Dylan's Lullaby* follows a boy as he sleeps and travels through the sky. In his dreams, he flies with birds, runs with a horse, and swims with fish. In *Malcolm's Runaway Soap,* a little boy loses his soap; it makes its way out of the bathtub and downtown. "Bogart has the soap pop in a great variety of places," noted Kathleen Corrigan in *Canadian Children's Literature,* "and she writes in nice descriptive detail about each one." The soap ends up in the fountain at city hall.

Two of Bogart's other books, *10 for Dinner* and *Two Too Many,* may be used as counting books. *10 for Dinner* features Margo's birthday dinner, following the antics of one unusual guest. Nancy Tully of *Canadian Materials* commented that the text of the book is "bold, simple" and "especially readable." *Two Too Many* demonstrates, as Catherine McInerney of *Canadian Materials* commented, "the nutty things that go on when there are simply two too many things." Children "will enjoy the high-spirited fun of this attractive book," concluded Kenneth Oppel of *Quill & Quire.*

While many of Bogart's books have won recognition from the Canadian Children's Book Centre, *Daniel's Dog* has garnered special attention. This book is about a young boy, Daniel, who finds himself feeling neglected and sad when a new baby sister joins his family. Daniel copes with his feelings by announcing that his grandfather (who has passed away) has sent him a ghost dog, Lucy. Although Lucy is an imaginary pet, Daniel spends a great deal of time with her and taking care of her needs, just as his mother cares for the new baby. Gradually, Daniel feels more comfortable about his role in the family, grows more accepting of his new sister, and gives Lucy less attention. "This is a fine book [that] gracefully covers topics ranging from the arrival of a

"Just the smell of rain
from a shady lane,
and a ride on a garden swing."

Follow Grandma as she tours the world, sharing her love of faraway places with her appreciative granddaughter. (From *Gifts*, written by Jo Ellen Bogart and illustrated by Barbara Reid.)

new sibling to imaginary companions to the resolution of inner conflict," noted *School Library Journal* contributor Anna DeWind. Bogart's empathetic portrayal of Daniel was likely influenced a great deal by her own childhood. She told *SATA* that she was an only child for the first five years of her life, and "had lots of time to make up games, make mudpies and play with the rabbits and chickens." She explained that "the experience of then having three siblings born in four years helped me understand how Daniel felt." *Sarah Saw a Blue Macaw* has also found favor with critics. Written in rhyme, with question and answer format, this book allows readers to see what Sarah (a spider monkey) sees during the course of a day in the Peruvian rainforest. All of the animals, like Sarah, are referred to by their first names; a "cast of characters" at the end of the book helps readers identify each animal and learn its species name. Sarah herself is featured on each page of the book, but readers have to search for her! A *Quill & Quire* critic, Frieda Wishinsky, wrote that the book "displays a fine use of verse." Many commentators appreciated the way Sylvie Daigneault illustrated the book. "It is difficult to exaggerate how beautifully designed a book *Sarah Saw a Blue Macaw* is," commented Ted McGee in *Canadian Children's Literature*. *Canadian Materials* contributor Jennifer Johnson added that the book "imparts a sense of wonder and appreciation for an endangered environment."

Bogart told *SATA* about the experiences that inspired *Sarah Saw a Blue Macaw*. "I have always been interest-ed in animals. I accompanied my Canadian zoologist husband on two scientific expeditions to South America to study amphibians and reptiles shortly after we were married. The setting for *Sarah Saw a Blue Macaw* is the Peruvian rainforest where we spent four months many years ago. During the development of that book, I spent lots of time in the university library studying the various animals. I wanted to feel familiar with their habits, even though the verses are more lyrical than realistic."

Bogart's talents were paired with those of illustrator Sylvie Daigneault once again in *Mama's Bed*. This book demonstrates all the ways a little girl finds security and fun in her mother's bed. She cuddles with her family, folds laundry, and even works on Halloween costumes, all on Mama's bed. Noting that the book has no plot, Janet McNaughton in *Quill & Quire* asserted that it "proves what a powerful device simplicity can be in a picture book." McNaughton added that "children age five and under will identify strongly with the small protagonist's feelings about the safety and comfort provided by her mother's bed."

As with *Sarah Saw a Blue Macaw*, *Gifts* is also told in verse and question and answer format. A little girl relates how she asks for gifts from her traveling grandmother, requesting among other things a memory, a piece of sky, and a rainbow to wear as a ring, and how her grandmother always manages to bring her just what she wants. In all, the grandmother takes nine trips, to places including Africa, the Arctic, Australia, England,

India, and Mexico. The Plasticine illustrations of Barbara Reid show how, with each trip, time passes and grandmother and daughter grow older. At the end of the book, the granddaughter has grown up and has a baby of her own, with whom she shares grandmother's treasured travel bag. Many critics enjoyed the presentation of the traveling, adventurous, and loving grandmother. Linda Granfield of *Quill & Quire* commented, "the text of *Gifts* is full of zing and zest, redolent with images of a child's limitless imagination." According to Jody McCoy of *School Library Journal,* the story "is a treasure to read alone, aloud, to a group, or to give to anyone who loves the unique."

Bogart explained how she came up with the idea for *Gifts:* "The book ... began in 1984 as a song. I was thinking of all of the things someone might bring back as a souvenir from a trip. I often collect shells and bits of driftwood, small stones and feathers. As well, I bring back books and records from the culture I have visited and make sketches in little notebooks with descriptions of what I see. When someone I know returns from a trip, what I most want is to hear stories about what happened. Stories take time and effort and make a wonderful gift. The gifts requested by the grandchild in *Gifts* show her special relationship with her grandma because the grandma knows how to understand the requests, and to be really involved in her granddaughter's imaginary life. Barbara Reid brought a blossoming of meaning to my text with her warm but lively illustrations."

Bogart told *SATA* about her work habits. "I often write a first draft or at least notes in pencil or ball-point, then transfer to computer disk for further writing and editing. In the cold weather, I like to walk my dog on a woodland trail and talk to myself about characters and plots. The fresh air and exercise are very invigorating and a necessary break from time at the computer. In our short warm season, I am so busy with gardening and other outdoor activities that I don't often get much writing done. I relax by enjoying nature, especially at the lake where we spend time in the summer. Sometimes I think about a story for quite a while, letting it simmer, then sit down and just write it. That's what I did with a story last summer. I finally gave birth to it in written form while sitting on a screened verandah at the lake listening to red squirrels scold each other."

■ Works Cited

DeWind, Anna, review of *Daniel's Dog, School Library Journal,* March, 1990, p. 188.

Corrigan, Kathleen, review of *Malcolm's Runaway Soap, Canadian Children's Literature,* no. 63, 1991, pp. 97-98.

Granfield, Linda, review of *Gifts, Quill & Quire,* September, 1994, p. 70.

Johnson, Jennifer, review of *Sarah Saw a Blue Macaw, Canadian Materials,* May, 1991, p. 170.

McCoy, Jody, review of *Gifts, School Library Journal,* March, 1996, p. 166.

McGee, Ted, review of *Sarah Saw a Blue Macaw, Canadian Children's Literature,* no. 66, 1992, p. 82.

McInerney, Catherine, review of *Two Too Many, Canadian Materials,* October, 1994, pp. 183-84.

McNaughton, Janet, review of *Mama's Bed, Quill & Quire,* October, 1993, pp. 38-39.

Oppel, Kenneth, review of *Two Too Many, Quill & Quire,* April, 1994, pp. 36, 38.

Tully, Nancy, review of *10 for Dinner, Canadian Materials,* September, 1989, p. 216.

Wishinsky, Frieda, review of *Sarah Saw a Blue Macaw, Quill & Quire,* March, 1991, pp. 20-21.

■ For More Information See

PERIODICALS

Booklist, February 1, 1996, p. 936.
Canadian Children's Literature, no. 51, 1988, p. 99.
Publishers Weekly, April 13, 1990, p. 63.

*   *   *

BULLOCK, Robert (D.) 1947-

■ Personal

Born October 23, 1947, in Eastman, GA; son of Cary and Sarah (a counselor; maiden name, Irvin) Bullock; married Kate Harrigan, October 18, 1981; children: Joshua, Daniel, SarahAnn. *Education:* University of North Carolina, B.A. (theater arts), 1969; Cleveland Institute of Art, B.A. (industrial design), 1979; Case Western Reserve University, M.A., 1979.

ROBERT BULLOCK

■ Addresses

Home—1715 Anna St., New Cumberland, PA 17070.
Office—The State Museum of Pennsylvania, Exhibition
Management, Third & North St., Harrisburg, PA 17108.

■ Career

Industrial/graphics designer, New York City, 1980-82;
St. John's, New York City, staff stage designer, 1981;
American Museum of Natural History, New York City,
preparator/designer, 1982-86; Creative Group, Inc.,
Orange, CT, vice-president/creative director, 1986; Yale
University, Peabody Museum, New Haven, CT, design-
er, 1986-91; Paier College of Art, Hamden, CT, adjunct
professor, 1989-90; The State Museum of Pennsylvania,
Harrisburg, chief of exhibits, 1991—. New Canaan
Nature Center, exhibit designer of children's interac-
tives; Roger Williams Museum, Providence, RI, exhibit
designer of galleries. Dodge Historical Society, Eastman,
GA, board of directors, 1989—; The Herman Fund,
Inc., New Cumberland, PA, board of directors and
CEO, 1994—. *Military service:* U.S. Navy, 1970-74.
Member: Society of Children's Book Writers and Illus-
trators; National Association of Museum Exhibition;
American Association of Museums.

■ Awards, Honors

Frederick Koch Award, University of North Carolina at
Chapel Hill, 1969; National Sculpture Competition
finalist, 1980.

■ Writings

(And illustrator) *The Ozarks,* Inglewood Discoveries,
1984.
(And illustrator) *The Great Plains: A Young Reader's
Journal,* Homestead Publishing, 1987.
(And illustrator) *The Rocky Mountains: A Young Read-
er's Journal,* Homestead Publishing, 1994.

Also author of scholarly articles.

■ Work in Progress

*Into the Wind, Rainbow Man, Welcome Home, Tall
Tree Tale, Silent Song,* and *Evergreen.*

■ Sidelights

Robert Bullock told *SATA:* "I credit my fascination with
history to my father, but my interest in education is due
to my mother. She was a counselor, and I saw how much
children appreciated what she did for them. She made
people feel good, and that's the idea behind my work at
the museum and the books I write—making people feel
good and happy.

"I plan every aspect of an exhibit, from the development
of the overall designs to the placement of specimens,
artifacts, and lighting. I worked on a dinosaur exhibit of
Deinonychus at Yale and designed the Narragansett Bay

Gallery in Rhode Island which featured several habitat
groups and hands-on activities, such as a Quahog
picture puzzle and a tugboat navigation area complete
with steering wheel. The most effective exhibits are
interactive, because they draw the viewer into the
learning process. As you walk through an exhibit, there's
a sense of discovery, a sense of change that takes place
as you round corners or look down to see something
that's not really where you expect to see it. It's a very
exciting way to communicate information.

"Writing is another way. I love children, and I like
developing products for children, especially ones that
require them to become actively involved. My first book
was prototyped with lift tabs so young readers could
discover hidden bits of information. This evolved into
'Clue-Q' where questions throughout the books are
answered by clues in the text.

"I read about a locality—its history and animal life—
and then I look at the animals in their habitats at the
museum and at zoos. I ask the curators to describe the
animals' particular characteristics, and I take careful
notes. I then use this information to write the books for
the 'Wilderness Habitat' series."

*   *   *

BULPIN, (Barbara) Vicki

■ Personal

Born April 13; daughter of Marietta (McPherson) May;
children: Richard, John (deceased). *Education:* Attended University of Washington and Bellevue Community
College. *Hobbies and other interests:* Dancing (West
Coast swing, ballroom, folk, country western).

■ Addresses

Home—1115 107th Ave. S. E., Bellevue, WA 98004.

■ Career

Kennedy Associates Real Estate Counsel, Seattle, WA,
construction loan administrator, 1995—. *Member:* Seattle Swing Dance Club.

■ Writings

Fuzzytail's Big Mistake, Carlton Press (New York),
1996.

■ Work in Progress

A sequel to *Fuzzytail's Big Mistake* and a science fiction
book for teenagers.

■ Sidelights

Vicki Bulpin told *SATA:* "Reading has always been an
important part of my life. I read mysteries, science
fiction, historical novels, fantasies, biographies, etc.

VICKI BULPIN

Usually there are two or three books that I am reading at the same time. The rest of my time is spent working full-time at my position with Kennedy Associates Real Estate Counsel, caring for my home and yard, and dancing. Dancing is the other passion in my life. I usually dance about two to four times a week. To keep in shape for dancing, I work out at the YMCA about two to three times a week.

"My children were my inspiration for writing my first book. When they were young I always read stories to them and usually did the 'voice' characters that were in the book (i.e., Swedish, Mexican, Cockney, cackling witches, dogs, etc.). I did not know the effect of this until one night, in a hurry, I forgot to do the Cockney voice for one of the characters in a Howard Pease adventure story. My son said, 'Mom, that wasn't him, because he didn't speak with a Cockney accent!'

"When we didn't have a current book to read, I made up stories for bedtime. These included stories of my childhood spent in the hills of southern Idaho and some of the adventures of my father. He had worked for the railroad, been a Forest Service Ranger, and a cattle and horse wrangler. Telling stories evolved into a desire to put some of them on paper. I answered an ad for the Children's Institute of Literature correspondence course. I did it to see if I could write. I felt good about the short stories I wrote but was leery of sending them

out to publishers. One day my son, by this time grown up, said, 'What have you got to lose?' So, I started submitting my short stories and children's stories to magazines and publishers. Carlton Press accepted *Fuzzytail's Big Mistake*. I have various other stories, a sequel to Fuzzytail, and the beginning of a story line for a science fiction book for teenagers. *Fuzzytail's Big Mistake* is my first children's book, but hopefully it will be just one of many in the future."

*   *   *

BURNS, Khephra 1950-

■ Personal

Born October 2, 1950, in Los Angeles, CA; son of Isham "Rusty" (a retired travel services manager) and Treneta Cecelia (a retired systems analyst; maiden name, Davis) Burns; married Susan L. Taylor (a writer and editor), August 19, 1989; children: Shana Nequai Taylor. *Education:* University of California, Santa Barbara, B.A., 1972. *Politics:* Independent. *Religion:* "Life." *Hobbies and other interests:* Art (mixed media) and music (tenor saxophone and flute).

■ Addresses

Office—Taylor Burns, Inc., 1 Lincoln Plaza, New York, NY 10023. *Agent*—Faith Childs, 132 West 22nd Street, New York, NY 10011.

■ Career

Freelance writer, New York City, 1978—. Writer and associate producer, WNET-13, New York City, 1978-80. *Member:* Writers Guild of America East, Authors Guild, Authors League of America, One Hundred Black Men, National Brotherhood of Skiers, Sigma Pi Phi.

■ Awards, Honors

Award of Excellence, Communications Excellence to Black Audiences, 1981; Books for the Teen Age selection, New York Public Library, 1996, for *Black Stars in Orbit: NASA's African American Astronauts*.

■ Writings

(With William Miles) *Black Stars in Orbit: NASA's African American Astronauts,* Harcourt, 1994.
(With wife, Susan L. Taylor) *Confirmation: Wisdom of the Ages,* Doubleday, 1997.

Writer of television programs *Black Champions,* PBS, 1986, and *Essence: The Television Program,* NBC, 1986-87; co-writer of television programs, including *Black Stars in Orbit,* PBS, 1990, *The Essence Awards,* CBS, 1991, 1992, FOX, 1993-96, *Images & Realities: African Americans,* NBC, 1992-94, and (senior writer) *Triple Threat,* BET, 1992. Author of screenplay, *Marie Laveau,* and musical, *Stackalee.*

Contributor to books, including *African Americans: Voices of Triumph,* Time-Life (New York City), 1994. Author of liner notes for recordings of jazz artists that include Miles Davis and Nancy Wilson. Contributor of articles to periodicals, including *Art & Auction, Essence, Omni,* and *Swing Journal;* author of "Legacy" (column), *Essence,* 1992-94. Editor, *Boule Journal.*

■ Work in Progress

Mansa Musa, Lion of Mali.

■ Sidelights

As a journalist and writer/producer of television specials and documentaries, Khephra Burns has been able to share his wide-ranging interests with a broad audience. His efforts extended to children when he and co-producer William Miles translated their popular 1990 PBS documentary *Black Stars in Orbit* into a book for young readers. An inspirational look at the black pilots who, since the formation of the Tuskegee Airmen during World War II, have gone on to achieve success and acceptance in the U.S. space program, *Black Stars in Orbit: NASA's African American Astronauts* has been praised by reviewers. Calling the book "a stirring portrait of a remarkable group of individuals," a *Kirkus Reviews* commentator noted that it not only provides a history of African Americans in the U.S. space program, but also "shows how the space race can be viewed as a

KHEPHRA BURNS

paradigm of the civil rights struggle." Carolyn Phelan of *Booklist* found *Black Stars in Orbit* "an interesting look at an untapped topic," while *School Library Journal* contributor Margaret M. Hagel asserted that co-authors Burns and Miles "tell the compelling and at times horrifying story in a full and lively manner."

Raised in Compton, California, Burns found inspiration in the lives of his parents. "Between the ages of eight and fifteen, when I wasn't in school, I spent all my time with my father at Compton Airport," he told *SATA,* "working on planes and learning to fly." The author's father was a Tuskegee Airman, one of the famed black fighter pilots of World War II. Still working in the field of aviation—he worked as a flight instructor, charter pilot, and stunt pilot for air shows, television, and feature films—Burns's father's "notoriety planted the seed that would inspire me to achieve something worthy of recognition," according to the author. His mother, who worked as a corporate systems analyst, was also exemplary; she was, in the early 1960s, "one of only a handful of women pilots in the United States."

A self-proclaimed "aspiring jazz musician" then in his early twenties, Burns "encountered two writers whose influence marked a turning point in my life: Michael Butler, who is known mostly among a small circle of artists and intellectuals in the East Bay area of San Francisco, and whose breadth of knowledge and poetic voice have left a lasting impression on me; and Ilunga Adell, a pioneering young television writer who, by example, showed me that it was possible to make a living as a writer."

Burns's first large-scale writing project was a screenplay titled *Marie Laveau* after the legendary Voodoo Queen of pre-Civil War New Orleans. The work attracted the interest of several New York producers, "including singer Harry Belafonte, who took a one-year option on the story and subsequently commissioned me to write *Stackalee,* a stage drama with music." Burns has since gone on to write or co-write several television productions, including, since 1991, the annual *Essence Awards* as well as several other programs that celebrate the diverse accomplishments of African Americans.

"To make a living while waiting for these projects to come to fruition, I wrote speeches for corporate executives, advertising copy, press releases, articles for teen fanzines, even bios for people seeking employment," explained Burns. He also wrote scripts for the Schomburg Center for Research in Black History and Culture's annual Heritage Celebration at the New York Public Library, as well as for the NAACP Legal Defense Fund's annual National Equal Justice Awards, the Manhattan Borough President's Awards for Excellence in the Arts, the Arthur Ashe Institute for Urban Heath's Annual Sports Ball, and several Carnegie Hall productions. In addition, Burns has authored the column "Legacy," a cultural commentary published in *Essence* magazine. Several of his columns have been excerpted in published anthologies and quoted by other writers. His poem, "Essence 25," recited by television talk-show host

Oprah Winfrey on the *25th Anniversary Essence Awards,* has since been performed by small theater groups around the United States.

"Writing, for me, is a means of sharing with others information I have run across in my researches that I have found fascinating, educational, inspiring, and fun," noted Burns. "Music, especially the rhythms and idiomatic nuances of jazz, informs my writing style at its best. I love language and what it is capable of, and writing gives me an opportunity to experiment with communicating on several levels simultaneously. It is the closest thing to real magic that I have found. But," he added, "it's also an 8 A.M.-to-midnight, seven-day-a-week obsession."

■ Works Cited

Review of *Black Stars in Orbit: NASA's African American Astronauts, Kirkus Reviews,* February 15, 1995, p. 222.

Hagel, Margaret M., review of *Black Stars in Orbit: NASA's African American Astronauts, School Library Journal,* February, 1995, p. 115.

Phelan, Carolyn, review of *Black Stars in Orbit: NASA's African American Astronauts, Booklist,* February 15, 1995, p. 1076.

■ For More Information See

PERIODICALS

Bulletin of the Center for Children's Books, February, 1995, p. 193.

Voice of Youth Advocates, December, 1994, p. 294.

C

KARIN CALLEY

CALLEY, Karin 1965-

■ Personal

Born July 24, 1965, in Brisbane, Australia; daughter of Malcolm John Chalmers Calley (an anthropologist) and Laila Birgita Haglund (an archaeologist); married Jan Arvid Gotesson (a science student), 1994. *Education:* Sydney College of the Arts, B.A., 1987; Sydney University, B.A., 1991. *Politics:* Aboriginal land rights supporter. *Religion:* None.

■ Addresses

Home and office—1 Cameron St., Balmain, Sydney, 2041 Australia. *Electronic mail*—100353.1614@com puserve.com.

■ Career

Cape York Land Council, writer and researcher, archaeological field assistant. *Exhibitions:* Exhibitor at group shows, including "9 Printmakers at the Wharf," Wharf Theatre, Sydney, 1987; miniatures show, London, 1988; Hugo Galleries, Canberra, 1988. Exhibitor in a solo show, 41 Cleveland Street Gallery, Sydney, 1988.

■ Illustrator

Keith Harrison (adapter), *Sir Gawain and the Green Knight,* Black Willow Press, 1993.
(And author) *Caden Walaa!* (translated by Noel Pearson into Guugu Yimithirr), University of Queensland Press, 1994, Jam Roll Picture Books, 1995.

■ Work in Progress

Stories, a movie script, and a documentary about an Aboriginal land claim.

■ Sidelights

Karin Calley told *SATA:* "My parents were both lecturers at Queensland University.... We lived in Brisbane, in a tall house on a hill with a big dog.

"From the age of eight, when we left my father and moved to Sydney, I was raised mostly by my mother. She became a consulting archaeologist, so my younger sister and I were dragged all over the Australian outback, missing most of our formal schooling and learning about a million types of prickle, eating damper from the camp fire and sleeping under the stars. I don't think we had any particular complaints about this lifestyle."

Calley studied visual arts and worked on lithography, relief, and etching at Sydney College of the Arts. She also studied prehistory, history, anthropology, and philosophy at Sydney University. "During my years of study, I began to spend a great deal of time with my friends the Pearsons at Hope Vale, an aboriginal community in far north Queensland," she told *SATA*. "In 1992 I began writing and illustrating stories for the Pearson kids, to be translated into Guugu Yimithirr (the local aboriginal language) by their uncle, Noel Pearson.

"The ideas for these stories have developed in response to both my desire to express something specifically about and for the kids I know, and to various areas of need which Noel Pearson and I have often discussed. One important consideration has been the dearth of written or broadcast material in the children's own language (or any aboriginal language for that matter). This is a lack which limits the children's access to their language and also undermines its perceived authority.

"Completely interconnected with questions of language are of course questions of culture and identity. Guugu Yimithirr is a living culture, a cultural heritage, and a personal resource, both in the sense of its meaning as a language and as a people of a particular place. For this reason I attempt to show and validate culture and language as both living (for example, by using aboriginal English in the English text and by referring to details of the children's contemporary existence) and as a heritage resource (by reminding them of and giving them some access to the richness which lies behind their contemporary existence).

"Lately I have been working for the Cape York Land Council as a writer and researcher and part-time as an archaeological field assistant. I have also been working with the Cape York Land Council and OZIRIS Productions on a documentary about an aboriginal land claim in Cape York Peninsula. This project has been accepted for pre-sale by SBSTV. I am also wishfully working on a movie script and have continued to work on my own stories and drawings whenever I can. There are so many pictures in my head.

"My father's father was a painter, and from my earliest days I have maintained that I would be one too. My mother's family is Swedish, so over the years I have spent a lot of time in Sweden and Europe. I think this Scandinavian heritage has contributed a certain romantic morbidity to the landscapes of my mind. The rest of course comes directly out of my Australian life and a sense of our bizarre history as it is expressed in the present."

■ For More Information See

PERIODICALS

Australian Book Review, June, 1995, p. 63.
Magpies, May, 1995, p. 28.*

CARLSTROM, Nancy White 1948-

■ Personal

Born August 4, 1948, in Washington, PA; daughter of William J. (a steel mill worker) and Eva (Lawrence) White; married David R. Carlstrom, September 7, 1974; children: Jesse David, Joshua White. *Education:* Wheaton College, Wheaton, IL, B.A., 1970; also studied at Harvard Extension and Radcliffe, 1974-76. *Religion:* Christian. *Hobbies and other interests:* Reading, tennis, cross-country skiing, and birding.

■ Addresses

Agent—Marilyn Marlow, Curtis Brown Ltd., 10 Astor Pl., New York, NY 10003.

■ Career

Writer, 1983—. A. Leo Weil Elementary School, Pittsburgh, PA, teacher, 1970-72; Plum Cove Elementary School, Gloucester, MA, teacher, 1972-74; Secret Garden Children's Bookshop, Seattle, WA, owner and manager, 1977-83. Worked with children in West Africa and the West Indies; worked at school for children with Down's Syndrome in Merida, Yucatan, Mexico. *Mem-*

NANCY WHITE CARLSTROM

ber: Society of Children's Book Writers and Illustrators, National Council of Teachers of English, Authors Guild, Authors League of America.

■ Awards, Honors

Editor's Choice, *Booklist*, 1986, and Children's Choice, International Reading Association/Children's Book Council (IRA/CBC), 1987, both for *Jesse Bear, What Will You Wear?*; American Booksellers Pick of the List, and Notable Book, National Council of Teachers of English (NCTE), both 1987, both for *Wild Wild Sunflower Child Anna*; Best Book of 1990, *Parents' Magazine*, for *Where Does the Night Hide?*; Children's Choice, IRA/CBC, and Parents' Choice, *Booklist*, both 1991, both for *Blow Me a Kiss, Miss Lilly*; Notable Book, NCTE, 1991, for *Goodbye Geese*.

■ Writings

Jesse Bear, What Will You Wear?, illustrated by Bruce Degen, Macmillan, 1986.
The Moon Came, Too, illustrated by Stella Ormai, Macmillan, 1987.
Wild Wild Sunflower Child Anna, illustrated by Jerry Pinkney, Macmillan, 1987.
Better Not Get Wet, Jesse Bear, illustrated by Bruce Degen, Macmillan, 1988.
Where Does the Night Hide?, illustrated by Thomas B. Allen and Laura Allen, Macmillan, 1988.
Blow Me a Kiss, Miss Lilly, illustrated by Amy Schwartz, Harper, 1989.
Graham Cracker Animals 1-2-3, illustrated by John Sandford, Macmillan, 1989.
Heather Hiding, illustrated by Dennis Nolan, Macmillan, 1990.
It's about Time, Jesse Bear, and Other Rhymes, illustrated by Bruce Degen, Macmillan, 1990.
I'm Not Moving, Mama!, illustrated by Thor Wickstrom, Macmillan, 1990.
Grandpappy, illustrated by Laurel Molk, Little, Brown, 1990.
No Nap for Benjamin Badger, illustrated by Dennis Nolan, Macmillan, 1990.
Light: Stories of a Small Kindness, illustrated by Lisa Desimini, Little, Brown, 1990.
Moose in the Garden, illustrated by Lisa Desimini, Harper, 1990.
Goodbye Geese, illustrated by Ed Young, Philomel, 1991.
Who Gets the Sun Out of Bed?, illustrated by David McPhail, Little, Brown, 1992.
Northern Lullaby, illustrated by Leo and Diane Dillon, Philomel, 1992.
Kiss Your Sister, Rose Marie!, illustrated by Thor Wickstrom, Macmillan, 1992.
How Do You Say It Today, Jesse Bear?, illustrated by Bruce Degen, Macmillan, 1992.
Baby-O, illustrated by Sucie Stevenson, Little, Brown, 1992.
The Snow Speaks, illustrated by Jane Dyer, Little, Brown, 1992.

What Does the Rain Play?, illustrated by Henri Sorensen, Macmillan, 1993.
Swim the Silver Sea, Joshie Otter, illustrated by Ken Kuori, Philomel, 1993.
Rise and Shine, illustrated by Dominic Catalano, HarperCollins, 1993.
How Does the Wind Walk?, illustrated by Deborah K. Ray, Macmillan, 1993.
Fish and Flamingo, illustrated by Lisa Desimini, Little, Brown, 1993.
Wishing at Dawn in Summer, illustrated by Diane Wolfolk Allison, Little, Brown, 1993.
Does God Know How to Tie Shoes?, illustrated by Lori McElrath-Eslick, Eerdmans, 1993.
What Would You Do If You Lived at the Zoo?, illustrated by Lizi Boyd, Little, Brown, 1994.
Jesse Bear's Yum-Yum Crumble, Aladdin Books, 1994.
Jesse Bear's Wiggle-Jiggle Jump-Up, Aladdin Books, 1994.
Jesse Bear's Tum Tum Tickle, Aladdin Books, 1994.
Jesse Bear's Tra-La Tub, Aladdin Books, 1994.
Happy Birthday, Jesse Bear!, illustrated by Bruce Degen, Macmillan, 1994.
Barney Is Best, illustrated by James G. Hale, HarperCollins, 1994.
Who Said Boo?: Halloween Poems for the Very Young, illustrated by R. W. Alley, Simon & Schuster, 1995.
I Am Christmas, illustrated by Lori McElrath-Eslick, Eerdmans, 1995.
Let's Count It Out, Jesse Bear, illustrated by Bruce Degen, Simon & Schuster, 1996.
Ten Christmas Sheep, illustrated by Cynthia Fisher, Eerdmans, 1996.
Raven and River, illustrated by Jon Van Zyle, Little, Brown, 1997.
Midnight Dance of the Snowshoe Hare, illustrated by Ken Kuori, Philomel, 1997.
Glory, illustrated by Lori McElrath-Eslick, Eerdmans, in press.

■ Work in Progress

A historical novel for young adults, tentatively titled *The Shape of Waiting*.

■ Sidelights

Author of the popular "Jesse Bear" series, Nancy White Carlstrom decided to become a writer of children's books at an early age; she worked in the children's department of her local library during her high school years, and "that's where my dream of writing children's books was born," she once told *SATA*. Known for her tight lines of verse filled with vivid description and evocation of the everyday, Carlstrom presents hopeful and humorous picture and board books for very young readers, books with simple vocabulary and subjects ranging from counting and colors to more sophisticated topics like inter-generational and multicultural relationships.

Carlstrom's themes reflect her own life and interests. The popular "Jesse Bear" books grew out of a poem written for her first son, Jesse. In these and other works, the author's concerns with society and nature are a reflection of her own upbringing and world view. Growing up without television, Carlstrom learned early on to create her own fantasies and to entertain herself. She loved books and writing from an early age, and as she reported in an interview with Jeffrey S. and Vicky L. Copeland in *Speaking of Poets,* "I primarily grew up on the Bible. Even as a young child I enjoyed the language of the Psalms." Another favorite of Carlstrom's was *Little Women.* After earning a B.A. in education from Wheaton College, Carlstrom taught primary school in Pittsburgh while working summers with children in the West Indies and in West Africa. She also studied art and children's literature, then moved with her husband to the Yucatan where she worked at a school for children with Down's Syndrome. Upon their return to the United States, the couple moved to Seattle, where Carlstrom became proprietor of The Secret Garden, a children's bookstore. "As owner and manager of the bookshop I was constantly surrounded by children's books," Carlstrom once recalled for *SATA,* "and spent a good portion of my time promoting quality children's literature through book fairs, presentations at churches and parent groups, and in our shop newsletter. In 1981 the urge to write resurfaced and I participated in a two-week workshop led by children's book author Jane Yolen." During that workshop Carlstrom wrote the poem that forms the text of *Wild Wild Sunflower Child Anna,* although several years passed before this text found a publisher. In the meantime, Carlstrom wrote

Jesse Bear, What Will You Wear? "My husband and I often called our son Jesse Bear," Carlstrom told *SATA,* "and the book ... began as a little song I sang while dressing him. I finished the picture book text for Jesse's first birthday." The book progresses through the day as little Jesse dresses and then messes and must dress again. Liza Bliss, writing in *School Library Journal,* noted in particular that "the rhymes, besides having a charming lilt to them, are clean and catchy and beg to be recited." A *Bulletin of the Center for Children's Books* reviewer drew attention to Carlstrom's lyrics, as well, and determined that, "without crossing the line into sentimentality, this offers a happy, humorous soundfest that will associate reading aloud with a sense of play." Lines like Jesse's reply to his mother—"I'll wear the sun / On my legs that run / Sun on the run in the morning"—tempt one "to sing Carlstrom's words aloud," commented a *Kirkus Reviews* critic, who added: "[Carlstrom] has a rich imagination which, hopefully, will create many more books for children."

Carlstrom has, in fact, created many more books for children, a large number of which are further adventures of Jesse Bear, with illustrations by Bruce Degen. *Better Not Get Wet, Jesse Bear* is a "winsome picture book," according to a *Publishers Weekly* reviewer, with "lilting, strongly rhymed text"; Ellen Fader of *Horn Book* commented that "the book never loses its claim to the sensibility of young children, who will be won over by Jesse Bear's delight in water play and his final triumphant splash." Clocks and the times of the day are at the

In her most recent Jesse Bear book, Carlstrom encourages children to count along with her rhyming verse and Bruce Degen's colorful illustrations. (From *Let's Count It Out, Jesse Bear.*)

Sing a song of Baby-O,
Sing it loud, now, watch it grow.

Carlstrom leads readers through all the sights and sounds of a family selling their goods at a market in the West Indies. (From *Baby-O*, illustrated by Sucie Stevenson.)

heart of Carlstrom's third "Jesse Bear" title, *It's about Time, Jesse Bear, and Other Rhymes,* a book that "children are sure to enjoy," according to Patricia Pearl in *School Library Journal. How Do You Say It Today, Jesse Bear?* celebrates the holidays of the year, from Independence Day to Halloween and Christmas. Ilene Cooper of *Booklist* commented on this work: "A good way to learn about the months and holidays, or read it just for fun." The sixth in the series, a Main Selection of the Children's Book-of-the-Month Club, *Let's Count It Out, Jesse Bear,* finds the playful bear "in a high-impact counting game," according to a *Publishers Weekly* reviewer. The rhyme for number two in this counting book is indicative of the humor and joy of the whole: "Jumping high, / Landing loud. / New shoes dancing, / New shoes proud." At six titles and counting, the "Jesse

Bear" series has prompted spin-off board books and toys as well as a loyal following among readers.

Carlstrom has also written many books outside of the "Jesse Bear" series. The first text she wrote, *Wild Wild Sunflower Child Anna,* about a child's exploration and discovery of the natural world around her, found a publisher in 1987 and is, according to Carlstrom, "still my favorite book of all I have written." Denise M. Wilms of *Booklist* maintained that "audiences young and old will find [Anna's] pleasure in the day most contagious." Ellen Fader, writing in *Horn Book,* concluded that "an exceptional treat awaits the parent and child who lose themselves in this book." Carlstrom further celebrated the lives of preschoolers in books such as *Heather Hiding,* the tale of a hide-and-seek game, *Graham Cracker Animals 1-2-3,* and *Blow Me a Kiss, Miss Lilly,* which deals with the death of a loved one. *Light: Stories of a Small Kindness* draws somewhat on Carlstrom's time spent in Mexico, in that the gathered tales all have Hispanic settings and all deal with a small kindness. "Tender, thought-provoking, moving are just a few of the words to describe these seven short stories," commented Ilene Cooper in a *Booklist* review.

Much the same format is employed in *Baby-O,* in which the rhythms of the West Indies are celebrated in a rhyming cumulative story of a family on its way to market to sell their produce. "Sing it, chant it, clap it, or stamp it," Jane Marino declared in a *School Library Journal* review. "Just don't miss it." Carlstrom has dealt with topics as various as the relationship between a young boy and his grandfather in *Grandpappy,* unlikely friendships in *Fish and Flamingo,* a child's fears of a trip to the hospital in *Barney Is Best,* and even "new baby syndrome" in *Kiss Your Sister, Rose Marie!* Also, harking back to her own childhood enjoyment of the Bible and religion, she wrote a book to encourage a child's questions about God—*Does God Know How to Tie Shoes?*—as well as Christmas books such as *I Am Christmas* and *Ten Christmas Sheep.*

Carlstrom practices the craft of writing with care and intelligence. "A picture book, like a poem, is what I call a bare bones kind of writing," Carlstrom once explained to *SATA.* "Usually I start with many more words than I need or want. I keep cutting away until I am down to the bare bones of what I want to say. It is then up to the illustrator to create pictures that will enlarge and enhance the text.... Often a title of a story will come first. I write it down and tend to think about it for a long time before actually sitting down to work on it. Sometimes I just get a few pieces of the story and they have to simmer on the back burner, like a good pot of soup. When the time is right, the writing of the story comes easily." Carlstrom also explained, in *Books That Invite Talk, Wonder, and Play,* that she often sings her words to get the correct rhythm. "Language is a musical experience for me. Rhythm, rhyme and cadence all become an important part of the process. I love the way a young child, just learning the language, rolls a word around on her tongue and, if she likes the sound of it, may chant it over and over."

Moving to Alaska in 1987 provided the author with new settings and themes for her writing—"freely wandering moose, northern lights, and extreme seasonal changes to name a few," she told *SATA.* Books such as *Moose in the Garden, The Snow Speaks, Northern Lullaby,* and *Goodbye Geese* have all been inspired by the wilderness and wildlife of the far north. "A first-rate choice for toddlers" is how *School Library Journal* contributor Ellen Fader described *Moose in the Garden,* which tells of a moose invading a garden and—to the delight of the young boy of the family—eating all the vegetables the boy does not like. The northern winter is lovingly examined in *Goodbye Geese* through the question and answer exchange between a father and his curious child:

Illustrated by Leo and Diane Dillon, *Northern Lullaby* sings a gentle good night to all the creatures on the vast Alaskan landscape. (Written by Carlstrom.)

"Papa, is winter coming? / Yes, and when the winter comes, she'll touch every living thing." *Booklist* reviewer Carolyn Phelan found *Goodbye Geese* to be "an effective mood book for story hour ... a vivid introduction to personification." In *Northern Lullaby,* Carlstrom also personifies the natural elements such as the moon and stars, along with wild creatures to conjure up a vision of the vastness of the far north. "The end effect," commented *Bulletin of the Center for Children's Books* reviewer Betsy Hearne, "is both simple and sophisticated." A *Kirkus Reviews* critic noted the book's "gently cadenced verse," and a *Publishers Weekly* reviewer concluded that *Northern Lullaby* was a "stunning, seamlessly executed work." Wintertime in Alaska also inspired Carlstrom's *The Snow Speaks,* in which two children experience the first snowfall of the season. *Booklist* reviewer Carolyn Phelan noted that Carlstrom used "lyrical language to turn down-to-earth experiences into something more," and Jane Marino in *School Library Journal* thought that it was "a book to be enjoyed all winter, long after the decorations have been packed away."

Natural phenomena form the core of many of Carlstrom's books, as she has been a nature lover since her own childhood. In books such as *Where Does the Night Hide?, Who Gets the Sun Out of Bed?, What Does the Rain Play?,* and *How Does the Wind Walk?,* Carlstrom uses question and answer rhymes and riddles to look at nature. With *Who Gets the Sun Out of Bed?,* the author reverses the goodnight story, relating instead a tale about waking up. *School Library Journal* contributor Ruth K. MacDonald found this work to be "an altogether successful story about the coming of the day," noting that "the persistent gentle patterns of questions and answers leads up to a climax that is warm but not boisterous—a fitting, final ending to a story that, despite its message, functions as an appropriate bedtime tale." The sounds of rain take center stage in *What Does the Rain Play?*, as the little boy in the tale loves all the various noises rain makes, even at night. Emily Melton in *Booklist* noted that "the gently calming writing and softly lulling rhythms of the rain sounds make this book a perfect bedtime choice." In *How Does the Wind Walk?*, a little boy looks at the different moods of the wind in different seasons in a question-and-answer format. *Kirkus Reviews* noted that Carlstrom's text employed "lots of alliteration and some subtle internal rhymes" to produce "wonderfully evocative effects."

All of Carlstrom's books share the common denominator of humor and hope. "No matter how bad things get, in this world or in my life," Carlstrom commented in her *Speaking of Poets* interview, "I do believe in joy and hope because I believe there's someone greater than myself in charge. It is my own religious faith that affects both the way I live my life and the way I write." The mystery of creation and of art are at the center of Carlstrom's inspiration, as she explained in the same interview: "I can't always explain exactly why my poems come out the way they do, but there is a joy that I have that I do want to express. And for me, writing is my way of celebrating."

■ Works Cited

Review of *Better Not Get Wet, Jesse Bear, Publishers Weekly,* March 11, 1988, p. 102.

Bliss, Liza, review of *Jesse Bear, What Will You Wear?, School Library Journal,* April, 1986, pp. 68-9.

Carlstrom, Nancy White, *Jesse Bear, What Will You Wear?,* Macmillan, 1986.

Carlstrom, Nancy White, *Goodbye Geese,* Philomel, 1991.

Carlstrom, Nancy White, interview in *Speaking of Poets,* Volume 2, edited by Jeffrey S. Copeland and Vicky L. Copeland, NCTE, 1994, pp. 194-202.

Carlstrom, Nancy White, "Of Memory and Language That Sings with Young Children," *Books That Invite Talk, Wonder, and Play,* edited by Amy A. McClure and Janice V. Kristo, NCTE, 1996, pp. 236-238.

Carlstrom, Nancy White, *Let's Count It Out, Jesse Bear,* Macmillan, 1996.

Cooper, Ilene, review of *Light: Stories of a Small Kindness, Booklist,* December 15, 1990, p. 855.

Cooper, Ilene, review of *How Do You Say It Today, Jesse Bear?, Booklist,* September 15, 1992, p. 154.

Fader, Ellen, review of *Wild Wild Sunflower Child Anna, Horn Book,* November-December, 1987, pp. 721-22.

Fader, Ellen, review of *Better Not Get Wet, Jesse Bear, Horn Book,* May-June, 1988, pp. 338-39.

Fader, Ellen, review of *Moose in the Garden, School Library Journal,* October, 1990, p. 86.

Hearne, Betsy, review of *Northern Lullaby, Bulletin of the Center for Children's Books,* October, 1992, p. 40.

Review of *How Does the Wind Walk?, Kirkus Reviews,* September 1, 1993, p. 1141.

Review of *Jesse Bear, What Will You Wear?, Bulletin of the Center for Children's Books,* May, 1986, p. 162.

Review of *Jesse Bear, What Will You Wear?, Kirkus Reviews,* February 15, 1986, p. 300.

Review of *Let's Count It Out, Jesse Bear, Publishers Weekly,* June 17, 1996, p. 63.

MacDonald, Ruth K., review of *Who Gets the Sun Out of Bed?, School Library Journal,* September, 1992, p. 199.

Marino, Jane, review of *Baby-O, School Library Journal,* April, 1992, p. 89.

Marino, Jane, review of *The Snow Speaks, School Library Journal,* October, 1992, p. 38.

Melton, Emily, review of *What Does the Rain Play?, Booklist,* April 1, 1993, p. 1436.

Review of *Northern Lullaby, Kirkus Reviews,* October 15, 1992, p. 1307.

Review of *Northern Lullaby, Publishers Weekly,* October 19, 1992, p. 75.

Pearl, Patricia, review of *It's about Time, Jesse Bear, and Other Rhymes, School Library Journal,* April, 1990, p. 87.

Phelan, Carolyn, review of *Goodbye Geese, Booklist,* November 15, 1991, p. 628.

Phelan, Carolyn, review of *The Snow Speaks, Booklist,* September 15, 1992, p. 154.

Wilms, Denise M., review of *Wild Wild Sunflower Child Anna, Booklist,* October 1, 1987, p. 257.

■ For More Information See

PERIODICALS

Booklist, December 1, 1989, pp. 740-41; March 15, 1990, p. 1443; December 15, 1990, p. 860; November 1, 1991, p. 530; March 15, 1993, p. 1358; April 1, 1993, p. 1436; December 1, 1993, p. 692; November 1, 1994, p. 505; September 1, 1995, p. 54.

Bulletin of the Center for Children's Books, May, 1990, p. 210; October, 1996, p. 51.

Horn Book, May-June, 1990, p. 319.

Kirkus Reviews, April 1, 1993, p. 453; April 15, 1993, p. 525; October 15, 1994, p. 1406; October, 1995, p. 1424.

New York Times Book Review, July 20, 1986, p. 24; December 20, 1992, p. 19; April 18, 1993, p. 25; September 19, 1993, p. 36.

Publishers Weekly, February 27, 1987, p. 162; March 22, 1993, p. 78; April 12, 1993, p. 62; May 17, 1993, p. 77; July 5, 1993, p. 72; April 25, 1994, p. 76; October 3, 1994, p. 67.

Quill & Quire, October, 1992, p. 39.

School Library Journal, June-July, 1987, p. 78; February, 1988, p. 58; May, 1988, p. 81; December, 1989, p. 77; June, 1990, p. 97; July, 1990, p. 56; December, 1990, p. 100; December, 1991, p. 80; May, 1993, p. 82; March, 1994, p. 190; July, 1994, p. 74; December, 1994, p. 72; September, 1995, p. 192. *Times Literary Supplement,* April 3, 1987, p. 356.*

—*Sketch by J. Sydney Jones*

* * *

CHANDONNET, Ann 1943-

■ Personal

Born February 7, 1943, in Lowell, MA; daughter of Leighton Fox (a dairy farmer) and Barbara Cloutman Curran (a licensed practical nurse); married Fernand L. Chandonnet (a writer), June 11, 1966; children: Yves, Alexandre. *Education:* Lowell State College, B.S., 1964; University of Wisconsin-Madison, M.S., 1965. *Hobbies and other interests:* Reading, backpacking, listening to Afro-Pop music.

■ Addresses

Home—6552 Lakeway Dr., Anchorage, AK 99502-1949.

■ Career

Lowell State College, Lowell, MA, English instructor, 1966-69; *Anchorage Times,* Anchorage, AK, feature writer, 1982-92; Chandonnet Editing & Research, partner, 1992—; Alaska Northwest Books, Anchorage, publicist, 1993—; *Alaska,* Anchorage, contributing editor, 1993—; *Left Bank,* advisor for Alaska, 1993-96. *Member:* Women's National Book Association, Walden Forever Wild.

■ Awards, Honors

Awards from the Alaska Press Club, the Alaska Press Women, and Rocky Mountain Booksellers.

■ Writings

FOR CHILDREN

Chief Stephen's Parky, Indian Council for Education, 1989, reprinted, Roberts Rinehart, 1993.
The Birthday Party, McRoy & Blackburn, 1995.

OTHER

The Complete Fruit Cookbook, 101 Productions, 1972.
The Cheese Guide and Cookbook, Nitty Gritty Productions, 1973.
Ptarmigan Valley: Poems of Alaska, The Lightning Tree, 1980.
Alaska Heritage Seafood Cookbook, Alaska Northwest Books, 1995.

Chandonnet wrote the preface to Leila Kiana Oman's *The Epic of Qayac,* University of Ontario Press, 1995.

ANN CHANDONNET

■ Work in Progress

"A historical cookbook about gold rushes in Alaska and California"; two children's books.

■ Sidelights

A former English instructor and journalist, Ann Chandonnet shares her love of Alaska and its original inhabitants in her books of historical fiction for children. Understanding the need to record the unique and varied lives of Native Americans, Chandonnet decided to write a story about the Athapascan Indians who live in south central Alaska. *Chief Stephen's Parky,* Chandonnet's first children's work, follows the efforts of a young Athapascan bride who decides to make her husband, Chief Stephen, a new fur parka. Olga spends a year gathering all the materials and equipment she needs to fashion the tribal leader an outercoat which will allow him to survive the fierce Alaska climate when hunting and trapping. While illustrating how Olga will collect everything she needs for the coat, Chandonnet also provides insight into the everyday lives of the Athapascans. In *School Library Journal,* Lisa Mitten praised Chandonnet's research, presentation, and exploration into the lives of Alaskan Indian women, calling the "activities of the women and girls ... a refreshing perspective that makes this especially valuable for collections seeking gender balance." Describing the story as well written, Ann M. Burlingame says in a *Kliatt* review that "readers will identify with the characters" and suggests the book would be useful in "supplementing school assignments on Native Americans."

Ann Chandonnet told *SATA:* "I've been a published poet since I was sixteen.

"I decided to write *Chief Stephen's Parky* after doing ten years of spare-time research on the Athapascan Indians of Cook Inlet, Alaska. I realized that there were no children's books for the children who were members of that ethnic group and that the Athapascan unit was being taught in local schools without any supplemental texts whatsoever. The book, set in the village of Knik in 1898, has been enthusiastically received, and I plan to write a sequel set in the 1940s. I'm very proud to have written this 'first.'

"*The Birthday Party* is a very different project—written as a lesson in bad manners. My rhymed verse is influenced by an Odgen Nash poem which my husband and I used to read to our sons at the dinner table.

"I admire *Catherine called Birdy* by Karen Cushman; reading historical fiction is one of my first loves. I also admire [Shel Silverstein's] *Light in the Attic.*

"As a kid, I used to read under the covers with my Girl Scout flashlight. Therefore, no 'lights out' for *my* kids. They could keep their lights on for as long as they wished—as long as they were reading.

"Writing assignments have taken me to Barrow, where I saw a fifty foot bowhead whale hauled in and divided among villagers, and to Gambell, where I ate murre eggs gathered from the cliffs. In the summer of 1993, I visited a five-thousand-year-old fishing site on an island in Prince William Sound and helped to sift through layers of dirt to find evidence of prehistoric diets such as seal knuckle bones and fish bones. It's amazing how a fish bone the size of a tiny needle can be preserved as a fossil!"

■ Works Cited

Burlingame, Ann M., review of *Chief Stephen's Parky,* *Kliatt,* September, 1993, p. 6.
Mitten, Lisa, review of *Chief Stephen's Parky, School Library Journal,* August, 1993, p. 163.

■ For More Information See

PERIODICALS

Booklist, September 1, 1993, p. 59.

CHASE, Alyssa 1965-

■ Personal

Born December 23, 1965; daughter of John Churchill (a businessman) and Alexandra (an artist/illustrator; maiden name, de Monsabert) Chase, Jr.; married Robert Brian Rebein (a writer), July 1, 1995. *Education:* University of Kansas, B.A. (English literature), 1988; State University of New York at Buffalo, B.A. (studio art; magna cum laude), 1994. *Hobbies and other interests:* Painting, travel, gardening, folklore, running, hiking, cross-country skiing.

■ Addresses

Home—7130 Dartmouth Ave., University City, MO 63130.

■ Career

Dial Books for Young Readers, New York City, assistant editor, 1989-90; Holiday House, New York City, associate editor, 1990-92; freelance copy writer, proofreader, copy editor, and researcher, 1990—; *Buffalo Spree* (magazine), Buffalo, NY, associate editor, 1992-95; *Riverfront Times* (newspaper) and *St. Louis Magazine,* St. Louis, MO, copy editor/writer, 1995—. Arts in Education Institute of Western New York, Cheektowaga, teaching artist, docent coordinator, and tour guide, 1995. *Member:* Phi Beta Kappa.

■ Writings

Jomo and Mata, illustrated by her mother, Andra Chase, Marsh Media, 1993.
Tessa on Her Own, illustrated by Itoko Maeno, Marsh Media, 1994.

■ Sidelights

Alyssa Chase told *SATA:* "Currently, I'm developing my writing by simply writing as much as I can at the weekly newspaper where I work. I'm also a painter (I have abstract canvases bigger than I am in my basement). I hope to continue developing as a writer and artist, and that these skills will evolve into books that I've both written and illustrated, because I think I express myself best using both forms together. I'm an obsessive gardener, and I am very interested in nature. I hope to create picture books that will share my sense of wonder about plants and animals and mud and rocks—all the small, wonderful details of life—with kids."

■ For More Information See

PERIODICALS

Publishers Weekly, November 14, 1994, p. 67.
School Library Journal, February, 1995, p. 72.

CHESS, Victoria (Dickerson) 1939-
(Anne Dothers)

■ Personal

Born November 16, 1939, in Chicago, IL; daughter of William Leard (an engineer) and Virginia (a jeweller; maiden name, Slade) Chess; married Bernhard Hoffmann (a financial analyst), 1983; children: Sam William Dickerson. *Education:* Attended Kokoshka School of Art, Salzburg, Austria, 1957, and Boston School of the Museum of Fine Arts, 1959-61. *Politics:* "Democrat/Bipartisan." *Religion:* Episcopalian.

■ Addresses

Home—80 Valley Rd., Warren, CT 06777; and 27 rue Ledru Rollin, Cadenet, 84160, France.

■ Career

Author and illustrator of books for children, 1965—. Member of Board of Directors, Warren (CT) Public Library, and Shepaug River Association. Member, Les Amis du Biblioteque, Cadenet, France. *Member:* Bull Terrier Club of New England.

■ Awards, Honors

Brooklyn Art Books for Children Citation, the Brooklyn Museum and the Brooklyn Public Library, 1973, for *Fletcher and Zenobia;* American Institute of Graphic Arts Book Show Award, 1976, for *Bugs;* Parents' Choice Awards, 1980, for *Taking Care of Melvin,* 1985, for *Tales for the Perfect Child,* and 1992, for *Slither McCreep and His Brother Joe.*

■ Writings

SELF-ILLUSTRATED

(With Edward Gorey) *Fletcher and Zenobia,* Hawthorn, 1967.
Alfred's Alphabet Walk, Greenwillow Books, 1979.
Poor Esme, Holiday House, 1982.

ILLUSTRATOR

Mary Lystad, *Millicent the Monster,* Quist, 1968.
Miriam Young, *The Witch Mobile,* Lothrop, 1969.
Jan Wahl, *The Animals' Peace Day,* Crown, 1970.
Will Stanton, *Once Upon a Time Is Enough,* Lippincott, 1970.
Edward Gorey, *Fletcher and Zenobia Save the Circus,* Dodd, 1971.
Stan J. Goldberg, *The Adventures of Stanley Kane,* Harcourt, 1973.
Miriam Young, *King Basil's Birthday,* Franklin Watts, 1973.
Benjamin Elkin, *The King Who Could Not Sleep,* Parents Magazine Press, 1975.
Mary Ann Hoberman, *Bugs: Poems,* Viking, 1976.
Sue Alexander, *Peacocks Are Very Special,* Doubleday, 1976.

VICTORIA CHESS

Norma Farber, *A Ship in a Storm on the Way to Tarshish,* Greenwillow, 1977.
Florence Parry Heide and Sylvia W. Van Clief, *Fables You Shouldn't Pay Any Attention To,* Lippincott, 1978.
Jack Prelutsky, *The Queen of Eene,* Greenwillow, 1978.
Noelle Sterne, *Tyrannosaurus Wrecks: A Book of Dinosaur Riddles,* Crowell, 1979.
Jane Werner Watson (under pseudonym W. K. Jasner), *Which Is the Witch?,* Pantheon, 1979.
Jack Prelutsky, *Rolling Harvey down the Hill,* Morrow, 1980.
Marjorie Sharmat, *Taking Care of Melvin,* Holiday House, 1980.
Ron Roy, *The Great Frog Swap,* Pantheon, 1981.
Larry Bograd, *Lost in the Store,* Macmillan, 1981.
Jack Prelutsky, *The Sheriff of Rottenshot,* Greenwillow, 1982.
David Greenberg, *Slugs,* Little, Brown, 1983.
Alice Schertle, *Bim Dooley Makes His Move,* Lothrop, 1984.
Florence Parry Heide, *Tales for the Perfect Child,* Lothrop, 1985.
David A. Adler, *The Twisted Witch and Other Spooky Riddles,* Holiday House, 1985.
Emily Lampert, *A Little Touch of Monster,* Atlantic Monthly Press, 1986.
Hilaire Belloc, *Jim, Who Ran away from His Nurse, and Was Eaten by a Lion: A Cautionary Tale,* Little, Brown, 1987.
Kevin Henkes, *Once around the Block,* Greenwillow, 1987.

Verna Aardema, *Princess Gorilla and a New Kind of Water: A Mpongwe Tale*, Dial, 1988.

Bill Grossman, *Tommy at the Grocery Store*, Harper, 1989.

John W. Ivimey, *The Complete Story of the Three Blind Mice*, Joy Street, 1990.

J. Patrick Lewis, *A Hippopotamusn't and Other Animal Verses*, Dial, 1990.

Alvin Schwartz, *Ghosts: Ghostly Tales from Folklore*, HarperCollins, 1991.

Florence Parry Heide, *Grim and Ghastly Goings-On*, Lothrop, 1992.

Tony Johnston, *Slither McCreep and His Brother Joe*, Harcourt, 1992.

Mary Pope Osborne, *Spider Kane and the Mystery under the May-Apple*, Knopf, 1992.

Mary Pope Osborne, *Spider Kane and the Mystery at Jumbo Nightcrawler's*, Knopf, 1993.

William Wise, *Ten Sly Piranhas: A Counting Story in Reverse*, Dial, 1993.

Florence Parry Heide, *The Bigness Contest*, Joy Street, 1994.

J. Patrick Lewis, *The Fat-Cats at Sea*, Knopf, 1994.

Judy Sierra, *Good Night, Dinosaurs*, Clarion, 1995.

J. Patrick Lewis, *Ridicholas Nicholas: More Animal Verses*, Dial, 1995.

Verna Aardema, *This for That: A Tonga Tale*, Dial, 1995.

Jane Yolen, *King Long Shanks*, Harcourt, 1997.

J. Patrick Lewis, *The Little Buggers: Insect and Spider Poems*, Dial, 1997.

"CAT AND DOG" SERIES; BY ELIZABETH MILLER AND JANE COHEN; PUBLISHED BY FRANKLIN WATTS:

Cat and Dog and the Mixed-Up Week, 1980.
Cat and Dog Have a Contest, 1980.
Cat and Dog Have a Party, 1980.
Cat and Dog Raise the Roof, 1980.
Cat and Dog Take a Trip, 1980.
Cat and Dog and the ABC's, 1981.
Cat and Dog Have a Parade, 1981.

■ Work in Progress

Research on frogs.

■ Sidelights

In a career spanning three decades, Victoria Chess has graced the pages of over forty children's picture books with her expressive and witty illustrations. Award-winning author and editor Jane Yolen, who collaborated with Chess for the first time on the 1997 book *King Long Shanks*, posted a message to an online newsgroup proclaiming, "I adore her work and it is a dream come true to have her doing something of mine."

Chess was born in Chicago in 1939, but she soon moved with her family to Washington, Connecticut, where she spent most of her childhood. She loved to draw from an early age, especially horses. "All children draw, but I think illustrators are the ones who keep doing it after fifth grade," Chess commented in *Talking with Artists*.

She continually worked to hone her talent—first adding background scenery of castles and princes to her horse pictures, then learning to make other creatures by studying a book called *How to Draw Animals* for hours on end. She also pored over comic strips and the engravings that illustrated a favorite book of stories by the Brothers Grimm.

In her youth, Chess attended girls' schools in Rhode Island and Switzerland. She was not a very attentive student, however, and often found herself in trouble. Eventually, she was asked to leave both schools. After studying at the Boston School of the Museum of Fine Arts for two years, she was asked to leave there as well in 1959. Despite her unimpressive academic career, Chess soon happened upon an opportunity to illustrate her first children's book. From this point on, her need to earn a living helped her to develop better work habits.

As Chess's reputation as an illustrator grew, her clever, mischievous watercolor pictures enhanced the books of a number of well-known children's authors, including Edward Gorey, Jack Prelutsky, and Florence Parry Heide. Her illustrations are distinguished by her keen, often wicked sense of humor; in Kevin Henkes's *Once around the Block*, for instance, "Chess' unique pop-eyed characters add just the right bit of tartness to a sweet tale," Judith Gloyer asserted in *School Library Journal*. Chess used Victorian backdrops to illustrate Hilaire Belloc's cautionary poem from 1908, *Jim, Who Ran*

Poor Beasley cannot win any contest until his Aunt Emerald helps him find a special talent of his very own. (From *The Bigness Contest*, written by Florence Parry Heide and illustrated by Victoria Chess.)

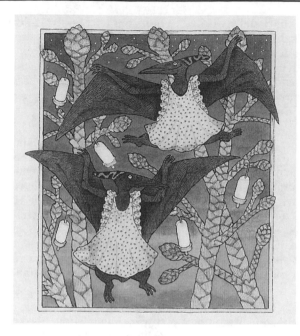

In this picture book written by Judy Sierra, Chess illustrates how baby dinosaurs once prepared for sleep. (From *Good Night, Dinosaurs.*)

away from His Nurse, and Was Eaten by a Lion. According to *School Library Journal* contributor Yvonne A. Frey, "Chess' clever comic illustrations capture the witty black humor of Belloc's verse," a tale of the grisly but deserved end of a spoiled brat.

Chess's artwork has also added humor to other texts, as with Alvin Schwartz's collection *Ghosts!* This series of ghost stories taken from folklore "seems tailor-made for Chess's friendly, funny, ever-mischievous art," according to a *Publishers Weekly* critic. In Mary Pope Osborne's lighthearted *Spider Kane and the Mystery under the May-Apple,* the artist portrayed a kidnapping among a community of insects. A *Publishers Weekly* reviewer hailed Chess's "antic drawings" as the "highlight" of the book, adding that "her eccentricity shines through even in black-and-white." William Wise's *Ten Sly Piranhas* offered a further opportunity to display the artist's "trademark wicked wit," according to another *Publishers Weekly* writer. A concept counting book, *Ten Sly Piranhas* demonstrates subtraction as a school of piranhas consumes each other one by one, all portrayed in Chess's "gleefully fiendish illustrations," as Mary M. Burns wrote in *Horn Book.* The critic concluded: "Victoria Chess's work has never been more colorful or more delightfully mischievous."

The 1990s saw Chess establish a particularly productive relationship with poet J. Patrick Lewis, beginning with *A Hippopotamusn't* (1990) and encompassing *The Fat-Cats at Sea* (1994), *Ridicholas Nicholas* (1995), and *The Little Buggers* (1997). Each book contains a series of offbeat, rhyming verses about the crazy antics of a group of animals. In a review of *A Hippopotamusn't,* a *Publishers Weekly* contributor noted that the poems "are brimming with wordplay and good fun," adding

that Chess's "distinctive, wittily drawn animals ... cavort and grin from every page." Mary M. Burns, reviewing the same volume for *Horn Book,* called Chess's illustrations "colorful, expressive, and at times oh-so-subtly wicked."

In *The Fat-Cats at Sea,* a group of cats is sent on a mission by the Queen of Catmandoo to retrieve sticky-buns from the Island of Goo. After a hilarious sea voyage in which various members of the feline crew hide from a thunderstorm or become seasick, they finally reach their destination, where the beaches are made of cinnamon sand and icing rivers run to a caramel sea. After loading their ship with fourteen tons of sticky-buns, the cats return to the high seas, only to be forced to defend their cargo from an enemy ship full of poodles. When they finally make it home, the queen proclaims them Fat-Cat Knights. Calling Chess's contributions to the book "devilishly droll" and "a treat," a reviewer for *Publishers Weekly* claimed that the illustrations provided "an indispensable element of the journey's great allure."

In 1995, Chess worked with Judy Sierra on *Good Night, Dinosaurs,* another book of nonsense animal verse. Each poem gives readers a lighthearted look at what baby dinosaurs might do when they get ready for bed and go to sleep. Many problems that the dinosaurs encounter, such as being scared of the dark or not wanting to take a bath, are the same ones that human children experience. Though several reviewers praised Sierra's concept and wordplay, most agreed that Chess's illustrations added significantly to the text. Stephanie Zvirin, writing in *Booklist,* called Chess's work "wonderfully expressive," noting that "it's the art that makes this [book] special." Similarly, a writer for *Kirkus Reviews* stated that "the offbeat charm of these watercolor scenes compensates for any imperfections in the poems."

Chess eventually returned to Connecticut to live near the town where she grew up. "I lived for a total of fifteen years in Manhattan and made occasional forays into odd corners of the world," she related in *Talking with Artists,* noting that she had lived in Beirut for three years and visited such countries as Jordan, Syria, Iraq, and Turkey. Her house in Connecticut features a river running past the yard, and is shared with her husband and a variety of pets, including a dog, two cats, a tortoise, and four lizards. Chess claims that she awakes each morning eager to begin working on the illustrations for a new book. "I only hope that children will enjoy my pictures," she has commented, "and learn to laugh at the world and not take themselves too seriously."

■ Works Cited

Burns, Mary M., review of *A Hippopotamusn't, Horn Book,* May-June, 1990, p. 344.

Burns, Mary M., review of *Ten Sly Piranhas, Horn Book,* July-August, 1993, p. 452.

Chess, Victoria, autobiographical statement in *Talking with Artists,* compiled and edited by Pat Cummings, Bradbury Press, 1992, pp. 10-14.

Review of *The Fat-Cats at Sea, Publishers Weekly,*
    September 5, 1994, p. 111.
Frey, Yvonne A., review of *Jim, Who Ran away from
    His Nurse, and Was Eaten by a Lion, School Library
    Journal,* June-July, 1987, p. 76.
Review of *Ghosts!, Publishers Weekly,* July 5, 1991, p.
    64.
Gloyer, Judith, review of *Once around the Block, School
    Library Journal,* June-July, 1987, p. 83.
Review of *Good Night, Dinosaurs, Kirkus Reviews,*
    January 1, 1996.
Review of *A Hippopotamusn't, Publishers Weekly,* May
    18, 1990, p. 83.
Review of *Spider Kane and the Mystery under the May-
    Apple, Publishers Weekly,* March 23, 1992, p. 72.
Review of *Ten Sly Piranhas, Publishers Weekly,* May 31,
    1993, p. 54.
Yolen, Jane, online posting to *rec.arts.books.children,*
    May 4, 1996.
Zvirin, Stephanie, review of *Good Night, Dinosaurs,
    Booklist,* January 1, 1996, p. 841.

■ For More Information See

BOOKS

Holtze, Sally Holmes, editor, *Sixth Book of Junior
    Authors and Illustrators,* Wilson, 1989, pp. 55-56.
Kingman, Lee, *Illustrators of Children's Books, 1967-76,*
    Horn Book, 1978.

PERIODICALS

Booklist, May 1, 1992, p. 1287; March 15, 1993, p.
    1319; May 1, 1993, p. 1597; March 15, 1994, p.
    1372; December 1, 1995, p. 638.
Bulletin of the Center for Children's Books, May, 1986.
Horn Book, September-October, 1989, p. 610; Septem-
    ber-October, 1991, p. 607.
New York Times Book Review, June 7, 1992, p. 22;
    January 15, 1995, p. 25.
Publishers Weekly, April 24, 1987, p. 69; May 29, 1987,
    p. 77; October 13, 1989, p. 51; March 2, 1992, p. 64;
    March 14, 1994, p. 72; October 30, 1995, p. 62;
    January 29, 1996, p. 99.
School Library Journal, December, 1989, p. 78; May,
    1990, p. 99; September, 1991, p. 294; April, 1992,
    pp. 94, 118; April, 1993, p. 102; October, 1993, p.
    114; May, 1994, p. 95; September, 1994, p. 188;
    November, 1995, p. 91; April, 1996, p. 118.*

*   *   *

CLIFFORD, David
See CLIFFORD, Eth

CLIFFORD, Eth 1915-
(Ruth Bonn Penn, Eth Clifford Rosenberg, Ethel Rosenberg; David Clifford, a joint pseudonym)

■ Personal

Born in 1915 in New York City; married David
Rosenberg (a publisher), October 15, 1941; children:
Ruthanne.

■ Addresses

Home—1075 Miami Gardens Drive #102W, North
Miami Beach, FL 33179-4600. *Agent*—Ted Chichak,
1040 First Ave., Suite 175, New York, NY 10022.

■ Career

Writer. David-Stewart Publishing Co., Indianapolis, IN,
editor and writer, 1959-70.

■ Awards, Honors

Best Children's Books selection, *Saturday Review* and
New York Times, 1961, for *Red Is Never a Mouse;*
Young Hoosier Award, Association for Indiana Media
Educators, 1982, for *Help! I'm a Prisoner in the Library;*
Sequoyah Award, Oklahoma Library Association, 1986,
for *Just Tell Me When We're Dead.* Clifford also
received an Artist's Fellowship Award from the state of
Florida in 1987 for her body of work.

■ Writings

FOR CHILDREN; FICTION

The Year of the Second Christmas, illustrated by Stan
    Learner, Bobbs-Merrill, 1959.

ETH CLIFFORD

Red Is Never a Mouse, illustrated by Bill Heckler, Bobbs-Merrill, 1960.

(With husband, David Rosenberg, under name David Clifford) *No Pigs, No Possums, No Pandas*, Putnam, 1961.

A Bear Before Breakfast, illustrated by Kelly Oechsli, Putnam, 1962.

A Bear Can't Bake a Cake for You, illustrated by Jackie Lacy, E. C. Seale (Indianapolis, IN), 1962.

(Under name Ruth Bonn Penn) *Mommies Are for Loving*, illustrated by Ed Emberley, Putnam, 1962.

Pigeons Don't Growl and Bears Don't Coo, illustrated by Esther Friend, E. C. Seale, 1963.

(With husband, David Rosenberg, under name David Clifford) *Your Face Is a Picture*, E. C. Seale, 1963.

(Under name Ruth Bonn Penn) *Simply Silly*, illustrated by Joseph Reisner, E. C. Seale, 1964.

The Witch That Wasn't, illustrated by Jean Dorion Kauper, E. C. Seale, 1964.

(With Leo C. Fay) *Curriculum Motivation Series: A Necessary Dimension in Reading* (contains *Blue Dog, and Other Stories; The Flying Squirrels, and Other Stories; The Almost Ghost, and Other Stories; The Barking Cat; Better Than Gold;* and *Three Green Men*), illustrated by Carol Burger, Lyons and Carnahan, 1965.

Why Is an Elephant Called an Elephant?, illustrated by Jackie Lacy, Bobbs-Merrill, 1966.

The King Who Was Different, illustrated by Francoise Webb, Bobbs-Merrill, 1969.

The Year of the Three-Legged Deer, illustrated by Richard Cuffari, Houghton, 1972.

Search for the Crescent Moon, illustrated by Bea Holmes, Houghton, 1973.

Burning Star, illustrated by Leo and Diane Dillon, Houghton, 1974.

The Wild One, illustrated by Arvis Stewart, Houghton, 1974.

The Curse of the Moonraker: A Tale of Survival, Houghton, 1977.

The Rocking Chair Rebellion, Houghton, 1978.

The Killer Swan, Houghton, 1980.

The Strange Reincarnations of Hendrik Verloon, Houghton, 1982.

The Remembering Box, illustrated by Donna Diamond, Houghton, 1985.

I Never Wanted to Be Famous, Houghton, 1986.

The Man Who Sang in the Dark, illustrated by Mary B. Owen, Houghton, 1987, published as *Leah's Song*, Scholastic, 1989.

I Hate Your Guts, Ben Brooster, Houghton, 1989.

The Summer of the Dancing Horse, Houghton, 1991.

Will Somebody Please Marry My Sister?, illustrated by Ellen Eagle, Houghton, 1992.

Family For Sale, Houghton, 1996.

"JO-BETH AND MARY ROSE" SERIES; ILLUSTRATED BY GEORGE HUGHES; PUBLISHED BY HOUGHTON

Help! I'm a Prisoner in the Library, 1979.
The Dastardly Murder of Dirty Pete, 1981.
Just Tell Me When We're Dead, 1983.
Scared Silly, 1988.
Never Hit a Ghost with a Baseball Bat, 1993.

"HARVEY" SERIES; PUBLISHED BY HOUGHTON

Harvey's Horrible Snake Disaster, 1984.
Harvey's Marvelous Monkey Mystery, 1987.
Harvey's Wacky Parrot Adventure, edited by Patricia MacDonald, 1990.
Harvey's Mystifying Raccoon Mix-Up, 1994.

"FLATFOOT FOX" SERIES; ILLUSTRATED BY BRIAN LIES; PUBLISHED BY HOUGHTON

Flatfoot Fox and the Case of the Missing Eye, 1990.
Flatfoot Fox and the Case of the Nosy Otter, 1992.
Flatfoot Fox and the Case of the Missing Whoooo, 1993.
Flatfoot Fox and the Case of the Bashful Beaver, 1995.
Flatfoot Fox and the Case of the Missing Schoolhouse, 1997.

NONFICTION

(With Willis Peterson) *Wapiti, King of the Woodland*, Follett, 1961.

Ground Afire: The Story of Death Valley, photographs by Ansel Adams, Follett, 1962.

(Under name Ruth Bonn Penn) *Unusual Animals of the West*, photographs by Willis Peterson, Follett, 1962.

(With Raymond Carlson) *The Wind Has Scratchy Fingers*, Follett, 1962.

(With Richard E. Kirk and James N. Rogers) *Living Indiana History: Heartland of America*, illustrated by George Armstrong and David Kinney, David-Stewart, 1965.

(With Leo C. Fay) *Curriculum Enrichment Series: A New Dimension in Reading* (contains *Look at the Moon* and *Tommy Finds a Seed*), illustrated by Carol Burger, Lyons and Carnahan, 1965.

(With others) *War Paint and Wagon Wheels: Stories of Indians and Pioneers*, illustrated by David Kinney, Bill Harris, and Polly Woodhouse, David-Stewart, 1968.

(Compiler) *The Magnificent Myths of Man*, edited by Leo C. Fay, Globe Book Company, 1972.

(Editor) *The Third Star: The Story of New Jersey* (textbook), Third Star Publishing, 1974.

Show Me Missouri: A History of Missouri and the World Around It, illustrated by George Armstrong, Russell E. Hollenbeck, and Gene Jarvis, Unified College Press, 1975.

Also contributor of four books to "Reading for Concepts" series, McGraw-Hill, 1970. Contributor to *Basic Science Series*, McGraw-Hill, 1968; *Reading Incentive Series*, McGraw-Hill (Webster Division), 1968; *Pacesetters in Personal Reading*, Lyons and Carnahan, 1969; *Health and Safety Series*, Globe Book Company, 1970; *Living City Adventures*, Globe Book Company, 1970; *Pathways to Health*, Globe Book Company, 1970; and *Pre-Primer Stories for Series 360*, Ginn and Company, 1971. Also lexicographer for *Compton's Illustrated Science Dictionary*, Compton's Encyclopedia Company, 1963; *Dictionary of Natural Science* (2 volumes), Compton's Encyclopedia Company, 1966; and *Discovering Natural Science*, Encyclopedia Britannica, 1967.

FOR ADULTS

Go Fight City Hall (fiction), Simon & Schuster, 1949.

Uncle Julius and the Angel with Heartburn (fiction),
    Simon & Schuster, 1951.
(As Eth Clifford Rosenberg; with Molly Picon) *So
    Laugh a Little* (fiction), Messner, 1962.

Also contributor to *Best Humor Annual, 1949-50,* 1950,
and *Best Humor Annual, 1951,* 1951, both edited by
Louis Untermeyer and Ralph E. Shikes and published
by Holt. Contributor to *A Treasury of Jewish Humor,*
edited by Nathan Ausubel, Doubleday, 1951, and *Tales
of Our People,* edited by Jerry D. Lewis, Bernard Geis
Associates, 1969.

Some of Clifford's papers and manuscripts have been
collected by the Division of Rare Books and Special
Collections of the University of Wyoming, the Bicentennial Library of California State College in California,
and the Kerlan Collection at the Walter Library of the
University of Minnesota.

■ **Adaptations**

The Rocking Chair Rebellion was adapted for film by
NBC-TV.

■ **Sidelights**

The author of more than eighty books, Eth Clifford is
best known for her children's fiction, including the well-
received *Year of the Three-Legged Deer, The Killer
Swan, The Remembering Box,* and mysteries with a
humorous twist such as *Help! I'm a Prisoner in the
Library* and *Just Tell Me When We're Dead.* Clifford
has, however, written a wide range of books, both fiction
and nonfiction, for children and adults. Her adult
fiction bestseller, *Go Fight City Hall,* appeared in 1949
and a sequel soon thereafter, but those would be the first
and last adult fiction titles Clifford wrote independent-
ly. Turning her hand to children's books, she has since
written everything from classroom reading primers to
picture books and humorous mystery fiction.

"I never, ever thought I would be a writer," Clifford
confided in an essay for *Something about the Author
Autobiography Series* (*SAAS*). "Writers I regarded as a
race apart. They were tall, and handsome, and male.
They were brilliant, and witty, and flawless .... Then I
made an extraordinary discovery. All writers were not
necessarily male! ... But of course, I told myself, these
women were tall and beautiful. I was tiny, and certainly
not beautiful, so I automatically disqualified myself....
I wrote, of course, very early on. I accepted the fact that
this did not make me an author. Authors were very
special people. I was very class-conscious!"

Whether or not she considered herself a writer, Clifford
was a reader from an early age. Born in Manhattan, she
moved with her family to rural New Jersey for a time,
and then to Philadelphia where her father's employment
took him. Clifford was eight when her father died, and
the family moved to Brooklyn to live among their
relatives. Clifford's father's death was a defining moment of her childhood. "I understood that I would never

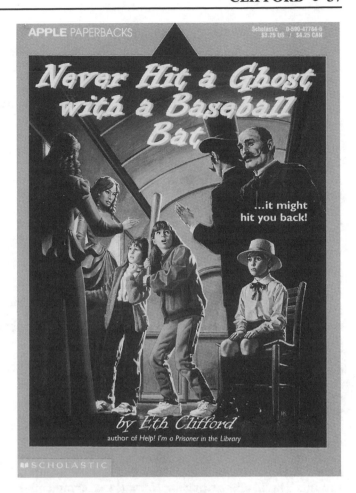

**Expecting to find the museum boring, Jo-Beth and her
sister Mary Rose are startled when the mannikins come
to life in this suspenseful mystery.**

see him again," she wrote in *SAAS*. "Never hear his
voice, never see him smile." It was then that Clifford
turned to the solace of fiction—both reading and
writing. "I think that somehow that was when I became
a writer. Making up stories gave me power—power to
create people and situations, power to control what they
said and did."

At age seventeen, Clifford met the man she would later
marry, someone who loved books as much as she. After
marriage and the turmoil of the war years in the 1940s,
the two started the David-Stewart Publishing Company,
which developed a range of books and educational
materials from inception to writing to packaging. Clifford had been writing short stories and publishing them
in magazines throughout the 1940s, and the success of
her first two novels, *Go Fight City Hall* and its sequel,
Uncle Julius and the Angel with Heartburn, were encouraging. "And then suddenly, my direction changed,"
Clifford explained in *SAAS*. "My husband listened each
evening as I told stories to our daughter at bedtime. She
snuggled down in her pillow, thumb in mouth, ready for
story time. One evening, when she was fast asleep,
David told me, 'You ought to write those stories
down.'" Thus was launched a career in children's books
that has lasted nearly four decades.

One of her first children's books, *Red Is Never a Mouse,* was about colors. Chosen as one of the 100 best books of the year by *Saturday Review* and the *New York Times,* that book convinced Clifford to devote full time to writing for children "of all ages," as she put it in *SAAS.* Her early efforts were mainly picture books for young children as well as first readers for school curricula. By the 1970s, however, she was writing longer novels for middle-grade and young adult readers. *The Year of the Three-Legged Deer,* inspired by Clifford's visit to a pioneer museum in Indiana where the family had moved, was set on the Indiana frontier in 1819 and based on actual events. In this story, trader Jesse Benton is married to a Lenni Lenape Indian and has a son and daughter by her. His son brings home an injured deer which his daughter, Chilili, raises. Jesse purchases the freedom of a slave who has saved his son's life, but intolerance and bigotry soon rip the family apart, and Chilili is killed by Indian-hunting whites. Jesse's wife and son decide to go back to their people, joining their removal westward to Missouri. Jeanette Swickard of *Booklist* thought that Clifford's novel presented a "thought-provoking dramatization of the evils of prejudice." Clifford commented in *SAAS* that readers still complain about the death of Chilili: "'Why did you let Chilili die? Can you write the book over again and let her live?' one child begged." Another frontier story—based on the life of Frances Slocum—informs *Search for the Crescent Moon,* the tale of a 15-year-old boy who, along with his grandfather, goes on a search for the old man's twin sister, kidnapped by Indians as a child. Virginia Haviland, writing in *Horn Book,* commented that in this work Clifford "is in full command of her historical material and knows how to invent and present dramatic actions."

Clifford expanded on this technique of fictional biography and history with two books somewhat further afield: one set in Spain, the other in the South Pacific, and both in the nineteenth century. *The Wild One* is the embellished partial biography of young Santiago Ramon y Cajal, winner of the Nobel Prize for medicine in 1906, and of his punishing upbringing that nearly squelched his genius. Desiring to be an artist, the young Santiago was sent to strict schools by his stern doctor father, and became interested in medicine only when his father sought his help in the infirmary and allowed him to use his artistic skills to sketch anatomy drawings. "Santiago's escapades as embellished here make lively reading," noted a *Kirkus Reviews* critic, "and Clifford brings the time and place of his teen-age years to dramatic life." Zena Sutherland of the *Bulletin of the Center for Children's Books* concluded in her review that "the book has good period detail, a sensitive treatment of relationships, strong characterization, and a vigorous style." Clifford's South Pacific novel, *The Curse of the Moonraker,* was based on a true incident: the sinking of a passenger ship in the South Pacific in 1866. Just fifteen passengers survived on the Auckland Islands for a year and a half until being rescued. Told from the point of view of a thirteen-year-old cabin boy, Clifford's Robinson Crusoe narrative "is a gripping one," according to *Horn Book* reviewer Mary M. Burns, "because of the

ingenuity by which [the shipwrecked people] battled and defeated the emotional and physical obstacles to their survival." *School Library Journal* contributor Robert Unsworth felt that the novel, on balance, was "a good story, well told, and it deserves a reading."

With *The Rocking Chair Rebellion,* Clifford left the realms of history for contemporary fiction. In this story, protagonist Opie is fourteen and a somewhat reluctant volunteer at the Maple Ridge Home for the Aged where a former neighbor, Mr. Pepper, is an unwilling guest. Pepper and some other residents try to buy a house of their own in Pepper's former neighborhood and set up a communal home for the aged. The neighbors, however, dig in their heels and take the seniors to court. Opie's lawyer father successfully handles the case in this novel which has, according to *Bulletin of the Center for Children's Books* reviewer Zena Sutherland, "a crisp style, sharp characterizations, and humor." *The Rocking Chair Rebellion* was adapted for television by NBC-TV, and several months after publication, a "rebellion" mirroring that in Clifford's book actually took place in Chicago. "Fiction turned into fact!" Clifford wrote in *SAAS.* "That was a joyous moment for me."

Lighthearted, often humorous adventures form the core of some of Clifford's most popular books, those center-

ETH CLIFFORD · THE Remembering Box

Grandma tells the best stories!

Joshua looks forward to Saturday afternoon when his grandmother shares stories and mementos from her childhood. (Cover illustration by Kathy Coville.)

ETH CLIFFORD

Harvey's Mystifying Raccoon Mix-Up

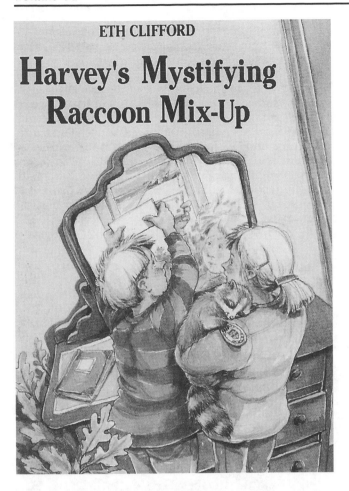

Startled by a mysterious figure lurking under his window, Harvey Willson teams with his cousin Nora to investigate. (Cover illustration by Margot Apple.)

ing on the exploits of sisters Jo-Beth and Mary Rose. Their first adventure, *Help! I'm a Prisoner in the Library,* has the two accidentally locked overnight in a children's library after their father has run out of gas in a blizzard. Spooky sounds abound, the pair save the injured librarian who lives upstairs, and by morning all is well when their father shows up to rescue them. Mary I. Purucker in *School Library Journal* called it a "funny, fast-moving, suspenseful, and engaging easy-to-read tale," and a *Kirkus Reviews* critic noted that the book is a "cozy adventure, easy to read in a sitting." A runaway cousin and bank robbers at an amusement park figure in another Mary Rose and Jo-Beth romp, *Just Tell Me When We're Dead.* Craighton Hippenhammer commented in *School Library Journal* that "lots of laughs and fast-paced action follow," and *Bulletin of the Center for Children's Books* reviewer Zena Sutherland noted that there was "plenty of danger and action for thrill-lovers." A deserted mining town in California with a very life-like ghost fuels the engine of *The Dastardly Murder of Dirty Pete,* a novel with "verve and suspense," according to *Publishers Weekly,* and an unscheduled visit to a bizarre shoe museum gets Jo-Beth and Mary Rose in hot water in *Scared Silly.* With the fifth novel in the series, *Never Hit a Ghost with a Baseball Bat,* Clifford has the sisters explore a haunted

trolley museum, fashioning a book which *Booklist* dubbed "another great in the series."

Two distinctive books by Clifford from the 1980s deal with loss and remembrance, handling serious problems with poignancy while avoiding sentimentality. *The Killer Swan* presents something of a paradox with a male white swan, a cob, that attacks its young. Lex, the young protagonist, whose father recently committed suicide, saves one of the cygnets from its father's attack, and ultimately is forced to kill the cob after it attacks a friend's dog. Clifford draws the analogy between the behavior of the cob—actually set off because of the pain it is experiencing from an injured eye—and Lex's father who took his own life. *Publishers Weekly* declared that "Clifford is at her impressive best," and Frank Perry, writing in *Voice of Youth Advocates,* while noting Clifford's "keen insight and sensitivity," concluded that *The Killer Swan* was more than just an animal story: "It is a human story for all persons fortunate enough to read it." *The Remembering Box* also deals with loss, when young Joshua's grandmother dies. But she has left Joshua with a legacy of memories in her trunk full of mementos, a heritage that bridges the generational and cultural gaps between the two. Hanna B. Zeiger of *Horn Book* noted that "Eth Clifford has succeeded in opening a remembering box for her readers, giving them a glimpse into the world of their grandparents." A *Bulletin of the Center for Children's Books* commentator called the book a "moving remembrance within a remembrance," and Micki S. Nevett in *School Library Journal* wrote that "this warm and loving relationship between a boy and his grandmother is beautifully depicted."

Two separate series also employ Clifford's blend of zany humor and action/mystery writing. The "Harvey" series features young Harvey Willson and sometimes his cousin Nora, with whom he has a tenuous relationship. The books also feature adventures with various animals: a snake, a monkey, a parrot, a raccoon. *Horn Book* reviewer Elizabeth S. Watson commented of *Harvey's Marvelous Monkey Mystery* that "the real focus is on plenty of action. Children who are looking for the next step after easy readers will find new friends in these books...." Ilene Cooper of *Booklist* found the book "warm, realistic, and certainly funny." Reviewing *Harvey's Wacky Parrot Adventure* for *Booklist,* Deborah Abbott noted that this was "another breezy read for Harvey fans," and Christina Dorr in *School Library Journal* concluded that *Harvey's Mystifying Raccoon Mix-Up* is a "lively page-turner that draws readers into the action and won't disappoint them." The second series to employ Clifford's penchant for mysteries with a light touch are the "Flatfoot Fox" books for younger readers, featuring the Fox as a great detective. These easy-to-read chapter books involve cases ranging from recovering the owl's missing "whoooo" to the otter's missing child, and combine the best of mystery and animal stories. Flatfoot Fox and his sidekick, Secretary Bird, team up initially in *Flatfoot Fox and the Case of the Missing Eye* to create a "clever and funny first chapter book," according to Kay Weisman in *Booklist.*

In this book for beginning readers, Flatfoot Fox and Secretary Bird join forces to discover who stole Bashful Beaver's missing buttons. (From *Flatfoot Fox and the Case of the Bashful Beaver*, written by Clifford and illustrated by Brian Lies.)

They have continued to please through five further installments in their adventures with a mixture of "tongue-twisting alliterations" and "dry comedy," as Stephanie Zvirin noted in a *Booklist* review of *Flatfoot Fox and the Case of the Bashful Beaver*.

Clifford is at her best when she infuses her work with a quirky humor that has become a hallmark of her writing. She can tackle serious themes but, with a dash of humor, turn such books into easy-reads. A strained relationship between cousins once again comes to play with *I Hate Your Guts, Ben Brooster*, in which near-genius Ben arrives to spend a year with his older cousin, Charlie. Rivalry is put on hold while the mystery of a suitcase Ben has mistakenly taken is solved. "Dollops of humor add fun to a book that demonstrates how children can learn to get along without having to be best friends," according to Deborah Abbott in *Booklist*. Pure fun fills the pages of *I Never Wanted to Be Famous*, in which thirteen-year-old Goody is jarred out of his ambition-less state when he saves an infant from choking. A sudden celebrity, Goody now has to deal with the pressures that fame brings as well as the plans his mother has for him. "*I Never Wanted to Be Famous* is a sheer delight to read," commented Civia Tuteur in *Voice of Youth Advocates*. "It is filled with humor."

A *Publishers Weekly* critic, reviewing *I Never Wanted to be Famous*, noted that "Clifford's quick wit and likable characters have won the hearts of fans who revel in such gems as *Help! I'm a Prisoner in the Library, The Dastardly Murder of Dirty Pete*, etc."—which is high praise for someone who thought she could never be one of those "authors". Over the years, Clifford has created a body of work that has pleased, amused, delighted, and encouraged children to read. "Words are the bridges to communication," Clifford wrote in *SAAS*. "Words on the page say: listen, I've been thinking and I want to share my thoughts with you. Perhaps you've had these same thoughts (and feelings) but haven't been able to express them. But when you read these words, you can say to yourself—that's it. She's got it exactly right."

■ Works Cited

Abbott, Deborah, review of *I Hate Your Guts, Ben Brooster, Booklist,* September 1, 1989, p. 68.

Abbott, Deborah, review of *Harvey's Wacky Parrot Adventure, Booklist,* March 15, 1990, p. 1444.

Burns, Mary M., review of *The Curse of the Moonraker: A Tale of Survival, Horn Book,* April, 1978, pp. 162-63.

Clifford, Eth, essay in *Something about the Author Autobiography Series,* Volume 22, Gale, 1996, pp. 23-38.

Cooper, Ilene, review of *Harvey's Marvelous Monkey Mystery, Booklist,* June 1, 1987, p. 1520.

Review of *The Dastardly Murder of Dirty Pete, Publishers Weekly,* December 11, 1981, p. 62.

Dorr, Christina, review of *Harvey's Mystifying Raccoon Mix-Up, School Library Journal,* October, 1994, p. 120.

Haviland, Virginia, review of *Search for the Crescent Moon, Horn Book,* October, 1973, p. 464.

Review of *Help! I'm a Prisoner in the Library, Kirkus Reviews,* December 15, 1979, pp. 1429-30.

Hippenhammer, Craighton, review of *Just Tell Me When We're Dead, School Library Journal,* December, 1983, p. 64.

Review of *I Never Wanted to Be Famous, Publishers Weekly,* April 25, 1986, p. 83.

Review of *The Killer Swan, Publishers Weekly,* December 12, 1980, pp. 47-48.

Review of *Never Hit a Ghost with a Baseball Bat, Booklist,* April 15, 1994, p. 1540.

Nevett, Micki S., review of *The Remembering Box, School Library Journal,* December, 1985, p. 87.

Perry, Frank, review of *The Killer Swan, Voice of Youth Advocates,* April, 1981, pp. 31-2.

Purucker, Mary I., review of *Help! I'm a Prisoner in the Library, School Library Journal,* November, 1979, p. 63.

Review of *The Remembering Box, Bulletin of the Center for Children's Books,* December, 1985, p. 64.

Sutherland, Zena, review of *The Wild One, Bulletin of the Center for Children's Books,* March, 1975, p. 107.

Sutherland, Zena, review of *The Rocking Chair Rebellion, Bulletin of the Center for Children's Books,* March, 1979, p. 111.

Sutherland, Zena, review of *Just Tell Me When We're Dead, Bulletin of the Center for Children's Books,* February, 1984, p. 104.

Swickard, Jeanette, review of *The Three-Legged Deer, Booklist,* November 1, 1972, p. 246.

Tuteur, Civia, review of *I Never Wanted to Be Famous, Voice of Youth Advocates,* August, 1986, p. 140.

Unsworth, Robert, review of *The Curse of the Moonraker: A Tale of Survival, School Library Journal,* March, 1978, p. 125.

Watson, Elizabeth S., review of *Harvey's Marvelous Monkey Mystery, Horn Book,* July-August, 1987, p. 461.

Weisman, Kay, review of *Flatfoot Fox and the Case of the Missing Eye, Booklist,* December 15, 1990, p. 861.

Review of *The Wild One, Kirkus Reviews,* October 15, 1974, pp. 1109-10.

Zeiger, Hanna B., review of *The Remembering Box, Horn Book,* March-April, 1986, p. 200.

Zvirin, Stephanie, review of *Flatfoot Fox and the Case of the Bashful Beaver, Booklist,* March 1, 1995, p. 1242.

■ For More Information See

BOOKS

Sixth Book of Junior Authors and Illustrators, H. W. Wilson, 1989.

PERIODICALS

Booklist, December 15, 1993, p. 753; September 15, 1994, p. 135; February 1, 1996, p. 932.

Bulletin of the Center for Children's Books, January, 1973, p. 73; March, 1975, p. 107; May, 1978, p. 139; April, 1980, p. 148; March, 1981, p. 129; February, 1983, p. 104; April, 1988, p. 152; July, 1990, p. 261; March, 1992, p. 177; November, 1992, p. 70; November, 1993, p. 77.

Horn Book, February, 1979, p. 59; April, 1981, p. 189.

Kirkus Reviews, November 15, 1994, p. 1524; December 15, 1995, p. 1768.

New York Times Book Review, June 18, 1972, p. 8.

School Library Journal, October, 1978, p. 153; November, 1980, p. 84; January, 1982, p. 61; May, 1986, p. 89; April, 1987, p. 92; October, 1987, p. 124; June, 1988, p. 103; October, 1989, p. 116; March, 1991, p. 170; July, 1991, p. 72; September, 1991, p. 201; June, 1992, p. 112; June, 1993, p. 104; August, 1993, p. 140; April, 1995, p. 100; April, 1996, p. 132.

—Sketch by J. Sydney Jones

*   *   *

COFFEY, Brian
    See KOONTZ, Dean R(ay)

COTTONWOOD, Joe 1947-

■ Personal

Born August 19, 1947, in Washington, DC; married an occupational therapist, 1969. *Education:* Washington University (St. Louis), B.A., 1970. *Hobbies and other interests:* Outdoor life: hiking, canoeing, camping.

■ Addresses

Home—P.O. Box 249, La Honda, CA 94020. *Electronic mail*—joecot@well.com.

■ Career

Computer operator, 1968-76; self-employed building contractor, 1976—. Has worked variously as a dishwasher, fry cook, and bus driver. *Member:* Authors Guild, Society of Children's Book Writers and Illustrators.

■ Awards, Honors

Best Children's Book designation, 1992, Bay Area Book Reviewers Association (BABRA), for *Danny Ain't;* Best Books for the Teen Age selection, New York City Public Library, 1995, for *Quake!,* and 1996, for *Babcock.*

■ Writings

The Adventures of Boone Barnaby, Scholastic, 1990.
Danny Ain't, Scholastic, 1992.
Quake!, Scholastic, 1995.
Babcock, Scholastic, 1996.

Also author of novels for adults, including *Famous Potatoes,* 1976, and *Frank City (Goodbye),* c. 1977; author of a poetry book, *Son of a Poet.*

■ Work in Progress

A novel about abortion protestors.

■ Sidelights

Having written novels for adults, author Joe Cottonwood was inspired to write for a younger audience after reading aloud to his own children. He found many books for children "written without respect for kids," as he told interviewer Stacy Trevenon in the *Half Moon Bay Review,* "like Saturday morning TV." Breaking with that trend, Cottonwood's first novel for young readers, *The Adventures of Boone Barnaby,* features realistic characters and true-to-life situations, and illuminates a young boy's growing understanding of the way the world really works. The author has followed *Boone Barnaby* with the sequels *Danny Ain't* and *Babcock;* all three novels depict small-town life in Northern California. While the adventures of Cottonwood's young protagonists may be fictitious, each novel's setting is not; it is based on the author's own hometown of La Honda, California.

"When I was young, I didn't know there was such a thing as a novel written for children," Cottonwood explained to *SATA*. "I read adult books. My father loved to buy novels and usually picked up three, four, even six paperbacks every day on the way home from work." At this rate, Cottonwood's home was soon full to overflowing with books. "We filled up shelves, and then we built more shelves, and then we filled up closets, and then we stored them in the basement. So I had plenty to read—from classics to science fiction," he recalled.

The ideas that he gleaned from his father's novels shaped Cottonwood's view of the adult world. "When I was young, I thought a lot of adults were strange, dishonest, mean, bossy. (I still do.) The world of my childhood seemed a mysterious and hostile place full of nuclear bombs aimed, I thought, right at my house, which was near Washington, D.C. The adult world was trying to kill me. Trying to be reassuring, my father built a bomb shelter in our basement—and filled it with boxes of books. The shelter was no comfort, but it was a nice place to read." Young Cottonwood would perch on top of boxes filled with books stacked next to shelves of emergency equipment—canned food, candles, a first aid kit, gas masks—and devour novels. He searched for

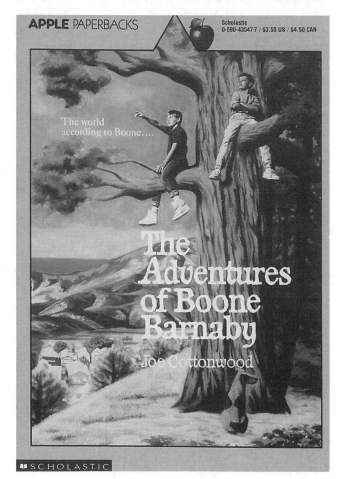

In his first work for middle school readers, Joe Cottonwood tells the story of Boone Barnaby, a boy slowly learning how to fit into the world of responsible adults.

answers to life's important questions "in hopes of figuring out:

1) Why the adult world was trying to kill me; 2) How to stay safe; 3) How to get girls."

It wasn't until Cottonwood began raising his own family that he was introduced to the "undiscovered universe of books for kids." He read books aloud to his children, and "in silence to myself. Here, it seemed, were the answers I had forgotten I was searching for." By this time, he had become a published author, with novels for adults and a book of poetry to his credit. "Now I wanted to try to write a novel that my own son, my oldest, would enjoy and that would answer some of the problems he was pondering, the same questions we all ponder: 'Who am I? What do I stand for? Why isn't life fair?'"

Cottonwood's first novel for young people was geared toward middle-school readers and published in 1990 as *The Adventures of Boone Barnaby*. Taking place in the less-affluent suburb of a wealthy town in the redwood mountains of Northern California, the book features sixth grader Boone, his best pal Danny, and Babcock, the new kid in town, who is quickly inducted into Boone's one-player-short soccer team. Events unfold that help each boy gain an awareness of the larger world around him; the boys act on their growing social conscience by organizing a Trashathon to both clean up their town and pay their team's way to the soccer playoffs. They also begin to puzzle over the same personal and social issues that concern their parents: drugs, politics, and tradeoffs between ideology and personal action. Praising *Boone Barnaby* for its thoughtfulness, humor, and upbeat resolution, reviewer Joel Shoemaker noted in *School Library Journal* that the novel "leaves open a variety of problems to be faced in the search for justice that will continue throughout the lives of these characters."

After writing *Boone Barnaby* for his oldest son, Cottonwood recalled to *SATA* that "my youngest son wanted a book about foxes." During the course of writing the story, foxes were somehow transformed into coyotes, the author explained, and *Danny Ain't* was the result. Featuring the protagonists from his previous novel, *Danny Ain't* focuses on streetwise Danny, who lives "on the other side of the tracks." He shares a trailer with his father, a Vietnam War veteran whose flashbacks of the violence he experienced in Southeast Asia eventually cause a mental breakdown. With his dad now in the VA hospital, Danny finds himself one step away from being placed in a shelter, where he definitely does not want to be. The resourceful young man manages to make it on his own while also befriending two coyotes that have begun to live beneath the family trailer. Danny feels a kinship with these two wild animals; both he and they are survivors keeping one step ahead of capture by learning to trust. "This ultimate tale of latchkey-life gone wild provides some obvious potential for book talks," according to *Voice of Youth Advocates* contributor Kevin Kenny. *Booklist* reviewer Sheilamae O'Hara

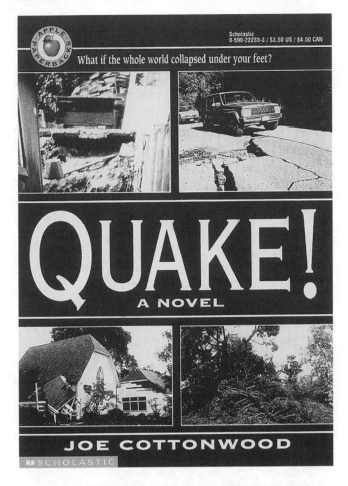

What if the whole world collapsed under your feet?

Scholastic
0-590-22233-3 / $3.50 US / $4.50 CAN

QUAKE!
A NOVEL

JOE COTTONWOOD

After an earthquake levels her mountainside home, Franny must act quickly to help her younger brother and other residents in her town survive the disaster.

concurred, asserting: "Complex, with well-developed characters and a fast-paced plot, the novel not only has appeal as a solitary reading experience, but also may stimulate discussions on ethical and environmental issues."

Cottonwood's third children's novel was inspired by Mother Nature. "We had an earthquake [in 1989]; it was terrifying; but we survived and were stronger for the experience. From this, I wrote *Quake!*" In the novel, two bored teens, left in charge of a bratty little brother for the weekend while their parents go to a baseball game in nearby San Francisco, find their slumber party slide into disaster after an earthquake occurs. When her little brother panics as he sees his home start to break apart, Fran shoulders adult responsibility for him and takes charge. Using their heads and keeping themselves out of danger, Fran and her friend Jennie also rally to the aid of neighbors in their mountain town, providing readers with a positive view of young women successfully coping in an emergency situation. A *Publishers Weekly* critic lauded *Quake!* for portraying a frightening "geological phenomenon in accessible you-are-there terms," and noted that Cottonwood has designed his story to "build his reader's skills rather than exploit their fears." Julie Yates Walton of *Booklist* praised Cottonwood's

survival story as "grippingly told," adding that it "fleshes out the newspaper headlines [of California's 1989 earthquake] in fascinating detail." *School Library Journal* contributor Anne Connor also offered a favorable assessment of *Quake!*, asserting: "Cottonwood spins his tale with great immediacy and power. Characters and relationships are multidimensional and convincing."

"A fourth grader who read one of my novels asked me, 'Are you a real writer, or did you just make those stories up?,'" Cottonwood told *SATA*. "I'm not sure what he believed a writer does, but he got me thinking. I make up all my characters, but many of the events in my novels were inspired by something that really happened. Just as a real fox became an imaginary coyote as I was writing *Danny Ain't*, a real earthquake became an imaginary story in *Quake!*, and a real family became something entirely different in *The Adventures of Boone Barnaby*." Keeping his writing "real" remains a top priority for Cottonwood. As he told Stacy Trevenon, "There isn't any one set way a book is read. If you write a book that's true and real, people will look at it from different points of view, like they look at life from different points of view.... If there's only one way to write a book," Cottonwood added, "it's probably not a real book."

Throughout the pages of Cottonwood's books for preteen readers, values and a growing understanding of life take center stage. "I like to write about the relationships between children and adults in which some kid is trying to make sense out of the behavior and attitudes of some adult," he explained to *SATA*. "All children are trying to puzzle out who they are and what they stand for. I hope my books will help them find the answers."

■ Works Cited

Connor, Anne, review of *Quake!*, *School Library Journal*, May, 1995, p. 104.

Kenny, Kevin, review of *Danny Ain't*, *Voice of Youth Advocates*, October, 1992, p. 222.

O'Hara, Sheilamae, review of *Danny Ain't*, *Booklist*, September 1, 1992, p. 48.

Review of *Quake!*, *Publishers Weekly*, June 19, 1995, p. 61.

Shoemaker, Joel, review of *The Adventures of Boone Barnaby*, *School Library Journal*, February, 1991, p. 25.

Trevenon, Stacy, "Writer Joe Cottonwood Branches Out," *Half Moon Bay Review*, June 12, 1991, p. 17A.

Walton, Julie Yates, review of *Quake!*, *Booklist*, May 1, 1995, p. 1572.

■ For More Information See

PERIODICALS

Bulletin of the Center for Children's Books, February, 1991, p. 139; April, 1995, p. 268.

Horn Book, September, 1995, p. 638.

Kirkus Reviews, November 15, 1990, p. 1600; July 15, 1992, p. 919.

Publishers Weekly, September 28, 1992, p. 80.

School Library Journal, December, 1990, p. 279; October, 1992, p. 114.

Voice of Youth Advocates, December, 1990, p. 279; August, 1995, p. 155.

Wilson Library Bulletin, May, 1991, p. 3.

*   *   *

COUSINS, Margaret 1905-1996
(Avery Johns, William Masters, Mary Parrish)

OBITUARY NOTICE—See index for *SATA* sketch: Born January 26, 1905, in Munday, TX; died July 30, 1996, in San Antonio, TX. Author and editor. Cousins gained prominence as a magazine writer and editor and as the author of children's books. She began her career in 1927 as an associate editor, and eventually editor in chief, of *Southern Pharmaceutical Journal* in Dallas, Texas. In 1937, Cousins moved to New York City, and soon joined the staff of the Hearst Promotion Service as a copywriter. After four years with Hearst, she accepted a position with *Good Housekeeping* magazine, serving as editor from 1945 until 1958. At that time, Cousins was hired by *McCall's,* where she remained for about three years until accepting a position with Doubleday and Co. in 1961. During her earlier stint with *Good Housekeeping,* Cousins began to write children's stories. Her first, *Uncle Edgar and the Reluctant Saint,* was published in 1948. Others include *We Were There at the Battle of the Alamo,* and *Souvenir: Margaret Truman's Own Story* (with Margaret Truman). One of the many short stories she wrote, "The Life of Lucy Gallant," was produced as a film in 1955. Cousins also wrote under several pseudonyms—including William Masters and Mary Parrish. She also penned *Traffic with Evil* under the name Avery Johns.

OBITUARIES AND OTHER SOURCES:

PERIODICALS

New York Times, August 2, 1996, p. B7.

D–E

DELANY, Samuel R(ay, Jr.) 1942-
(K. Leslie Steiner)

■ Personal

Born April 1, 1942, in New York, NY; son of Samuel R. (a funeral director) and Margaret Carey (a library clerk; maiden name, Boyd) Delany; married Marilyn Hacker (a poet), August 24, 1961 (divorced, 1980); children: Iva Alyxander. *Education:* Attended City College (now of the City University of New York), 1960 and 1962-63.

■ Addresses

Agent—Henry Morrison, Inc., Box 235, Bedford Hills, NY 10507.

■ Career

Author, editor, and educator. Butler Professor of English, State University of New York at Buffalo, 1975; professor of comparative literature, University of Massachusetts—Amherst, 1988—. Senior fellow at the Center for Twentieth Century Studies, University of Wisconsin—Milwaukee, 1977; senior fellow at the Society for the Humanities, Cornell University, 1987; senior fellow at the Institute for the Humanities, University of Michigan, 1993; visiting Penny and Michael Winton scholar, University of Minnesota, 1995.

■ Awards, Honors

Nebula Award for best novel, Science Fiction Writers of America, 1966, for *Babel-17,* 1967, for *The Einstein Intersection;* Nebula Award for best short story, 1967, for "Aye and Gomorrah"; Nebula Award for best novelette, 1969, for "Time Considered as a Helix of Semi-Precious Stones"; Hugo Award for best short story, Science Fiction Convention, 1970, for "Time Considered as a Helix of Semi-Precious Stones"; American Book Award nomination, 1980, for *Tales of Neveryon;* Pilgrim Award, Science Fiction Research Association, 1985; The Dark Room Award for Lifetime Contribution to Black Literature, 1989; William Whitehead

Memorial Award, Lifetime Contribution to Gay and Lesbian Writing, 1993.

■ Writings

SCIENCE FICTION

The Jewels of Aptor (abridged edition bound with *Second Ending* by James White), Ace Books, 1962, hardcover edition, Gollancz, 1968, complete edition published with an introduction by Don Hausdorff, Gregg Press, 1976.
The Ballad of Beta-2 (also see below; bound with *Alpha Yes, Terra No!* by Emil Petaja), Ace Books, 1965,

SAMUEL R. DELANY

45

hardcover edition published with an introduction by David G. Hartwell, Gregg Press, 1977.

Empire Star (also see below; bound with *The Three Lords of Imeten* by Tom Purdom), Ace Books, 1966, hardcover edition published with an introduction by Hartwell, Gregg Press, 1977.

Babel-17, Ace Books, 1966, hardcover edition, Gollancz, 1967, published with an introduction by Robert Scholes, 1976.

The Einstein Intersection, slightly abridged edition, Ace Books, 1967, hardcover edition, Gollancz, 1968, complete edition, Ace Books, 1972.

Nova, Doubleday, 1968.

Driftglass: Ten Tales of Speculative Fiction, Doubleday, 1971.

The Tides of Lust, Lancer Books, 1973.

Dhalgren, Bantam, 1975, hardcover edition published with an introduction by Jean Mark Gawron, Gregg Press, 1978.

The Ballad of Beta-2 [and] *Empire Star,* Ace Books, 1975.

Triton, Bantam, 1976.

Empire: A Visual Novel, illustrations by Howard V. Chaykin, Berkley Books, 1978.

Distant Stars, Bantam, 1981.

Stars in My Pocket Like Grains of Sand, Bantam, 1984.

The Complete Nebula Award-Winning Fiction, Bantam, 1986.

The Star Pits (bound with *Tango Charlie and Foxtrot Romeo* by John Varley), Tor Books, 1989.

They Fly at Ciron, Incunabula, 1992.

"FALL OF THE TOWERS" SERIES; SCIENCE FICTION

Captives of the Flame (bound with *The Psionic Menace* by Keith Woodcott), Ace Books, 1963, revised edition published under author's original title *Out of the Dead City,* Sphere Books, 1968.

The Towers of Toron (bound with *The Lunar Eye* by Robert Moore Williams), Ace Books, 1964.

City of a Thousand Suns, Ace Books, 1965.

The Fall of the Towers (trilogy; contains *Out of the Dead City, The Towers of Toron,* and *City of a Thousand Suns*), Ace Books, 1970, hardcover edition published with introduction by Joseph Milicia, Gregg Press, 1977.

"RETURN TO NEVERYON" SERIES; SWORD AND SORCERY NOVELS

Tales of Neveryon, Bantam, 1979.

Neveryona; or, The Tale of Signs and Cities, Bantam, 1983.

Flight from Neveryon, Bantam, 1985.

The Bridge of Lost Desire, Arbor House, 1987.

OTHER

The Jewel-Hinged Jaw: Notes on the Language of Science Fiction (criticism), Dragon Press, 1977, revised edition, Berkley Publishing, 1978.

The American Shore: Meditations on a Tale of Science Fiction by Thomas M. Disch—"Angouleme" (criticism), Dragon Press, 1978.

Heavenly Breakfast: An Essay on the Winter of Love (memoir), Bantam, 1979.

Starboard Wine: More Notes on the Language of Science Fiction (criticism), Dragon Press, 1984.

The Motion of Light in Water: Sex and Science Fiction Writing in the East Village, 1957-1965 (memoir), Arbor House, 1988.

Wagner/Artaud: A Play of Nineteenth and Twentieth Century Critical Fictions (criticism), Ansatz Press, 1988.

Straits of Messina (essays; essays by Delany as well as originally published in magazines under pseudonym K. Leslie Steiner), Serconia Press, 1989.

The Mad Man (fiction), Richard Kasek, 1994.

Silent Interviews: On Language, Race, Sex, Science Fiction, and Some Comics (essays), University Press of New England, 1994.

Atlantis: Three Tales (novella), University Press of New England, 1995.

Hogg (fiction), Illinois State University/Black Ice Books, 1995.

Longer Views: Extended Essays (essays), University Press of New England, 1996.

Also author of scripts, director, and editor of two short films, *Tiresias,* 1970, and *The Orchid,* 1971; author of two scripts for the *Wonder Woman* comic book series, 1972, and of the radio play *The Star Pit,* based on his short story of the same title. Editor, *Nebula Winners 13,* Harper and Row, 1989, and coeditor with Marilyn Hacker of *Quark,* issues 1-4, Paperback Library, 1970-71. In addition, Delany contributed to the *Green Lantern/Green Arrow Anthology.*

■ Sidelights

"Samuel R. Delany," comments Jane Branham Weedman in her study of the author, "is one of today's most innovative and imaginative writers of science fiction." *School Library Journal* critic John Adams adds, "Delany's not for everyone.... But his writing offers one of the most heady, rewarding experiences in modern fiction today." Considered among the most successful of the New Wave writers of science fiction, a group of English and American authors who emerged in the 1960s and favor stylistic experimentation over traditional narratives, Delany is praised as one of the most gifted authors in the genre as well as one of the few African Americans working in his field to have achieved both critical and popular success. Regarded as a brilliant stylist and compelling storyteller whose complex, often demanding novels and stories have expanded the scope of science fiction, Delany uses elements of mythology, anthropology, psychology, sociology, history, and philosophy to probe the natures of language and art, the role of the artist, sexual identity, and societal issues such as racism and sexism while telling action-filled adventure stories often set in alien worlds. Filling his works with intricate meanings, literary and cultural symbols and allusions, flashbacks, and unusual page designs, the author attempts to provide experiences for his readers that parallel the quests of his protagonists. Delany's audience is invited to question themselves and their societies while participating in the act of reading to its fullest extent. In his essay on Delany in *Dictionary of*

Literary Biography, Peter S. Alterman notes, "His are stories in which the creative experience of the reader is as important as the narrative. They invite, wheedle, and bully the reader into confronting the process of his reading and thereby participating in both the creation and the experience of the story." At the center of the web of personal, cultural, artistic, and intellectual concerns that provides the framework for his books is Delany's examination of how language and myth influence reality by shaping perceptions. In his science fiction, the author "creates new myths, or inversions of old ones, by which his protagonists measure themselves and their societies against the traditional myths that Delany includes," observes Jane Branham Weedman. In this way, as Alterman notes, Delany confronts "the questions of the extent to which myths and archetypes create reality." In addition to his contributions to science fiction, Delany has written adult novels and plays, memoirs, and collections of essays as well as scripts for films, comic books, and a radio play; a professor of comparative literature, he is also the author of several well-received volumes of literary criticism, much of it assessing science fiction as literature. He has also taught writing, coedited a magazine, and written and directed two short films.

Although Delany does not characteristically address his books to young adults, several of his novels have been adopted by this audience; for example, a reviewer in *School Library Journal* notes that reissues of some of his early paperbacks in hardcover "are primarily for school libraries supporting s-f programs." Adolescent readers have been attracted to the author's imaginative detailing of alternative societies as well as by his fascination with myth and language. In addition, young adults can identify with his characters as they search for selfhood and may relate to Delany's vision of future worlds, including our own, in which, as the author says, things have changed. "In most of my futures," he has noted, "the racial situation has changed and changed for the better." Many of Delany's protagonists are teenage poets or musicians in the process of self-discovery. In these quests, the characters—who are both male and female, are often black or of mixed race, and suffer from some physical or psychological problem—resolve their personal issues while they seek meaning in their respective worlds. These young people are often involved in criminal activities ranging from petty theft to assassination; critics note that Delany equates the artist and the criminal because both figures operate outside mainstream society. In Delany's view, the presence of both archetypes is crucial, since the actions of the artist/ criminals push society's values to their limits and provide the experimentation needed to prepare for eventual change.

Delany was born and raised in Harlem, the son of Samuel R. Delany, Sr., a prominent businessman and funeral director, and Margaret Carey Boyd Delany, a library clerk with the New York Public Library whose friends included some of the Harlem Renaissance figures of the 1920s and 1930s. He received most of his education in predominantly white settings, such as the

► First paperback publication ◄

SAMUEL R. DELANY

THEY FLY AT CIRON

"Vintage Delany in his finest fantasy mode."
—Ursula K. Le Guin

Delany returns to the struggle of the enslaved Cironians against their brutal oppressors, the Myetrans, in this well-received fantasy novella. (Cover illustration by Thomas Canty.)

Dalton Elementary School on Park Avenue and the Bronx High School of Science. Expressing his awareness of the differences in the speech he heard at home and at school, Delany noted that he became attuned to "language as an intriguing and infinitely malleable modeling tool." The dichotomies in his daily life affected Delany's behavior, causing him to run away several times between the ages of five and seventeen and to receive psychological counseling. Accepted by his classmates, he was named Most Popular in his last year at Dalton. However, his teachers failed to recognize his dyslexia. In a letter to bibliographers Michael W. Peplow and Robert S. Brayard, Delany describes his youth as a "virtually ballistic trip through a socio-psychological barrier of astonishingly restrained violence," adding that "it wouldn't be too far afield to say that within the metaphorical, or more accurately, the analogical freedom science fiction provides, I have written nothing about nothing but the trip through such socio-psychological barriers ever since."

While at Dalton, Delany began writing short stories. After graduation, he enrolled at the Bronx High School of Science, concentrating on math and physics as well as pursuing extracurricular interests in music, acting, and ballet; at fourteen, he wrote a complete violin concerto. He also continued his writing, winning first place for a short story and second place for an essay in the National Scholastic Writing Awards contest. While a teenager, Delany became enthralled by science fiction writers such as Robert Heinlein, Ray Bradbury, and Alfred Bester and by European and African American writers such as Jean Genet, Albert Camus, Jean Cocteau, Lawrence Durrell, Alexander Trocchi, James Baldwin, Chester Himes, and John O'Killins—as well as James Joyce and William Faulkner. At nineteen, he married former classmate Marilyn Hacker, with whom he had edited their school's literary magazine. Hacker had begun working as an assistant editor at Ace Books, a major publisher of science fiction. When she complained to her husband about the poor quality of some of the manuscripts she was seeing, Delany responded by writing a novel inspired by a series of recent nightmares. That story, *The Jewels of Aptor* (1962), became his first published work.

While working for a few years as a singer and musician in Greenwich Village, Delany wrote four additional novels, including *Captives of the Flame* (1963), the first volume of his popular "Fall of the Towers" trilogy that also includes *The Towers of Toron* (1964) and *City of a Thousand Suns* (1965).

Over this time, he published *Babel-17* (1966), *Empire Star* (1966), *The Einstein Intersection* (1967), and *Nova* (1968), the first of his works to be printed originally in hardcover. Douglas Barbour, writing in *Dictionary of Literary Biography,* describes these early novels as "colorful, exciting, entertaining, and intellectually provocative to a degree not found in most genre science fiction." Barbour adds that although they do adhere to science fiction conventions, the books "begin the exploration of those literary obsessions that define [Delany's] oeuvre: problems of communication and community; new kinds of sexual/love/family relationships; the artist as social outsider ...; cultural interactions and the exploration of human social possibilities these allow; archetypal and mythic structures in the imagination."

With the publication of *Babel-17* in 1966, Delany began to gain recognition as a writer of science fiction. The novel, which earned its author his first Nebula Award, is a story of galactic warfare between the forces of the Alliance, which includes the Earth, and the forces of the Invaders. The poet Rydra Wong is enlisted by Alliance intelligence to decipher communications intercepted from its enemy. When she discovers that these dispatches contain not a code but rather an unknown language, her quest becomes one of learning the mysterious tongue labeled Babel-17. While leading an interstellar mission in search of clues, Rydra gains insights into the nature of language and, in the process, discovers the unique character of the enigmatic new language of the Invaders. When the poet discovers that Babel-17 is the

secret weapon of the Invaders, she and her allies use the language to end the war. After *Babel-17,* Delany wrote *Empire Star* (1966), a novel that is considered specifically directed to young adults. *Empire Star* relates the history of a galactic civilization by portraying its characters at different ages and performing different functions throughout the narrative. The protagonist, teenager Comet Jo, meets older versions of himself who help him as he grows and travels toward Empire Star, the center of the galaxy, to bring word of the freeing of an enslaved alien race, the L11. On his way to Empire Star, he acquires a sophisticated understanding of the cyclical nature of time and history. At the end of the novel, Comet Jo dies, only to be reborn so that he can begin his journey once again. In her essay in *Dictionary of Literary Biography,* Sandra Y. Govan says that *Empire Star,* "ostensibly for younger readers, is actually an allegory of the cycle of oppression, guilt, and responsibility which the enslavement of any group imposes on the free." Delany's second Nebula winner, *The Einstein Intersection,* introduces his theme of the power and influence of myth. The story describes a strange race of beings that occupies a post-apocalyptic Earth thirty thousand years in the future where humans are extinct. The aliens assume the economic, political, and religious traditions of the humans in an attempt to make sense of the remnant world in which they find themselves. The key figure in the novel is Lobey, a musician. The power of Lobey's music is its ability to create order, to destroy the old myths and usher in the new. Lobey is on a quest to find his lost love Friza and to assassinate Kid Death, who is killing the race of beings struggling to become human. At the end of the novel, Lobey participates in the murder of Kid Death, finds and loses Friza, and prepares to leave Earth for other galaxies.

After the publication of his next science fiction novel, the well-received *Nova* (1968), in which the mulatto hero Lorq Von Ray locates a rare element from an exploding star in order to prevent oppression in his galaxy, Delany went through several major changes in lifestyle; Sandra Y. Govan describes his personal life of this period as "a model of Bohemian flexibility." Coming out as a gay man with his Hugo and Nebula Award-winning story "Time Considered as a Helix of Semi-Precious Stones" (1968), he also engaged himself in conceiving, writing, and polishing what would become his longest, most complex, and most controversial novel, *Dhalgren* (1975). On its shifting surface, this novel, which is set on Earth in the near future, represents the experience of a nameless amnesiac, an artist/criminal, during the period of time he spends in an isolated city that has been scarred by destruction and decay. The central theme of this massive work, which is nearly nine hundred pages long, is the search for identity undertaken by the protagonist, who comes to be called Kid. Throughout the story, Kid, who is usually regarded as Delany's characterization of himself, has many adventures, including a variety of sexual escapades, and becomes both a poet and the leader of a teenage gang. At the end of the book, Kid is disgorged from the city during a cataclysm, but he leaves with both life experience and a name. Dazzlingly varied in structure, *Dhal-*

gren is considered both rich and overblown; some critics, in fact, do not consider it science fiction at all. "Nobody, however," writes Peter S. Alterman, "criticized Delany's masterful use of language in *Dhalgren.* Indeed, his prose style is brilliant." In the *New York Times Book Review,* Gerald Jonas notes, "If the book can be said to be about anything, it is about nothing less than the nature of reality," and adds, "One thing is certain; *Dhalgren* is not a conventional novel, whether considered in terms of S.F. or the mainstream."

In the late 1970s and 1980s, Delany continued to experiment with his fiction while contributing to a variety of other genres; he and Hacker separated in 1975, and he began to teach at the university level. A book from this period with special appeal for young adults is *Empire: A Visual Novel* (1978), a space opera in comic strip form with illustrations by Howard V. Chaykin, an artist who had worked on *Star Wars* and several Marvel comics. Another group of Delany's books that is especially popular with young audiences is his "Neveryon" quartet, a series of heroic fantasies set in an ancient past filled with dragons, treasures, and fabulous cities; the quartet includes *Tales of Neveryon* (1979), which was nominated for an American Book Award, *Neveryona; or, The Tale of Signs and Cities* (1983), *Flight from Neveryon* (1985), and *The Bridge of Lost Desire* (1987). Reviewing the third novel, a *Publishers Weekly* critic notes, "Like Nabokov, Delany has created a grand, mirrored mythology around versions of himself. Both may write about dispossessed artists, but instead of Russian exiles, Delany's protagonists tend to be black, homosexual outcasts." The reviewer notes that Delany's "variegated fantasy world" contains flying dragons, gods, and a child empress and that the author describes "its sexual life and its economic life, its waning slavery and gaining literacy, its architecture, politics, religion and children's games." In an assessment of the fourth novel, a *Publishers Weekly* reviewer states, "Around [the] paradigmatic action ... Delany constructs a world so distant and romantic that it contains dragons and barbarians, yet so close and recognizable that it suffers an AIDS epidemic. In the best entries, he gives us an enthralling tale and at the same time a challenging critique—of sword and sorcery and of the social systems that fantasy so often ignores or trivializes: politics, economics, language, history, sexuality, slavery, and power." Throughout the series, Delany tells the story of Gorgik, a boy enslaved at fifteen who becomes known as the Liberator when he defeats the Child Empress and abolishes slavery. In the novel-length "Tale of Plagues and Carnivals," one of the first novels published in the United States to deal with AIDS, the author shifts in time from his primitive world to present-day New York and back to examine the devastating effects of AIDS. In the appendices that accompany each of these books, Delany reflects on the creative process itself. Of the four volumes in the series, *Neveryona* has perhaps received the most critical attention. The novel describes how Pryn, a girl who flees her mountain home on the back of a dragon, meets a storyteller who teaches her to write her name and tells her of a hidden treasure in a sunken town. On her journey, Pryn meets Gorgik and finally discovers the city, Neveryona. *Science Fiction and Fantasy Book Review* contributor Michael R. Collings calls the novel "a stirring fable of adventure and education, of heroic action and even more heroic normality in a world where survival itself is constantly threatened." Faren C. Miller finds the book groundbreaking; she writes in *Locus:* "Combining differing perspectives with extraordinary talent for the details of a world—its smells, its shadows, workaday furnishings, and playful frills—Delany has produced a sourcebook for a new generation of fantasy writers."

With the publication of *The Motion of Light in Water* (1988), Delany turned to writing about himself. This memoir of his early days as a writer in New York's East Village is "an extraordinary account of life experienced by a precocious black artist of the 1960s," as E. Guereschi writes in *Choice.* The book details Delany's sexual adventures and nervous breakdown while reflecting the sense of living on the edge in an exciting social and cultural period. Moreover, *The Motion of Light in Water* describes Delany's realization and eventual acceptance of his homosexuality. Thomas M. Disch, writing in the *American Book Review,* finds that Delany "can't help creating legends and elaborating myths. Indeed, it is his forte, the open secret of his success as an SF writer. [Delany's] SF heroes are variations of an archetype he calls The Kid.... In his memoir, the author himself [is] finally assuming the role in which his fictive alter-egos have enjoyed their success. That is the book's strength even more than its weakness." Disch concludes that *The Motion of Light in Water* "has the potential of being as popular, as representative of its era, as [Jack Kerouac's] *On the Road.*" In the 1990s, Delany has continued to contribute to the genres of both fiction and nonfiction. Young adults may be most interested in *They Fly at Ciron,* a fantasy novella combined with two related short stories that describes how the peaceful village of Ciron fights against domination by the army of Myetra, who kill and enslave many of the Cironians; a main character in the novel is Rahm, a village boy who joins the Cironian resistance. *Booklist* reviewer Carl Hays calls *They Fly at Ciron* "must reading for Delany's fans and, for newcomers, a good introduction to an enduring talent."

Beginning as a wunderkind of science fiction, Delany is now regarded as one of the genre's grand masters. Despite their sophistication and multilayered levels of meaning, his works have found an appreciative audience among both adults and young adults for their literary quality, dynamic structures, and relevant subtexts. Jane Branham Weedman notes, "Few writers approach the lyricism, the command of language, the powerful combination of style and content that distinguishes Delany's works. More importantly," she concludes, "few writers, whether in science fiction or mundane fiction, so successfully create works which make us question ourselves, our actions, our beliefs, and our society as Delany has helped us do." Writing in the *Washington Post Book World,* John Clute places Delany in a central position in modern science fiction. In his best work, Clute believes, Delany "treated the interstellar venues of space opera as analogues of urban life in the decaying hearts of the great American cities. As a black gay New Yorker much too well educated for his own good, Delany ... illuminated the world the way a torch might cast light in a cellar."

■ Works Cited

Adams, John, review of *Distant Stars, School Library Journal,* November, 1981, p. 114.

Alterman, Peter S., "Samuel R. Delany," in *Dictionary of Literary Biography, Volume 8: Twentieth-Century American Science Fiction Writers,* Gale, 1981.

Review of *The Ballad of Beta-2, Driftglass, Empire Star,* and *Nova, School Library Journal,* May, 1978, p. 94.

Barbour, Douglas, "Cultural Invention and Metaphor in the Novels of Samuel R. Delany," *Foundation,* March, 1975, pp. 105-21.

Review of *The Bridge of Lost Desire, Publishers Weekly,* October 23, 1987, p. 49.

Clute, John, *Washington Post Book World,* August 25, 1991, p. 11.

Collings, Michael R., review of *Neveryona, Science Fiction and Fantasy Book Review,* July-August, 1983, p. 31.

Delany, Samuel R., letter to Michael W. Peplow and Robert S. Brayard reprinted in their *Samuel R. Delany: A Primary and Secondary Bibliography 1962-1979,* G. K. Hall, 1980.

Disch, Thomas M., review of *The Motion of Light in Water, American Book Review,* January, 1989, p. 1.

Review of *Flight from Neveryon, Publishers Weekly,* April 26, 1985, p. 79.

Govan, Sandra Y., "Samuel R. Delany," in *Dictionary of Literary Biography, Volume 33: Afro-American Fiction Writers after 1955,* Gale, 1984.

Guereschi, E., review of *The Motion of Light in Water, Choice,* February, 1989, p. 938.

Hays, Carl, review of *They Fly at Ciron, Booklist,* December 15, 1994, p. 740.

Jonas, Gerald, review of *Dhalgren, New York Times Book Review,* February 16, 1975, p. 22.

Miller, Faren C., review of *Neveryona, Locus,* summer, 1983.

Weedman, Jane Branham, *Samuel R. Delany,* Starmont House, 1982.

■ For More Information See

BOOKS

Bleiler, E. F., editor, *Science Fiction Writers: Critical Studies of the Major Authors from the Early Nineteenth Century to the Present Day,* Scribner, 1982.

Contemporary Literary Criticism, Gale Research, Volume 8, 1978, Volume 14, 1980, Volume 38, 1986.

Kostelanetz, Richard, editor, *American Writing Today,* Whitston, 1991.

McCaffery, Larry, and Sinda Gregory, editors, *Alive and Writing: Interviews with American Authors of the 1980s,* University of Illinois Press, 1987.

McEvoy, Seth, *Samuel R. Delany,* Ungar, 1984.

Platt, Charles, editor, *Dream Makers: The Uncommon People Who Write Science Fiction,* Berkley Books, 1980.

Slusser, George Edgar, *The Delany Intersection: Samuel R. Delany Considered as a Writer of Semi-Precious Words,* Borgo, 1977.

Smith, Nicholas D., editor, *Philosophers Look at Science Fiction,* Nelson-Hall, 1982.

Weedman, Jane Branham, *Reader's Guide to Samuel R. Delany,* Starmont House, 1979.

PERIODICALS

Analog Science Fiction/Science Fact, April, 1985.
Black American Literature Forum, summer, 1984.
Commonweal, December 5, 1975.
Extrapolation, fall, 1982; winter, 1989; fall, 1989.
Fantasy Review, December, 1984.
Globe and Mail (Toronto), February 9, 1985.
Library Journal, May 1, 1995, p. 134.
Locus, October, 1989.
Los Angeles Times Book Review, March 13, 1988.
Kirkus Reviews, November 1, 1994, p. 1488.
Magazine of Fantasy and Science Fiction, November, 1975; June, 1980; May, 1989.
Mother Jones, August, 1976.
New York Review of Books, January 29, 1991.
New York Times Book Review, March 28, 1976; October 28, 1979; February 10, 1985.
Publishers Weekly, January 29, 1988; October 19, 1992; April 3, 1995, p. 47.
Science Fiction Chronicle, November, 1987; February, 1990.
Science-Fiction Studies, November, 1981; July, 1987; November, 1990.
Voice Literary Supplement, February, 1985.
Washington Post Book World, January 27, 1985.

—Sketch by Gerard J. Senick

*   *   *

DEMIJOHN, Thom
See DISCH, Thomas M(ichael)

*   *   *

DEVON, Paddie 1953-

■ Personal

Born February 19, 1953, in Belfast, Northern Ireland; daughter of George (a private fruit wholesaler) and Martha (an elocution teacher; maiden name, Jones) McCormick; married Michael Devon (the managing director of a retail decor business), August 11, 1977; children: Kate, Steen Michael, Hanna Lara, Sian Rachael. *Education:* Attended Belfast Art College, 1970. *Politics:* "Any party which promises and *gives* peace and honesty, helps negate poverty, and promotes fair trade!" *Religion:* Methodist. *Hobbies and other interests:* Acoustic guitar, reading, sewing, sketching, watching medical programs/documentaries on television, "refurbishing and enhancing with T.L.C. our 200-year-old cottage home—from knocking down walls to painting wall murals!"

Addresses

Home and office—Ballywooley Cottage, 175 Crawfordsburn Rd., Bangor, County Down, BT19 1BT, Ireland.

Career

Photographic and fashion model, 1967-74; Tudor Publications, Belfast, Northern Ireland, graphic artist and art director, until 1982; Sweet Inspirations, Bangor, Ireland, interior design consultant, 1984—. Youth leader in local church; helps with riding for the disabled on a voluntary basis.

■ Writings

(Self-illustrated) *The Grumpy Shepherd,* Scripture Union, 1995.

The Grumpy Shepherd has been translated into other languages.

Adaptations

The Grumpy Shepherd has been released by Scripture Union as a short video.

Work in Progress

The Soldier's Sword, a book for four- to seven-year-old children; re-telling of the parables; a musical package (cassette tape, musical score, and script for actors) for educational sector; and an educational book about Northern Ireland for primary school children.

PADDIE DEVON

■ Sidelights

Paddie Devon told *SATA:* "I had no inspirations to write at all, or indeed illustrate, until after I had become a committed Christian a few short years ago. I had always, through my life, used my artistic skills in some form or other, whether it was commercial graphics (through my workplace), portrait sketching, or attacking some poor unsuspecting bare wall with one of my creations in paint! But writing and illustrating children's books had never crossed my mind. It wasn't until I recognized and accepted that my talents were in fact a gift from my Heavenly Father that I had the desire to do something for Him in return.

"This fresh awakening and need, along with my negative childhood recall of children's Christian literature, urged me toward the path I am now on of writing and illustrating. It provides me with the instrument to play my very small part of filling young minds with all things good and encouraging and to perhaps help make some sense and offer focus within this crazy world we live in.

"Being convinced that I should forge ahead, I felt that to start at the *beginning* was the best concept (and now you know I'm Irish!). So, *The Grumpy Shepherd* (the well-known Christmas story) came about—told from the viewpoint of a very discontented, grumpy fellow! The birth of Christ, like many other biblical stories, is well known to children. I wondered, if I retold them from a different angle (like *The Grumpy Shepherd*), and possibly with a sprinkling of humour, would this treatment of the too familiar 'been there, read it, forgotten it' stories help to re-awaken children's interest, and bring the old and known alive again? Backed up with very vibrant and sometimes comical illustrations, I'm pleased to say, thankfully, that this notion is a relative success. My hope now is to go forward with more stories, using the same concept. If I can touch one person's heart with one of my books, whether it be a child or a grown-up, and stir his or her tired spirit, then *that* would be wonderful!

"Hopefully this is just the beginning, and years from now I will still be found at our cottage, sitting at our huge kitchen table, strewn with pencils and papers, still busy producing. Our four children and my husband Michael, all of whom I love very much, are tremendous encouragers. My greater family circle adopts this same positive attitude, and none more so than my two older sisters, both successful in their own fields. It's not uncommon to walk into our home, which always has an open door, and find at least two of our offspring sharing the table with me, paintbrushes in hand, creating their own exhibits. Our youngest, Sian Rachael, would love me to sometime write her an adventure book with colourful drawings.

"So perhaps one day, I'll venture into the more secular field. If I were to try to emulate any writer/illustrator in that area, it would be Jane Hissey. Her illustrations are fabulous. I love her attention to detail and the impact her work has on the page. Her written content is simple and innocent and fun to read. I never have any hesitation giving any of her work to a child, as I know there would not be anything I would consider negative or a bad influence within its pages. Young minds are like sponges, and I believe that as parents, guardians, teachers, we should take great care in what they absorb.

"Any writing talent that I may have, I inherited from my gifted mother, the matriarch of our family. She has lived with us in our country cottage for some years now, since the death of our dad, whom we all adored. Our children enjoy the unique benefit and privilege of experiencing her great wisdom and love; 'Nanny' plays a vital role in their growing up. My mother can still, even in her eighty-first year, write a letter or piece which can break your heart, spill your tears, and put encouragement and belief where there was doubt, all with a swift movement of her pen. She is a great lady.

"My sense of humour, which I try to make an ingredient of my books, comes from my father, or 'Vince,' as was his nickname. He was a wonderful character, with a healthy, vivacious appetite for fun and life itself. Humour is an inspiring gift. It can lift the spirit and help put adversity into new perspective. My father used his gift well; he lightened many peoples' hearts with his quick wit, and even now, as I sit and think of him, he makes me smile."

■ For More Information See

PERIODICALS

Booklist, December 1, 1995, p. 640.

* * *

DISCH, Thomas M(ichael) 1940-
(Tom Disch; Leonie Hargrave; Thom Demijohn and Cassandra Knye, joint pseudonyms)

■ Personal

Born February 2, 1940, in Des Moines, IA; son of Felix Henry and Helen (Gilbertson) Disch. *Education:* Attended Cooper Union and New York University, 1959-62.

■ Addresses

Office—31 Union Square West, No. 11E, New York, NY 10003. *Agent*—Karpfinger Agency, 500 Fifth Ave., Suite 2800, New York, NY 10110.

■ Career

Freelance writer, 1964—. Majestic Theatre, New York City, part-time checkroom attendant, 1957-62; Doyle Dane Bernbach, New York City, copywriter, 1963-64; theater critic for *Nation,* 1987-91; theater critic for the *New York Daily News,* 1993—. Artist-in-residence, College of William and Mary, 1996—. Lecturer at universities. *Member:* PEN, National Book Critics Circle (board member, 1988-91), Writers Guild East.

■ Awards, Honors

O. Henry Prize, 1975, for story "Getting into Death," and 1979, for story "Xmas"; John W. Campbell Memorial Award, and American Book Award nomination, both 1980, both for *On Wings of Song;* Hugo Award and Nebula Award nominations, 1980, and British Science Fiction Award, 1981, all for novella *The Brave Little Toaster; The Castle of Indolence* was a finalist for the National Book Critics Circle Award for a work of criticism, National Book Critics Circle, 1996.

■ Writings

FOR CHILDREN

The Tale of Dan de Lion: A Fable, Coffee House Press, 1986.
The Brave Little Toaster: A Bedtime Story for Small Appliances, Doubleday, 1986.
The Brave Little Toaster Goes to Mars, Doubleday, 1988.
A Children's Garden of Grammar, University Press of New England, 1997.

NOVELS

The Genocides, Berkley, 1965.
Mankind under the Leash (expanded version of his short story, "White Fang Goes Dingo" [also see below]),

THOMAS M. DISCH

Ace, 1966, published in England as *The Puppies of Terra*, Panther Books, 1978.

(With John Sladek under joint pseudonym Cassandra Knye) *The House That Fear Built*, Paperback Library, 1966.

Echo Round His Bones, Berkley, 1967.

(With Sladek under joint pseudonym Thom Demijohn) *Black Alice*, Doubleday, 1968.

Camp Concentration, Hart-Davis, 1968, Doubleday, 1969.

The Prisoner, Ace, 1969.

334, MacGibbon & Kee, Avon, 1974.

(Under pseudonym Leonie Hargrave) *Clara Reeve*, Knopf, 1975.

On Wings of Song, St. Martin's, 1979.

Triplicity (omnibus volume), Doubleday, 1980.

(With Charles Naylor) *Neighboring Lives*, Scribner, 1981.

The Businessman: A Tale of Terror, Harper, 1984.

Amnesia (computer-interactive novel), Electronic Arts, 1985.

The Silver Pillow: A Tale of Witchcraft, M. V. Ziesing (Willimantic, CT), 1987.

The M.D.: A Horror Story, Knopf, 1991.

The Priest: A Gothic Romance, Knopf, 1995.

STORY COLLECTIONS

One Hundred and Two H-Bombs and Other Science Fiction Stories (also see below), Compact Books (Hollywood, FL), 1966, revised edition published as *One Hundred and Two H-Bombs*, Berkeley, 1969, published in England as *White Fang Goes Dingo and Other Funny S.F. Stories*, Arrow Books, 1971.

Under Compulsion, Hart-Davis, 1968, also published as *Fun with Your New Head*, Doubleday, 1969.

Getting into Death: The Best Short Stories of Thomas M. Disch, Hart-Davis, 1973, revised edition, published as *Getting into Death and Other Stories*, Knopf, 1976.

The Early Science Fiction Stories of Thomas M. Disch (includes *Mankind under the Leash* and *One Hundred and Two H-Bombs*), Gregg (Boston, MA), 1977.

Fundamental Disch, Bantam, 1980.

The Man Who Had No Idea, Bantam, 1982.

POETRY

(With Marilyn Hacker and Charles Platt) *Highway Sandwiches*, privately printed, 1970.

The Right Way to Figure Plumbing, Basilisk Press, 1972.

ABCDEFG HIJKLM NPOQRST UVWXYZ, Anvil Press Poetry (Millville, MN), 1981.

Orders of the Retina, Toothpaste Press (West Branch, IA), 1982.

Burn This, Hutchinson, 1982, revised edition published as *Burn This and Other Essays in Criticism*, WiseAcre Books, 1995.

Here I Am, There You Are, Where Were We?, Hutchinson, 1984.

Yes, Let's: New and Selected Poetry, Johns Hopkins University Press, 1989.

Dark Verses and Light, Johns Hopkins University Press, 1991.

The Dark Old House, Bob Barth, 1996.

EDITOR

The Ruins of the Earth: An Anthology of Stories of the Immediate Future, Putnam, 1971.

Bad Moon Rising: An Anthology of Political Foreboding, Harper, 1975.

The New Improved Sun: An Anthology of Utopian Science Fiction, Harper, 1975. (With Naylor) *New Constellations: An Anthology of Tomorrow's Mythologies*, Harper, 1976.

(With Naylor) *Strangeness: A Collection of Curious Tales*, Scribner, 1977.

CRITICISM

The Castle of Indolence: On Poetry, Poets, and Poetasters, Picador (New York City), 1995.

OTHER

(Ghost editor with Robert Arthur) *Alfred Hitchcock Presents: Stories that Scared Even Me*, Random House, 1967.

(Librettist) *The Fall of the House of Usher* (opera), produced in New York City, 1979.

(Librettist) *Frankenstein* (opera), produced in Greenvale, NY, 1982.

Ringtime (short story), Toothpaste Press, 1983.

(Author of introduction) Michael Bishop, *One Winter in Eden*, Arkham House (Sauk City, WI), 1984.

Torturing Mr. Amberwell (short story), Cheap Street (New Castle, VA), 1985.

(Author of preface) Pamela Zoline, *The Heat Death of the Universe and Other Stories*, McPherson & Company (New Paltz, NY), 1988.

(Author of introduction) Philip K. Dick, *The Penultimate Truth*, Carroll & Graf, 1989.

Ben Hur (play), first produced in New York City, 1989.

The Cardinal Detoxes (verse play), first produced in New York City by RAPP Theater Company, 1990.

The Stuff Our Dreams Is Made Of: How Science Fiction Conquered the World, Free Press, 1997.

Contributor to *Science Fiction at Large*, edited by Peter Nicholls, Harper, 1976.

Contributor to numerous anthologies. Also contributor to periodicals, including *Playboy*, *Poetry*, and *Harper's*. Regular reviewer for *Times Literary Supplement* and *Washington Post Book World*.

■ Adaptations

The Brave Little Toaster was produced as an animated film by Hyperion-Kushner-Lockec, 1987. A full-length animated feature of *The Brave Little Toaster Goes to Mars* is in production by Hyperion.

■ Work in Progress

The Teddy Bear's Tragedy; *The Pressure of Time*; *The Sub: A Study in Witchcraft*.

■ Sidelights

An author of science fiction, poetry, historical novels, opera librettos, and computer-interactive fiction, Thomas M. Disch has been cited as "one of the most remarkably multi-talented writers around" by a reviewer for the *Washington Post Book World.* Disch began his career writing science fiction stories that featured dark themes and disturbing plots. Many of Disch's early themes reappear in his short stories and poetry; the result, according to Blake Morrison in the *Times Literary Supplement,* is "never less than enjoyable and accomplished." While many of his best-known works are aimed at an adult audience, Disch is also the author of well-received children's fiction, including two fantasies, *The Brave Little Toaster* and *The Brave Little Toaster Goes to Mars.* Describing the diversity of Disch's work in *Dream Makers: The Uncommon People Who Write Science Fiction,* Charles Platt notes that the author "has traveled widely, through almost every genre and technique.... And in each field [Disch] has made himself at home, never ill-at-ease or out-of-place, writing with the same implacable control and elegant manners."

Hard to pigeon-hole, Disch's versatility has made both marketing his work and developing a loyal following of readers difficult. In refusing to let critics stamp his work with labels, Disch has been granted a relative anonymity, a phenomenon that led *Newsweek* critic Walter Clemons to call the author "the most formidably gifted unfamous American writer."

Disch grew up in Minnesota and graduated from high school in St. Paul. As a youngster he devoured horror comic books and science fiction magazines, including the influential *Astounding Science Fiction;* he learned his craft by reading and re-reading the work of authors such as Robert A. Heinlein and Isaac Asimov found in the pages of that journal. Although Disch did not publish his first short story until 1962, he had been writing science fiction for a decade or more under the inspiration of his favorite childhood authors.

After a series of low-paying jobs in Minnesota (including employment as a night watchman in a funeral parlor), Disch moved to New York City. While living in New York, he worked as a checkroom attendant and advertising copywriter. His first fiction appeared in a magazine called *Fantastic Stories* in 1962; that periodical and another one called *Amazing Stories* would publish nine more of his works that year and the next. Although Disch has admitted that he did not think very highly of his first publishing success, he found his second effort at writing a full-length story more satisfactory. This story, entitled "White Fang Goes Dingo," was first published in its short form, then in an expanded version as the author's second novel, *Mankind under the Leash* (later published under the title Disch prefers, *The Puppies of Terra*).

In 1964, having secured an advance from Berkley, Disch left advertising to become a full-time writer. He published his first novel the following year, a science fiction tale entitled *The Genocides.* In large part the story of an alien invasion of Earth, *The Genocides* describes the last grim days of human existence, an existence where people are reduced to little more than insects in the aliens' global garden. Critics found the book frightening. "The novel ... is powerful in the way that it forces the reader to alter his perspective, to reexamine what it means to be human," writes Erich S. Rupprecht in *Dictionary of Literary Biography.* Disch followed *The Genocides* with a series of thought-provoking science fiction tales, such as *Camp Concentration* and *334,* as well as horror novels such as *The Businessman* and *The M.D.*

Confident of his continued success as a writer, Disch would soon find himself near the center of an upheaval in the world of science fiction. Having published stories in the influential British magazine *New Worlds,* he became a force in what has since been labeled the New Wave of science fiction. Brian Aldiss, in his *Trillion Year Spree: The History of Science Fiction,* noted: "At the heart of *New Worlds's* New Wave—never mind the froth at the edges—was a hard and unpalatable core of message, an attitude to life, a skepticism about the benefits of society or any future society." More specifically, the New Wave was interested in new forms of expression and new themes never dreamed of by the older generation of science fiction writers. "In a broad sense," write Robert Scholes and Eric S. Rabkin in *Science Fiction: History, Science, Vision,* "the New Wave represents an attempt to find a language and a social perspective for science fiction that is as adventurous and progressive as its technological vision." The skepticism of its writers made their works on a whole pessimistic, and Disch was no exception. Although the New Wave has been followed by succeeding generations of writers, its impact on Disch's work—and the reverse—is undeniable.

Camp Concentration, 334, and *On Wings of Song* are widely considered Disch's best works. All three appeared in a mid-1980s survey by David Pringle entitled *Science Fiction: The 100 Best Novels.* Scholes and Rabkin describe *Camp Concentration* as Disch's "first major breakthrough" under the influence of the New Wave. It is set at a secret prison camp run by the U.S. Army where selected prisoners are being treated with a new drug that increases their intelligence. Unfortunately, this drug also causes the prisoners' early deaths. The novel is in the form of a diary kept by one of the prisoners. The diary's style grows more complex as the narrative develops, reflecting the prisoner's increasing intelligence. According to Scholes and Rabkin, the novel "combines considerable technical resources in the management of the narrative ... with a probing inquiry into human values." Rupprecht draws a parallel between *Camp Concentration* and *The Genocides.* In both novels, he argues, the characters must survive inescapable situations. Disch's continuing theme, Rupprecht summarizes, is "charting his characters' attempts to keep themselves intact in a world which grows increasingly hostile, irrational, inhuman."

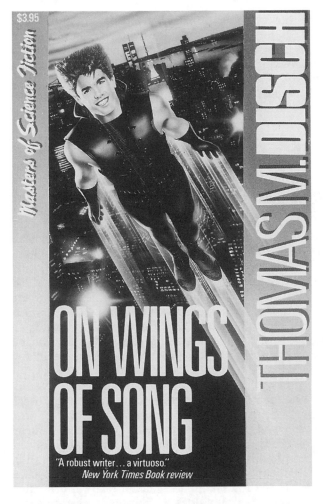

$3.95

Masters of Science Fiction

ON WINGS OF SONG

THOMAS M. DISCH

"A robust writer... a virtuoso."
New York Times Book review

Stifled by the rigid police state of 21st-century Iowa, Daniel Weinreb and his bride escape to New York looking for adventure in this critically acclaimed science fiction.

This theme is also found in *334,* a novel set in a New York City housing project of the future. Divided into six loosely-related sections, the novel presents the daily lives of residents of the building, which is located at 334 East Eleventh Street. The characters live in boredom and poverty; their city is rundown and dirty. The world of the novel, Scholes and Rabkin believe, "is not radically different from ours in many respects but is deeply troubling for reasons that apply to the present New York as well. Above all, the aimlessness and purposelessness of the lives chronicled is affecting." In his analysis of the book Rupprecht also notes the similarity between the novel's setting and the world of the present. He finds *334* to be "a slightly distorted mirror image of contemporary life." Although a *Washington Post Book World* contributor judges the setting to be "an interesting, plausible and unpleasant near-future world where urban life is even more constricted than now," he nonetheless believes that "survival and aspiration remain possible." Rupprecht praises *334* as Disch's "most brilliant and disturbing work .... One can think of few writers—of science fiction or other genres—who could convey a similar sense of emptiness, of yearning, of ruin with this power and grace .... Like all great

writers, Disch forces his readers to see the reality of their lives in a way that is fresh, startling, disturbing, and moving." Speaking of *Camp Concentration* and *334,* David Lehman of the *Times Literary Supplement* states that these two novels "seem to transcend their genre without betraying it; they manage to break down the barriers separating science fiction from 'literature,' and they do so by shrewdly manipulating the conventions of the former."

Like *334, On Wings of Song* deals with a future time that resembles our own. In his autobiographical essay for *Something about the Author Autobiography Series* (*SAAS*), Disch says the "book is about a boy from the Iowa Corn Belt who wants more than anything to sing (because in his future world that is a means of achieving out-of-body flight), but who just doesn't have the knack." *On Wings of Song* follows the story of Daniel Weinreb as he challenges the repressive police state controlled by the "undergoders." Hearing of a new technological advance in the form of a "flight apparatus" that allows people to escape from their bodies, Daniel decides to head to New York in search of the device. However, his attempts to fly are grounded because he cannot achieve the one requirement needed to find release—the ability to lose oneself in song.

Describing the general atmosphere of the novel in the *New York Times Book Review,* Gerald Jonas notes: "Politically and economically, things seem to be going downhill, but in between crises, people can still assure themselves that they are living in 'normal' times." In the *Village Voice,* John Calvin Batchelor calls *On Wings of Song* Disch's "grandest work." The critic maintains that the novel links Disch with other great social critics of the past, including H. G. Wells and George Orwell. "Disch," he writes, "is an unapologetic political writer, a high-minded liberal democrat, who sees doom in Western Civilization and says so, often with bizarre, bleak scenarios."

Along with his novels, Disch has also contributed numerous short stories to periodicals. These have been gathered in several well-received short story collections and have appeared in anthologies, including several volumes of *The Best from Fantasy & Science Fiction.* Reviewers of his short stories have also been reluctant to classify Disch as "merely" a science fiction writer. *Time* reviewer Paul Gray, for instance, observes that in Disch's collection *Getting into Death and Other Stories,* there is only one story that is traditional, space-oriented science fiction, while the others are deemed comparable to the work of Lewis Carroll, creator of *Alice's Adventures in Wonderland.* Finding yet another notable author with whom to compare Disch, *Voice of Youth Advocates* contributor Wain Saeger refers to the stories in *Fundamental Disch* as "somber, even eerie, more like Edgar Allan Poe than today's space opera."

Continuing to explore many literary avenues, in the 1980s and 1990s Disch published novels, stories, poetry, a libretto and an interactive computer novel. Three novels published during this period further the social criticism evident in his earlier works. In *The Business-man: A Tale of Terror, The M.D.: A Horror Story,* and *The Priest: A Gothic Romance,* Disch combines classic thriller techniques with a critical look at the corruption he sees in the three professions mentioned in the titles. The plots are replete with the type of strange occurrences Disch's readers have grown to expect, and the works show Disch's usual blend of styles. Writing about *The M.D.* in *Kliatt,* Larry W. Prater notes: "The novel combines elements of the macabre, of fantasy and of SF." Evidently, in life as well as literature, categories aren't important to Disch. In a *Publishers Weekly* interview with David Finkle, Disch refuses to see *The M.D.* as just a horror novel and with equal fervor defends his right to remain unburdened by a convenient label. "Every book has its own slightly different ground rules from the others," he maintains. "As long as the book plays by its own rules and those are clear, I don't think genre borderlines are especially helpful. I don't spend my life trying to determine what category I'm in." Disch tells Platt: "Part of my notion of a proper ambition is that one should excel at a wide range of tasks."

Thinking they have been abandoned, a toaster and other household appliances begin a journey to a far away city in search of their master. (From *The Brave Little Toaster,* written by Disch and illustrated by Karen Schmidt.)

The variety found in Disch's novels and stories also extends to his poetry and work for children. Lehman praises Disch's poetry by noting that "the distinctive qualities of Disch's prose fiction—wit, invention, and the gift of gab—are the virtues of his verse as well.... [Disch has] an excellent ear and clever tongue." Disch has also enjoyed success as a children's author with such works as *The Brave Little Toaster* and *The Tale of Dan de Lion.* In these books, Disch fully embraces the fantastic. *The Brave Little Toaster* tells the story of a group of small appliances (including a toaster, a clock radio, and an electric blanket) who come to life in order to search for their missing master. Claiming *The Brave Little Toaster* "may prove to be a modern classic," Michael Dirda wrote in the *Washington Post Book World* that different aspects of the book would appeal to different audiences: "though kids will get a real charge out of the story ... the adult reader's joy will be more literary." A critic in *Publishers Weekly* applauds "the human vulnerability of the hero and his friends" and believes that for some, *The Brave Little Toaster* will be fondly remembered as "a *Velveteen Rabbit* with extension cords." *The Brave Little Toaster* gained further recognition when it was produced as an animated film in 1987.

In 1988, familiar appliances return to action in Disch's sequel to his first children's book, *The Brave Little Toaster Goes to Mars,* and a few new characters are introduced, including a ceiling fan and a microwave. When the Earth is threatened by a hostile band of Martian appliances, the toaster takes it upon himself to travel to the red planet and make peace with the alien appliances. Not only does the toaster succeed in securing peace, but the Martians even elect him president of their planet. A reviewer in *Publishers Weekly* claims "the epic elements will more than appease readers awaiting this sequel."

For those critics who scoffed at his talking appliances, Disch commented in his *SAAS* entry: "The thing is, as everyone below the age of ten knows quite well, anything and everything can talk quite clearly, if one just has the patience, and imagination, to listen. It's all a matter of pretending. Children are the best pretenders, and writers of children's books are probably the next best.... I'd go so far as to say that to write children's books well, some part of you has to remain a child and stay behind in first grade forever."

The Tale of Dan de Lion, Disch's collection of children's poetry presented in a series of couplets, concerns the adventures of a dandelion, his weedy family, and the rose breeder who wants to destroy them. Again, *The Tale of Dan de Lion* can be enjoyed by different generations with adults catching jokes that are out of the grasp of young minds and children finding entertaining tidbits overlooked by older readers. In his *SAAS* essay, Disch admits that "a goodly portion of all the poems I've written are probably as suitable for kids as for grown-ups.... Once again I find myself impatient with the notion that kids and grown-ups should live in separate literary worlds."

In most evaluations of his work, Disch is lauded for his great imagination, the diversity of his narrative style, and the ease with which he works in a number of different genres. Because Disch is able to move so effortlessly through these different thematic and stylistic concerns, Rupprecht concludes that Disch is "one of the finest writers of fiction today," a writer who "seems to delight ... in blurring easy distinctions."

■ Works Cited

Aldiss, Brian W., *Trillion Year Spree: The History of Science Fiction,* Atheneum, 1986.

Batchelor, John Calvin, "Weird Worlds of Thomas Disch," *Village Voice,* August 27-September 2, 1980, pp. 35-36.

Review of *The Brave Little Toaster, Publishers Weekly,* May 30, 1986, p. 68.

Review of *The Brave Little Toaster Goes to Mars, Publishers Weekly,* May 20, 1988, p. 93.

Clemons, Walter, "The Joyously Versatile Thomas Disch," *Newsweek,* July 11, 1988, pp. 66-67.

Dirda, Michael, review of *The Brave Little Toaster, Washington Post Book World,* April 13, 1986, p. 11.

Disch, Thomas M., "My Life as a Child: A Mini-Autobiography," *Something about the Author Autobiography Series,* Volume 15, Gale, 1993, pp. 107-23.

Finkle, David, "Thomas M. Disch," *Publishers Weekly,* April 19, 1991, pp. 48-49.

Gray, Paul, review of *Getting into Death and Other Stories, Time,* February 9, 1976, pp. 83-84.

Jonas, Gerald, review of *On Wings of Song, New York Times Book Review,* October 28, 1979, p. 15.

Lehman, David, review of *Burn This, Times Literary Supplement,* August 27, 1982, p. 919.

Review of *The Man Who Had No Idea, Washington Post Book World,* October 31, 1982, p. 12.

Morrison, Blake, review of *Here I Am, There You Are, Where We Were,* May 25, 1984, p. 573.

Platt, Charles, *Dream Makers: Uncommon People Who Write Science Fiction,* Berkley Publishing, 1980.

Prater, Larry W., review of *The M.D., Kliatt,* September, 1992, p. 20.

Rupprecht, Erich S., "Thomas M. Disch," *Dictionary of Literary Biography, Volume 8: Twentieth-Century American Science Fiction Writers,* Part 1, Gale, 1981, pp. 148-154.

Saeger, Wain, review of *Fundamental Disch, Voice of Youth Advocates,* April, 1981, p. 39.

Scholes, Robert and Eric S. Rabkin, *Science Fiction: History, Science, Vision,* Oxford University Press, 1977, pp. 88, 96.

Review of *334, Washington Post Book World,* July 26, 1981, pp. 6-7.

■ For More Information See

BOOKS

Bleiler, E. F., editor, *Science Fiction Writers: Critical Studies of the Major Authors from the Early Nineteenth Century to the Present Day,* Scribner, 1982, pp. 351-56.

Children's Literature Review, Volume 18, Gale Research, 1989.

Contemporary Literary Criticism, Gale Research, Volume 7, 1977, pp. 86-87; Volume 36, 1986, pp. 123-28.

Contemporary Poets, St. James Press (Chicago), 5th edition, 1991.

Delany, Samuel R., *The American Shore: Meditations on a Tale of Science Fiction by Thomas M. Disch,* Dragon (Elizabethtown, NY), 1978.

Disch, Thomas M., *334,* Gregg, 1976, pp. v-xiii.

Nee, David, *Thomas M. Disch: A Preliminary Bibliography,* Other Change of Hobit (Berkeley, CA), 1982.

Nicholls, Peter, editor, *Science Fiction at Large,* Harper, 1976, pp. 141-55. Stephens, Christopher P., *A Checklist of Thomas M. Disch,* Ultramarine (Hastings-on-Hudson, NY), 1991.

PERIODICALS

Chicago Tribune Book World, March 22, 1982.

Los Angeles Times, February 3, 1981; November 21, 1982, p. 13; August 13, 1989, p. 3.

New Statesman, July 13, 1984, p. 28.

Newsweek, March 9, 1981; July 2, 1984.

New York Times Book Review, March 21, 1976, p. 6; August 26, 1984, p. 31; April 20, 1986, p. 29.

Publishers Weekly, January 7, 1974, p. 56; January 5, 1976, p. 59; August 29, 1980, p. 363.

Science Fiction Chronicle, February, 1993, p. 35.

Spectator, May 1, 1982, p. 23.

Time, July 28, 1975; July 9, 1984, pp. 85-86.

Times Literary Supplement, February 15, 1974, p. 163; June 12, 1981, p. 659; August 27, 1982, p. 919; November 28, 1986, p. 343; September 15-21, 1989, p. 1000; November 11, 1994, p. 19.

Washington Post, September 23, 1979, p. 7.

Washington Post Book World, January 27, 1980, p. 13; August 6, 1989, p. 5.*

*   *   *

DISCH, Tom
See DISCH, Thomas M(ichael)

*   *   *

DOTHERS, Anne
See CHESS, Victoria (Dickerson)

*   *   *

DUNTON, Dorothy 1912-

■ Personal

Born November 7, 1912; daughter of Robert Blaisdell and Nell (Rollins) Magune; married Robert Gilley Dunton, April 29, 1939; children: Robert Jr., John Magune. *Politics:* Republican. *Religion:* Protestant. *Hobbies and other interests:* Travel.

Addresses

Home—300 Nautilus Court, Fort Myers, FL 33908-1610.

Career

Worked as a registered nurse and a head nurse for a private hospital. Organizer and president of Jefferson County Mental Health Care Association; volunteer for Jefferson County Health Department.

Writings

City Cat Goes to the Country, illustrated by Megan Elizabeth Tuttle, Carlton Press, 1995.

Work in Progress

Mellie, The Cap'n's Wife, from diaries.

Sidelights

Dorothy Dunton told *SATA:* "*City Cat Goes to the Country* is a true story about Ringo, who was such a 'people' cat that his language became understandable and it was fun to interpret. There are a lot of cat books, but Barbara Bush's *Millie's Book* inspired me. My advice to aspiring writers would be to have lots of patience, to accept disappointments, and to recognize that there are thousands of cat books out there. Publishing your first is very frustrating and expensive and not a great deal of editorial assistance is offered."*

* * *

DURRETT, Deanne 1940-

■ Personal

Born February 3, 1940, in Oklahoma City, OK; daughter of David Martin (a farmer) and June (Capps) Grantham; married F. Dan Durrett (an engineer), August 28, 1959; children: Timothy Dan, Joy Lynn Parker. *Education:* Attended Southwestern State College, 1958-59. *Politics:* Republican. *Religion:* Baptist.

Career

Writer, wife, and mother. *Member:* Society of Children's Book Writers and Illustrators (regional advisor, 1989-94).

Writings

NONFICTION

Organ Transplants, Lucent Books, 1993.
Jim Henson, Lucent, 1994.
Angels: Opposing Viewpoints, Greenhaven Press, 1996.
Norman Rockwell, Lucent, 1996.
Healers, Facts on File, 1997.

DEANNE DURRETT

FICTION

My New Sister, the Bully, Abingdon, 1985.

■ Work in Progress

Navajo Codetalkers, expected 1997. Biography of Dommique Moceanu.

■ Sidelights

Deanne Durrett told *SATA:* "I love to write! Fiction is pure pleasure but nonfiction is discovery!

"I never know what the day will bring or who will enrich my life—a Muppeteer or a transplant surgeon? A medicine man or an artist? Who will be next—a Navajo code talker? Maybe I will unearth a gold nugget of information everyone else overlooked. Perhaps it will add the perfect touch to my chapter or lead to the mother lode and another idea for a book. One thing is for sure, something will excite me. I love discovery and sharing the adventure with my readers.

"Although I attended college only one year, my education did not stop there. For more than twenty-five years I've studied on my own and taken many writing classes at the college level. I count the information I gain from researching the books I write, the books I read for pleasure, and life experience as my continuing education. It is my plan to never stop learning."

■ For More Information See

PERIODICALS

Horn Book Guide, fall, 1993, p. 352; spring, 1995, p. 148.
School Library Journal, May, 1996, p. 138.

* * *

DWYER, Deanna
See KOONTZ, Dean R(ay)

* * *

DWYER, K. R.
See KOONTZ, Dean R(ay)

* * *

DYGARD, Thomas J. 1931-1996

OBITUARY NOTICE—See index for *SATA* sketch: Born August 10, 1931, in Little Rock, AK; died of heart failure, September 30, 1996, in Hazelton, PA. Children's author and journalist. A reporter and bureau chief for the Associated Press, Dygard was best known for his sports and adventure novels for children. His most recent book, *Running Wild,* features a teenager who finds happiness and acceptance after joining a football team. Dygard began his career writing sports for the *Arkansas Gazette* after earning his degree from the University of Arkansas at Fayetteville. In 1954 he was offered a job with the Associated Press and went on to work in several of their bureaus, including those in the southern cities of Little Rock, Birmingham, and New Orleans. He was also bureau chief in Tokyo, Chicago, Indianapolis, and Little Rock. Dygard started writing sports novels for young adults as a hobby and had his first one, *Running Scared,* published in 1977. He went on to publish a book every year until 1986; some of the best-known of these stories are *Outside Shooter, Point Spread* and *Soccer Duel.* Dygard retired from the Associated Press in 1993 and moved to Evansville, Indiana, but continued writing children's novels.

OBITUARIES AND OTHER SOURCES:

BOOKS

Something about the Author Autobiography Series, Volume 15, Gale, 1993.

PERIODICALS

New York Times, October 5, 1996, p. 52.
Publishers Weekly, October 14, 1996, p. 32.

* * *

EARLY, Jack
See SCOPPETTONE, Sandra

F

FARTHING-KNIGHT, Catherine 1933-

■ Personal

Born May 2, 1933, in Bendigo, Victoria, Australia; daughter of Kenneth Stuart (a solicitor) Smalley and Reta Maude Showers-Smalley; married Brian Farthing (a naval officer), July 31, 1954; married Robert John Knight (an anesthesiologist), April 27, 1991; children: (first marriage) Stephen Farthing, Catherine Barrow, Sally Ann Wilcox, Adam Farthing. *Education:* Bendigo Technical School, certificate of art, 1954; Tafe Holmesgren, associate diploma of professional writing and editing, 1993. *Politics:* Liberal Party. *Religion:* Church of England. *Hobbies and other interests:* Music (classical and jazz), painting on silk, scuba diving, tennis.

■ Addresses

Home and office—34 College St., Hawthorn, Victoria 3122, Australia.

■ Career

C.S.I.R.O., Melbourne, Victoria, Australia, map drawing, 1953; writer, painter, and poet. Girl Guide leader in Papua New Guinea, 1967-71, and in Melbourne, 1972-84; "Meal on Wheels" district commissioner in Papua New Guinea, 1967-71. Pianist for Spastic Society, 1972-86, and for Villa Maria School for the Blind, 1994-96. *Exhibitions:* Silk painting exhibitions, 1996. *Member:* National Gallery Society, Writers Group, Arts and Crafts Victoria, Melbourne Symphony Orchestra Society.

■ Awards, Honors

Various awards for piano performance, 1947-53; short story award, 1995.

■ Writings

Days with Gran, illustrated by Anne-Maree Althaus, University of Queensland Press, 1995.

■ Work in Progress

A children's novel; *The Tethered Birds,* poetry; painting of silk scarves, wall hangings, and children's scenes.

■ Sidelights

Catherine Farthing-Knight told *SATA:* "As a child I liked to escape into an imaginary world, writing stories, plays, and poetry in a school exercise book. I wrote adventure stories, rhyming poetry, anything to do with castles and knights and dragons, which explains my later fascination for Arthurian tales, myths, and legends. Sketching, listening to music, I was a dreamer who liked playing the piano and making up tunes.

"Having six granddaughters, whose company I find joyous, I wanted to share my childhood with them, and all other readers, especially the relationship I enjoyed

CATHERINE FARTHING-KNIGHT

with my grandmother. *Days with Gran* was written to reclaim my past. It was a warm and happy time, and I loved writing about it. *Days with Gran* has not, as yet, been adapted to another medium. Here's hoping!

"I write when the mood takes me, usually at our beach house where I spend a lot of my time. There are pelicans to watch, and the sound of the sea makes it an inspiring place. I had pure enjoyment in writing the book, as recalling one anecdote led to remembering another. My only advice to aspiring writers is to keep writing and send manuscripts in.

"I enjoy Alison Lester's stories and colorful illustrations and her simple yet effective style. Ida Rentoul's illustrations appeal to me. I like contemporary children's writers' work but find little value in contemporary poetry. I am obsessed with murder mysteries by such authors as Ruth Rendell, Elizabeth George, Sara Paretsky, and Sue Grafton, and like to watch mystery/drama films.

"I have a husband who encourages my writing, four children, and granddaughters. My interests are listening to classical music and jazz, painting on silk (scarves and wall hangings) which I sell to galleries and shops. I enjoy scuba diving, watching fish, gazing at pelicans, and being with the very young and with the older generation. Other pleasures are tennis, gardening, and travelling, particularly in Norway and Turkey. I have lived in England and Ireland for three years and in Papua New Guinea for six."

She concludes: "I worry that we are moving too quickly without taking the time to stop and listen and care for others. The loneliness of other people is a great concern."

*   *   *

FERRY, Charles 1927-

■ Personal

Born October 8, 1927, in Chicago, IL; son of Ignatius Loyola (a postal clerk) and Madelyn Anne (Bartholemew) Ferry; married Ruth Louise Merz (an executive travel coordinator), September 26, 1958; children: Ronald Edmund Richardson (stepson). *Education:* Attended University of Illinois, 1952. *Politics:* Republican. *Religion:* Episcopalian. *Hobbies and other interests:* "I cook, bake bread, and tutor persons of all ages in writing."

■ Addresses

Home—Rochester Hills, MI. *Office*—Daisy Hill Press, P.O. Box 1681, Rochester, MI 48308.

■ Career

Radio and newspaper journalist, 1949-71; writer, 1971—. *Military service:* U.S. Navy, 1944-49.

CHARLES FERRY

■ Awards, Honors

Best Children's Book, Friends of American Writers, Best Books of the Year selection, *School Library Journal,* and Best Books for Young Adults, American Library Association (ALA), all 1983, all for *Raspberry One;* Best Book for Young Adults, ALA, 1993, Books for the Teen Age, New York Public Library, 1994, and Best Book for High School Seniors, National Council of Teachers of English, 1995, all for *Binge.*

■ Writings

Up in Sister Bay, Houghton, 1975.
O Zebron Falls!, Houghton, 1977.
Raspberry One, Houghton, 1983.
One More Time!, Houghton, 1985.
Binge, Daisy Hill Press (Rochester, MI), 1992.
A Fresh Start, Proctor Publications (Ann Arbor, MI), 1996.
Love, Proctor Publications, in press.

■ Adaptations

Binge was optioned for film by Walt Disney Educational Productions.

■ Sidelights

A career as a children's book writer came relatively late in life for Charles Ferry. After working as a journalist and in related fields for several years, Ferry began writing his first book for young readers after he had reached his forties. Prompted by recollections of his own wide-ranging life experiences—from happy childhood vacations in the northern United States to tragic adult years during which his life was controlled by a growing dependence on alcohol—Ferry published the first of several novels that would vividly recreate young peoples' movement toward adulthood. While his early novels take place during the years surrounding World War II, his later fiction deals with contemporary—and controversial—topics, including alcoholism. "I have no interest in writing for adults," Ferry once told *SATA*. "In general, I think the best writing is being done in the children's field. Authors have the freedom to give of themselves and to dream a little."

"I began writing vignettes about my boyhood summers in northern Wisconsin," Ferry once explained to *SATA*, describing how he "eased into the role of author." He eventually collected these vignettes into the manuscript of his first novel, *Up in Sister Bay*, which was published in 1975. Set in northern Wisconsin in the year 1939, the story revolves around the challenges facing four teens during wartime. "In *Up in Sister Bay*, Hitler's armies invade Poland," the author noted, "triggering the war and changing the lives of simple people."

Up in Sister Bay would be the first of Ferry's books to illuminate the events of everyday life during the World War II era. 1977's *O Zebron Falls!* portrays a young woman approaching high school graduation, whose efforts to find a direction in her life are complicated by an unresolved conflict with her father and the onset of the Second World War. Sixteen-year-old Lukie Bishop tries to get the most from her last year in school, knowing her future as a woman in a small Midwestern town is limited. At a glance, Lukie's life seems idyllic— she's elected Class Sweetheart, serves as homecoming chairman, and enjoys the company of Billy Butts, football hero and school valedictorian. However, readers soon understand Lukie's sorrows. Her relationship with Billy, an African American, can never become serious because of the townspeople's prejudices; her uncle dies in a munitions factory while contributing to the war effort; and her elders suggest she should limit her goals to teaching or nursing, respectable professions for women. Critics praised Ferry for writing about times long past without sugarcoating or ignoring the difficulties young adults experienced. Marianne M. Rafalko, writing in *Best Sellers*, commended Ferry for his perceptive portrayal of a teenage girl of the 1940s, saying "today's young reader may readily identify with her problems and fears: growing up, falling in love, maturing sexually, relating to one's parents, and deciding one's future." In a *Horn Book* review, Ann A. Flowers applauded *O Zebron Falls!*, asserting that it "contains the sweetness of a simpler time but emphasizes that every era has its unsolvable problems."

Ferry's award-winning *Raspberry One*, published in 1983, also focuses on the tensions young Americans felt during the Second World War. The young protagonist, Nick Enright, attempts to deal with the brutalizing effects of combat while serving aboard a U.S. Navy torpedo bomber destined to fight in the bloody battle for control of the island of Iwo Jima. "*O Zebron Falls!* deals with life on the wartime home front, while *Raspberry One*, a hard look at the horrors of war, ends with V-J Day and victory," explained Ferry. "Prior to that war, in 1936, President Franklin Delano Roosevelt had told his countrymen, 'To some generations, much is given. Of some generations, much is expected. This generation of Americans has a rendezvous with destiny.' That generation had an awesome rendezvous, with history's greatest war," Ferry maintained, "and it acquitted itself admirably." Because he had never actually experienced a combat situation, Ferry put an enormous amount of effort into researching the historic backdrop of *Raspberry One*. He once said in a *Horn Book* article, "For two years ... I relived the war, in all of its theaters. God, what a horror! ... *Raspberry One* is my little prayer that it will never happen again." Ferry expects that his first four titles will soon be reissued, in a boxed set, as "The Rendezvous Quartet."

Calling the characters in *Raspberry One* "well-realized," Micki S. Nevett in *Voice of Youth Advocates* remarked on Ferry's ability to dramatize war without glorifying it and suggested the novel will give new readers an idea of "what a generation of young people in the 1940s experienced." In *School Library Journal*, reviewer David A. Lindsey appreciated Ferry's war narrative as a refreshing change of pace and described *Raspberry One* as being "long on action and strong in characterization."

Another of Ferry's historical novels, 1985's *One More Time!*, takes place during the same period, depicting the impact of the Japanese attack on Pearl Harbor on an older group of Americans: the members of a popular Big Band dance orchestra. Ferry details the life of a musician and American culture in general during the Big Band era. Writing in *Booklist*, Stephanie Zvirin complimented Ferry on "capturing the nostalgia and the trepidation of the American people" during the 1940s as they prepared for the "unknown." While admitting *One More Time!* may appeal to a smaller audience because of its subject, *School Library Journal* contributor Lindsey praised the novel's "well-crafted narrative," adding that Ferry presents solidly constructed characters and provides readers "a detailed knowledge of the milieu in which [these characters] live."

"In the writing of my first four titles, I was keenly aware that I was probably creating the most important body of work on life in America during World War II ever written for young people," Ferry once disclosed to *SATA*. "I knew that because I was drawing heavily from personal experience and was confident of the integrity of my work." While providing his readers with a vivid recreation of life in the United States during wartime, Ferry also accomplished something of a personal nature while writing those first four novels. "I had an ambivalent relationship with my father," he explained to *SATA.* "As a result, when I started my creative writing, I couldn't handle a father as a fictional character, even though my own father had passed away fifteen years earlier.

"And so in *Up in Sister Bay,* I wrote the father out of the story. He is away in Chicago looking for work. We learn about him indirectly through his son, Robbie, who remembers unkind things about him: his meanness, his drinking, things that applied to my own father. Yet it is clear that Robbie loves his father and looks up to him—again reflecting my own situation.

"In my second book, I could handle a father, but he is a gruff man who embarrasses his daughter in front of her friends, which my father often did. Then, in my third book, *Raspberry One,* the character George Enright is a marvelous father. The self-therapy had worked; I had come to terms with my own father. In researching that book, I learned about the horrors he had experienced in World War I. I came to understand him and to realize that I loved him dearly—and still do."

At this point in his career as an author, all of Ferry's books had focused on the lives of young people during the period of his own adolescence. A change in direction came in the 1990s with the publication of *Binge.* Considering it "the most personally important book" he would ever write, Ferry bravely confronted the reality of the addiction that had diminished his own life, career, and relationships with family and friends for more than two decades. "For much of my life I was plagued by the ravages of alcohol," he told *SATA.* "I could fill a large volume, recounting the horrors it caused in my life. [In the early 1970s], I finally whipped the problem. Still, hardly a night goes by that some bad memory of that period doesn't return to haunt me." In his essay for *Something about the Author Autobiography Series,* Ferry shares how alcohol consumed his life for over twenty-five years, leading him to commit crimes and even spend time in prison. "Why was I sent to prison in the first place? Forgery, and uttering, and publishing—three-and-a-half to fourteen years. The sentence ... may seem rather harsh, but it wasn't. [It] was merely the tip of the iceberg. [It] was the disgraceful culmination of my six-month, nine-state drinking binge. During that time I was a mini crime wave. Two stolen cars, one abandoned, one totaled. Five break-ins, most of them senseless. Bad checks, whenever I got my hands on a blank one. Larceny, whenever there was an opportunity. Anything to keep alcohol flowing through my bloodstream."

Ferry wanted to write these experiences out of his system; he did, publishing *Binge* in 1992. The story of Weldon Yeager, an eighteen-year-old petty criminal with a serious drinking problem, *Binge* follows its dissolute protagonist on a colossal binge that has tragic consequences. Waking up in a hospital ward under police guard—and not remembering how he got there—Weldon must eventually accept responsibility for actions that resulted in not only the loss of his own right

In his award winning book, Ferry chronicles the life of Weldon Yeager, an eighteen-year-old alcoholic, after he kills his girlfriend while driving drunk.

foot, but in the deaths of two people struck and killed by the car he was driving. "If the book spares one young person the ravages of alcohol, I will consider it the greatest achievement of my life," Ferry declared. "You see, when I set out to write a young adult novel about how alcohol destroys young lives, my primary target was not young people who already have a drinking problem (although some would surely be influenced by such a book) but those who *don't,*" the author said in his *SAAS* essay. "Hopefully the images in *Binge* would remain fixed in the minds of some of them and spare them the horrors of alcoholism in future years. I would achieve that effect, I decided, with a short novel that could be read in one sitting and have a stunning impact on the reader."

Since its publication, critical reception has marked *Binge* a success: Mary K. Chelton in a review for *Voice of Youth Advocates* called the novel "an incredibly powerful, mesmerizing, tragic, read-in-one-sitting little book with an authenticity and understanding rare in adolescent literature." In the same publication, critic Carol Otis Hurst termed the work "a brutal book with a strong moral impact. It walks a thin line between being a tract on the evils of alcohol and a novelette and, thanks to the skills of Mr. Ferry, it succeeds."

Binge proved to be pivotal, both in the field of publishing as a whole—it was the first self-published book in the history of the American Library Association to receive an ALA Best Book citation—as well as in its author's personal life. "I had gone public with my troubled background: my twenty-five-year battle against alcohol, which had been a torment in my life: lost jobs, wrecked cars, dirty jail cells, prison. *Binge,* which tells a powerful story about how alcohol destroys young lives, was written as my personal redemption. When sixty-one mainstream publishers rejected it, I published the book myself ... [and] when the American Library Association chose it as a Best Book for Young Adults, almost overnight I became something of a legend."

Ferry has continued writing in the candid, forthright vein characteristic of *Binge;* he released *A Fresh Start* in 1996. "*A Fresh Start* points the way to recovery from alcoholism [using] my Eight Steps to Sobriety and a Better You," the author explained. "This time, I ignored establishment publishers and went directly to small presses." The novel recounts the efforts of four high school seniors in fighting the demons of alcohol and regaining sobriety through an eight-step program that Ferry devised during his own recovery from alcoholism. After failing courses during their final year in school, these four students struggle to earn their diploma, all the while reflecting on how alcohol abuse has affected their relationships with friends, family, and classmates. In *Voice of Youth Advocates,* C. A. Nichols emphasized that *A Fresh Start*'s message would be lost if it were viewed as "a novel or short story." Instead the reviewer insisted the work be used "to empower teens (or adults) to examine and take control of their own lives."

A more recent novel, *Love,* departs from the topic of alcohol to focus on two terminally ill children—Robbie and Sue Ellen, both age eleven—and the strong bond of love that develops between them in a hospital cancer ward. "I think ... *Love* is my best work to date," the author explained to *SATA,* although he believes that, like *Binge, Love* will be regarded as controversial for dealing with issues that are not typical of children's literature.

Despite the controversy surrounding his most recent novels, Ferry remains dedicated to his work. "To one degree or another, all good fiction involves truth," he once told *SATA.* "As William Faulkner put it, 'Truth is what a person holds to his or her heart.' What do my books offer that young people can hold to their hearts? It's not for me to say, really. My strong suit appears to

be evoking mood and atmosphere. I tell stories of young people coming of age.... My books come from deep inside of me, and they are slow to develop." After more than two decades as a published author, Ferry continues to live modestly, researching, lecturing, and writing from his home in Rochester Hills, a suburb of Detroit, Michigan. There, he explains, "our gregarious Belgian sheepdog, Emily Anne, rules the household. My wife, Ruth, who is a partner in my work, and I have touched a lot of young lives throughout America. We feel privileged."

■ Works Cited

Chelton, Mary K., review of *Binge, Voice of Youth Advocates,* June, 1993, p. 8.

Ferry, Charles, article in *Horn Book,* December, 1983, p. 651.

Ferry, Charles, essay in *Something about the Author Autobiography Series,* Vol. 20, Gale Research, 1995, pp. 201-18.

Flowers, Ann A., review of *O Zebron Falls!, Horn Book,* October, 1977, p. 539.

Hurst, Carol Otis, review of *Binge, Voice of Youth Advocates,* August, 1994.

Lindsey, David A., review of *Raspberry One, School Library Journal,* September, 1983, pp. 132-33.

Lindsey, David A., review of *One More Time!, School Library Journal,* August, 1985, p. 74.

Nevett, Micki S., review of *Raspberry One, Voice of Youth Advocates,* April, 1984, p. 30.

Nichols, C. A., review of *A Fresh Start, Voice of Youth Advocates,* October, 1996, p. 208.

Rafalko, Marianne M., review of *O Zebron Falls!, Best Sellers,* December, 1977, p. 293.

Zvirin, Stephanie, review of *One More Time!, Booklist,* May 15, 1985, p. 1325.

■ For More Information See

PERIODICALS

Booklist, May 15, 1983, p. 1196; March 15, 1993, p. 1342.

Children's Literature in Education, spring, 1985, pp. 15-20.

Horn Book, December, 1975, p. 601; June, 1983, p. 310; September-October, 1985, p. 563.

Kirkus Reviews, August 15, 1975, p. 924.

New York Times Book Review, November 2, 1975, p. 10; March 5, 1978, p. 26.

Publishers Weekly, March 29, 1985, p. 73.

School Library Journal, December, 1975, p. 59; October, 1977, p. 123; May, 1996, p. 132.

Voice of Youth Advocates, August, 1985, p. 183; October, 1993, pp. 206-08; December, 1994, p. 272.

G

GARNER, James Finn 1960(?)-

■ Personal

Born c. 1960; married Lies Vander Ark (a bank executive); children: Liam. *Education:* University of Michigan, B.A., 1982. *Politics:* Democrat.

■ Addresses

Home—Chicago, IL. *Office*—c/o Simon & Schuster, 1230 Avenue of the Americas, New York, NY 10020.

JAMES FINN GARNER

■ Career

Author and improvisational theater artist. Has appeared on Chicago Public Radio.

■ Writings

Politically Correct Bedtime Stories, Macmillan, 1994.
Once Upon a More Enlightened Time: More Politically Correct Bedtime Stories, Macmillan, 1995.
Politically Correct Holiday Stories: For an Enlightened Yuletide Season, Macmillan, 1995.

Also the author of an improvisational theater collection titled *Kafka for Kinder.* Contributor to periodicals, including *Chicago Tribune Magazine.*

■ Adaptations

Politically Correct Bedtime Stories was adapted for CD-ROM.

■ Work in Progress

An animated *film noir* about one of his improvisational characters, Rex Koko, a private-eye clown.

■ Sidelights

When James Finn Garner heard that classic children's fairy tales were being revised to avoid material that might be considered offensive by various groups, "he was appalled," according to Jon Elsen, an interviewer for the *New York Times Book Review.* Garner decided to make fun of this trend, and the result is his *Politically Correct Bedtime Stories.* In this volume Garner has rewritten thirteen popular stories, inserting politically correct terminology wherever he could. For instance, Rumpelstiltskin is not a dwarf but variously "vertically challenged" or a "man of nonstandard height," who is scolded for attempting to "interfere" with Esmeralda's "reproductive rights" by demanding her first-born child as payment for teaching her how to spin straw into gold.

In Garner's version of "Little Red Riding Hood," the wolf manages to don Grandma's nightgown after eating her because he is "unhampered by rigid, traditionalist notions of what was masculine or feminine," and after Jack trades his mother's cow for three magic beans, Garner writes of Jack's mother: "She used to think her son was merely a conceptual rather than a linear thinker, but now she was sure that he was downright differently abled."

Critics have applauded Garner's satire; Patricia T. O'Conner in the *New York Times Book Review* asserted that "somebody had to do it. And James Finn Garner has met the challenge manfully—or, rather, like a fully realized individual, secure in his personhood and in touch with his inner child." Jonathan Yardley in the *Washington Post Book World* was even more lavish in his praise of *Politically Correct Bedtime Stories;* he declared that "Garner isn't a mere writer, he's a virtuoso, a necromancer, a master of the tour de force— a Hans Nonsectarian Andersen for our very own time." Yardley further judged that Garner, in satirizing the extremes of political correctness, has committed "a public service of truly epic dimensions." Garner himself has defended stories like the ones he altered, commenting to *New York Times Book Review* interviewer Elsen: "There's magic to storytelling, and fear and wonder, and when you tie obvious little agendas to it, kids see that. I don't think a kid was ever made sexist because he or she read 'Snow White.' I think they were made sexist because of how they were raised and what they see in society around them."

■ Works Cited

Elsen, Jon, "Kafka for Children," *New York Times Book Review,* May 15, 1994, p. 3.

Garner, James Finn, *Politically Correct Bedtime Stories,* Macmillan, 1994.

O'Conner, Patricia T., review of *Politically Correct Bedtime Stories, New York Times Book Review,* May 15, 1994, p. 3.

Yardley, Jonathan, review of *Politically Correct Bedtime Stories, Washington Post Book World,* April 27, 1994, p. B2.

■ For More Information See

PERIODICALS

Detroit News, December 25, 1995, pp. C1, 5.

People Weekly, September 26, 1994, p. 90; June 19, 1995, p. 31.

Publishers Weekly, February 14, 1994, pp. 78-9.*

* * *

GEISERT, Arthur 1941-

■ Personal

Born September 20, 1941, in Dallas, TX; son of Leonard (an engineer) and Doris (a homemaker; maiden name, Boland) Geisert; married Bonnie Meier (a teach-

ARTHUR GEISERT

er), June 1, 1963; children: Noah. *Education:* Concordia College, Seward, NE, B.S., 1963; University of California, Davis, M.A., 1965; additional study at Chouinard Art Institute, Otis Art Institute, and Art Institute of Chicago.

■ Addresses

Home—P.O. Box 3, Galena, IL 61036.

■ Career

Printmaker and artist. Art teacher at Concordia College, River Forest, IL, Concordia College, Seward, NE, and Clark College, Dubuque, IA, 1965—. Invitational lecturer at many colleges, universities, and institutions, including University of Wisconsin, Madison, University of Minnesota, Minneapolis, and the Smithsonian. *Exhibitions:* Has exhibited artwork at galleries and exhibitions, including the Society of American Graphic Artists, New York City, 1986, 1991, and 1993; and the Society of Illustrators Museum of American Illustration, New York City, 1991, 1992, and 1996. *Member:* National Artist's Equity Association, Los Angeles Printmaking Society, Boston Printmakers.

■ Awards, Honors

Illinois Arts Council fellow, 1986; Ten Best Illustrated Children's Books selection, *New York Times,* 1986, for *Pigs from A to Z,* 1996, for *Roman Numerals I to MM; Reading Rainbow* Review Book selection and Reading Magic Award, *Parenting,* both 1991, both for *Oink;* Honor Book, *Parents Choice,* Ten Recommended Picture Books selection, *Time,* and Honor Book, *Boston Globe-Horn Book,* all 1995, all for *Haystack.*

■ Writings

SELF-ILLUSTRATED

Pa's Balloon and Other Pig Tales, Houghton, 1984.
Pigs from A to Z, Houghton, 1986.
The Ark, Houghton, 1988.
Oink, Houghton, 1991.
Pigs from 1 to 10, Houghton, 1992.
Oink Oink, Houghton, 1993.
After the Flood, Houghton, 1994.
Roman Numerals I to MM: Numerabilia Romana Uno Ad Duo Mila, Houghton, 1996.
The Etcher's Studio, Houghton, 1997.

ILLUSTRATOR

Barbara Bader, *Aesop and Company: With Scenes from His Legendary Life,* Houghton, 1991.

Bonnie Geisert, *Haystack,* Houghton, 1995.

OTHER

Contributor to numerous books, including *Paradis Perdu,* Atelier Contraste Fribourg, 1991; *Children's Book Illustration and Design,* edited by Julie Cummins, P.B.C. International, 1992; *World Book Encyclopedia,* 1993; and *The Very Best of Children's Book Illustration,* compiled by the Society of Illustrators, North Light Books, 1993. Geisert's books have been published in Japan, France, Spain, and Germany.

■ Work in Progress

Prairie Town, for Houghton.

■ Sidelights

Arthur Geisert combines etching with wry humor to produce award-winning children's books. A resident of the midwest, Geisert has become an expert on pigs, and five of his picture books feature the porcine critters. "My main interest is illustration," Geisert once commented. "I'm trying to combine a classic etching style inspired by Piranesi, Rembrandt, and Callot with humor and narrative."

Illustrated with Geisert's own etchings, *After the Flood* explores how Noah and his family begin life anew after surviving the Great Flood. (Written by Geisert.)

Once Mama Pig lays down for a nap, the piglets are free to run off and explore the barnyard. (From *Oink,* written and illustrated by Geisert.)

Trained as a teacher for both primary grades and art, Geisert soon discovered that his real passion lay in the studio, not in the classroom. Taking up residence in rural Galena, Illinois, Geisert and his wife and child lived for many years a "dirt poor" existence, as he wrote in *Something about the Author Autobiography Series* (*SAAS*). While his wife taught at a local school, Geisert worked selling etchings and building two homes for the family. As he explained in *SAAS,* his early etching subjects focused on "Noah's Ark, with a lot of detailed cutaway pieces, pigs, views of Galena, and humorous prints." Beginning with a small business loan of $800, Geisert was able to develop a lucrative business in prints. For many years he also submitted proposals to publishers for children's books. Over the years he managed to collect a drawer full of rejections for his troubles.

In the end, publishers came to him, however. An editor at Houghton Mifflin, after seeing his etchings in an exhibition, took a look at his portfolio and the happy result was Geisert's first picture book, *Pa's Balloon and Other Pig Tales.* "It was illustrated with etchings," Geisert explained in *SAAS,* "a rarely used technique in children's books, and the color was done with manual color separations." Relatively long for a picture book, *Pa's Balloon and Other Pig Tales* "has the look of a short novel," according to Karen Stang Hanley writing in *Booklist.* It contains three stories about a pig family: a disastrous picnic; a balloon race; and a journey to the North Pole. All are "narrated with childlike economy by a plucky piglet," Hanley noted. Writing in *Horn Book,* Karen Jameyson commented that while the stories themselves were slight, the illustrations "distinguish the book," utilizing "an array of perspectives to record the activity." A *Publishers Weekly* reviewer concluded that "Geisert's first book is sure to leave children wanting more from him."

Children did not have to wait long. Geisert's second title was a puzzle alphabet book, *Pigs from A to Z,* illustrated as all his books are, with original etchings. Minimal text accompanies full-page etchings in which various letters are hidden. A story line about the building of a tree house recalls Geisert's own boyhood carpentry efforts as well as his adult construction of houses. Denise M. Wilms in *Booklist* noted that the book was an "intriguing venture for curious, ambitious browsers," and *Horn Book*'s Jameyson concluded that "the graphically pleasing and very clever book may fascinate even those well beyond the picture-book age." *Pigs from A to Z* was selected by the *New York Times* as one of ten Best Illustrated Picture Books of 1986.

Animals figure in most of Geisert's graphic productions, and with *The Ark*, there is a definite plethora of all sorts of beasts in a retelling of the story from Genesis. "A dignified, somber retelling of the flood story," Ellen D. Warwick dubbed the book in a *School Library Journal* review. "I drew on material from many of my earlier etchings that deal with a Noah's Ark theme," Geisert wrote in *SAAS*. "I was especially interested in the interior views of the ark. I liked combining the rigid discipline of perspective with the organic chaos of the animals, birds, sacks of feed, etc." *Horn Book* reviewer Elizabeth S. Watson noted that "children will love finding the beasts who have wandered from their proper spaces. Parents and religious educators will welcome Geisert's handsome rendition of the story." Geisert, educated as an undergraduate at a Lutheran teacher's college, returned to this biblical theme with *After the Flood*, a story of what happens after the waters recede and the animals leave the Ark. "A glowing, impelling, visually stimulating panorama of hope and affirmation of life," is how Mary M. Burns described the book in *Horn Book*. Classical mythology forms the basis of another book, *Aesop and Company*, written by Barbara Bader, for which Geisert provided illustrations.

But Geisert never strays far from his beloved pigs. Four further titles have employed playful porkers: *Oink* and its sequel, *Oink Oink*, and two counting books, *Pigs from 1 to 10* and *Roman Numerals I to MM*. "Oink ... was a silly one-word (oink, oink, oink, etc.) book," Geisert reported in *SAAS*. "Earlier versions done on a single etching-plate date back fifteen years. *Oink* was the culmination of an idea that I had worked at, on and off, for years. I used our neighbor's pigs for models. It was a popular little book which received several awards and was translated into Spanish, German, and Japanese." As the sound that a pig makes is rendered the same in those languages as in English, it was not much of a translation effort. *Publishers Weekly* noted that the book's "droll illustrations exude an understated hilarity," and *Kirkus Reviews* dubbed its wordless sequel, *Oink Oink*, "a joyful adventure." *Pigs from 1 to 10* is a sequel to Geisert's earlier *Pigs from A to Z*, and a suspension bridge that Geisert had been building on his property played an integral part in this counting puzzle book. Numbers from 0 to 9 are hidden in each double-page, black-and-white etching. These etchings in turn tell the story of a pig family searching for a lost land. Each of the illustrations shows the piglets building elaborate machinery that will allow them to explore from mountain top to mountain top. "Few will be able to resist the

game," concluded Nancy Vasilakis in *Horn Book*. Geisert also illuminated the world of Roman numerals in *Roman Numerals I to MM*. "You have to count pigs to find the value of the Roman numeral," explained Geisert in *SAAS*. "The total number of pigs in the book is MMMMDCCCLXIV or 4,864." Jennifer Fleming, writing in *School Library Journal*, commented that "there is plenty of visual detail for early-elementary children to pore over," and *Booklist*'s Carolyn Phelan concluded that "Geisert's etchings, tinted with washes, make lively and beautifully detailed illustrations for this unusual book."

Teaming up with his wife, Geisert created a "quiet tribute to a bygone era," according to *Publishers Weekly*, with the picture book *Haystack*. The narrative explains the cycle of hay, from growth to cutting and stacking. Eventually the hay is used for feed and to provide warmth, while the animals give back to the cycle with their manure which fertilizes the next crop of hay. Leone McDermott in *Booklist* concluded that "readers will gain not only knowledge about haystacks, but also a sense of the atmosphere of farm life," while *School Library Journal* contributor Lee Bock noted that "the prose is brisk and straightforward and the text is superbly illustrated." *Haystack* went on to win several awards, including Honor Book listings from *Parents Choice* and *Boston Globe-Horn Book*. In another non-pig book, 1997's *The Etcher's Studio*, Geisert's etching technique wins pride of place. "It shows how an etching is made and the studio equipment used in the etching process," Geisert wrote in *SAAS*. "For me there is no more beautiful way of putting line on paper than by etching." With his blend of humor and classical method, Geisert has made believers of the publishing industry as well as the book-buying public.

■ Works Cited

Bock, Lee, review of *Haystack, School Library Journal*, September, 1995, p. 193.

Burns, Mary M., review of *After the Flood, Horn Book*, July-August, 1994, pp. 440-41.

Fleming, Jennifer, review of *Roman Numerals I to MM, School Library Journal*, September, 1996.

Geisert, Arthur, essay in *Something about the Author Autobiography Series*, Volume 23, Gale, 1997, pp. 95-109.

Hanley, Karen Stang, review of *Pa's Balloon and Other Pig Tales, Booklist*, August, 1984, p. 1625.

Review of *Haystack, Publishers Weekly*, August 28, 1995, p. 112.

Jameyson, Karen, review of *Pa's Balloon and Other Pig Tales, Horn Book*, August, 1984, p. 457.

Jameyson, Karen, review of *Pigs from A to Z, Horn Book*, January-February, 1986, p. 43.

McDermott, Leone, review of *Haystack, Booklist*, September 15, 1995, p. 161.

Review of *Oink Oink, Kirkus Reviews*, February 1, 1993, p. 146.

Review of *Oink, Publishers Weekly*, March 29, 1991, p. 92.

Review of *Pa's Balloon and Other Pig Tales, Publishers Weekly,* June 22, 1984, p. 100.

Phelan, Carolyn, review of *Roman Numerals I to MM, Booklist,* May 1, 1996, p. 1509.

Vasilakis, Nancy, review of *Pigs from 1 to 10, Horn Book,* September-October, 1992, p. 575.

Warwick, Ellen D., review of *The Ark, School Library Journal,* October, 1988, p. 120.

Watson, Elizabeth S., review of *The Ark, Horn Book,* January-February, 1989, pp. 52-53.

Wilms, Denise M., review of *Pigs from A to Z, Booklist,* November 15, 1986, p. 509.

■ For More Information See

BOOKS

Silvey, Anita, ed., *Children's Books and Their Creators,* Houghton Mifflin, 1995.

PERIODICALS

Bulletin of the Center for Children's Books, October, 1984, p. 25; February, 1987, p. 106; September, 1988, p. 7; February, 1993, p. 176; February, 1994, p. 185; October, 1995, p. 54.

Kirkus Reviews, May 1, 1984, p. J30; August 15, 1985, p. 1290; July 1, 1988, p. 972; August 1, 1992, p. 989; February 1, 1994, p. 142; July 15, 1995, p. 1023; January 15, 1996, p. 133; February 15, 1997, p. 299.

New York Times Book Review, July 29, 1984, p. 146; November 9, 1986, p. 39; November 27, 1988, p. 36; July 14, 1991, p. 25; January 31, 1993, p. 22; March 27, 1994, p. 21; January 28, 1996, p. 27; November 10, 1996.

—*Sketch by J. Sydney Jones*

*　　*　　*

GEISERT, Bonnie 1942-

■ Personal

Born November 17, 1942, in Hartley, IA; daughter of Anton (a farmer) and Leona (Johnson) Meier; married Arthur Geisert (an author and illustrator), June 1, 1963; children: Noah. *Education:* Concordia College (Seward, NE), B.S., 1963; Concordia University (River Forest, IL), M.A., 1968.

■ Addresses

Home—Galena, IL.

■ Career

Writer and photographer. Has worked as a teacher. *Freeport Journal-Standard,* Freeport, IL, feature writer and columnist, 1991-95. *Exhibitions:* Photographs have appeared in group shows at the Dubuque Museum of Art, Eagle Ridge Inn and Resort, Freeport Art Museum, Galena City Hall, Galena Art Festival, 1995, Group Photography Show-Galena, 1996 and 1997.

■ Writings

Haystack, illustrated by Arthur Geisert, Houghton, 1995.

Has contributed articles to *The Lutheran, Cobblestone, The Galenian, Julien's Journal,* and *The Freeport (Ill.) Journal-Standard.*

■ Work in Progress

Prairie Town, another picture book with husband Arthur Geisert.

■ Sidelights

Bonnie Geisert told *SATA:* "I find that the camera is a powerful tool in exploring the world around me—whether I'm taking photos of Galena architecture, rolling hills, people, animals, or flowers.

"My interest in photography started in 1991 while writing feature stories for the *Freeport Journal-Standard.* I could count on my fingers the times I held a camera before I started stringing for the *Journal-Standard.* Jim Quick was a great help in getting me started with equipment and fundamentals.

"Recently I've been shooting butterflies and other insects with a macro lens, and that has lured me into abstract photography."

■ For More Information See

PERIODICALS

Booklist, September 15, 1995, p. 165.
Bulletin of the Center for Children's Books, October, 1995, p. 54.
Horn Book, November, 1995, p. 756.
Kirkus Reviews, July 15, 1995, p. 1023.
New York Times Book Review, January 28, 1996, p. 27.
Publishers Weekly, August 28, 1995, p. 112.
School Library Journal, September, 1995, p. 193.
Time, December 11, 1995, p. 77.

*　　*　　*

GILLILAND, (Cleburne) Hap 1918-

■ Personal

Born August 26, 1918, in Willard, CO; son of Samuel Smith (a teacher) and Esther J. (an artist; maiden name, Sandstedt) Gilliland; married Erma L. Rodreick (a secretary), April 21, 1946; children: Lori Sargent, Diane Bakun, Dwight. *Education:* Western State College (Colorado), A.A., 1948, B.A., 1949, M.A., 1950; University of Northern Colorado, Ed.D., 1958; attended University of Colorado, Philippine Teachers College, and Eastern Montana College. *Religion:* Protestant.

HAP GILLILAND

■ Addresses

Home—2032 Woody Dr., Billings, MT 59102.

■ Career

Public school teacher in Richland, WA, 1950-53; Humboldt State University, Arcata, CA, supervising teacher, 1953-60; Montana State University—Billings, professor, 1960-80; Lake and Peniasual Schools, Alaska, bilingual and multicultural specialist, 1980-84. Council for Indian Education (a publisher of educational and children's books), president and editor, 1970—. Has directed various educational programs serving Indian reservations and chaired numerous committees dealing with Indian and general education. Has conducted teacher training workshops. Has been a visiting lecturer and speaker at numerous institutions. *Military service:* U.S. Air Force, 1942-46. *Member:* International Reading Association (Montana state president, 1963-75), Montana Writers Coalition, Billings Arts Association (vice-president, 1963-64, 1988-90; president, 1990-92), Billings Friendship Force (vice-president, 1988-90, 1994-95), Kiwanis.

■ Awards, Honors

Merit Award for Research and Creative Endeavor, Committee on Evaluation of Faculty, Eastern Montana College, 1977; Bronze Plaque in recognition of outstanding contributions to child's rights and education, Billings Committee for International Year of the Child, 1978; Outstanding Alumnus Award, Western State

College of Colorado, 1979. Professor Emeritus, Montana State University—Billings.

■ Writings

FOR CHILDREN

No One Like a Brother, Council for Indian Education, 1970.
Broken Ice, Council for Indian Education, 1972.
Coyote's Pow-wow, Council for Indian Education, 1972.
The Flood, Montana Reading Publications, 1972.
Bill Red Coyote Is a Nut, Council for Indian Education, 1981.
(With Betty Greison and Sam Bloom) *Black Hawk and Jim Thorp: Super Heroes,* Council for Indian Education, 1983.
Drums of the Head Hunters (novel), Winston-Derek, 1987.
O'Kohome: The Coyote Dog, illustrated by Tanya Hardgrove, Council for Indian Education, 1989.
Mystery Tracks in the Snow: A Guide to Animal Tracks, Naturegraph, 1990.
(With others) *When We Went to the Mountains,* Council for Indian Education, 1991.

After leaving his beloved Cheyenne reservation, Flint Red Coyote must help his new friends defend themselves when they are blamed for vandalism and accused of cheating.

Flint's Rock (novel), illustrated by Pauline Livers-Lambert, Roberts Rhinehart, 1994.

Also author of *We Live on an Indian Reservation, How the Dogs Saved the Cheyennes, The Dark Side of the Moon,* and *Jumper;* author, with Royce Holland, Virginia Kroll, and Sylvia Mularchyk, of *Search for Identity* (stories).

TEXTBOOKS

Materials for Remedial Reading, Montana Reading Publications, 1965, revised, 1966, 1967, 1972, 1976.
Establishment and Operation of a Remedial Reading Program, Alpine, 1967.
Analysis Skills, Alpine, 1968.
A Practical Guide to Remedial Reading, C. E. Merrill, 1974.
Corrective and Remedial Reading, Alpine, 1973.

OTHER

Chant of the Red Man, Council for Indian Education, 1976.
(With others) *Teaching the Native American,* Kendall/Hunt (Dubuque, IA), 1988.
(With Bill Walters) *Challenging Education: A Positive Approach to Teaching Maori Students in New Zealand Schools,* Kupenga O Te Matouranga (New Zealand), 1994.
Voices of Native America, Kendall/Hunt, 1997.

Also author of *The Road to Happiness* (poetry), Council Publications. Author of three standardized tests. Contributor to *Reading Teacher, Reading Horizons,* and *Journal of the Reading Association of Ireland.* Editor of *Montana Journal of Reading,* 1962-68; member of editorial board of *Journal of Reading,* 1972-74, *ERIC Research Materials,* beginning 1973, *Reading Teacher,* beginning 1974, and *Reading Horizons,* beginning 1974.

Editor of "Indian Culture Series" for Montana Reading Publications, beginning 1970.

■ Work in Progress

Enhancing Your Wilderness Experience; Cooperative Learning for Hispanic and Native American Students.

■ Sidelights

Hap Gilliland told *SATA:* "My two main interests for the last thirty years have been writing children's books and studying world cultures. Believing that the way to learn about and understand a culture is to live in it, I have lived in the homes of indigenous peoples on all five continents and the Pacific islands.

"I grew up on a horse ranch in Southeast Colorado. I still love to do ranch work and ride horseback. I also hike and climb, and spend one to two weeks each summer backpacking in the Montana wilderness areas."

GINSBURG, Mirra

■ Personal

Born in Bobruisk (formerly Russia; now Belarus); daughter of Joseph and Bronia (Geier) Ginsburg. *Education:* Attended schools in Russia, Latvia, Canada, and the United States. *Hobbies and other interests:* Poetry, cats (big and little), birds, ballet, baroque, folk, and early music, early and primitive art.

■ Addresses

Home and office—150 West 96th St., Apt. 9-G, New York, NY 10025.

■ Career

Freelance writer, editor, and translator from Russian and Yiddish. Served on translation juries. *Member:* American Literary Translators Association, Authors Guild, Authors League of America, PEN.

■ Awards, Honors

National Translation Center grant, 1967; Lewis Carroll Shelf Award, 1972, for *The Diary of Nina Kosterina;* Mildred L. Batchelder nomination, 1973, for *The Kaha Bird: Folk Tales from the Steppes of Central Asia,* and 1974, for *The White Ship;* Children's Book Showcase Title, 1973, for *The Chick and the Duckling;* Guggenheim fellow, 1975-76.

MIRRA GINSBURG

■ Writings

PICTURE BOOKS; AUTHOR, ADAPTOR, TRANSLATOR

The Fox and the Hare (Russian folktale), Crown, 1969.

Vladimir Grigor'evich Suteyev, *The Chick and the Duckling,* illustrated by Jose Aruego and Ariane Dewey, Macmillan, 1972.

What Kind of Bird Is That?, illustrated by Guilio Maestro, Crown, 1973.

Vladimir Grigor'evich Suteyev, *The Three Kittens,* illustrated by Guilio Maestro, Crown, 1973.

Mushroom in the Rain: Adapted from the Russian of V. Suteyev, illustrated by Jose Aruego and Ariane Dewey, Macmillan, 1974.

The Proud Maiden, Tungak, and the Sun (Russian Eskimo tale), illustrated by Igor Galanin, Macmillan, 1974.

How the Sun Was Brought Back to the Sky (adapted from a Slovenian folktale), illustrated by Jose Aruego and Ariane Dewey, Macmillan, 1975.

The Two Greedy Bears: Adapted from a Hungarian Folk Tale, illustrated by Jose Aruego and Ariane Dewey, Macmillan, 1976.

Pampalche of the Silver Teeth (based on a Mari tale), illustrated by Rocco Negri, Crown, 1976.

Pyotr Dudochkin, *Which Is the Best Place?,* illustrated by Roger Duvoisin, Macmillan, 1976.

The Strongest One of All (based on a Kumyk tale), illustrated by Jose Aruego and Ariane Dewey, Greenwillow, 1977.

Kirill Bulychev, *Alice: Some Incidents in the Life of a Little Girl of the Twenty-first Century, Recorded by Her Father on the Eve of Her First Day in School* (science fiction), illustrated by Igor Galanin, Macmillan, 1977.

Little Rystu (an Altai tale), illustrated by Tony Chen, Greenwillow, 1978.

Striding Slippers (based on an Udmurt folktale), illustrated by Sal Murdocca, Macmillan, 1978.

The Fisherman's Son (adapted from a Georgian tale), illustrated by Tony Chen, Greenwillow, 1979.

The Night It Rained Pancakes (based on a Russian folktale), illustrated by Douglas Florian, Greenwillow, 1979.

Ookie-Spooky (based on a verse of Korney Chukovsky), illustrated by Emily McCully, Crown, 1979.

Good Morning, Chick (based on a verse of Korney Chukovsky), illustrated by Byron Barton, Greenwillow, 1980.

Kitten from One to Ten, illustrated by Guilio Maestro, Crown, 1980.

Where Does the Sun Go at Night? (based on an Armenian song), illustrated by Jose Aruego and Ariane Dewey, Greenwillow, 1980.

The Sun's Asleep behind the Hill (based on an Armenian poem), illustrated by Paul O. Zelinsky, Greenwillow, 1982.

Across the Stream (based on a verse of Daniil Kharms), illustrated by Nancy Tafuri, Greenwillow, 1982.

The Little Magic Stove (Russian tale), illustrated by Linda Heller, Putnam, 1983.

Four Brave Sailors (based on a verse of Daniil Kharms), illustrated by Nancy Tafuri, Greenwillow, 1987.

The Chinese Mirror (adapted from a Korean fairy tale), illustrated by Margot Zemach, Harcourt, 1988.

Asleep, Asleep (based on a verse by A. Vvedensky), illustrated by Nancy Tafuri, Greenwillow, 1992.

Merry-Go-Round, Four Stories, illustrated by Jose Aruego and Ariane Dewey, Greenwillow, 1992.

The King Who Tried to Fry an Egg on His Head (based on a Russian tale), illustrated by Will Hillenbrand, Macmillan, 1994.

The Old Man and His Birds (based on a riddle by Vladimir Dal), illustrated by Donna Huff, Greenwillow, 1994.

Clay Boy and the Little White Goat with the Golden Horns (adapted from a Russian folktale), illustrated by Joseph Smith, Greenwillow, 1997.

FOLKTALE COLLECTIONS; EDITOR, ADAPTOR, TRANSLATOR

Three Rolls and One Doughnut: Fables from Russia, illustrated by Anita Lobel, Dial, 1970.

The Master of the Winds and Other Tales from Siberia, illustrated by Enrico Arno, Crown, 1970.

The Kaha Bird: Folk Tales from the Steppes of Central Asia, illustrated by Richard Cuffari, Crown, 1971.

One Trick Too Many: Fox Stories from Russia, illustrated by Helen Siegl, Dial, 1973.

The Lazies: Tales of the Peoples of Russia, illustrated by Marian Parry, Macmillan, 1973.

How Wilka Went to Sea: Folk Tales from West of the Urals, illustrated by Charles Mikolaycak, Crown, 1975.

The Twelve Clever Brothers and Other Fools: Folk Tales from Russia, illustrated by C. Mikolaycak, Lippincott, 1979.

FOR ADULTS; TRANSLATOR

Roman Goul, *Azef,* Doubleday, 1962.

Vera Alexandrova, *A History of Soviet Literature,* Doubleday, 1963.

Mikhail Bulgakov, *Heart of a Dog,* Grove, 1968.

Fyodor Dostoyevsky, *Notes from Underground,* introduction by Donald Fanger, Bantam, 1974.

Lydia Obukhova, *Daughter of Night: A Tale of Three Worlds* (science fiction), Macmillan, 1974.

EDITOR AND TRANSLATOR

(And author of introduction) *The Fatal Eggs and Other Soviet Satire,* Macmillan, 1965, Grove Press, 1968.

(And author of introduction) *The Dragon: Fifteen Stories by Yevgeny Zamyatin,* Random House, 1966, second edition, University of Chicago Press, 1976.

(And author of introduction) *The Last Door to Aiya: Anthology of Soviet Science Fiction,* S. G. Phillips, 1968.

A Soviet Heretic: Essays by Yevgeny Zamyatin, introduction by Alex Shane, University of Chicago Press, 1970.

(And author of introduction) *The Ultimate Threshold: Anthology of Soviet Science Fiction,* Holt, 1970.

The Air of Mars and Other Stories of Time and Space (Soviet science fiction anthology), Macmillan, 1976.

TRANSLATOR AND AUTHOR OF INTRODUCTION

Mikhail Bulgakov, *The Master and Margarita,* Grove, 1967.

The Diary of Nina Kosterina, Crown, 1968.

Mikhail Bulgakov, *Flight* (play), Grove, 1969.

Mikhail Bulgakov, *The Life of Monsieur de Molière,* Funk and Wagnalls, 1970.

Chingiz Aitmatov, *The White Ship,* Crown, 1972.

Yevgeny Zamyatin, *We,* Viking, 1972.

Andrey Platonov, *The Foundation Pit,* Dutton, 1975.

Mikhail Bulgakov, *Flight and Bliss* (two plays), New Directions, 1985.

Yuri Tynyanov, *Lieutenant Kije/Young Vitushishnikov,* Eridanos/Marsilio, 1991.

Also translator of stories by Isaac Bashevis Singer, Alexey Remizov, Isaac Babel, and Zoshchenko and for various anthologies and collections by periodicals; co-translator of Isaac Babel's play, "Sunset," produced in 1966 and 1972.

Many of Ginsburg's books have also been published in England, and translated into various languages, including Afrikaans, Chinese, Danish, French, German, Japanese, Portuguese, Swedish, and Zulu.

■ Sidelights

Although Mirra Ginsburg is a well-respected translator and editor of adult novels, stories, anthologies, and

A villager becomes shocked and confused upon seeing his face in a mirror for the first time in this Korean folktale retold by Ginsburg. (From *The Chinese Mirror,* illustrated by Margot Zemach.)

plays, she is also recognized for her charming adaptations and succinct translations of folktales for children. Among her works are several collections of Russian and non-Russian folktales from the former Soviet Union, such as *The Twelve Clever Brothers and Other Fools: Folk Tales from Russia* and *The Master of the Winds and Other Tales from Siberia.* A large number of her individual titles are also adapted from or inspired by Russian and non-Russian tales, poems, and songs. An avid lover of folktales, Ginsburg once commented that "folk literature, to me, is among the purest and most profound creations humans have been capable of."

A Russian immigrant, Ginsburg once described growing up in a small Russian town. "I was born and spent my early childhood in Bobruisk, a small town in Byelorussia (now Belarus), which seems centuries away from my present home in New York. It was a town of small one-story wooden houses, with only three brick buildings two stories high. It was surrounded by woods and fields, and we lived simply. We had no running water and no plumbing. Most streets were not paved. When it rained, barrels were put out to collect the water, for washing and cleaning. Drinking water was brought from a neighbor's well. After the rains there were huge puddles in the street, where pigs, big and little, came to wallow and luxuriate. Neighboring women often rinsed their wash in rivulets that ran along board sidewalks." Ginsburg's family eventually left Russia and lived in Latvia and Canada before settling in the United States.

A wearer of many hats in the publishing world, Ginsburg started her career as a translator of Russian literature. "I have been fortunate in my work," Ginsburg once commented. "I have translated into English a number of books by some of the greatest Russian writers of the twentieth century." Some of the early works for adult readers which she translated were *Azef* by Roman Goul, *A History of Soviet Literature* by Vera Alexandrova, *We,* by Yevgeny Zamyatin, and *The Diary of Nina Kosterina.* For this latter title she also wrote the introduction. And in addition to translating acclaimed writer Fyodor Dostoyevsky's *Notes from Underground,* Ginsburg also translated a number of Mikhail Bulgakov's works, including *Heart of a Dog, The Life of Monsieur de Molière,* his two plays *Flight and Bliss,* and the celebrated novel *The Master and Margarita.*

In 1965 Ginsburg became an editor and translator of anthologies, particularly in the Russian science fiction genre. Her early works in this genre include *The Last Door to Aiya: Anthology of Soviet Science Fiction.* Another of her works, *The Air of Mars and Other Stories of Time and Space,* which contains nine short stories about time and space travel by various authors from the Soviet Union, was well received by critics. Paul Heins complimented Ginsburg on her translating skills in his review for *Horn Book,* stating, "The translator has skillfully turned the original writing into excellently clear and flowing English."

One of Ginsburg's later science fiction translations is *Alice: Some Incidents in the Life of a Little Girl of the*

And the fish in the deep?
Asleep, asleep.

Inspired by a verse of A. Vvedensky, *Asleep, Asleep* contains Ginsburg's poem about a mother gently persuading her young child to go to sleep. (Illustrated by Nancy Tafuri.)

Twenty-first Century, Recorded by Her Father on the Eve of Her First Day in School by Kirill Bulychev. This work, written for children, features four-year-old Alice and her father, a zoo director, who records his daughter's unusual adventures. Making friends with a baby brontosaurus and getting lost on Mars are among the highlights of Alice's day.

Alice, however, was not Ginsburg's first work for children. She had previously adapted the Russian folktale *The Fox and the Hare,* which was published in 1969. Ginsburg, who is no stranger to folktales, once told *SATA:* "I have loved folktales since childhood, and have gone on collecting them and delighting in them ever since. I place folktales among the greatest works of literature. To me they are a distillation of man's deepest experience into poetry, wisdom, truth, sadness, and laughter. The folktale preserves values that have been largely crushed in the 'modern,' material world. It means truth as opposed to bare fact, wisdom as opposed to mere knowledge, imagination as opposed to sterile, utilitarian (and often destructive) reason. It holds, in all its aspects, the truth about us. And it is play and magic at their purest and most delightful."

Drawing again on her wide knowledge of Russian folktales, as well as those of the non-Russian peoples inhabiting the vast expanses of the former Soviet Union, Ginsburg began editing, adapting, and translating other folktales and placed them in a series of collections. She grouped some by location, for example, *Three Rolls and*

One Doughnut: Fables from Russia and *The Master of the Winds and Other Tales from Siberia,* and some by theme, such as *One Trick Too Many: Fox Stories from Russia* and *The Lazies: Tales of the Peoples of Russia.* Ginsburg once explained that she considered these collections "a labor of love and joy."

Published in 1970, Ginsburg's first book in this series of folktale collections was *Three Rolls and One Doughnut.* Among the twenty-eight humorous short Russian folktales, fables, and riddles is the title story in which a hungry peasant buys three rolls and eats them. Still hungry, he buys a doughnut and eats it. Finally full, he's annoyed at himself for wasting his money on the rolls rather than buying the doughnut first. As with many of Ginsburg's selections, the "wise" person is really the fool and the "fool" is really the wise person. And in some cases, as in the above story, it is the reader who turns out to be the wisest.

"A distinctive volume in every detail of bookmaking," is how Virginia Haviland, writing for *Horn Book,* described *The Master of the Winds and Other Tales from Siberia.* This second collection of tales contains fourteen stories from fourteen Siberian cultures, including Eskimo. Another collection in the series, *The Twelve Clever Brothers and Other Fools: Folk Tales from Russia,* also contains fourteen stories and spotlights, again, some who at first appear wise but really are fools or vice versa. "A very pleasant collection, adapted in sprightly style," noted Zena Sutherland in her review for *Bulletin of the Center for Children's Books.*

One Trick Too Many contains nine folktales featuring the fox trying to outsmart people and animals, sometimes successfully, sometimes not. A *Kirkus Reviews* critic noted that sometimes reading stories with the same theme can become dull. In this case, however, the reviewer noted that Ginsburg "tells them all with dispatch." *The Lazies,* a collection of fifteen tales revolving around the theme of lazy people or animals, includes among its array of idle characters princesses, peasants, beasts, and jesters. "Told in a pithy manner, the lively collection should delight both storytellers and listeners," according to Mary M. Burns in a review for *Horn Book.*

Over a span of more than twenty-five years, Ginsburg has edited, translated, adapted, and sometimes authored a score of other tales, including *The Night It Rained Pancakes, Good Morning, Chick,* and *How the Sun Was Brought Back to the Sky,* which have been published as individual picture books for children. Ginsburg once described her approach to retelling or adapting folktales for children. "Although I usually begin with a Russian original, it is necessary to work freely—change, delete, and invent, *letting the story sing out* as something fresh and new and strange, so that it speaks directly to the child—here and now. I never try to teach or draw a moral. I love poetry and wit and play, and I hope that what delights me will in turn delight the reader and the

listener. And if there is a lesson in the story, let it speak for itself. And if there isn't, let the story play and sing as it will."

Two of Ginsburg's early picture books, *The Chick and the Duckling* and *Mushroom in the Rain,* were translated from the Russian of Vladimir Suteyev. Children ages three through seven have enjoyed these tales for many years. *The Chick and the Duckling* is about two different types of birds hatched at the same time. The two are inseparable, and the chick does exactly what the duckling does. When the duckling decides to go swimming, the chick follows, only to find it can't swim. Fortunately the duckling swims for both of them and saves the young chick. In the simple, yet crowded tale *Mushroom in the Rain,* an ant is caught in the rain and seeks shelter under a mushroom. A butterfly, a mouse, a sparrow, and a rabbit also seek shelter under the same mushroom and succeed. When a fox comes along looking for the rabbit, the group convinces the fox that it won't fit, saving the rabbit's hide. Later, a wise frog explains to the perplexed ant how the group fit under that tiny mushroom.

Like the folktales published in her collections, a number of Ginsburg's titles are of non-Russian origin. Examples include the simple, well-known tale *How the Sun Was Brought Back to the Sky,* adapted from a Slovenian folktale, and the fable *The Two Greedy Bears: Adapted from a Hungarian Folk Tale.* The first tale, which has been translated into a number of other languages, describes how five chicks set off to find the sun after it

"Come here, wife," he said when he got home. "Look at these lovely presents. We won't be poor from now on. And look at what I've learned from our clever son-in-law."

He told her to buy some eggs. "Now watch me," he said. "I will make you the tastiest omelette you have ever eaten."

He sat down, and he broke an egg, and poured it on his head. It trickled down his face and neck, and got into his collar. But "Wait," he said to his wife. "Just wait and see."

"I married a fool," she said. And she went to the stove and made herself the tastiest omelette she had ever eaten.

Trying to imitate his son-in-law, the Sun, a foolish king tries to fry an egg on his head for his wife's breakfast. (From *The King Who Tried to Fry an Egg on His Head,* retold by Ginsburg and illustrated by Will Hillenbrand.)

hasn't shown itself for three days. Zena Sutherland, commenting in the *Bulletin of the Center for Children's Books,* noted that the story was "silly, merry, and sunny." Similarly, critics appreciated Ginsburg's adaptation of *The Two Greedy Bears*—the story of two bears who fight over two equally split pieces of cheese and wind up losing both pieces to a sly fox. Virginia Haviland, writing for *Horn Book,* complimented Ginsburg on her "smooth text containing the fewest possible words."

Little Rystu, an Altai folktale adapted by Ginsburg, is a tale from Central Asia containing "rhythms and poetic language," as noted by a reviewer for *Junior Bookshelf.* Rystu (which means happy) is an orphan who loves to play his reed pipe. Tricked into slavery by Khan—a mean-spirited, selfish man—Rystu is magically rescued by ants and returns to his blue mountain paradise, where he lives in harmony with the birds and animals. In the retelling of the Korean tale *The Chinese Mirror,* Ginsburg describes the individual reactions people have after seeing themselves for the first time in a strange looking piece of glass, which the reader immediately knows is a mirror. Zena Sutherland, who wrote that the book was "nicely done" in a review for the *Bulletin of the Center for Children's Books,* also noted how the "message to the reader is one children appreciate: you are smart enough to understand although the characters in the story are not."

The Night It Rained Pancakes, The Little Magic Stove, and *The King Who Tried to Fry an Egg on His Head* are a few of Ginsburg's adaptations of Russian tales. The titles alone are silly enough to intrigue any child. *The Night It Rained Pancakes* features a peasant, Ivan, who finds a pot of gold while plowing his landlord's field. To keep his simple-minded brother Stepan from telling the landlord, Ivan shows Stepan a bunch of strange occurrences—including pancakes falling from the sky—and then tells him about the gold. When Stepan tells the landlord about the strange happenings and then about the gold, the landlord, of course, doesn't believe him. A reviewer for *School Library Journal* applauded Ginsburg for her "witty adaptation of a Russian folktale." A *Publishers Weekly* critic also enjoyed the "humor and wisdom" of this tale. *The Magic Stove* is the story of a rooster that helps its poor, old owners get back their stove—which bakes any kind of pie when asked—from a selfish king. In *The King Who Tried to Fry an Egg on His Head,* a king tries to imitate the sun by frying an egg on his head. Both books were praised by reviewers for their humor and noodlehead characters.

Not all of Ginsburg's works for children are based on folktales. *Ookie-Spooky* and *Good Morning, Chick,* two books for pre-schoolers, are based on separate verses by Korney Chukovsky. *Where Does the Sun Go at Night?,* a story filled with humorous answers written in a child-like voice, is based on an Armenian song. A story that celebrates the change of season, *The Old Man and His Birds,* was based on a riddle by Vladimir Dal, a nineteenth-century Russian who, like Ginsburg, loved to collect folklore. And finally, a few titles, such as *Kitten*

from One to Ten, are Ginsburg's original creations. In this book, Ginsburg introduces toddlers to the concept of counting. A reviewer commenting in *Publishers Weekly* stated that the author's verses are "as frisky as her little hero."

Reflecting on her years as a translator, editor, adaptor, and author, Ginsburg once explained to *SATA:* "What I try to do in my work . . . is to offer a counterbalance to the merely 'useful,' to extend horizons, to restore dimensions suppressed or eliminated by 'progress.'"

■ Works Cited

Burns, Mary M., review of *The Lazies: Tales of the Peoples of Russia, Horn Book,* April, 1974, p. 145.

Haviland, Virginia, review of *The Master of the Winds and Other Tales from Siberia, Horn Book,* April, 1971, p. 165.

Haviland, Virginia, review of *The Two Greedy Bears, Horn Book,* February, 1977, pp. 37-38.

Heins, Paul, review of *The Air of Mars and Other Stories of Time and Space, Horn Book,* August, 1976, pp. 410-11.

Review of *Kitten from One to Ten, Publishers Weekly,* June 13, 1980.

Review of *Little Rystu, Junior Bookshelf,* December, 1978, p. 293.

Review of *The Night It Rained Pancakes, Publishers Weekly,* April 11, 1980, p. 77.

Review of *The Night It Rained Pancakes, School Library Journal,* May, 1980, p. 81.

Review of *One Trick Too Many: Fox Stories from Russia, Kirkus Reviews,* April 15, 1973, p. 454.

Sutherland, Zena, review of *How the Sun Was Brought Back to the Sky, Bulletin of the Center for Children's Books,* November, 1975, p. 44.

Sutherland, Zena, review of *The Twelve Clever Brothers and Other Fools, Bulletin of the Center for Children's Books,* April, 1980, p. 152.

Sutherland, Zena, review of *The Chinese Mirror, Bulletin of the Center for Children's Books,* May, 1988, p. 176.

■ For More Information See

PERIODICALS

Booklist, February 15, 1971, p. 492; June 15, 1983, p. 1338; February 15, 1994, p. 1084.

Bulletin of the Center for Children's Books, October, 1971, p. 25; January, 1974, p. 78; February, 1994, p. 187.

Horn Book, April, 1971, p. 165; December, 1971, p. 607; April, 1974, p. 145; June, 1978, p. 269; May-June, 1988, p. 365; November-December, 1994, p. 718.

Kirkus Reviews, January 1, 1974, p. 3; May 15, 1975, p. 562; September 15, 1976, p. 1034; May 1, 1983, pp. 519-20; March 1, 1988, p. 362; October 15, 1994, pp. 1407-08.

New York Times Book Review, June 6, 1976; September 13, 1992.

Publishers Weekly, October 9, 1972, p. 112; February 4, 1974, p. 72.
School Library Journal, March, 1978, p. 118; March, 1980, p. 131; April, 1988, p. 95.

—*Sketch by Kathleen L. Witman*

* * *

GOLDIN, Barbara Diamond 1946-

■ Personal

Born October 4, 1946, in New York, NY; daughter of Morton (an accountant) and Anna (a medical secretary) Diamond; married Alan Goldin (a soil scientist), March 31, 1968 (divorced 1990); children: Josee Sarah, Jeremy Casey. *Education:* University of Chicago, B.A., 1968; Boston University, teaching certificate in primary and special education, 1970; attended Western Washington University, 1980. *Religion:* Jewish.

■ Addresses

Office—P.O. Box 981, Northampton, MA 01061. *Agent*—Virginia Knowlton, Curtis Brown Ltd., 10 Astor Pl., New York, NY 10003.

■ Career

Special education teacher at public schools in Gloucester and Ipswich, MA, 1970-72; preschool teacher in Missoula, MT, and Yellow Springs, OH, 1972-75; Children's Bookshop, Missoula, co-owner and operator, 1975-76; Goldendale Public Library, Goldendale, WA, library assistant in children's section, 1976-78; preschool teacher in Bellingham, WA, 1980-82; Congregation B'nai Israel Preschool, Northampton, MA, head teacher, 1986-89; Heritage Academy, Longmeadow, MA, middle school English teacher, 1990—; freelance writer. *Member:* Society of Children's Book Writers and Illustrators.

■ Awards, Honors

National Jewish Book Award, 1989, for *Just Enough Is Plenty: A Hanukkah Tale;* Association of Jewish Libraries Award, 1992, for *Cakes and Miracles: A Purim Tale;* American Library Association Notable Book, 1995, for *The Passover Journey: A Seder Companion.*

■ Writings

JUVENILE

Just Enough Is Plenty: A Hanukkah Tale, illustrated by Seymour Chwast, Viking, 1988.
The World's Birthday: A Story About Rosh Hashanah, illustrated by Jeanette Winter, Harcourt, 1990.
The Family Book of Midrash: Fifty-two Stories from the Sages, J. Aronson, 1990.
Cakes and Miracles: A Purim Tale, illustrated by Erika Weihs, Viking, 1991.

BARBARA DIAMOND GOLDIN

Fire!: The Beginnings of the Labor Movement, illustrated by James Watling, Viking, 1992.
The Magician's Visit: A Passover Tale, illustrated by Robert Andrew Parker, Viking, 1993.
The Passover Journey: A Seder Companion, illustrated by Neil Waldman, Viking, 1994.
Red Means Good Fortune: A Story of San Francisco's Chinatown, illustrated by Wenhai Ma, Viking, 1994.
Night Lights: A Sukkot Story, illustrated by Louise August, Harcourt, 1995.
Bat Mitzvah: A Jewish Girl's Coming of Age, illustrated by Erika Weihs, Viking, 1995.
Creating Angels: Stories of Tzedakah, J. Aronson, 1996.
Coyote and the Fire Stick: A Pacific Northwest Indian Tale, illustrated by Will Hillenbrand, Harcourt, 1996.
While the Candles Burn: Eight Stories for Hanukkah, illustrated by Elaine Greenstein, Viking, 1996.
The Girl Who Lived with the Bears, illustrated by Andrew Plewes, Gulliver Books, 1997.

Author of retelling of Tchaikovsky's ballet *The Sleeping Beauty* for boxed editions of compact discs, BMG Music, 1993. Contributor of story to *The Haunted House,* edited by Jane Yolen and Martin H. Greenberg, HarperCollins, 1995; also contributor of articles and reviews to children's magazines and newspapers, including *Highlights*, *Cricket*, *Shofar*, *Seattle's Child*, *Child Life*, and *Jack and Jill*.

■ **Work in Progress**

Meeting Elijah: Tales of the Prophet, illustrated by Jerry Pinkney, Harcourt, expected 1998; *Kids Talk about Religion*, for Viking; *What Is Hidden Is Revealed: Tales of Revelation*, for Aronson.

■ **Sidelights**

Barbara Diamond Goldin is an author of children's picture books, novels for older children, story collections, and nonfiction. Her popular picture books deal mainly with holidays and the retelling of folktales, and they often emphasize her Jewish heritage. Her first picture book, *Just Enough Is Plenty: A Hanukkah Tale*, set the tone for much of her subsequent work: well researched stories often set in the "old country" of Eastern Europe, in the shtetls where three of Goldin's grandparents came from. Growing up in New York and Pennsylvania, Goldin was partially cut off from these beloved grandparents because of a language barrier. Yiddish was still their first language, and thus young Goldin was not able to share in their rich heritage. It was only with the research for her first children's book that she began to understand their histories.

This first book was a long time coming, however. Teaching, motherhood, and stints as a bookshop owner and librarian all came first. Then, in 1981, Goldin took a writing workshop with Jane Yolen and spent the next years placing articles and stories in magazines, but also in gathering rejection slips from book publishers. Increasingly, she became fascinated with the Eastern European origins of her relations and researched memoirs as well as the writings of Shalom Aleichem and Isaac Bashevis Singer. Black and white photographs of pre-Holocaust Eastern Europe also aided in this reconstruction, and such researches ultimately coalesced into the story of a poor shtetl family who take in a peddler at Hanukkah to share their holiday meal. The peddler repays their kindness by leaving behind a bag of gifts, just as the prophet Elijah does in the traditional stories. The book, *Just Enough Is Plenty*, is a "satisfying tale of traditional values," according to Hanna B. Zeiger in *Horn Book*, and a *Publishers Weekly* reviewer noted that "Goldin's tale and Chwast's vibrant, primitive paintings are masterfully combined." *Junior Bookshelf* critic Marcus Crouch offered a favorable estimation of "this admirable picture-book," commenting that "the simple story is told briefly but with due regard to the importance of its message." *Just Enough Is Plenty* went on to win the National Jewish Book Award.

Goldin continued with holiday themes in her later picture books. *The World's Birthday: A Story about Rosh Hashanah* explores the Jewish New Year, through the story of young Daniel who decides to throw a birthday party for the world and buys a birthday cake for the occasion. Zeiger, writing in *Horn Book*, noted that the

blend of text and illustrations created a "tale that captures the spirit of the holiday." *Cakes and Miracles: A Purim Tale* returns to an Eastern European shtetl to tell a story of Purim, a celebration of spring. The young blind boy Hershel finds a place for himself in the life of his village when he helps his mother bake cakes for the holiday, shaping the dough with a special sensitivity he has as a result of his lack of sight. A *Booklist* reviewer stated that *Cakes and Miracles* is "a heartwarming story that is really about using one's special gifts," and Zeiger, in *Horn Book*, concluded that it is a "loving story." Betsy Hearne of the *Bulletin of the Center for Children's Books* called the work a "blessedly unsentimental picture of a blind boy" and also noted that an afterword to the book summarized the origins and customs of Purim.

The important Jewish holiday of Passover is depicted in two books by Goldin. *The Magician's Visit: A Passover Tale* is a picture book in which the prophet Elijah himself comes to provide a feast for a poor couple, while *The Passover Journey: A Seder Companion*, a nonfiction work, looks at the history and customs of this holiday and the ceremonial evening meal, or Seder. Goldin explained that she worked on *The Passover Journey* on and off for four years in an attempt to organize her material and get it exactly right. Betsy Hearne of the *Bulletin of the Center for Children's Books* offered a favorable estimation of Goldin's efforts, stating: "More

Malka and her family watch closely as candle number one is lit for the first night of Hanukkah in Goldin's *Just Enough Is Plenty*, **illustrated by Seymour Chwast.**

Wise, crafty Coyote is able to bring fire to the People in Goldin's engaging porquoi tale *Coyote and the Firestick.*
(Illustrated by Will Hillenbrand.)

thorough than many children's books on *Pesach,* this takes great care to explore Jewish tradition and to encourage individual response to it." In a starred review, *Booklist*'s Stephanie Zvirin commended the intricate blending of text and illustration in the work, calling *The Passover Journey* "a beautiful wedding of the work of two talented individuals.... A book for family sharing as well as a rich source of information." Goldin has also compiled a collection of tales and retellings to be read aloud, one each night, for the Hanukkah season. *While the Candles Burn: Eight Stories for Hanukkah* is, according to Janice M. Del Negro of the *Bulletin of the Center for Children's Books,* "a solid addition to collections looking for something a little more unusual than typical holiday fare."

A departure from such picture books with strictly Jewish themes are two short novels for older readers focusing on historical issues such as the labor movement and immigration. *Fire!: The Beginnings of the Labor Movement* is a view of the 1911 Triangle Shirtwaist factory fire through the eyes of eleven-year-old Rosie who wants to quit school and go to work in the garment factory like her older sister. When a fire destroys the building and kills 146 workers, Rosie, the daughter of Russian immigrants, wakes up to her need for an education and for the labor movement to win strength. "Rosie and her friends will appeal to readers looking for a good story as well as to those needing information on the era," commented *School Library Journal* contributor Joyce Adams Burner. Goldin explores the lives of Chinese Americans in *Red Means Good Fortune: A Story of San Francisco's Chinatown,* set in 1869. Jin Mun, a twelve-year-old boy, helps out in his father's laundry, but when he discovers a young Chinese girl sold into slavery, he sets a new mission for himself: to free the girl. Carla Kozak, writing in *School Library Journal,* noted that the book was "well-researched and clearly written," while Carolyn Phelan of *Booklist* commented that the "characters and story are involving." Phelan, however, also felt that the book was "too short and the ending will leave the readers wondering what happened next."

Goldin has continued her eclectic mix of story material with a retelling of a Native American tale in *Coyote and the Fire Stick: A Pacific Northwest Indian Tale,* as well as further explication of Jewish tradition and customs in *Bat Mitzvah: A Jewish Girl's Coming of Age.* The former, a retelling of a pourquoi tale explaining the origin of fire, is raised "above the common" variety of such retellings, according to Patricia Lothrop Green in *School Library Journal,* by Goldin's characterization of Coyote and the illustrations of Will Hillenbrand. *Horn Book* reviewer Ann A. Flowers concurs, describing *Coyote and the Fire Stick* as "a well-told story with inventive oil and oil pastel illustrations." With the nonfiction *Bat Mitzvah,* Goldin explains the relatively recent ceremony of the celebration of a girl's coming of age at twelve or thirteen. Ellen Mandel of *Booklist* called the work "relevant, informative, and highly readable," and *School Library Journal* contributor Marsha W. Posner concluded that *Bat Mitzvah* would be "an insightful addition to all collections."

Goldin, whose favorite place to work is at a local college library, enjoys the process of research and writing. "I still love to write and research and discover new worlds on paper," she once said. "Writing is still an exciting process for me. I'm never certain when I sit down to write what the next few hours bring."

■ **Works Cited**

Burner, Joyce Adams, review of *Fire!: The Beginnings of the Labor Movement, School Library Journal,* July, 1992, p. 73.

Review of *Cakes and Miracles: A Purim Tale, Booklist,* January 15, 1991, p. 1062.

Crouch, Marcus, review of *Just Enough is Plenty, The Junior Bookshelf,* April, 1989, p. 60.

Del Negro, Janice M., review of *While the Candles Burn: Eight Stories for Hanukkah, Bulletin of the Center for Children's Books,* November, 1996, pp. 96-97.

Flowers, Ann A., review of *Coyote and the Fire Stick: A Pacific Northwest Indian Tale, Horn Book Magazine,* November-December, 1996, p. 748.

Goldin, Barbara Diamond, comments in pamphlet from Viking Children's Books, c. 1994.

Green, Patricia Lothrop, review of *Coyote and the Fire Stick: Pacific Northwest Indian Tale, School Library Journal,* October, 1996, p. 114.

Hearne, Betsy, review of *Cakes and Miracles: A Purim Tale, Bulletin of the Center for Children's Books,* February, 1991, p. 141.

Hearne, Betsy, review of *The Passover Journey: A Seder Companion, Bulletin of the Center for Children's Books,* April, 1994, pp. 257-58.

Review of *Just Enough Is Plenty: A Hanukkah Tale, Publishers Weekly,* September 30, 1988, p. 66.

Kozak, Carla, review of *Red Means Good Fortune: A Story of San Francisco's Chinatown, School Library Journal,* May, 1994, p. 114.

Mandel, Ellen, review of *Bat Mitzvah: A Jewish Girl's Coming of Age, Booklist,* September 1, 1995, p. 56.

Phelan, Carolyn, review of *Red Means Good Fortune: A Story of San Francisco's Chinatown, Booklist,* December, 15, 1993, p. 754.

Posner, Marcia W., review of *Bat Mitzvah: A Jewish Girl's Coming of Age, School Library Journal,* November, 1995.

Zeiger, Hanna B., review of *Just Enough Is Plenty: A Hanukkah Tale, Horn Book,* November-December, 1988, p. 763.

Zeiger, Hanna B., review of *The World's Birthday: A Rosh Hashanah Story, Horn Book,* November-December, 1990, pp. 718-19.

Zeiger, Hanna B., review of *Cakes and Miracles: A Purim Tale, Horn Book,* July-August, 1991, p. 447.

Zvirin, Stephanie, review of *The Passover Journey: A Seder Companion, Booklist,* March 1, 1994, p. 1260.

■ **For More Information See**

PERIODICALS

Bulletin of the Center for Children's Books, April, 1992, p. 206; March, 1993, p. 233.

Kirkus Reviews, September 15, 1988, p. 1403; July 15, 1990, p. 1011; December 1, 1990, p. 1671; May 15, 1992, p. 677; January 1, 1993, p. 67; January 1, 1994, p. 67.

Publishers Weekly, August 31, 1990, p. 64; December 7, 1990, p. 90; January 4, 1993, p. 72; January 24, 1994, p. 57; February 14, 1994, p. 65; November 13, 1995, p. 65.

Sunday Republican (Springfield), September 1, 1996, p. D5.

—*Sketch by J. Sydney Jones*

*   *   *

GRAHAM, Arthur Kennon
See HARRISON, David L(ee)

*   *   *

GRAHAM, Kennon
See HARRISON, David L(ee)

H

HAHN, Michael T. 1953-

■ Personal

Born April 11, 1953, in Fort Bragg, NC; son of Thomas J. (in timber management) and Janice (a teacher; maiden name, Darby) Hahn; married Robin Tarwater (a registered nurse), August 4, 1990. *Education:* Attended Bradford Academy, 1968-71, Berklee College of Music, 1971-72, and Wildbranch Writers Workshop and Bennington Writers Workshop, both 1993. *Politics:* Independent. *Religion:* Independent. *Avocational interests:* "Devoted hunter, fisherman, and gardener."

■ Addresses

Home—RR 2 Box 248, Orleans, VT 05860.

■ Career

Performing musician; writer. Softball and basketball coach. *Member:* Bass Anglers Sportsman Society, National Rifle Association, Connecticut River Bass Anglers.

■ Awards, Honors

Special Merit Award, Vermont Book Publishers Association, 1994, for *Ethan Allen: A Life of Adventure.*

■ Writings

Ethan Allen: A Life of Adventure, New England Press, 1994.
Ann Story: Vermont's Heroine of Independence, New England Press, 1996.

Contributor of chapters on antlers and bass fishing to *The Sports Encyclopedia of North America,* 1988; also contributor of humor stories to *The Chronicle.* Author of columns, "Chasing Rainbows," *Vermont Sportsman,* 1996—, and "Four Season Angler," *Vermont Outdoors,* 1996—.

■ Work in Progress

Butte, a literary western novel; *Champ's Mate,* a contemporary fantasy featuring sea serpents and dragons.

■ Sidelights

Michael T. Hahn told *SATA:* "When I was in my twenties, playing in a rock-and-roll band was the perfect career; but as my thirtieth birthday came and went, the wild life seemed less exciting. I grew tired of arriving home at 4:30 in the morning, and I developed respiratory problems from breathing so much second-hand smoke. When a drunken woman stumbled to the stage one evening and puked on me, I knew that it was time to find a new line of work. Fortunately, music was not the only passion in my life.

MICHAEL T. HAHN

"I've always loved to read. Entertainment, information, and a magical enrichment of life are hidden between the covers of books, waiting to be discovered. If I can produce a little magic for my readers, my life will be well spent."

For More Information See

PERIODICALS

Horn Book Guide, spring, 1995, p. 151.

* * *

HAMILTON, Anita 1919-

Personal

Born November 16, 1919, in Wichita Falls, TX; daughter of Herbert B. (a contractor) and Rachel Louise (a homemaker; maiden name, Howard) Hayes; married Robert S. Hamilton (a sales manager in photography); children: Neil H. Olsen. *Education:* Hardin Simmons University, B.A., 1941.

Addresses

Home—21406 North 138th Ave., Sun City West, AZ 85375-5812.

Career

Teacher and writer. *Member:* Writer's Club—Sun City West, AZ.

Writings

(Self-illustrated) *Dempsey,* Carlton Press, 1995.

Work in Progress

Two sequels to *Dempsey: Dempsey Goes to Mexico,* and *Dempsey Meets Sydney.*

Sidelights

Anita Hamilton told *SATA:* "Actually, I believe that my parents put a pencil, instead of a rattle, in my hands when I was small, because I have always had the urge to put my thoughts on paper.

"If ever there was any kind of a writing contest, I'd enter it! And I usually won! For example, the first one was 'Why Texans Should Eat Texas Grapefruit.' I wrote them why, and won! A crate of Texas ruby reds! I was about 10 years old. That was the beginning.

"Teaching children in the elementary grades for many years naturally enhanced my love and interest in children's literature. In my first book, *Dempsey,* our handsome little rooster, and I hope the readers, learn some very important lessons on life. I have tried to make evident the love between animals and people, as well as the strong love that exists in the family and in the

ANITA HAMILTON

home. I do not talk down to the children in my writings; I simply try to 'chat' with them.

"The illustrations in *Dempsey* were intended to be just sketches to the publishers so that they could visualize what I wanted my characters to look like. Imagine my surprise when they informed me that they were 'charming' and would do nicely. Thus an artist was born!

"In Abilene, Texas, a children's theater group is planning a play around *Dempsey*'s characters. In Alameda, California, a third-grade class is using *Dempsey* as a 'science project' in watching baby chicks being hatched. They plan to name one of the chicks 'Dempsey.'

"I am sending Dempsey on two more adventures; my second fable is *Dempsey Goes to Mexico* and in the third (and last!) I am getting him involved with an Australian ostrich named Sydney, of course. Since I couldn't figure out how to get a rooster to Australia, I am bringing 'down under' to Dempsey!

"Writing these children's books has been hard work but *very* rewarding! I felt I was getting rejection notices even when I wrote for guidelines! But it has been worth it if I have made just a few people get a hoot from our little rooster!"

HARGRAVE, Leonie
See DISCH, Thomas M(ichael)

*   *   *

HARRISON, David L(ee) 1937-
(Arthur Kennon Graham, Kennon Graham)

■ Personal

Born March 13, 1937, in Springfield, MO; son of John Alexander (a businessman) and Laura Neva (a homemaker; maiden name, Justice) Harrison; married Sandra Sue Kennon (a high school counselor), May 23, 1959; children: Robin Lynn Harrison Williams, Jeffrey Scott. *Education:* Drury College, A.B., 1959; Emory University, M.S., 1960; Evansville University, graduate studies, 1960-63.

■ Addresses

Home—2634 Skyline Dr., Springfield, MO 65804. *Office*—928 South Glenstone, Springfield, MO 65802. *Electronic mail*—dharriso@mail.orion.org (Orion).

■ Career

Mead Johnson Co., Evansville, IN, pharmacologist, 1960-63; Hallmark Cards, Kansas City, MO, editorial manager, 1963-73; Glenstone Block Co. (manufacturer and supply house of building materials), Springfield, MO, president and owner, 1973—. President and member of Springfield Board of Education, 1983-88; member of board, Springfield Public Schools Foundation, 1988-96; member of board of trustees, Ozarks Technical Community College, 1992-94; member of advisory board, *Springfield Parent* magazine, 1994—. Has been a professional musician, music teacher, and principal trombonist in the Springfield Symphony. Active in various activities supporting literacy, 1982—; presenter and speaker at workshops and conferences. *Member:* Society of Children's Book Writers and Illustrators, Missouri Writers Guild.

■ Awards, Honors

Christopher Award, Christopher Foundation, 1973, for *The Book of Giant Stories;* award for Outstanding Contributions to Children's Literature, Central State University, 1978; Distinguished Alumni Award, Drury College, 1981; Kentucky Blue Grass Award nominee, Kentucky State Reading Association, 1993, for *Somebody Catch My Homework;* Celebrate Literacy Award, Missouri State Reading Association, 1994; Friend of Education Award, Missouri State Teachers Association, 1994; Children's Choice Award, International Reading Association and Children's Book Council (IRA/CBC), 1994, for *Somebody Catch My Homework,* and 1995, for *When Cows Come Home;* inclusion on Recommended Reading List, Kansas State Reading Association, 1995, and Master List of the Virginia Young Readers Pro-

DAVID L. HARRISON

gram, Virginia State Reading Association, 1996-97, both for *When Cows Come Home.*

■ Writings

The Boy with a Drum, Golden Press (Racine, WI), 1969.
Little Turtle's Big Adventure, Random House, 1969.
The Little Boy in the Forest, Whitman Publishing (Racine, WI), 1969.
About Me, Childcraft Education Corp., 1969.
The World of American Caves, Reilly & Lee, 1970.
The Case of Og the Missing Frog, Rand McNally, 1972.
(With Mary Loberg) *The Backyard Zoo,* Hallmark, 1972.
(With Loberg) *The Kingdom of the Sea,* Hallmark, 1972.
(With Loberg) *The World of Horses,* Hallmark, 1972.
(With Loberg) *The Terrible Lizards,* Hallmark, 1972.
The Book of Giant Stories, illustrated by Philippe Fix, McGraw, 1972.
The Little Boy and the Giant, Golden Press, 1973.
Let's Go Trucks!, Golden Press, 1973.
Children Everywhere, Rand McNally, 1973.
Piggy Wiglet and the Great Adventure, Golden Press, 1973.
The Huffin Puff Express, Whitman Publishing, 1974.
The Busy Body Book, Whitman Publishing, 1975.
Monster! Monster!, Golden Press, 1975.
The Pink Panther in Z-Land, Whitman Publishing, 1976.
The Circus Is in Town, Golden Press, 1978.

Detective Bob and the Great Ape Escape, illustrated by Ned Delaney, Parents' Magazine Press, 1980.

My Funny Bunny Phone Book, illustrated by Lyn McClure Butrick, Golden Press, 1980.

What Do You Know! Mind-Boggling Questions: Astonishing Answers, illustrated by Rod Ruth, Rand McNally, 1981.

The Snoring Monster, illustrated by Richard Walz, Golden Book, 1985.

Busy Machines, illustrated by Walz, Golden Book, 1985.

Wake Up, Sun!, illustrated by Hans Wilhelm, Random House, 1986.

Little Boy Soup, Ladybird Books (England), 1989.

Somebody Catch My Homework: Poems, illustrated by Betsy Lewin, Boyds Mills Press, 1993.

When Cows Come Home, illustrated by Chris L. Demarest, Boyds Mills Press, 1994.

The Boy Who Counted Stars: Poems, illustrated by Betsy Lewin, Boyds Mills Press, 1994.

A Thousand Cousins, Poems of Family Life, illustrated by Betsy Lewin, Boyds Mills Press, 1996.

The Animals' Song, Boyds Mills Press, 1997.

UNDER PSEUDONYM KENNON GRAHAM

Smokey Bear Saves the Forest, Whitman Publishing, 1971.

Lassie and the Big Clean-Up Day, Golden Press, 1971.

Eloise and the Old Blue Truck, Whitman Publishing, 1971.

Lassie and the Secret Friend, Golden Press, 1972.

My Little Book of Cars and Trucks, Whitman Publishing, 1973.

Woodsy Owl and the Trail Bikers, Golden Press, 1974.

Land of the Lost: Surprise Guests, Golden Press, 1975.

The Pink Panther in the Haunted House, Golden Press, 1975.

The Pink Panther Rides Again, Whitman Publishing, 1976.

My Little Book about Flying, Whitman Publishing, 1978.

Bugs Bunny in Escape from Noddington Castle, illustrated by Darrell Baker, Golden Press, 1979.

EDITOR; PUBLISHED BY HALLMARK

Peter Pan, 1964.

Cinderella, 1964.

Pinocchio, 1964.

The Adventures of Doctor Dolittle, 1965.

A Christmas Carol, 1965.

The Three Pigs, 1966.

Goldilocks and the Three Bears, 1966.

Also editor of other books for Hallmark.

OTHER

Contributor of stories and poems to anthologies. Contributor of short stories, under pseudonyms Arthur Kennon Graham and Kennon Graham, to *The Witch Book,* edited by Dorothy F. Haas, Rand McNally, 1976. Contributor to periodicals, including *Highlights for Children, Family Circle, Journal of Reading, Creative Classroom, Hello Reader!, Senior Living,* and *Springfield News-Leader.* Some of Harrison's work has been presented on cassettes, on television, and on radio throughout the world; *Somebody Catch My Homework* was produced on CD-ROM, Discis, 1994. Harrison's work has been translated into more than twelve languages.

■ Work in Progress

My Desk Is Haunted, "a collection of humorous school poems;" *The Purchase of Small Secrets,* "a collection of free verse comprising memories from teenage years;" *Farmer's Garden,* a picture book; *Don't Tell Said the Bell,* a picture book; a book for classroom teachers about writing poetry, with Bernice E. Cullinan.

■ Sidelights

Although the author of over fifty books for young people, David L. Harrison has not limited himself to the field of children's literature. He once told *SATA:* "By the time I was twenty-one I had worked in a pet shop, done yard work, taught music, dug ditches, unloaded boxcars, played in dance bands, poured concrete, worked in the entomology department at a university, mined uranium, and explored caves. I had also begun to write seriously, but it took nearly six more years before my first story was accepted for publication." Using these wide and varied experiences as inspiration, Harri-

Harrison's humorous poetry about school life fills the pages of *Somebody Catch My Homework,* illustrated by Betsy Lewin.

They somersault
And prance away
And laugh to hear
The donkeys bray.

Cows dance, swim, ride bicycles and more in Harrison's lively rhyming picture book *When Cows Come Home*. (Illustrated by Chris L. Demarest.)

son has produced award winning children's stories, poetry, and retellings of classic tales.

Harrison's 1972 work, *The Book of Giant Stories*, blends limericks and stories together to create a world where giants live among men. In this make-believe book, one young boy escapes from the hands of giants by telling them a secret; another clever lad calms a temperamental giant by teaching him to whistle; and a third boy helps a sorry giant who has been cursed by a wicked witch. A reviewer in *Publishers Weekly* described Harrison's book as "farfetched and funny," while Evelyn Stewart noted in *Library Journal* that the "believable fantasy is perfect for reading aloud" to younger readers. *Wake Up, Sun!,* an easy-to-read book published in 1986, chronicles the humorous attempts of barnyard animals to awaken the sun when they arise one morning before daybreak.

Somebody Catch My Homework features a variety of poems addressing the trials and tribulations children often have about school. Missing homework excuses, asking permission for restroom privileges, and complaints about playground bullies are set to verse with a sense of humor that is accessible to children. According to *School Library Journal* contributor Lee Bock, *Somebody Catch My Homework* is "reminiscent of the styles of Prelutsky and Silverstein." Writing in *Booklist,* Hazel Rochman applauded the book's "immediacy and slapstick." A critic in *Kirkus Reviews* remarked that the book is "all recognizable, neatly scanned, and genuinely

funny," further labeling the book "a winner—to read aloud, pass around, and chortle over again."

In his 1994 picture book, *When Cows Come Home,* Harrison reveals what really happens on the farm when the farmer's back is turned. As soon as the farmer tends to other business, all of his cows explode in silly and whimsical stunts, including square dancing, riding bicycles, and playing tag. A *Kirkus Reviews* critic complimented Harrison's "skillful versifying," while in *School Library Journal,* Mary Lou Budd admired "the motion in the rhythmic and evocative text." A *Publishers Weekly* reviewer described *When Cows Come Home* as "a bright, appealing volume with a mischievous nature."

Harrison's collection *A Thousand Cousins: Poems of Family Life* looks lightheartedly at numerous family situations which often confuse and confound children. The poet explores the relationships between siblings and extended family members and makes light of situations common to many children, such as fathers snoring loudly and mothers incessantly reminding their kids to keep clean. A critic in *Kirkus Reviews* observed that most of the poems "have punchy endings; each revolves around some gimmick." *School Library Journal* contributor Marjorie Lewis asserted that these poems will "elicit giggles from young readers and listeners."

About his work as a children's writer and poet, David L. Harrison told *SATA:* "I've always maintained two careers. First I worked in a pharmacology lab by day and wrote at night. Then came editing greeting cards by day and writing by night, followed by managing a business by day and writing at night. That used to seem normal to me. Now I'm not as sure. Years ago I'd come home from my day job and work on some manuscript until late at night. Late comes earlier than it once did.

"Something else that's changed is the way folks react if you tell them you write for young people. They used to say something like, 'Oh?' beneath arched eyebrows, signifying that it was a darned pity you couldn't make it as a real writer. Worse yet, sometimes there wasn't even the spark of a question mark. 'Oh,' they'd say simply, a touch of sadness pursing their lips, their attention turning to the broccoli dip.

"Thanks to our nation's well-founded concerns about educating and developing our newest generations, writing for young people is now recognized as a worthy goal. Writers have always known that they must grow with their work. What could be a better strategy for success than to choose an audience that also must keep growing?"

■ Works Cited

Bock, Lee, review of *Somebody Catch My Homework*, *School Library Journal*, January, 1993, p. 92.

Review of *The Book of Giant Stories*, *Publishers Weekly*, December 11, 1972, p. 36.

Budd, Mary Lou, review of *When Cows Come Home*, *School Library Journal*, February, 1994, p. 86.

Lewis, Marjorie, review of *A Thousand Cousins: Poems of Family Life*, *School Library Journal*, March, 1996, p. 209.

Review of *Somebody Catch My Homework*, *Kirkus Reviews*, December 15, 1992, p. 1573.

Rochman, Hazel, review of *Somebody Catch My Homework*, *Booklist*, January 15, 1993, p. 914.

Stewart, Evelyn, review of *The Book of Giant Stories*, *Library Journal*, January 15, 1973, p. 253.

Review of *A Thousand Cousins: Poems of Family Life*, *Kirkus Reviews*, December 15, 1995, p. 1770.

Review of *When Cows Come Home*, *Publishers Weekly*, November 29, 1993, p. 64.

Review of *When Cows Come Home*, *Kirkus Reviews*, January 1, 1994, p. 68.

■ For More Information See

PERIODICALS

Booklist, December 1, 1986, p. 583; May 1, 1994, p. 1608.

Reading Teacher, October, 1994.

St. Louis Post-Dispatch, June 5, 1994.

School Library Journal, November, 1994, p. 98.

HENNING, Ann 1948-

■ Personal

Born August 5, 1948, in Goteborg, Sweden; daughter of Gunnar Albert Filip (a physician) and Kerstin Lillemor (a teacher; maiden name, Kavland) Henning; married The Earl of Roden, February 13, 1986; children: Viscount Jocelyn. *Education:* Lund University, B.A., 1975.

■ Addresses

Home—4 The Boltons, London SW10 9TB, England.

■ Career

Author, playwright, and translator. Artistic Director, 4th International Women Playwrights Conference; Artistic Director, Connemara Theatre Co. *Member:* Society of Authors, Irish Writer's Union, Society of Irish Playwrights.

■ Writings

The Connemara Whirlwind, Poolbeg Press (Dublin, Ireland), 1990.
The Connemara Stallion, Poolbeg Press, 1991.
The Connemara Champion, Poolbeg Press, 1994.
The Cosmos & You (nonfiction), Poolbeg Press, 1995.
Honeylove the Bear Cub, illustrated by Laura Cronin, Poolbeg Press, 1995.

■ Sidelights

Ann Henning told *SATA:* "I started writing very early: my first book, *Honeylove the Bear Cub*, was written when I was seven, put away for forty years and then published in 1995. My first published story was in a magazine in 1957. My debut as a playwright was in 1972 with *Smile*, at Atelierteatern, Goteborg.

"From 1970 to 1983 I worked in London as a playwright and translator of plays, books, and films. In 1983 I moved to Connemara in the west of Ireland. My involvement with Connemara ponies resulted in the Connemara trilogy about my own stallion Cuaifeach, whom I still have much pleasure riding.

"At present I'm planning a return to writing for the theatre."

*   *   *

HERB, Angela M. 1970-

■ Personal

Born July 29, 1970, in Edmonds, WA; daughter of Michael W. (an attorney) and Donna M. (a pharmacist) Herb. *Education:* Washington State University, B.A., 1993.

■ Addresses

Home—6743 Sycamore Avenue NW, Seattle, WA 98117. *Electronic mail*—angieh@saltmine.com.

■ Career

Laing Communications, Inc., Redmond, WA, editor/project manager, 1993-95; Saltmine Creative Inc., Seattle, WA, editorial and content manager, 1996—.

■ Awards, Honors

Children's Books of the Year, Bank Street Child Study Children's Book Committee, 1996, and Washington State Governor's Writers Award, 1996, both for *For Home and Country*.

■ Writings

Alaska A to Z, Vernon Publications, 1993.
(With Norman Bolotin) *For Home and Country: A Civil War Scrapbook*, Lodestar Books, 1995.
Beyond the Mississippi: Early Westward Expansion of the United States, Lodestar Books, 1996.

■ Work in Progress

A book of poetry, *Conversations with Plants and Artists.*

■ Sidelights

Angela M. Herb has teamed with Norman Bolotin to create *For Home and Country: A Civil War Scrapbook*, a social history of the American Civil War for middle-grade readers that focuses on the daily experiences of soldiers during the conflict. "From the outset, the reader becomes absorbed in the portrayal of actual people as they lived through the realities of war," noted *Horn Book* reviewer Margaret A. Bush. Other reviewers similarly praised the unique perspective offered in *For Home and Country*. Carolyn Phelan of *Booklist* maintained: "Giving a close-up view of everyday life for Civil War soldiers, this book fills in the blanks left by more traditional history books." *Voice of Youth Advocates* contributor Suzanne Julian added that "the emotional impact of learning facts about the Civil War from accounts of people who experienced it, makes this book an intriguing and eye-opening experience."

Herb explores more nineteenth-century American history in her *Beyond the Mississippi: Early Westward Expansion of the United States*. Featuring numerous photographs and other illustrative materials, as well as maps, sidebars, a timeline, and other enhancements, Herb's work "makes history come alive," according to *Voice of Youth Advocates* contributor Debbie Earl, who described *Beyond the Mississippi* as "lively, entertaining supplementary material for junior high and high school history classes."

■ Works Cited

Bush, Margaret A., review of *For Home and Country: A Civil War Scrapbook, Horn Book,* November-December, 1995, pp. 753-54.
Earl, Debbie, review of *Beyond the Mississippi: Early Westward Expansion of the United States, Voice of Youth Advocates,* February, 1997, p. 348.
Julian, Suzanne, review of *For Home and Country: A Civil War Scrapbook, Voice of Youth Advocates,* December, 1995, p. 320.
Phelan, Carolyn, review of *For Home and Country: A Civil War Scrapbook, Booklist,* October 1, 1995, p. 306.

■ For More Information See

PERIODICALS
Bulletin of the Center for Children's Books, October, 1995, p. 47.
Kirkus Reviews, August 1, 1995, p. 1107.

* * *

HERMES, Jules 1962-

■ Personal

Born November 17, 1962, in St. Paul, MN; daughter of Vernon and Margaret (Garvey) Jules; married Steven Hersman, August 23, 1996. *Education:* University of California, Los Angeles, B.A., 1984. *Religion:* Catholic.

■ Addresses

Home—3549 Midland Ave., White Bear Lake, MN 55110.

■ Career

International Commentary Service, New York City, senior writer, 1989-90; F.L.I.P. Writers and Photographers, Manitou Springs, CO, writer/photographer, 1990-93; Carolrhoda Books, Inc., Minneapolis, MN, contract writer/photographer, 1991-95; Global Volunteers, St. Paul, MN, media coordinator, 1995—.

■ Writings

Children of India, Carolrhoda Books, 1993.
Children of Micronesia, Carolrhoda Books, 1994.
Children of Morocco, Carolrhoda Books, 1995.
The Dalai Lama: A Biography, Lerner Publications, 1995.
Children of Bolivia, Carolrhoda Books, 1996.
Children of Guatemala, Carolrhoda Books, 1997.

■ Sidelights

Jules Hermes is the author and photographer of several titles in the "World's Children" series published by Carolrhoda. "When I was young," Hermes recalled for *SATA,* "I was very interested in the world—different

JULES HERMES

cultures and countries—probably because our family always had a subscription to National Geographic. I dreamed of taking photographs of people around the world. I finally had that chance when I went to live in New York City. There, I was hired to coordinate a documentary and was sent to India. After that, I decided to return to India on my own, and I started photographing the children and the country. I was in India for more than one year writing, photographing, and learning about that wonderful place. I wanted to write and photograph a book about India for children who want to know the world and children from other countries. The book was a labor of love—three years of my life. But it was worth every minute because it opened a door to a new world."

■ For More Information See

PERIODICALS

Booklist, February 1, 1994, p. 1004; May 1, 1995, p. 1570.
Bulletin of the Center for Children's Books, April, 1994, p. 258; September, 1994, p. 13.
Kirkus Reviews, June 15, 1994, p. 846.
School Library Journal, July, 1995, p. 86; May, 1996, p. 122.
Science Books and Films, May, 1994, p. 117.

HILL, John
See KOONTZ, Dean R(ay)

*   *   *

HIMLER, Ronald (Norbert) 1937-

■ Personal

Born November 16, 1937, in Cleveland, OH; son of Norbert and Grace (Manning) Himler; married Ann Danowitz, June 18, 1972 (divorced); children: Daniel, Anna, Peer. *Education:* Cleveland Institute of Art, diploma, 1960; graduate study in painting at Cranbrook Academy of Art, Bloomfield Hills, MI, 1960-61, and New York University and Hunter College, New York City, 1968-70.

■ Addresses

Home—11301 East Placita Cibuta, Tucson, AZ 85749.

■ Career

General Motors Technical Center, Warren, MI, technical sculptor (styling), 1961-63; artist and illustrator, 1963—. Toy designer and sculptor for Transogram Co., New York City, 1968, and Remco Industries, Newark, NJ, 1969. Cofounder and headmaster, Blue Rock School, NC, 1982-84. *Exhibitions:* Wolfe Galleries, Tucson, AZ, 1990.

■ Awards, Honors

Award for Graphic Excellence, American Institute of Graphic Arts, and citation of merit, Society of Illustrators, both 1972, both for *Baby;* Printing Industries of America citation, 1972, for *Rocket in My Pocket;* Children's Book Showcase selection, Children's Book Council, 1975, for *Indian Harvests;* New Jersey Institute of Technology award (with Ann Himler), 1976, for *Little Owl, Keeper of the Trees;* Best of Bias-free Illustration citation, American Institute of Graphic Arts, 1976, for *Make a Circle, Keep Us In;* Children's Choice selection, International Reading Association/Children's Book Council (IRA/CBC), 1979, for *Bus Ride;* Best Children's Books, *School Library Journal,* 1979, for *Curly and the Wild Boar,* 1990, for *The Wall,* and 1991, for *Fly Away Home;* Children's Books of the Year selection, Child Study Children's Book Committee at Bank Street College (CSCBC), 1982, for *Moon Song* and *Jem's Island,* and 1992, for *Fly Away Home; Best Town in the World* was exhibited at the Brataslava Biennale of Illustration, 1985; Best Books of 1985, New York Public Library, and Notable book selection, American Library Association, 1986, both for *Dakota Dugout;* Pick of the Lists, American Booksellers, 1987, for *Nettie's Trip South,* 1990, for *The Wall,* 1991, for *I'm Going to Pet a Worm Today,* and 1992, for *Fly Away Home* and *Katie's Trunk;* Notable Children's Book, American Library Association and Association for Library Services to Children (ALSC), 1990, and Journal of Youth Services

RONALD HIMLER

in Libraries, 1991, both for *The Wall;* Children's
Books—100 titles for reading and sharing, New York
Public Library, 1990, for *The Wall,* and 1992, for *The
Lily Cupboard;* Notable Children's Books, American
Library Association, 1991, and Editor's Choice, *Book-
list,* 1991, both for *Fly Away Home;* Silver Medal,
Society of Illustrators, 1992, for best western painting in
book cover art.

■ Writings

FOR CHILDREN; SELF-ILLUSTRATED

(Compiler) *Glad Day, and Other Classical Poems for
Children,* Putnam, 1972.
(With former wife, Ann Himler) *Little Owl, Keeper of
the Trees,* Harper, 1974.
The Girl on the Yellow Giraffe, Harper, 1976.
Wake Up, Jeremiah, Harper, 1979.

■ Illustrator

Robert Burgess, *Exploring a Coral Reef,* Macmillan,
1972.
Carl A. Withers, compiler, *Rocket in My Pocket* (poetry
anthology), revised edition, Western Publishing,
1972.
Fran Manushkin, *Baby,* Harper, 1972.
Elizabeth Winthrop, *Bunk Beds,* Harper, 1972.

Millicent Brower, *I Am Going Nowhere,* Putnam, 1972.
Charlotte Zolotow, *Janey,* Harper, 1973.
Marjorie Weinman Sharmat, *Morris Brookside, a Dog,*
Holiday House, 1973.
Tom Glazer, *Eye Winker, Tom Tinker, Chin Chopper,*
Doubleday, 1973.
Fran Manushkin, *Bubblebath,* Harper, 1974.
William C. Grimm, *Indian Harvests,* McGraw-Hill,
1974.
Robert Burch, *Hut School and the Wartime Homefront
Heroes,* Viking, 1974.
Marjorie Weinman Sharmat, *Morris Brookside Is Miss-
ing,* Holiday House, 1974.
Betsy Byars, *After the Goat Man,* Viking, 1974.
Polly Curran, *A Patch of Peas,* Golden Press, 1975.
Arnold Adoff, *Make a Circle, Keep Us In,* Delacorte,
1975.
Achim Broger, *Bruno,* William Morrow, 1975.
Marty Kelly, *The House on Deer-Track Trail,* Harper,
1976.
Crescent Dragonwagon, *Windrose,* Harper, 1976.
Betty Boegehold, *Alone in the Cabin,* Harcourt, 1976.
Yoshiko Uchida, *Another Goodbye,* Allyn & Bacon,
1976.
Richard Kennedy, *The Blue Stone,* Holiday House,
1976.
Jeanette Caines, *Daddy,* Harper, 1977.
Johanna Johnston, *Harriet and the Runaway Book: The
Story of Harriet Beecher Stowe and Uncle Tom's
Cabin,* Harper, 1977.
Eleanor Coerr, *Sadako and the Thousand Paper Cranes,*
Putnam, 1977.
Arnold Adoff, *Tornado,* Delacorte, 1977.
Louise Dickerson, *Good Wife, Good Wife,* McGraw-
Hill, 1977.
Arnold Adoff, *Under the Early Morning Trees,* Dutton,
1978.
Clyde Bulla and Michael Syson, *Conquista,* Crowell,
1978.
Nancy Jewell, *Bus Ride,* Harper, 1978.
Fred Gipson, *Little Arliss,* Harper, 1978.
Fred Gipson, *Curly and the Wild Boar,* Harper, 1979.
Richard Kennedy, *Inside My Feet: The Story of a Giant,*
Harper, 1979.
Carla Stevens, *Trouble for Lucy,* Houghton, 1979.
Arnold Adoff, *I Am the Running Girl,* Harper, 1979.
Douglas Davis, *The Lion's Tail,* Atheneum, 1980.
Elizabeth Parsons, *The Upside-Down Cat,* Atheneum,
1981.
Linda Peavy, *Allison's Grandfather,* Scribner, 1981.
Byrd Baylor, *Moon Song,* Scribner, 1982.
Katherine Lasky, *Jem's Island,* Scribner, 1982.
Byrd Baylor, *Best Town in the World,* Scribner, 1983.
Thor Heyerdahl, *Kon Tiki: A True Adventure of Survival
at Sea,* Random House, 1984.
Ann Turner, *Dakota Dugout,* Macmillan, 1985.
Ellen Howard, *Edith Herself,* Atheneum, 1987.
Ann Turner, *Nettie's Trip South,* Macmillan, 1987.
Susan Pearson, *Happy Birthday, Grampie,* Dial, 1987.
Emily Cheney Neville, *The Bridge,* Harper, 1988.
Alice Fleming, *The King of Prussia and a Peanut Butter
Sandwich,* Scribner, 1988.
Susan Nunes, *Coyote Dreams,* Atheneum, 1988.

Ann Herbert Scott, *Someday Rider*, Clarion, 1989.

(With John Gurney) Della Rowland, *A World of Cats*, Contemporary Books (Chicago), 1989.

Crescent Dragonwagon, *Winter Holding Spring*, Macmillan, 1990.

Eve Bunting, *The Wall*, Clarion, 1990.

Dorothy and Thomas Hoobler, *George Washington and Presidents' Day*, Silver Press (Englewood Cliffs, NJ), 1990.

Merry Banks, *Animals of the Night*, Scribner, 1990.

Liza Ketchum Murrow, *Dancing on the Table*, Holiday House, 1990.

Patricia Hubbell, *A Grass Green Gallop*, Atheneum, 1990.

Eve Bunting, *Fly Away Home*, Clarion, 1991.

Constance Levy, *I'm Going to Pet a Worm Today, and Other Poems*, McElderry Books, 1991.

Virginia T. Gross, *The Day It Rained Forever: A Story of the Johnstown Flood*, Viking, 1991.

Kathleen V. Kudlinski, *Pearl Harbor Is Burning*, Viking, 1991.

Shulamith Levey Oppenheim, *The Lily Cupboard*, HarperCollins, 1992.

Byrd Baylor, *One Small Blue Bead*, Scribner, 1992.

Ann Turner, *Katie's Trunk*, Macmillan, 1992.

Kate Aver, *Joey's Way*, McElderry Books, 1992.

Ann Herbert Scott, *A Brand Is Forever*, Clarion, 1993.

Eve Bunting, *Someday a Tree*, Clarion, 1993.

Virginia Driving Hawk Sneve, *The Sioux*, Holiday House, 1993.

Virginia Driving Hawk Sneve, *The Navajos*, Holiday House, 1993.

Virginia Driving Hawk Sneve, *The Seminoles*, Holiday House, 1994.

Virginia Driving Hawk Sneve, *The Nez Perce*, Holiday House, 1994.

Kathleen V. Kudlinski, *Lone Star*, Viking, 1994.

Kathleen V. Kudlinski, *Earthquake*, Viking, 1994.

Eve Bunting, *A Day's Work*, Clarion, 1994.

Nancy Luenn, *SQUISH! A Wetland Walk*, Atheneum, 1994.

Wendy Kesselman, *Sand in My Shoes*, Hyperion, 1995.

Virginia Driving Hawk Sneve, *The Hopis*, Holiday House, 1995.

Virginia Driving Hawk Sneve, *The Iroquois*, Holiday House, 1995.

D. Anne Love, *Bess's Log Cabin Quilt*, Holiday House, 1995.

D. Anne Love, *Dakota Spring*, Holiday House, 1995.

Sue Alexander, *Sara's City*, Clarion, 1995.

Virginia Driving Hawk Sneve, *The Cherokees*, Holiday House, 1996.

Virginia Driving Hawk Sneve, *The Cheyennes*, Holiday House, 1996.

Eve Bunting, *Train to Somewhere*, Clarion, 1996.

Barbara A. Steiner, *Desert Trip*, Sierra Club Books, 1996.

Ellen Howard, *The Log Cabin Quilt*, Holiday House, 1996.

Several of Himler's books have been translated into other languages, including Dutch and Japanese.

■ Sidelights

Artist and illustrator Ronald Himler is known for his work in a variety of artistic media. Watercolor, oils, gouache, and pencil have all been used by Himler to present his imaginative interpretation of popular children's books to young readers. Trained in both painting and illustration, Himler offers characteristically gentle and sensitive depictions of stories and poems that help open the eyes of preschoolers and primary graders to the world that surrounds them.

Raised in Cleveland, Ohio, Himler spent many childhood hours immersed in drawing, especially during the weekly trips he took to his grandmother's home. After graduating from high school, he studied painting at the Cleveland Institute of Art, and went on to attend graduate school at the Cranbrook Academy of Art in Bloomfield Hills, Michigan. After holding various positions as a commercial artist, Himler decided to travel throughout Europe and Scandinavia, doing independent research in such major museums as the Louvre in Paris, the Uffizi Galleries in Florence, and Amsterdam's Rijksmuseum. His tours through some of the world's finest collections of fine art broadened the scope of Himler's own painting, while the contacts he made with people of so many different cultures increased his sensitivity to the diversity of the world's peoples.

Upon returning to the United States, Himler was determined to pursue a career as an illustrator of children's books. His first project was a verse anthology called *Glad Day, and Other Classical Poems for Children*, which was published in 1972. The *Glad Day* illustrations were quickly followed by others, including drawings to accompany a work of nonfiction entitled *Exploring a Coral Reef*. Requests for illustrations for

A homeless boy living in an airport finds hope after seeing a trapped bird find its own freedom. (From *Fly Away Home* by Eve Bunting, illustrated by Himler.)

other books continued to come his way, and Himler found himself working with texts written by a wide variety of popular children's writers, including Betsy Byars, Tom Glazer, Marjorie Weinman Sharmat, and Charlotte Zolotow.

In 1974, Himler and his wife Ann collaborated on the children's book *Little Owl, Keeper of the Trees,* with Himler providing the illustrations. Three tales that center on a young owl living high up in a sycamore tree, *Little Owl* weaves magic into the world of forest-dwelling animals through the character of Jonas, a small, friendly monster who possesses special powers. Himler went on to write two other books, including his 1976 publication *The Girl on the Yellow Giraffe,* which features his pencil-sketch illustrations. Calling the book "an affectionate celebration of a child's imaginative powers," *Booklist* reviewer Denise M. Wilms praised the author/illustrator's picture book as an effective portrayal of a child's imaginary world. Himler wrote *The Girl on the Yellow Giraffe* for his daughter, Anna; four years later, he produced *Wake Up, Jeremiah* for his son, Peer. Accompanied by a minimum of text, Himler's impressionist-style, full-color illustrations depict a young boy's excitement at witnessing the start of a new day. Getting up extra early to watch the sunrise from the top of a hill near his home, Jeremiah then rushes home to share this fresh new day with his drowsy parents. "The evolution of dawn—from early murk to resplendent full light—in Mr. Himler's illustrations represent his best, most colorful performance to date," asserted *New York Times Book Review* contributor George A. Woods.

In the works he has illustrated since *Wake Up, Jeremiah,* Himler has focused on complex emotional issues. In Eve Bunting's *Fly Away Home,* for example, the homeless lifestyle of a young boy and his out-of-work dad is treated by Himler with muted shades of brown and blue watercolor, and the artist places father and son at the edge of his pictures as a way of reflecting their existence on the fringes of airport life. "Himler matches Bunting's understated text with gentle sensibility," noted a *Kirkus Reviews* commentator. Zena Sutherland of the *Bulletin of the Center for Children's Books* similarly noted that "Himler's quiet paintings echo the economy and the touching quality of the story," and *Horn Book* reviewer Ann A. Flowers commented: "The yearning sadness of the story, ameliorated only by the obvious and touching affection between father and son, is reflected in the subtle, expressive watercolors, dominated by shades of blue." In 1996 *Fly Away Home* was adapted as a major motion picture.

Other collaborations with Bunting have included the 1990 work *The Wall,* which sensitively presents a boy's impressions of a visit to Washington, D.C.'s Vietnam Memorial, and, in 1993, *Someday a Tree,* a gentle ecology message for primary graders centering on the fate of one sick tree. In a review of Bunting's highly regarded *The Wall,* Denise Wilms of *Booklist* maintained that "Himler's intense, quiet watercolors capture the dignity of the setting as Bunting's story reaches right

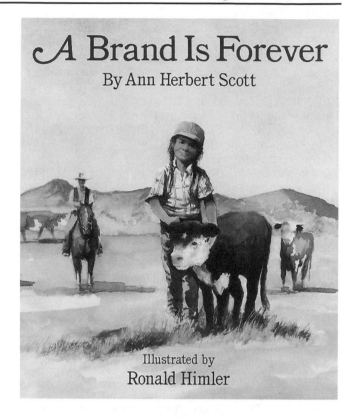

Raised on a cattle ranch, Annie must face the fact that her own adopted calf Doodle must be branded. (From *A Brand is Forever* by Ann Herbert Scott, illustrated by Himler.)

to the heart of deep emotions." In a *Booklist* review of *Someday a Tree,* Hazel Rochman commented favorably on yet another effective Bunting/Himler collaboration, noting that "Himler's watercolors express the quiet harmony of the green shady scene where you can dream and hear leaves whisper and see 'clouds change like smoke.'"

While Himler has enjoyed writing and illustrating books for young readers, painting has remained his first love. In 1982, while traveling through the U.S. Southwest, the artist was permitted to attend several ceremonial dances performed by Native Americans. The powerful psychological effect of witnessing these traditional dances opened Himler's eyes to a people and a time with which he felt an inexplicable empathy. As a result, he sensed a growing need to understand and give expression to what he perceived as two very different cultures and histories: Plains Indian traditions and the history of the white man who had invaded and altered those traditions. Himler has since worked to capture the essence of Native American ceremony in oil paintings. Many of these works have won him critical acclaim; Himler's Indian paintings have been featured in both *Art of the West* magazine and the PBS television program *Arizona Illustrated.*

Acknowledged for his beautifully executed children's book illustrations on a variety of topics, Himler's area of greatest interest is the life and history of the American west. He has executed illustrations for "The First Americans," a series of books written by Virginia Driving Hawk Sneve that focus on Native American tribal culture. Series titles include *The Nez Perce, The Sioux,* and *The Seminoles,* of which *School Library Journal* contributor M. Colleen McDougall noted: "Himler's illustrations are the book's high point.... [His] figures and landscapes are both aesthetically pleasing and pertinent to the discussion." A *Publishers Weekly* commentator praised "Himler's striking oil paintings" in a review of Sneve's *The Sioux* and *The Navajos,* while *School Library Journal* contributor Jacqueline Elsner, reviewing *The Cherokees,* asserted: "Himler's familiar watercolors, rich, warm, and serene, grace the text." And the ranch stories of Ann Herbert Scott—*Someday Rider* in 1989 and *A Brand Is Forever*

in 1993—have also benefited from Himler's artistic vision; each reflects the artist's sensitivity to western surroundings. Of *A Brand Is Forever,* Marianne Partridge noted in the *New York Times Book Review* that Himler's illustrations "capture the essentially unchanging nature of ranching while giving [the book] a thoroughly modern flavor." And Himler's illustrations for Byrd Baylor's stories of the U.S. southwest have also been hailed by reviewers: a *Publishers Weekly* critic refers to his illustrations for Baylor's *Moon Song* as "harmonious, lovely drawings, dominated by the touching presence of the lonely coyote." With scores of children's books to his credit, and hundreds of book cover illustrations, Himler continues to inspire young people through his artistic talents.

Illustrated by Himler, this work describes the traditional lifestyles of the Sioux Indians and their various tribes. (From *The Sioux,* by Virginia Driving Hawk Sneve.)

■ Works Cited

Elsner, Jacqueline, review of *The Cherokees, School Library Journal,* April, 1996, p. 130.

Flowers, Ann A., review of *Fly Away Home, Horn Book,* July-August, 1991, p. 445.

Review of *Fly Away Home, Kirkus Reviews,* February 1, 1991, p. 172.

McDougall, M. Colleen, review of *The Seminoles, School Library Journal,* April, 1994, p. 146.

Review of *Moon Song, Publishers Weekly,* June, 1982.

Partridge, Marianne, review of *A Brand Is Forever, New York Times Book Review,* May 30, 1993, p. 19.

Rochman, Hazel, review of *Someday a Tree, Booklist,* March 1, 1993, p. 1234.

Review of *The Sioux* and *The Navajos, Publishers Weekly,* November 8, 1993, p. 80.

Sutherland, Zena, review of *Fly Away Home, Bulletin of the Center for Children's Books,* May, 1991, p. 212.

Wilms, Denise M., review of *The Girl on the Yellow Giraffe, Booklist,* October 1, 1976, p. 252.

Wilms, Denise, review of *The Wall, Booklist,* April 1, 1990, p. 1544.

Woods, George A., review of *Wake Up, Jeremiah, New York Times Book Review,* October 28, 1979, p. 18.

■ For More Information See

PERIODICALS

Art of the West, January/February, 1989.

Booklist, September 15, 1979, p. 120; December 15, 1993, p. 759; November 1, 1994, p. 505.

Bulletin of the Center for Children's Books, May, 1975, p. 148; February, 1980, p. 111; October, 1994, pp. 38-39.

Horn Book, July-August, 1990, pp. 442-43; March-April, 1992, p. 193; May-June, 1996, p. 353.

Kirkus Reviews, October 15, 1974, p. 1103; February 15, 1993, p. 223; September 15, 1994, p. 1266.

New York Times Book Review, June 25, 1972; November 12, 1972; February 19, 1989.

Publishers Weekly, September 30, 1974, p. 60; January 1, 1992, p. 55; August 8, 1994, pp. 434-35; February 5, 1996, p. 89.

Quill & Quire, June, 1993, p. 40.

School Library Journal, June, 1991, p. 74; January, 1995, p. 82; March, 1996, p. 166.

* * *

HOPKINS, Jackie (Mims) 1952-

■ Personal

Born October 2, 1952, in Tyler, TX; daughter of Levi Jackson (a geologist) and Rhebajo (a homemaker; maiden name, Rogers) Mims; married Jeffrey Van Hopkins (commercial insurance manager), July 28, 1972; children: Jonathan, Katie. *Education:* Attended Texas Tech University, 1971-72; University of Arkansas, B.S., 1976; Texas A & M University, M.A., 1993. *Politics:* Republican. *Religion:* Christian.

JACKIE HOPKINS

■ Addresses

Home—13223 Golden Valley, Cypress, TX 77429.

■ Career

Eastdale Academy, Memphis, TN, elementary school teacher, 1976-78; Lamkin Elementary, Houston, TX, elementary school teacher, 1978-81; Building Rainbows, Houston, kindergarten teacher, 1985-88; Matzke Elementary, Houston, elementary school teacher, 1988-91, librarian/media specialist, 1994—; Horne Elementary, Houston, librarian/media specialist, 1991-93. *Member:* Society of Children's Book Writers and Illustrators, Association of Texas Professional Educators, Texas Library Association.

■ Writings

Tumbleweed Tom on the Texas Trail, illustrated by Kay Salem, Charlesbridge, 1994.

■ Work in Progress

Seasons of the Cowboy, Charlesbridge.

■ Sidelights

Jackie Hopkins told *SATA:* "The first book I can remember reading as a child is *The Cat in the Hat Comes Back* by Dr. Seuss. I loved the rhythm and the silliness of the words. Dr. Seuss's books were fast-paced like me. I didn't enjoy reading any book of length because I was so hyperactive and couldn't sit still long enough to read. I liked picture books, but when I was old enough to begin reading chapter books like *Nancy Drew,* I continued to only want picture books that I could finish quickly. Who would have ever imagined that a kid who had no interest in reading would someday become a teacher and, later, a librarian? It was more than twenty years ago in a college children's literature class that I first fell in love with books.

"Over the years I've spent a good portion of my teacher paychecks on children's books to supplement the curriculum. It was during one of these searches for the perfect books on Texas that I discovered a real deficit. Like many native Texans, I take great pride in our state. It was this pride and a need for literature about Texas for younger students that sparked my interest in creating my first book, *Tumbleweed Tom on the Texas Trail.* The children loved my book, and eight years later, I found a publishing company that liked it, too.

"As an educator and a librarian I continue to firmly believe in using literature to enrich curriculum. I provide my teachers with as many books on a subject as I can find. In addition to helping out the teachers, I love reading aloud and story-telling to the children. It's wonderful to share literature just for the fun of it, too!

"I hope to write more books that teachers will find useful in their teaching, but it is also my desire to write books that will enchant and delight children of all ages. Hopefully they won't have to wait until they are in college to discover the magic of books."

■ For More Information See

PERIODICALS

Horn Book Guide, fall, 1995, p. 399.

I–J

IGNOFFO, Matthew 1945-

■ Personal

Born July 22, 1945, in Chicago, IL; son of Matthew, Sr. (a doctor) and Virginia (a nurse; maiden name, Fenelon) Ignoffo. *Education:* Loyola University, B.S., 1967, Ph.D., 1972; Northwestern University, M.A., 1968; Monmouth University, Reading Specialist Certification, 1981. *Politics:* Independent. *Religion:* Catholic.

■ Career

United States Military Academy Prep School, Ft. Monmouth, NJ, professor of English, 1972—. Counselor for terminally ill patients; neurolinguistics, hypnotherapy, and reality therapist. *Military service:* U.S. Army Adjutant General Corps, 1972-77; attained rank of captain. *Member:* Modern Language Association, Orton Dyslexia Society, American Counseling Association.

■ Awards, Honors

Woodrow Wilson Fellow.

■ Writings

FOR YOUNG ADULTS

Coping with Your Inner Critic, Rosen, 1989.
Everything You Need to Know about Self-Confidence, Rosen, 1996.

FOR ADULTS

What the War Did to Whitman, Vantage, 1975.
One Perfect Lover: A Story of the Resurrection, Resource Publications, 1987.

Has published articles in *Running Times, Journal of Reading, Christian New Age Quarterly, Sea Tails, Connecting Link, Muscle & Fitness, Men's Fitness, Journal of Military Prep Schools, International Journal of Professional Hypnosis,* and *Journal of Reality Therapy.*

■ Work in Progress

A movie script titled *Vortex.*

■ Sidelights

Matthew Ignoffo told *SATA:* "I have enjoyed writing imaginative stories since I was in grade school because I have a very active imagination which was nurtured by my parents. My mother read me stories and got me books about magical beings and fantasy. My father rented movies long before they were available on tape. He got the actual celluloid films themselves from a film

MATTHEW IGNOFFO

library in Chicago. We watched all the Hollywood classics.

"My romantic fascination with the sea, mermaids, and mermen comes from the fact that, when I was three years old, I fell in love with Lenore, the mermaid in the 1948 film *Mr. Peabody & the Mermaid.* My parents took me on a ship to Hawaii in 1958, the year before Hawaii became a state. This trip reinforced my love of the sea and tropical waters that could be inhabited by merfolk.

"I became fascinated with the poetry of Walt Whitman. I loved the unrestrained exuberance of his style. I also identified with the ideas about himself, America, and life which he expressed in his poems.

"Through my writing, I hope to help people become reacquainted with the magic and the mystery in the universe—the beautiful and mystical elements missing from everyday life. If we begin to see the spiritual elements that seem invisible to us, we will begin to really know who we are and why we are alive.

"I teach English, reading, and drama. From my students I learned that people too often sabotage themselves by expecting less of themselves than they are capable. Therefore, I have written articles and two books on how we can be in more control of ourselves and thus achieve much more of our potential.

"I write using a computer because it allows me to change, cut, add, and edit quickly and easily. I also use mood music that sets the atmosphere of what I am writing. I usually use classical music or movie soundtracks.

"A writer must write. If you feel that you are a writer, never let anyone tell you that you can't succeed. I have published numerous articles and four books without even having a literary agent."

■ For More Information See

PERIODICALS

Booklist, March 1, 1996, p. 1128.
School Library Journal, September, 1989, p. 281; March, 1996, p. 226.
Voice of Youth Advocates, December, 1989, p. 301.

*   *   *

IMMELL, Myra H. 1941-

■ Personal

Born March 23, 1941, in New Brunswick, NJ; daughter of Shim R. (a printer) and Sally (an administrative assistant; maiden name, Pellis) Hankins; married William Hopkins Immell (a certified public accountant), July 21, 1963; children: Seth Alan. *Education:* Ohio University, B.A. (cum laude); attended Ohio State University, University of Madrid, and Rutgers University. *Politics:* "Liberal/Democrat." *Religion:* Jewish.

Hobbies and other interests: "History in general—British and Native American in particular."

■ Addresses

Home—4391 Hansen Dr., Hilliard, OH 43026. *Office*—Meeks Heit Publishing Co., 374 Morrison Rd., Columbus, OH 43213.

■ Career

Merrill Publishing Co., Westerville, OH, member of foreign languages editorial staff, 1969-74, member of social studies editorial staff, 1976-85, managing editor—social studies, 1986-89, acting executive director—social studies, 1989-90; self-employed as consultant, project manager, author, and editor, 1990-93; Quest International, Newark, OH, director of high school programs, 1993-96; employed by Meeks Heit Publishing Co., Columbus, OH, 1996—.

■ Writings

Automobiles: Connecting People and Places, Lucent Books (San Diego), 1994.
Tecumseh, Lucent Books, 1996.

Also author, with Marion Sader, of *The Young Adult Reader's Adviser,* 1992.

■ Work in Progress

A suspense novel; a literary companion for young adults; a world history textbook; research on computer technology, the World Wide Web (WWW), and trial law.

■ Sidelights

Myra H. Immell told *SATA:* "Writing has been a way of life for me for more years than I care to acknowledge. When I was in high school, I decided I would be the next Marguerite Higgins, a female (wonder of all wonders) who did the impossible—became a foreign correspondent for the *New York Times.* I could—would—I determined, be even better and more famous than she was!

"One year as a journalism major burst that bubble. The trade-off was more than I was willing to tolerate. Clawing my way to the top, compromising some of my integral beliefs and values to stay there, giving up a family was too high a price for me to pay. This was the 1950s, and the truth of that era was that I'd probably end up doing the fashion news or some other equally thrilling topic. That wouldn't do for me either. So I switched my major, and love for writing soon took second place to languages other than English and people other than Americans. Writing was relegated to academic papers and private correspondence.

"In the late 1960s my husband and I moved to his home state of Ohio, where I ended up getting a job in educational publishing. Once again, writing reared its head. I became an editor—in two languages. I soon discovered that in that particular publishing arena at the grade levels on which I focused, the manuscript sent in by the 'author' often bore little or no resemblance to the final product that resided in our sons' and daughters' school desks or lockers. More often than not, the real author was the underpaid editor whose name never even appeared on the credits page and who never saw a cent of royalties. One day, I promised myself, I would actually be credited as author on a book that I wrote.

"Not until the 1990s did that promise to myself become a reality. I wrote two nonfiction books for young people. History is my avocation, and in history I have found a multitude of living, breathing individuals and fascinating 'stories' to tell young and old about. What happened yesterday is as much history as what happened years or centuries ago. On the other hand, the people of Richard Plantagenet's times were as individualistic and vibrant and three-dimensional as this week's movie or rock stars. I want others to share my enthusiasms and acknowledge why we are what we are today and what helps us be who we are.

"As I still work full-time in publishing, my writing has to be done at night and on weekends. Because of that, the research, development, and manuscript creation processes may take longer than I'd like and the books slower to appear on the market. But that's okay ... for now."

*　　*　　*

INGRAM, Scott 1948-

■ Personal

Born September 27, 1948, in Schenectady, NY; son of William Ingram (a consultant) and Winifred Sellick (a realtor); married, 1976; wife's name, Carol (an artist); children: Miles, Abby. *Education:* University of Connecticut, B.A.; Wesleyan University, M.A. *Hobbies and other interests:* Bicycling, guitar.

■ Addresses

Home—101 Culver Lane, Portland, CT 06480. *Office*—245 Long Hill Rd., Middletown, CT 06457. *Electronic mail*—singram@weeklyreader.com.

■ Career

Weekly Reader Corp., managing editor, 1979—. Member of Board of Education, Portland, CT.

■ Awards, Honors

Educational Press Awards, 1985, 1988, 1994, and 1995.

■ Writings

Bloody Waters: Terrorizing Shark Tales, illustrated by Ron Rundo, Lowell House, 1995.
Beast: Hair-Raising Horror Stories, Lowell House, 1996.
More Scary Stories for Stormy Nights, Lowell House, 1996.

■ Sidelights

Scott Ingram told *SATA:* "Reading and writing have always been at the center of my life. People who knew me thirty years ago would not be surprised to learn that I make my living with language. As an author, editor, and parent I get a great deal of enjoyment from passing my scary stories under my kids' stern eyes and seeing them make faces as they read something icky that I have invented.

"Oddly enough, I think writing gross stuff has increased my stature with my kids; before this, I was just a regular old dad who wrote news stories for Weekly Reader. Now that they know characters in my stories are filled with worms or eaten by sharks, they think I'm really onto something—they actually talk about my work with their friends. Ahhh ... success."

*　　*　　*

JACKSON, Woody 1948-

■ Personal

Born October 9, 1948, in Newark, NJ; son of Russell W. (a lawyer) and Emily (Barclay) Jackson; married Rebecca Gooch (a bookkeeper), December 29, 1984; children: Kelsey, Bjorn, Leif, Macon. *Education:* Middlebury College, B.A., 1970; Yale School of Art, M.F.A., 1980. *Hobbies and other interests:* Outdoor sports including skiing and soccer, reading, playing with children.

■ Addresses

Home—60 Seminary St., Middlebury, VT 05753. *Office*—P.O. Box 906, 52 Seymour St., Middlebury, VT 05753.

■ Career

Artist. Holy Cow Inc., Middlebury, VT, president, 1983—. Parent Child Center, Middlebury, VT, board member/treasurer 1982—; Middlebury Little League, coach. *Member:* Vermont Land Trust, American Farmland Trust, Heifer Project International.

■ Writings

Counting Cows, Harcourt, 1995.

■ Work in Progress

Two more books for children, *A Cow's Alfalphabet* and *Where Are We Going Daddy?*

WOODY JACKSON

■ Sidelights

After graduating from Middlebury College in 1970, Woody Jackson moved into a commune with some of his friends and did odd jobs on nearby farms to earn a living. After eight years, Jackson decided to enroll in the Yale School of Art, where he received his master's degree in fine arts in 1980.

Returning to Vermont, Jackson began designing cow tee-shirts to sell in local shops; one of these shirts turned his life around. Ben Cohen, co-founder of Ben and Jerry's ice cream, discovered one of Jackson's tee-shirts and licensed the design for use in promoting his popular product.

In an interview with Dan Chu and Martha Babcock of *People Magazine,* Cohen remarked that the cow "was an image that went with our ice cream."

The Ben & Jerry's Cow may long be the image for which Woody Jackson is best known. His picture book, *Counting Cows,* is a counting book for preschoolers that features the artist's favorite subject. In a review of the work in *Publishers Weekly,* the critic surmises: "Ice cream connoisseurs might recognize the black-and-white bovines in this picture book debut from another setting: Jackson's distinctive critters decorate a number of Ben and Jerry's ice cream parlors."

For Jackson, translating his art into books seemed a natural transition. He told *SATA,* "I have been making prints of cows and Vermont since 1972. I love the farmers, cows, and beauty of the Champlain Valley. *Counting Cows* was a natural extension of my work."

■ Works Cited

Chu, Dan, and Martha K. Babcock, "The Whole Country Cowtows as Woody Jackson Makes His Big Moove Toward Udder Success," *People Magazine,* August 28, 1989, pp. 100-101.
Review of *Counting Cows, Publishers Weekly,* August 7, 1995, p. 459.

■ For More Information See

PERIODICALS

School Library Journal, November, 1995, p. 91.

*   *   *

JOHNS, Avery
See COUSINS, Margaret

K

KALECHOFSKY, Roberta 1931-

■ Personal

Born May 11, 1931, in Brooklyn, NY; daughter of Julius
(a lawyer) and Naomi (maiden name, Jacobs) Kirchik;
married Robert Kalechofsky (a mathematician), June 7,
1953; children: Hal, Neal. *Education:* Brooklyn College,
B.A., 1952; New York University, M.A., 1956, Ph.D.,
1970. *Politics:* Liberal. *Religion:* Jewish. *Hobbies and
other interests:* Animal rights, vegetarianism, history.

■ Career

Publisher and writer. Micah Publications, Inc., Marble-
head, MA, publisher, 1975—. *Member:* Amnesty International, National Writers Union (charter member),
Association of Jewish Book Publishers, Anti-Slavery
Society, Jews for Animal Rights (founder).

■ Awards, Honors

Fellowship in creative writing, National Endowment for
the Arts, 1982; fellowship in fiction, Massachusetts
Council on Arts, 1987; Kind Writers Make Kind
Readers award, Fund for Animals, for *A Boy, a Chicken,
and the Lion of Judah.*

■ Writings

FOR CHILDREN

*A Boy, a Chicken, and the Lion of Judah: How Ari
Became a Vegetarian,* illustrated by Anselm Atkins,
Micah, 1996.

OTHER

*Bodmin, 1349: An Epic Novel of Christians and Jews in
the Plague Years,* Micah, 1982.
(Editor with Robert Kalechofsky) *South African Jewish
Voices,* Micah, 1982.
*Haggadah for the Liberated Lamb: Bilingual Edition,
Hebrew and English,* revised edition, Micah, 1988.
(Editor with Robert Kalechofsky) *The Global Anthology
of Jewish Women Writers,* Micah, 1990.

ROBERTA KALECHOFSKY

*Autobiography of a Revolutionary: Essays on Animal and
Human Rights,* Micah, 1991.
(Editor) *Judaism and Animal Rights: Classical and
Contemporary Responses,* Micah, 1992.
*Haggadah for the Vegetarian Family: An Egalitarian
Traditional Service,* Micah, 1993.
*Justice, My Brother, My Sister: Life and Death in a
Mexican Family,* Micah, 1993.
K'tia, A Savior of the Jewish People (short stories),
Micah, 1996.

The Jewish Vegetarian Year Cookbook: Reading and Recipes, Micah, 1996.

(Editor) *Rabbis and Vegetarianism: An Evolving Tradition,* Micah, 1996.

Also author of *George Orwell,* a monograph; *Rejected Essays and Other Matters;* and *Solomon's Wisdom.* Works have been translated into Italian, including the novella *La Hoya* (translated as *Veduta Di Toledo*).

■ Work in Progress

Job Enters a Pain Clinic, short stories; research on social reform movements of the nineteenth century: women's rights, abolition of slavery, liberation of Jews from ghettos and civic disabilities, animal rights.

■ Sidelights

Roberta Kalechofsky told *SATA:* "As a publisher, independent scholar, and writer, publishing and research feed my writing life as continuous acts of communication. I began Micah Publications as a small, independent press in 1975 to solve a specific publishing problem as a writer, but came to realize that publishing was another form of communication. In 1985, when I became actively involved with the Animal Rights movement, my press became a vehicle for publishing material for this movement, which I regard as the leading edge of a new sensibility. My children's book for vegetarian children, *A Boy, a Chicken, and the Lion of Judah,* was awarded the Kind Writers Make Kind Readers Award from the Fund for Animals.

"Unfortunately, publishing also seriously reduces one's time for writing, and there is a persistent tension between writing and publishing—as there is for me between being a wife and mother. I also like to garden, take dancing and aerobic classes, walk an hour a day, and be physically active. I like to cook and read cookbooks, and I have written one. I even like to clean house sometimes. These activities, or what I call 'living' as opposed to writing, also create tension and the need to search for balance between life and fiction, whose purpose is to create an alternative life.

"My fiction, which often is historical fiction, using original chronicles and documents, has found a particularly appreciative audience in Italy. My novella, *La Hoya,* was translated into Italian and published in Italy as *Veduta Di Toledo* by Palomar. It received excellent reviews in major Italian papers and has been used in several college courses on American writers at the University of Florence. Several other stories of mine have also been translated into Italian and published in Italian-language anthologies.

"My historical fiction deals with the inter-relationship between Jews and Christians, which I regard as a primary theme in European civilization."

KALISH, Claire M. 1947-

■ Personal

Born October 2, 1947, in New York, NY; daughter of Sy (an importer and exporter of fashion wear) and Roz (a bookkeeper) Goldberg; children: Adina, Michael, Alex. *Education:* Attended Syracuse University, 1965-66, Adelphi University, B.A., 1969; Queens College, 1970-71.

■ Addresses

Home—5530 West Idlewood Lane, Atlanta, GA 30327.

■ Career

Art educator, fashion and jewelry designer, illustrator. Art educator at a private school in Lawrence, Long Island, 1969-72, head of the summer program, 1967-72; art teacher and chair of the department at a private school in Atlanta, GA, 1971-78; consultant for art education methods and workshops for teachers, 1971-80. Jewelry design, 1970-71; interior design, ongoing; centerpiece business, 1988—; shirt design, 1995—. Travel consultant, 1985—. *Member:* Museum of Modern Art, High Museum of Art (Atlanta, GA), Kappa-Pi (National Art Honorary Society).

CLAIRE M. KALISH

ILLUSTRATOR; ALL WRITTEN BY RHONDA VANSANT AND BARBARA L. DONDIEGO

Cats, Dogs, and Classroom Pets: Science in Art, Song, and Play, TAB Books, 1995.
Moths, Butterflies, Insects and Spiders: Science in Art, Song and Play, TAB Books, 1995.
Seeds, Flowers, and Trees: Science in Art, Song and Play, McGraw-Hill, 1996.
Shells, Whales, and Fishtails: Science in Art, Song, and Play, McGraw-Hill, 1996.

■ Work in Progress

Dinosaurs and Endangered Species; illustrations for a book of quotes for a psychologist to better impart ideas to her patients visually.

■ Sidelights

Claire Kalish told *SATA:* "I write and illustrate journals of my travels as well as the memories of my life. I have found that it isn't always the significant event or the important day we remember, but often a feeling, a smell, a color. This becomes my challenge to express on the page. I am like a strainer with all of my life's experiences passing through the mesh. The most notable land on the pages of my journal.

"While raising a family took me away from full-time teaching, I continued with freelance design and illustration. Currently, my work with teaching science according to the learner's stage of development brings me back to teaching again, this time through illustration. With this innovative series, children learn through their five senses.

"I draw, I teach, children learn...."

* * *

KELLEY, True (Adelaide) 1946-

■ Personal

Born February 25, 1946, in Cambridge, MA; daughter of Mark E. (an illustrator) and Adelaide (an artist; maiden name, True) Kelley; spouse: Steven W. Lindblom (a writer and illustrator of children's books); children: Jada Winter Lindblom. *Education:* University of New Hampshire, B.A., 1968; attended Rhode Island School of Design, 1968-71. *Hobbies and other interests:* Skiing, biking, canoeing, travel.

■ Addresses

Home—79 Old Denny Hill, Warner, NH 03278.

■ Career

Free-lance illustrator, 1971—; writer, 1978—. *Member:* Society of Children's Book Writers and Illustrators, Authors Guild, Audubon Society, New Hampshire

TRUE KELLEY

Writers and Publishers Project, Warner Raconteur's Association.

■ Awards, Honors

Children's Choice, International Reading Association, 1982, for *A Valentine for Fuzzboom;* Outstanding Science Trade Book for Children citation, National Science Teachers Association, 1987, for *What the Moon is Like;* Children's Books of the Year, Child Study Children's Book Committee, 1995, for *I've Got Chicken Pox;* 100 Best Titles selection, New York Public Library, and Parent's Choice Honor book, both 1995, both for *Three Stories You Can Read to Your Dog.*

■ Writings

SELF-ILLUSTRATED

(With Steven Lindblom) *The Mouses' Terrible Christmas,* Lothrop, 1980.
(With Steven Lindblom) *The Mouses' Terrible Halloween,* Lothrop, 1980.
A Valentine for Fuzzboom, Houghton, 1981.
Buggly Bear's Hiccup Cure, Parents Magazine Press, 1982.
The Mystery of the Stranger in the Barn, Putnam, 1986.
Look, Baby! Listen, Baby! Do, Baby!, Dutton, 1987.
Let's Eat!, Dutton, 1989.
Day Care Teddy Bear, Random House, 1990.
(With Christel Kleitsch) *It Happened at Pickle Lake,* Dutton, 1993.
I've Got Chicken Pox, Dutton, 1994.
Hammers and Mops, Pencils and Pots: A First Book of Tools and Gadgets We Use around the House, Crown, 1994.
Look Again at Funny Animals, Candlewick, 1996.
Look Again at My Funny Family, Candlewick, 1996.

ILLUSTRATOR OF FICTION

Ann Cole, Carolyn Haas, Faith Bushnell, and Betty Weinburger, *I Saw a Purple Cow*, Little, Brown, 1976.

Michael Pellowski, *Clara Cow Joins the Circus*, Parents Magazine Press, 1981.

Steven Lindblom, *Let's Give Kitty A Bath*, Addison Wesley, 1982.

Ann Cole, Carolyn Haas, and Betty Weinburger, *Purple Cow to the Rescue*, Little, Brown, 1982.

Joanne Oppenheim, *James Will Never Die*, Dodd, 1982.

Riki Levinson, *Touch! Touch!*, Dutton, 1986.

Joanna Cole, *Mixed-Up Magic*, Scholastic, 1987.

Debra Meryl, *Baby's Peek-A-Boo Album*, Putnam, 1989.

Susan Breslow and Sally Blakemore, *I Really Want A Dog*, Dutton, 1989.

A. F. Bauman, *Guess Where You're Going, Guess What You'll Do*, Houghton, 1989.

Michaela Morgan, *Dinostory*, Dutton, 1991.

Wendy Lewison, *Where's Baby?*, Scholastic, 1992.

Wendy Lewison, *Uh-Oh Baby*, Scholastic, 1992.

Wendy Lewison, *Bye-Bye Baby*, Scholastic, 1992.

Stephanie Calmenson, *Rollerskates!*, Scholastic, 1992.

Raffi, *Spider on the Floor* (A Raffi Song Book), Crown, 1993.

Patricia Brennan Demuth, *In Trouble With Teacher*, Dutton, 1995.

Sara Swan Miller, *Three Stories You Can Read to Your Dog*, Houghton, 1995.

Sara Swan Miller, *Three Stories You Can Read to Your Cat*, Houghton, 1996.

ILLUSTRATOR OF NONFICTION

Franklyn Branley, *Sun Dogs and Shooting Stars: A Skywatcher's Calendar*, Houghton, 1980.

Gilda and Melvin Berger, *The Whole World of Hands*, Houghton, 1982.

Franklyn Branley, *Water for the World*, Crowell, 1982.

The Scribblers Play Book, *Sunshine and Snowflakes*, Western, 1982.

Ben Schneiderman, *Let's Learn Basic*, Little, Brown, 1984.

Joyce Mitchell, *My Mommy Makes Money*, Little, Brown, 1984.

Franklyn Branley, *Shivers and Goosebumps: How We Keep Warm*, Crowell, 1984.

Joanna Cole, *Cuts, Breaks, and Bruises: How Your Body Heals*, Crowell, 1985.

Eric Arnold and Jeffrey Loeb, *Lights Out! Kids Talk About Summer Camp*, Little, Brown, 1986.

Franklyn Branley, *What the Moon Is Like*, Crowell, 1986.

Patricia Lauber, *Get Ready for Robots*, Crowell, 1986.

Franklyn Branley, *It's Raining Cats and Dogs: All Kinds of Weather and Why We Have It*, Houghton, 1986.

James Deem, *How to Find a Ghost*, Houghton, 1988.

Philip Balestrino, *The Skeleton Inside You*, Crowell, 1989, published as *El esqueleto dentro de ti* (translated by Daniel Santacruz), Harper/ArcoIris, 1995.

(With Steven Lindblom) Niles, Gregory, and Douglas Eldredge, *The Fossil Factory: A Kid's Guide to Digging Up Dinosaurs, Exploring Evolution & Finding Fossils*, Addison/Wesley, 1989.

Franklyn Branley, *Superstar: The Supernova of 1987*, Crowell, 1990.

Paul Showers, *How Many Teeth?*, Harper, 1991.

James Deem, *How to Catch a Flying Saucer*, Houghton, 1991.

Judy Donnelly, *All Around the World*, Grosset & Dunlap, 1991.

Paul Showers, *Look At Your Eyes*, Harper, 1992.

James Deem, *How to Hunt Buried Treasure*, Houghton, 1992.

James Deem, *How to Read Your Mother's Mind*, Houghton, 1994.

James Deem, *How to Make a Mummy Talk*, Houghton, 1995.

Franklyn Branley, *What Makes a Magnet?*, Crowell, 1997.

Also illustrator of textbooks.

■ Work in Progress

Illustrations for Franklyn Branley's *Floating in Space*, for Crowell.

■ Sidelights

With more than twenty-five years as an illustrator to her credit, True Kelley continues to write and illustrate nonfiction books, chapter books, picture books, and baby books for children. Her black-and-white, pen and ink, or watercolor cartoons and drawings are designed to delight babies, teach lessons about science, and charm young readers. Whether she illustrates the texts of others, works with her husband, Steven Lindblom, or writes and illustrates her own books, Kelley maintains her reputation as the creator of humorous, expressive, and informative work.

Kelley once told *SATA* that she developed her interest in illustration when she was just a child. "My mother illustrated children's books and my father was art director for *Child Life* magazine. My first published self-illustrated story appeared there when I was four years old. After graduating from college with a degree in elementary education, I attended Rhode Island School of Design. I began working as an advertising illustrator and was greatly influenced by my father, who is still an illustrator. My interest in children led me to doing textbook illustrations."

Kelley's illustrations for the texts of other authors have won praise. In a review of *I Really Want a Dog*, a book written by Susan Breslow and Sally Blakemore, *Horn Book* contributor Hanna B. Zeiger concluded that "children will love the bright, humorous illustrations of dogs in every conceivable situation." The artist's canine portrayals in Sara Swan Miller's *Three Stories You Can Read to Your Dog* also received praise; a *Publishers Weekly* critic noted that Kelley demonstrates "familiarity with doggy expressions and gestures." Gale W. Sherman remarked in *School Library Journal* that

Kelley's work for this book makes the text "even funnier," and Ilene Cooper of *Booklist* described Kelley's watercolor illustrations as "clever and full of vigor." In a review of another animal book, Raffi's *Spider on the Floor, School Library Journal* contributor Joyce Richards commented that Kelley's "sumptuous watercolors ... seem to jump off the pages."

As several critics have noted, Kelley's cartoon-like illustrations make excellent supplements to the texts of nonfiction works, and make information more easily understood. *The Fossil Factory,* for example, which Kelley illustrated with her husband, Steven Lindblom, provides children with accessible scientific information about the petrified remains of dinosaurs and other ancient animals we now know only as fossils. In the words of a *Publishers Weekly* reviewer, Kelley's and Lindblom's work exhibits "a wealth of paleontological lore in a winning fashion." According to Malcolm W. Browne, writing in the *New York Times Book Review,* the drawings and diagrams in *The Fossil Factory* are "simple and delightful." Kelley's pictures for Franklyn Branley's *What Makes a Magnet?,* another nonfiction title, were favorably noted by *Booklist* reviewer Denia Hester, who commended her "bright, splashy watercolors that make scientific exploration look like the fun it ought to be."

Kelley has also illustrated a group of books written by James M. Deem which explore unusual subjects. *How to Make a Mummy Talk* explains what mummies are as well as their historical and cultural significance. Kelley's illustrations for this work are black and white, cartoon-like sketches. These drawings, according to Mary Harris Veeder of *Booklist,* "maintain some sense of humor" in this book. *How to Read Your Mother's Mind,* Deem's

Believe it or not, I'm actually sick of ginger ale.
The house is horribly quiet.
"YAH YAH chickle pickle poxle doxle!" I yell. "I can't STAND it!"

Jess starts to get stir-crazy after staying home for a couple of days with the chicken pox. (From *I've Got Chicken Pox,* written and illustrated by Kelley.)

book on extrasensory perception, also features Kelley's black and white cartoons. These "witty cartoons ... further clarify the text," noted a critic for *Kirkus Reviews.* Ilene Cooper of *Booklist* described the illustrations as "terrific," while *Bulletin of the Center for Children's Books* contributor Roger Sutton praised the "lively improvisational flair" of Kelley's artwork.

One of the first books Kelley both wrote and illustrated, *A Valentine for Fuzzboom,* tells about a rabbit who has a crush on another. Lima Bean admires the haughty Fuzzboom and makes valentines for him for months before she finally sends him the best one. Yet Fuzzboom fails to send Lima Bean a valentine in return. Lima Bean is so upset, she barely notices when she receives a lovely gift from another friend. Later, Lima Bean realizes her mistake and marches to Fuzzboom's house to tell him what she thinks of him. Fuzzboom responds by saying he likes her assertiveness and by asking Lima Bean to be his valentine. Lima Bean loudly tells him, "No!" *A Valentine for Fuzzboom* was selected as a Children's Choice book by the International Reading Association in 1982; Barbara Elleman of *Booklist* praised the book's open design, which provides "space for the humor in both text and drawing to come through."

Look, Baby! Listen, Baby! Do, Baby! showcases Kelley's illustrations and encourages babies to look, listen, and then act in three sections. In the first section, a baby can look at different kinds of baby mouths, noses, eyes, hands, and feet functioning in a variety of ways. The listening section provides an assortment of sounds accompanied by illustrations of the things (or creatures) that make them. The Do Baby! section features babies crying, crawling, playing, and doing other things babies do. The drawings of babies in this book, wrote Denise Wilms of *Booklist,* are "droll and cheerful." A *Publishers Weekly* critic praised the diverse "expressions and mannerisms" of the babies in the book. "Definitely and delightfully a book for sharing ... and enjoying many times over."

Let's Eat! gives readers an idea of what people eat everyday and on holidays. It tells where food comes from, where it is eaten, and how various people eat it. It describes favorite foods and even food tricks. This book with few words presents illustrations which, in the words of *School Library Journal* contributor Louise L. Sherman, are "clear, whimsical, simple yet expressive watercolor and pen-and-ink." "True Kelley has a marvelous eye for the funny and naughty little actions of children," Margaret A. Bush similarly commented in *Horn Book.* Barbara Elleman of *Booklist* concluded that the book is a "cornucopia of information to consume in nibbles or large bites."

I've Got Chicken Pox, according to *Booklist* critic Carolyn Phelan, is a "first-rate" introduction to the common childhood disease. This book provides "Pox Facts" on each page spread in addition to a story. The narrator of the story, Jess, is excited when she learns that she has chicken pox. She will miss a week of school!

The dog food was great!

"This is better than squirrels," you said to yourself.
"I think I will be a House Dog again."

Illustrated by Kelley, *Three Stories You Can Read to Your Dog* contains a collection of humorous stories written from a dog's perspective. (Written by Sara Swan Miller.)

But, despite the fact that she gets to drink ginger ale and eat ice cream, it is not too long before Jess gets tired of the chicken pox. She is feverish, itchy, and bored. Her brother, who is jealous of her pox, torments her. When Jess finally returns to school, she has a great time, especially since she gets to explain her illness to her friends. As Denise L. Moll of *School Library Journal* pointed out, Kelley's cartoon, watercolor illustrations "are vibrant and appealing." A critic for *Publishers Weekly* described the book as a "humorously illustrated, jaunty tale."

True Kelley lives in New Hampshire. When she is not writing and illustrating children's books, she enjoys skiing, biking, and canoeing.

■ Works Cited

Browne, Malcolm W., review of *The Fossil Factory, New York Times Book Review,* June 24, 1990, p. 28.

Bush, Margaret A., review of *Let's Eat!, Horn Book,* May-June, 1989, pp. 385-86.

Cooper, Ilene, review of *How to Read Your Mother's Mind, Booklist,* March 1, 1994, p. 1256.

Cooper, Ilene, review of *Three Stories You Can Read to Your Dog, Booklist,* April 15, 1995, p. 1500.

Elleman, Barbara, review of *A Valentine for Fuzzboom, Booklist,* March 15, 1981, pp. 1028, 1030.

Elleman, Barbara, review of *Let's Eat!, Booklist,* May 15, 1989, p. 1650.

Review of *The Fossil Factory, Publishers Weekly,* February 23, 1990, p. 219.

Hester, Denia, review of *What Makes a Magnet?, Booklist,* November 1, 1996.

Review of *How to Read Your Mother's Mind, Kirkus Reviews,* March 1, 1994.

Review of *I've Got Chicken Pox, Publishers Weekly,* May 2, 1994, p. 306.

Review of *Look, Baby! Listen, Baby! Do, Baby!, Publishers Weekly,* September 11, 1987, p. 90.

Moll, Denise L., review of *I've Got Chicken Pox, School Library Journal,* June, 1994, p. 107.

Phelan, Carolyn, review of *I've Got Chicken Pox, Booklist,* May 15, 1994, p. 1683.

Richards, Joyce, review of *Spider on the Floor, School Library Journal,* February, 1994, p. 90.

Sherman, Gale W., review of *Three Stories You Can Read to Your Dog, School Library Journal,* April, 1995, p. 113.

Sherman, Louise L., review of *Let's Eat!, School Library Journal,* March, 1989, p. 164.

Sutton, Roger, review of *How to Read Your Mother's Mind, Bulletin of the Center for Children's Books,* March, 1994.

Review of *Three Stories You Can Read to Your Dog,*
Publishers Weekly, February 20, 1995, p. 206.
Veeder, Mary Harris, review of *How to Make a Mummy
Talk,* Booklist, September 15, 1995.
Wilms, Denise M., review of *Look, Baby! Listen, Baby!
Do, Baby!,* Booklist, September 15, 1987, p. 150.
Zeiger, Hanna B., review of *I Really Want a Dog,* Horn
Book, July/August, 1990, p. 442.

■ For More Information See

PERIODICALS

Booklist, January 1, 1993, p. 807; March 15, 1994, p.
1368.
Kirkus Reviews, March 1, 1981, p. 280.
New York Times Book Review, May 22, 1994, p. 34.
Publishers Weekly, August 16, 1991, p. 58.
School Library Journal, October, 1987, p. 114; September, 1991, p. 263; May, 1995, p. 84.

* * *

KIDD, Ronald 1948-

■ Personal

Born April 29, 1948, in St. Louis, MO; son of Paul R.
and Ida Sue (Smith) Kidd; married Yvonne Leona
Martin (a marketing executive), October 1, 1977. *Education:* University of California, Los Angeles, B.A.,
1971; California State University, Long Beach, Certificate of Secondary Education, 1972.

■ Addresses

Home and office—2231 Chickering Lane, Nashville, TN
37215. *Agent*—Amy Berkower, Writers House, Inc., 21
West 26th St., New York, NY 10010.

■ Career

Educational Resource Associates, Los Angeles, CA,
production manager, 1972-75; Family Films, Panorama
City, CA, writer and producer, 1975-76; Bowmar/Noble
Publishers, Inc., Los Angeles, editor, 1976-79; RK
Associates, Altadena, CA, owner, 1979-85; Walt Disney
Records, Burbank, CA, creative director, 1985-89; Kidd
& Company, Inc., owner, 1989—. Member of Edgar
Award judging committee for young adult category,
1991. *Military service:* California Air National Guard,
1969-75.

■ Awards, Honors

Grammy Award nomination for best children's recording, National Academy of Recording Arts and Sciences,
1975, for *Mr. Popper's Penguins;* Learning Magazine
Awards, 1976, for best filmstrips; Family Circle Golden
Leaf Award, 1981, for nutrition education; Golden
Eagle Award, Council on International Nontheatrical
Events (CINE), 1982, for *Winnie the Pooh Discovers the
Seasons;* Children's Choice Award, International Reading Association, 1982, for *Dunker;* Best Books of the

RONALD KIDD

Year, *School Library Journal,* 1983, and California
Young Reader Medal nomination, 1989, both for *Sizzle
& Splat;* Books for the Teen Age, New York Public
Library, 1984, for *Who Is Felix the Great?;* Edgar Award
nomination for best young adult mystery, 1989, and
Young Hoosier Book Award nomination, 1989, both for
Second Fiddle: A Sizzle & Splat Mystery; five Gold
Records as producer (each for 500,000 records sold),
1989, 1990, 1996; finalist, Nantucket Short Play Competition, for *Shaker Loops,* 1994.

■ Writings

That's What Friends Are For, Lodestar, 1978.
Dunker, Lodestar, 1982.
Who Is Felix the Great?, Lodestar, 1983.
Sizzle & Splat, Lodestar, 1983.
The Glitch: A Computer Fantasy, Lodestar, 1985.
Second Fiddle: A Sizzle & Splat Mystery, Lodestar, 1988.
Sammy Carducci's Guide to Women, Lodestar, 1991.
(Compiler and editor) *On Top of Old Smoky: A Collection of Songs and Stories from Appalachia,* Ideals,
1992.
Little Big League (adapted from the motion picture),
Turner, 1994.
Family under Fire: A Story of the Civil War, Chattanooga Regional History Museum, 1995.

Also adaptor of "Sound Story Books" series (includes
*Beauty and the Beast, 101 Dalmatians, Bambi, The
Little Mermaid, Winnie the Pooh and Tigger Too, Snow
White, Batman in the Case of the Missing Egg, Disney's
Cinderella, Disney's The Lion King, Robin Hood, The*

Jungle Book, Aladdin, Goldilocks and the Three Bears, It's Time, Jack and the Beanstalk, and *Peter Pan*), Sight & Sound/Western Publishing, 1990-92.

"DANNY DORFMAN'S DREAM BAND" SERIES; ILLUSTRATED BY BOB JONES; PUBLISHED BY PUFFIN

A Legend in His Own Mind, 1992.
Meet Maximum Clyde, 1992.
The Case of the Missing Case, 1992.
Rapunzel, Sort of, 1992.

PICTURE BOOKS

(With Tom Sullivan) *Common Senses,* Ideals, 1982.
The Nutcracker, Ideals, 1985.
The Littlest Angel Earns His Halo, Ideals, 1985.
The Littlest Angel Meets the Newest Angel, Ideals, 1985.
Grandpa's Hammer, Habitat for Humanity International, 1995.
Raising the Roof, Habitat for Humanity International, 1995.
Building Friends, Habitat for Humanity International, 1996.
Doorway to the World, Habitat for Humanity International, 1996.

INTERACTIVE FICTION

Tiny, Pitman, 1985.
Hills of Gold, Pitman, 1985.
Downtown Detective, Pitman, 1985.
The Magic Record, Pitman, 1985.
Planet of Dreams, Pitman, 1985.

PLAYS

Sammy Carducci's Guide to Women, Dramatic Publishing, 1995.

Other plays include *Tough Call,* 1992, and *Christ of the Coopermans,* 1994, both produced at the Eugene O'Neill Theater Center; and *Shaker Loops,* 1994.

TELEPLAYS AND SCREENPLAYS

Welcome to Pooh Corner (television pilot), Disney Channel, 1982.
Winnie the Pooh Discovers the Seasons (film), Walt Disney Productions, 1982.
Skills for the New Technology (set of three educational films), Walt Disney Productions, 1983.
I Love a Computer (educational film), Walt Disney Productions, 1983.
"The Secret Life of Ricky Stratton" (series episode), *Silver Spoons,* NBC-TV, 1984.

OTHER

(With Lisa Eisenberg) *The Official Name-Caller's Handbook* (humor), Ace, 1981.
(With Verne Bauman) *Power Painting: Computer Graphics on the Macintosh,* Bantam, 1985.

Author of short stories and over 100 educational filmstrips. Author of more than 30 titles for Walt Disney Productions' book and tape programs, including *The Rocketeer, Dick Tracy,* and *Who Framed Roger Rabbit?.* Producer of sound recording *Mr. Popper's Penguins.* Also contributor to reading programs, including *Point 32 Reading Program, Crosswinds Reading Program, HILO Reading Program,* and *My Fun with Reading.*

■ Adaptations

Dunker was adapted into a drama for *Scholastic Scope* magazine.

■ Work in Progress

How Can I Keep from Singing?, a musical with composer Michael Silversher.

■ Sidelights

Ronald Kidd has had a varied career in entertainment and educational products for children, including the production of educational films and filmstrips, record production for the Disney corporation, and the writing of picture books and such popular juvenile novels as *Dunker* and *Danny Dorfman's Dream Band.* "I guess you could say I became a writer because of the 1971 Los Angeles earthquake," Kidd once told *SATA.* Kidd became a driver for a bookmobile that temporarily took the place of damaged branch libraries, and it was then that he discovered the world of children's literature and determined that he could write such a book himself.

Following the old adage of writing what you know about, Kidd constructed a story based on his own school years and a friend of his who died of leukemia. *That's What Friends Are For* is told by young Gary, who feels he let his friend Scott down by not visiting him in the hospital during his last two weeks of life. Disturbed by Scott's decline, Gary had simply convinced himself that Scott would not die and thus put off such a visit until it was too late. Gary writes this first person narrative in partial expiation for the guilt he feels. Karen Harris, writing in *School Library Journal,* found this first novel "thoughtful" and "convincing," while Zena Sutherland of the *Bulletin of the Center for Children's Books* noted that it was "well constructed" and "perceptive in dealing with a young teenager's adjustment to death."

Kidd's next novel, *Dunker,* was inspired by his work with child actors while producing films. He came to understand the conflicts such young performers have balancing their private lives with careers, with most losing prematurely the freedom and innocence of childhood. Bobby Rothman is Kidd's fictional personification of such conflicts. Pursuing a parent-driven career in radio commercials, Bobby also discovers a love for basketball. At only five-feet-four-inches tall, Bobby is scrappy on the court and wins a place on the varsity squad with one proviso from his parents: if a conflict arises between career and basketball, career must win. The inevitable happens, and Bobby is forced to fulfill this promise and miss a clutch game. Redemption also occurs, however, in the championship game. David Keyes in *Voice of Youth Advocates* commented that "play-by-play coverage of the games captures the excitement of the crowds and players," and *School Library Journal* concluded that Kidd "lends a light and readable style to this well-paced novel." *Dunker* went on to win a Children's Choice Award.

Sports also figured prominently in Kidd's third novel, *Who Is Felix the Great?*, a story of inter-generational conflict and understanding. "When I go to the ballpark and look down on the clipped grass and the white lines and the players moving in the sunshine, I feel like a boy again," Kidd explained to *SATA*. "I give myself over to the game. This book is the story of a young man and an old man who together try to do just that." Tim Julian tracks down a former player for the Chicago Cubs for a school project, a private memorial to his dead father who loved the shortstop, Felix the Great. But Felix turns out to be not so great; crusty and egotistical, the old man soon wants Tim to drive him all the way from Los Angeles to Chicago for an old-timers game. The subsequent trip provides lessons for both characters. Though Denise M. Wilms, in *Booklist,* found the story "marred by some contrived plotting," she noted that "Tim is quite sympathetic as a character." The character of Felix won the attention of *Horn Book* reviewer Ethel R. Twichell. Twichell concluded that with "defiant, pitiful Felix ... the author presents an interesting portrait of an old man whom success has ultimately eluded."

Kidd drew on more of his own youthful experiences with *Sizzle & Splat* and its sequel, *Second Fiddle,* both mysteries set in a youth orchestra. Sizzle, the female narrator, is the trumpet soloist for the youth orchestra, and Splat plays tuba. These two self-appointed detectives investigate what appears to be sabotage of their financially embattled orchestra. *Booklist*'s Wilms dubbed the first of the two novels "a lively mystery-adventure with high entertainment value," and *Voice of Youth Advocates* contributor Carmen Oyeneque noted that the sequel "should be as popular with readers as its predecessor." A *Kirkus Reviews* critic concluded that *Second Fiddle* was "comical, suspenseful, and thoroughly entertaining." More music is played up in *Danny Dorfman's Dream Band,* a four-part series about the adventures of a youthful guitarist who wants to be a rock star. Reviewing *A Legend in His Own Mind,* the first in the series, a reviewer for *Publishers Weekly* commented that "Kidd laces his brief caper with comical analogies and peppy dialogue bound to please his audience."

Other Kidd novels have explored the world of computers and boy and girl relations with humor and wonder. In *The Glitch,* which was a Junior Literary Guild selection, a computer unfriendly sixth-grader is literally sucked into a computer in an Alice-in-Wonderland sort of adventure which "moves quickly and holds a good measure of suspense," according to Barbara Elleman in *Booklist.* Sixth graders also figure in *Sammy Carducci's Guide to Women,* "an antic, lightweight tale about suburban [youth] in pursuit of the opposite sex," as *Kirkus Reviews* described the book. Eager to act older than he is and swagger more than his 4'2" frame allows, Sammy fixes his attentions on the voluptuous Becky,

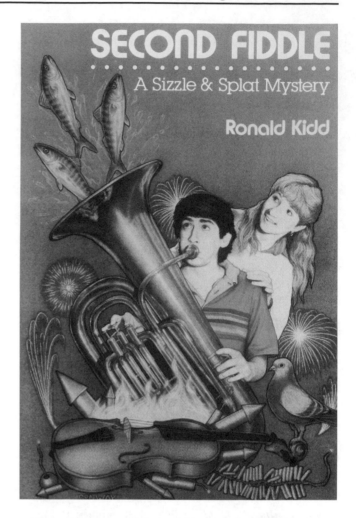

Sizzle (Prudence Szyznowski) and Splat, members of the Pirelli Youth Orchestra, are determined to find the pranksters who keep sabotaging their instruments. (Cover illustration by Michael Conway.)

who stands more than a foot taller than he. "Funny scenarios and sharp one-liners give this book instant appeal," concluded Todd Morning in *School Library Journal.*

In addition to novels for young readers, Kidd has also written text for numerous picture books and adapted popular cartoons and fairy tales for recorded books. In much of his work there is a unifying theme in the solace to be found in humor. Painful incidents become comical in Kidd's rendering; embarrassment and danger can both be alleviated with a touch of comedy. Researching the world of microcomputers for *The Glitch,* Kidd was at first put off with the plethora of technical terms, and in order to keep them straight, turned each of them into characters: the evil Delete, a dragon called GIGO (garbage in/garbage out). This fantastical, comic creation "somehow ... made the terms easier to remember, and a lot more fun," Kidd recalled for *SATA.* It was a lesson he learned well, and one he has taken with him in other titles.

■ Works Cited

Review of *Dunker, School Library Journal,* May, 1982, p. 86.

Elleman, Barbara, review of *The Glitch: A Computer Fantasy, Booklist,* February 15, 1986, p. 868.

Harris, Karen, review of *That's What Friends Are For, School Library Journal,* November, 1978, p. 76.

Keyes, David, review of *Dunker, Voice of Youth Advocates,* October, 1982, p. 44.

Review of *A Legend in His Own Mind: Danny Dorfman's Dream Band #1, Publishers Weekly,* May 18, 1992, p. 70.

Morning, Todd, review of *Sammy Carducci's Guide to Women, School Library Journal,* January, 1992, p. 114.

Oyeneque, Carmen, review of *Second Fiddle: A Sizzle & Splat Mystery, Voice of Youth Advocates,* October, 1988, p. 182.

Review of *Sammy Carducci's Guide to Women, Kirkus Reviews,* December 1, 1991, p. 1534.

Review of *Second Fiddle: A Sizzle & Splat Mystery, Kirkus Reviews,* May 15, 1988, p. 76.

Sutherland, Zena, review of *That's What Friends Are For, Bulletin of the Center for Children's Books,* May, 1979, p. 157.

Twichell, Ethel R., review of *Who Is Felix the Great?, Horn Book,* April, 1983, p. 171.

Wilms, Denise M., review of *Who Is Felix the Great?, Booklist,* August, 1983, pp. 1465-6.

Wilms, Denise M., review of *Sizzle & Splat, Booklist,* November 15, 1983, p. 498.

■ For More Information See

BOOKS

Helbig, Alethea K., and Agnes Regan Perkins, *Dictionary of American Children's Fiction: Books of Recognized Merit, 1985-1989,* Greenwood Press, 1993.

Reginald, Robert, *Science Fiction and Fantasy Literature, 1975-1991,* Gale, 1992.

PERIODICALS

Bulletin of the Center for Children's Books, July, 1983, p. 212; March, 1984, p. 130; February, 1986, p. 111; July, 1988, p. 232; January, 1992, p. 130.

Horn Book Guide, Spring, 1992, p. 67; Spring, 1993, p. 129.

School Library Journal, May, 1982, p. 86; December, 1982, p. 29; September, 1983, p. 136; March, 1986, p. 164.

—*Sketch by J. Sydney Jones*

*   *   *

KNYE, Cassandra
See DISCH, Thomas M(ichael)

KOERTGE, Ron(ald) 1940-

■ Personal

Surname is pronounced "*kur*-chee"; born April 22, 1940, in Olney, IL; son of William Henry (an owner of an ice cream store and school janitor) and Bulis Olive (a homemaker; maiden name, Fiscus) Koertge; married Bianca Richards (a counselor), November 4, 1992. *Education:* University of Illinois, B.A., 1962; University of Arizona, M.A., 1965.

■ Addresses

Home—1115 Oxley St., S. Pasadena, CA 91030. *Office*—Department of English, Pasadena City College, 1570 Colorado Blvd., Pasadena, CA 91106. *Agent*—William Reiss, John Hawkins and Associates, 71 West 23rd St., #1600, New York, NY 10010.

■ Career

Writer, 1962—. Pasadena City College, Pasadena, CA, professor of English, 1965—.

■ Awards, Honors

Books of the Decade citation, *Booklist,* 1988, for *The Arizona Kid;* Young Adult Author of the Year, Detroit Library System, 1990; Young People's Literature Award, Friends of American Writers, c. 1990, for *The Boy in the Moon;* Fellowship in literature (poetry), National Endowment for the Arts, 1991; Books for the

RON KOERTGE

Teen Age, New York Public Library, and Maine Student Book Award Master List citation, both 1992, both for *Mariposa Blues;* Books for the Teen Age, New York Public Library, and American Library Association (ALA) notable book citation, both 1993, both for *The Harmony Arms; Where the Kissing Never Stops, The Arizona Kid, The Boy in the Moon, The Harmony Arms,* and *Tiger, Tiger, Burning Bright* were all named ALA Best Books for Young Adults.

■ Writings

FOR YOUNG ADULTS

Where the Kissing Never Stops, Atlantic Monthly, 1986.
The Arizona Kid, Joy Street, 1988.
The Boy in the Moon, Little, Brown, 1990.
Mariposa Blues, Little, Brown, 1991.
The Harmony Arms, Little, Brown, 1992.
Tiger, Tiger, Burning Bright: A Novel, Orchard Books, 1994.
Confess-O-Rama, Orchard Books, 1996.

POETRY FOR ADULTS

The Father-Poems, Sumac Press, 1973.
Meat: Cherry's Market-Diary, MAG Press, 1973.
The Hired Nose, MAG Press, 1974.
My Summer Vacation, Venice Poetry, 1975.
Sex Object, Country Press, 1975, revised edition, Little Caesar, 1979.
(With Charles Stetler and Gerald Locklin) *Tarzan and Shane Meet the Toad,* Haas, 1975.
Cheap Thrills, Wormwood Review, 1976.
Men under Fire, Duck Down, 1976.
12 Photographs of Yellowstone, Red Hill, 1976.
How to Live on Five Dollars a Week, etc., Venice Poetry, 1977.
The Jockey Poems, Maelstrom, 1980.
Diary Cows, Little Caesar, 1981.
Fresh Meat, Kenmore, 1981.
Life on the Edge of the Continent: Selected Poems of Ronald Koertge, University of Arkansas Press, 1982.
High School Dirty Poems, Red Wind, 1991.
Making Love to Roget's Wife: Poems New & Selected, University of Arkansas Press, 1997.

Also a contributor to *The Maverick Poets: An Anthology,* Steve Kowit, editor, Gorilla Press, 1988.

OTHER

The Boogeyman (novel for adults), Norton, 1980.
100 Things to Write About (college textbook), Holt, 1990.

■ Work in Progress

The Heart of the City, Orchard Books.

■ Sidelights

Author Ron Koertge has not forgotten what it feels like to be young. The heroes of his stories for young adults suffer anxieties over acne pimples or being too short.

They ponder their futures and quarrel with eccentric or domineering parents. Most of all, they learn how to manage their sexual longings and their romantic impulses as they become seriously involved with girls they care about. While Koertge frequently uses humor to reveal a character, he never downplays the seriousness of these universal adolescent concerns. Jane Hoogestraat, in an essay for the *Dictionary of Literary Biography,* maintains that Koertge has made a name for himself with books that are "remarkable for the realism with which they present tough and not-so-tough teenage characters coming of age in a world of AIDS and widespread divorce, but often in a world in which tenderness and love are not absent."

Koertge was born in 1940, in Olney, Illinois. Both of his parents had grown up on working farms, and were then employed at a large dairy farm. While Koertge was still a youngster, his parents moved to Collinsville, Illinois, and opened an ice cream business. It flourished until the town's first supermarket opened, and then—like so many other specialty stores—it could not keep up with the new competition. Koertge's father became a janitor in the public school system while his mother stayed at

Gabriel's move to L.A. with his father proves to be a very eye-opening experience, as he learns to appreciate individuality and diversity in this comical coming-of-age story. (Cover illustration by Amy L. Wasserman.)

home. They were comfortable financially and, as the author once commented, "fairly happy."

An only child, Koertge said that he was "a pretty normal kid" who enjoyed sports and school. As a teenager he discovered a special talent—he had a "way with words." He could express himself well, and beyond that, he found himself open to the vast possibilities words offered as a means to communicate feelings. "I discovered I was more glib than most of my friends," he once commented, "but I also somehow sensed that my gift wouldn't be really valuable until I was older. Very early on, words seemed to have lives of their own. Still today, the way the words fit together and the way they lie on the music they generate is more interesting to me than the so-called arc of the story." In this way, Koertge was laying the groundwork for a career as a poet and novelist.

He also loved attention and had a flair for drama. Though not the class clown, he enjoyed saying and doing outrageous things. "I would say out loud things that other kids seemed reluctant to say," he once recalled. "I liked to shock people—to leave them lurching, not laughing." His sense of life's quirks was heightened by a serious bout of rheumatic fever when he was a young teen. The illness, which had the potential to debilitate him with a weakened heart for the rest of his life, or even kill him, left Koertge with a "sense of the insubstantiality of my body and made me alternately tentative and foolishly bold."

Koertge began writing in high school. "It was certainly something I was drawn to partly because it was something I could do," he remembered. His interest in the field led him to the University of Illinois, where he earned his bachelor's degree in 1962, and then on to the University of Arizona, where he received a master's degree in 1965. He began writing poetry during graduate school and soon became confident enough to seek publication for his work. "I didn't so much plan to be a writer," he said. "Mostly I wrote a lot. Then people started to call me a writer."

In 1965 Koertge took a position as a professor of English at Pasadena City College, where he still teaches today. He began publishing poems in magazines as early as 1970 and a few years after that released the first of many chapbooks of verse. In 1980 he published his only novel for adults, *The Boogeyman*. "But the two novels after that were pitiful. Embarrassing," Koertge revealed. "Then a friend suggested that I try young adults since I'm a chronic smart ass. I went to the library, read a couple, and figured I could do at least that well. Sure enough: the two failed grown-up novels became *Where the Kissing Never Stops* and *The Arizona Kid*."

Both of these humorous and touching coming-of-age stories ignited controversy for their frank and realistic depiction of sexual encounters and alternative lifestyles. "It might have been naive of me to think that straight talk about sex would be universally welcomed in the secret garden of children's books or that a gay character

After phoning the Confess-O-Rama hotline more times than he'd care to admit, Tony is surprised to find out who's been on the receiving end of his calls. (Cover illustration by Leslie Cober-Gentry.)

in a YA would be treated like any other character," Koertge admitted in the *Los Angeles Times Book Review*. "But I was simply looking for something interesting to write...."

In *Where the Kissing Never Stops* seventeen-year-old Walker is plagued with problems—his cravings for junk food run unchecked, his girlfriend has left town, and, worst of all, his mother has taken a job as a stripper in a nearby burlesque parlor. At his lowest ebb he meets Rachel, a mall-loving, cosmopolitan girl. Different as they are, Walker and Rachel begin a romance and ultimately learn to trust one another. *School Library Journal* contributor Marjorie Lewis wrote, "Walker's attempts to keep his mother's occupation a secret and make his romance with Rachel a rich, fulfilling one are believable and engrossing." In *The Arizona Kid* sixteen-year-old Billy faces a summer of change and discovery as he experiences firsthand the colorful world of horse-racing, falling in love, losing his virginity, and learning about the gay lifestyle of his Uncle Wes, with whom he is spending the summer in Tucson.

Koertge has continued his humorous tales featuring young male coming-of-age stories in his other novels. For example, in *The Harmony Arms,* Gabriel McKay moves temporarily with his divorced father to Los Angeles, where in the Harmony Arms apartment complex he becomes acquainted with a host of individuals with eccentric personalities—including his new friend Tess, an aspiring young filmmaker who carries a camcorder with her everywhere in order to document her life. "Koertge's brash, outrageous characters give new meaning to the word *diversity,*" noted *Horn Book* critic Nancy Vasilakis, who added: "[Koertge] offers a lively defense of the West Coast's let-it-all-hang-out spirit in his funniest novel to date." *Voice of Youth Advocates* contributor John Lord offered a similar estimation of *The Harmony Arms,* asserting: "The strength of this book lies in its characters. They are well-drawn and believable." In *Tiger, Tiger, Burning Bright,* Jesse tries to conceal his almost senile grandfather's lapses of memory to keep his mother from putting him into a nursing home. A reviewer writing for *Publishers Weekly* appreciated Koertge's "imaginative characterizations, wacky humor and crackling, authentically adolescent dialogue" in this story. And more recently in *Confess-O-Rama,* protagonist Tony meets up with an unusual circle of friends when he and his mother move to a new town after his fourth stepfather dies. Deborah Stevenson, writing for the *Bulletin of the Center for Children's Books,* maintained that Koertge "blend[s] humor and genuine emotion in a way many YA authors essay but fail: Tony's quips and the outrageousness of the plot are genuinely funny but never superficial...."

Critics in general comment enthusiastically about Koertge's work. Michael Cart, writing for *School Library Journal,* declared that "Koertge is a brilliant writer who is emerging as one of America's finest authors for young adults." About writing for young adults, Koertge explained to *SATA,* "I never think of myself as writing for children; I never think I know anything special about young people. I don't have children and am not much interested in them as such. But I like to write. And writing YA's is obviously what I'm up to at the moment. I'm as surprised as anyone else at the success I've had. Maybe more."

■ Works Cited

Cart, Michael, review of *Tiger, Tiger, Burning Bright,* *School Library Journal,* March, 1994, p. 236.

Hoogestraat, Jane, "Ronald Koertge," *Dictionary of Literary Biography, Volume 105: American Poets since World War II,* Gale, 1992, pp. 137-42.

Koertge, Ron, "Sex and the Single Kid," *Los Angeles Times Book Review,* March 21, 1993.

Lewis, Marjorie, review of *Where the Kissing Never Stops, School Library Journal,* December, 1986, p. 119.

Lord, John, review of *The Harmony Arms, Voice of Youth Advocates,* October, 1992, pp. 224-25.

Stevenson, Deborah, review of *Confess-O-Rama, Bulletin of the Center for Children's Books,* November, 1996, p. 102.

Review of *Tiger, Tiger, Burning Bright, Publishers Weekly,* April 18, 1994, p. 63.

Vasilakis, Nancy, review of *The Harmony Arms, Horn Book,* November/December, 1992, p. 727.

■ For More Information See

BOOKS

Twentieth-Century Young Adult Writers, St. James Press, 1994.

PERIODICALS

Booklist, October 15, 1992, p. 418; February 15, 1994, p. 1075.

English Journal, Deccember, 1993, p. 73.

Horn Book, July-August, 1990, p. 462; July-August, 1991, p. 464; September-October, 1994, p. 600.

Kirkus Reviews, October 1, 1992, p. 1256; February 15, 1994, p. 228.

New York Times Book Review, August 21, 1988, p. 25.

Publishers Weekly, April 13, 1990, p. 67; May 10, 1991, p. 284; September 14, 1992, p. 126.

School Library Journal, May, 1990, p. 122; May, 1991, p. 111; August, 1992, p. 178.

Voice of Youth Advocates, June, 1994; December, 1996, p. 271-72.

Wilson Library Bulletin, April, 1989, p. 97; September, 1991, p. 106; March, 1993, p. 84.

*   *   *

KOONTZ, Dean R(ay) 1945-
(David Axton, Brian Coffey, Deanna Dwyer, K. R. Dwyer, John Hill, Leigh Nichols, Anthony North, Richard Paige, Owen West)

■ Personal

Born July 9, 1945, in Everett, PA; son of Ray and Florence Koontz; married Gerda Ann Cerra, October 15, 1966. *Education:* Shippensburg State College, B.A., 1966. *Religion:* Catholic.

■ Addresses

Home—Orange, CA. *Agent*—Robert Gottlieb, William Morris Agency Inc., 1325 Avenue of the Americas, New York, NY 10019.

■ Career

Writer. Teacher-counsellor with Appalachian Poverty Program, 1966-67; high school English teacher in Mechanicsburg, PA, 1967-69.

■ Awards, Honors

Atlantic Monthly creative writing award, 1966, for story "The Kittens"; Hugo Award nomination, World Science Fiction Convention, 1971, for novella *Beastchild;* Daedalus Award, 1988, for *Twilight Eyes;* Litt.D., Shippens-

DEAN R. KOONTZ

burg State College, 1989. Several of Koontz's works have been Literary Guild selections.

■ Writings

FOR CHILDREN

Oddkins: A Fable for All Ages, illustrated by Phil Parks, Warner, 1988.
Santa's Twin, illustrated by Parks, HarperPrism, 1996.

NOVELS

Star Quest, Ace Books, 1968.
The Fall of the Dream Machine, Ace Books, 1969.
Fear That Man, Ace Books, 1969.
Anti-Man, Paperback Library, 1970.
Beastchild, Lancer Books, 1970.
Dark of the Woods, Ace Books, 1970.
The Dark Symphony, Lancer Books, 1970.
Hell's Gate, Lancer Books, 1970.
The Crimson Witch, Curtis Books, 1971.
A Darkness in My Soul, DAW Books, 1972.
The Flesh in the Furnace, Bantam, 1972.
Starblood, Lancer Books, 1972.
Time Thieves, Ace Books, 1972.
Warlock, Lancer Books, 1972.
A Werewolf among Us, Ballantine, 1973.
Hanging On, M. Evans, 1973.
The Haunted Earth, Lancer Books, 1973.
Demon Seed, Bantam, 1973.
(Under pseudonym Anthony North) *Strike Deep,* Dial, 1974.
After the Last Race, Atheneum, 1974.
Nightmare Journey, Putnam, 1975.

(Under pseudonym John Hill) *The Long Sleep,* Popular Library, 1975.
Night Chills, Atheneum, 1976.
(Under pseudonym David Axton) *Prison of Ice,* Lippincott, 1976, revised edition published under name Dean R. Koontz as *Icebound,* Random House, 1995.
The Vision, Putnam, 1977.
Whispers, Putnam, 1980.
Phantoms, Putnam, 1983.
Darkfall, Berkley, 1984 (published in England as *Darkness Comes,* W. H. Allen, 1984).
Twilight Eyes, Land of Enchantment, 1985.
(Under pseudonym Richard Paige) *The Door to December,* New American Library, 1985.
Strangers, Putnam, 1986.
Watchers, Putnam, 1987.
Lightning, Putnam, 1988.
Midnight, Putnam, 1989.
The Bad Place, Putnam, 1990.
Cold Fire, Putnam, 1991.
Dean R. Koontz: Three Complete Novels, The Servants of Twilight, Darkfall, Phantoms, Outlet Book Company, 1991.
Dean R. Koontz: A New Collection, Wings Books, 1992.
Hideaway, Putnam, 1992.
Dragon Tears, Putnam, 1992.
Winter Moon, Ballantine Books, 1993.
Mr. Murder, Putnam, 1993.
Dark Rivers of the Heart, Knopf, 1994.
Strange Highways, Warner Books, 1995.
Intensity, Knopf, 1996.
Tick-Tock, Ballantine, 1996.
Beautiful Death, Viking, 1996.
Sole Survivor, Random House, 1996.

UNDER PSEUDONYM DEANNA DWYER

The Demon Child, Lancer, 1971.
Legacy of Terror, Lancer, 1971.
Children of the Storm, Lancer, 1972.
The Dark of Summer, Lancer, 1972.
Dance with the Devil, Lancer, 1973.

UNDER PSEUDONYM K. R. DWYER

Chase, Random House, 1972.
Shattered, Random House, 1973.
Dragonfly, Random House, 1975.

UNDER PSEUDONYM BRIAN COFFEY

Blood Risk, Bobbs-Merrill, 1973.
Surrounded, Bobbs-Merrill, 1974.
The Wall of Masks, Bobbs-Merrill, 1975.
The Face of Fear, Bobbs-Merrill, 1977.
The Voice of the Night, Doubleday, 1981.

Also author, under pseudonym Brian Coffey, of script for *CHIPs* television series, 1978.

UNDER PSEUDONYM LEIGH NICHOLS

The Key to Midnight, Pocket Books, 1979.
The Eyes of Darkness, Pocket Books, 1981, revised edition published under name Dean R. Koontz, Berkley, 1996.

The House of Thunder, Pocket Books, 1982.
Twilight, Pocket Books, 1984.
Shadowfires, Avon, 1987.

UNDER PSEUDONYM OWEN WEST

The Funhouse (novelization of screenplay), Jove, 1980.
The Mask, Jove, 1981.

OTHER

(With wife, Gerda Koontz) *The Pig Society* (nonfiction),
Aware Press, 1970.
(With Gerda Koontz) *The Underground Lifestyles
Handbook,* Aware Press, 1970.
Soft Come the Dragons (story collection), Ace Books,
1970.
Writing Popular Fiction, Writer's Digest, 1973.
How to Write Best-Selling Fiction, Writer's Digest,
1981.
Trapped (graphic novel), illustrated by Anthony Bilau,
Eclipse Books, 1992.

Contributor to anthologies, including *Again, Dangerous
Visions,* edited by Harlan Ellison, Doubleday, 1972;
Future City, edited by Roger Elwood, Simon & Schus-
ter, 1973; *Children of Infinity,* edited by Elwood,
Putnam, 1974.

■ Adaptations

Demon Seed was filmed by Metro-Goldwyn-Mayer/
Warner Bros. in 1977; *Shattered* was filmed by Warner
Bros. in 1977; and *Watchers* was adapted as a motion
picture by Universal in 1988; *Hideaway* was produced
as a motion picture in 1995; *Phantoms* was produced as
a motion picture by Miramax/Dimension for 1997
release; *Intensity* was filmed by Mandalay Entertainment as a two-part miniseries for broadcast on Fox,
1997. CBS-TV has rights to *Dark Rivers of the Heart.*

■ Sidelights

Dean R. Koontz is an acknowledged master of a hybrid
class of books that combine suspense, horror, romance,
and science fiction. His more than seventy books have
sold in the millions and have been adapted for such
successful movies as *Demon Seed, Watchers,* and *Shattered.* Though often dubbed a horror novelist, Koontz
himself rejects such labels. In an interview for a critical
analysis of his work, *Sudden Fear: The Horror and Dark
Suspense Fiction of Dean R. Koontz,* the author noted
that "you can't find much hope, love, or optimism in
current horror, but you can find all the nihilism you
want, enough doom-saying and cynicism and pessi-
mism." Koontz views his own work as basically optimistic, showing hard-fought battles between good and evil.
A favorite Koontz theme is the conflict between emotion and reason, and the emotional level of his books—a
step beyond the usual plot-heavy nature of much of the
genre—has drawn in a wide variety of readers, including
young adults. *Watchers* was chosen as one of the
American Library Association's Best Books for Young
Adults in 1987, and his novels *Lightning* and the
juvenile *Oddkins* were both selected by the Enoch Pratt

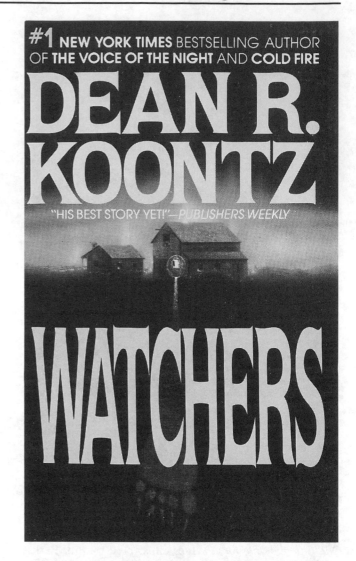

No one is safe after two genetically altered life forms,
one good and one evil, escape from a secret government
laboratory in this Koontz thriller.

Free Library's Young Adult Advisory Board in its
Youth-to-Youth reading list.

Koontz's own youth was one he was happy to escape. An
only child, he grew up in Pennsylvania. As he once
commented, "I began writing when I was a child, for
both reading and writing provided much needed escape
from the poverty in which we lived and from my father's
frequent fits of alcohol-induced violence." While still in
college, Koontz started selling his fiction and won an
Atlantic Monthly fiction contest. Having married and
graduated from college in the same year, Koontz took
teaching positions for a while, writing in his spare time
and selling stories and then novels. Finally he decided to
make a try at full-time writing, using an assortment of
pseudonyms in various genres, including science fiction,
mystery, and thrillers. "The curse lies in the fact that
much of the early work is of lower quality that what
came after," Koontz remarked, "both because I was so
young and unself-critical and because the low earnings
from each book forced me to write a lot of them in order
to keep financially afloat."

Koontz marks *Chase,* a suspense novel written under the pseudonym K. R. Dwyer about the after-effects of Vietnam on a veteran, as "the beginning of my *real* career as a writer." He left science fiction behind with that book, and never looked back. Another early book that Koontz looks to as a watershed in terms of technique was the 1973 novel *Hanging On,* about a group of U.S. Army Engineers constructing a bridge in Nazi-held France. *Publishers Weekly* commented that "this book has suspense and, more important, some of the most hilarious scenes that have come along in a long time." Throughout the 1970s Koontz continued to produce several books per year under various pseudonyms, depending upon genre. However, as Koontz pointed out in an interview with Stanley Wiater in *Writer's Digest,* "I began to realize that all these books that were being well-reviewed under pen names were doing absolutely nothing to build *my* name." His first bestseller, *The Key to Midnight,* was written under the pseudonym Leigh Nichols, and the invisible Mr. Nichols has produced four further titles since then, though in the main Koontz now writes solely under his own name.

"I have attempted, book by book, to speak to the reader's intellect and emotions as well as to his desire for a 'good read'," Koontz once stated. "I believe the best fiction does three things well: tells an involving story, makes the reader think, and makes the reader feel." Koontz's early work in several genres was instrumental in his development of his own unique form of dark suspense, and his addition of humor, romance, and the occult to the brew has created a distinctive niche for him among other writers such as Stephen King and Peter Straub. "My real breakthrough came in 1980 with *Whispers,*" Koontz noted. A bestseller with over five million copies in print worldwide, *Whispers* is a dark and violent story of a childhood cruelty, rape, and murder. Hilary Thomas is a survivor of abusive alcoholic parents who has become a successful screenwriter; she is attacked by millionaire Bruno Frye, whom she subsequently stabs to death. Bruno, however, returns from the grave to stalk Hilary, and it is left to Hilary's police officer boyfriend to help her unravel the twisted tale of Bruno's childhood to reveal the powers at work in this "slick tale of horror," as Rex E. Klett described the book in *Library Journal.* A *Publishers Weekly* reviewer noted that the "psychological portrait of the sick, sick Bruno makes skin crawl."

With *Phantoms* and *Darkfall,* Koontz made what he termed "sidesteps in my career," novels of horror and the supernatural which were long investigations of rational versus irrational belief, of technology versus emotion. The 1986 work *Strangers* forms a duo with *Whispers* that Koontz sees as benchmarks that he strives to maintain. "Without doubt, both novels have strong suspenseful plots, as well, and I intend that all of my future novels will be what are called 'page-turners'," Koontz once remarked. "However, the older I get the more I find that well-drawn characters and vivid backgrounds are just as important as plot to the success of a book."

The misuse of science is at the heart of the author's 1987 novel, *Watchers,* a book which also began to win Koontz a large audience among young adult readers. Recombinant DNA experiments go wrong at a government lab, and suddenly two mutants—one with human intelligence to be used for spying and the other a killer—are on the loose in Southern California. The intelligent mutant, a golden retriever, is pursued by the killer mutant, named Outsider, a blend of ape and dog. Soon two humans become involved helping the dog, nicknamed Einstein, as well as themselves, escape the wrath of Outsider. Subplots abound and a love interest figures between the two human protagonists, Travis and Nora. In short, Koontz had produced a blockbuster novel, and one which was chosen for the ALA Best Books for Young Adults list that year. As with all bestsellers, however, Koontz's books have their critics, including Audrey B. Eaglen, who described *Watchers* in *School Library Journal* as "about as horrifying as warm milk toast." Others disagreed, including *New York Times Book Review* contributor Katherine Weber, who had

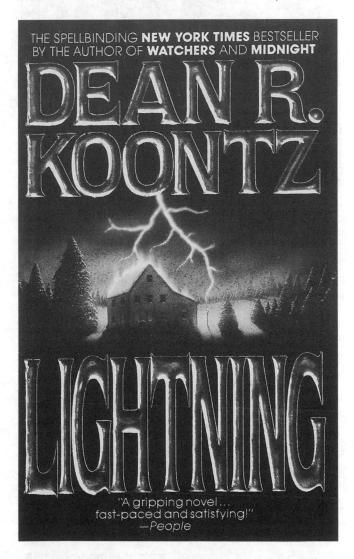

THE SPELLBINDING **NEW YORK TIMES** BESTSELLER BY THE AUTHOR OF **WATCHERS** AND **MIDNIGHT**

DEAN R. KOONTZ

LIGHTNING

"A gripping novel... fast-paced and satisfying!"
—*People*

Lightning strikes twice—with very mysterious results—in Koontz's suspenseful 1988 novel.

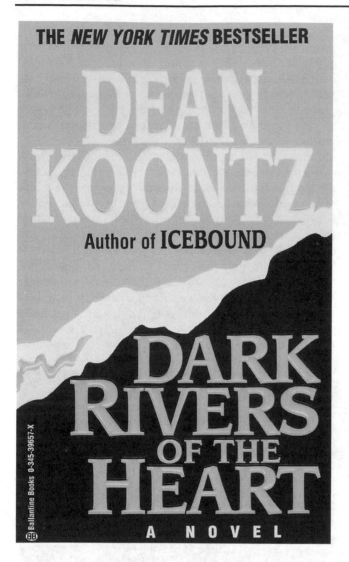

THE *NEW YORK TIMES* BESTSELLER

DEAN KOONTZ

Author of ICEBOUND

DARK RIVERS OF THE HEART

A NOVEL

Ballantine Books 0-345-39657-X

In this high-tech Koontz thriller, a powerful secret agency is formed to cover up illegal and tainted operations within the government.

special praise for Einstein, calling the dog "the most richly drawn character in the book."

In a tale somewhat reminiscent of *Whispers,* Koontz next told the story of Laura Shane, a successful novelist who has overcome a difficult childhood. *Lightning* tells the story of a blond man who has helped Shane out at various difficult and dangerous times of her life and now reveals to her that he is a time traveller and is being pursued by killers from his own era. While some reviewers complained of over-plotting in this suspense novel, Dick Lochte noted in the *Los Angeles Times Book Review* that Koontz was "particularly skilled at setting up believable characters and situations." The novel was included on one list of recommended books for young adults. Christy Tyson, reviewing a later Koontz novel in *Voice of Youth Advocates,* analyzed the trend of Koontz's increasing YA popularity. She commented that YA horror readers looking for something beyond Stephen King were more and more turning to Koontz. "His stories are smoothly told, his premises well-developed, and his characters often more approachable . . . .

In addition he often features characters and themes that strike home with young adult readers and adds touches of genuine warmth and humor."

One Koontz creation aimed specifically at the juvenile market, though called by the publishers "a fable for all ages," is *Oddkins.* A fantastic setting is the venue for the author's usual theme of the battle between good and evil. Magical toys have been created for the children in *Oddkins,* toys which help kids when they need a special secret friend. These Oddkins are actually alive and have the power of speech, though they look and feel like simple stuffed toys. When the child is old and strong enough to be on his or her own, the Oddkins return once again to their inanimate state, and for the child they are simply a fond memory. But when evil toys created by another toymaker escape from the cellar of the toy factory, they must be stopped by the Oddkins. Once again, Koontz sends an optimistic message through his fiction, though painted in rather black and white terms. A *Publishers Weekly* commentator noted that *Oddkins* has "enough excitement and humor to hold a child's attention" although it might not appeal as much to adult readers. In 1996 Koontz again produced a picture book dealing with themes of good vs. evil; *Santa's Twin* presents the story of Father Christmas as he tries to save the holiday season from his evil double.

Throughout the 1990s, Koontz has maintained a string of bestsellers, from *The Bad Place,* which *Los Angeles Times Book Review* critic Don G. Campbell described as being "as close to actual physical terror as the printed word can deliver," to *Hideaway, Mr. Murder, Dragon Tears, Winter Moon, Dark Rivers of the Heart,* and *Intensity.* With all these titles Koontz continues to employ his blending of genres. As Edward Bryant noted in *Locus,* "Koontz successfully does what most editors warn their writers not to do. He crosses genre boundaries with impunity . . . . He simply does pretty much what he wants, and the novels are then categorized as 'Dean R. Koontz books.'" In any genre, the critic added, Koontz "knows how to sink a narrative hook." Additionally, the author peppers his books with his own particular message. As he once remarked, he finds "the human species—and Western culture—to be primarily noble, honorable, and admirable. In an age when doomsayers are to be heard in every corner of the land, I find great hope in our species and in the future we will surely make for ourselves . . . . I think we live in a time of marvels, not a time of disaster, and I believe we can solve every problem that confronts us if we keep our perspectives and our freedom."

If the dangers of rampant technology is one of the major themes of his earlier works, a foreboding of social decay runs like a thread through later books. In *Dragon Tears,* two police officers have to battle a serial killer with mutant powers, a stand-in for modern rot. "Koontz gets a bit preachy about social decay," commented a *Kirkus Reviews* critic, "but his action never flags in this vise-tight tale." Evil stalks a family in *Mr. Murder,* in the guise of a monster killer. Similarly urban evil seems to follow a family as it resettles from Los Angeles to

Montana in *Winter Moon,* as creatures from another dimension give this ex-urban family no peace. A *Publishers Weekly* reviewer called *Winter Moon* a "gripping parable about the real cost of 'getting away from it all.'"

A libertarian theme comes through in *Dark Rivers of the Heart,* in which a secret federal agency is trying to take over the country. The villain of the piece is not a right-wing extremist, but a liberal sociopath. And as in *Watchers* and *Dragon Tears,* there is a lovable dog to round out the human protagonists. "Expect this yarn to be denounced as right-wing alarmist trash by some," noted Ray Olson in *Booklist,* "hailed as a libertarian warning by others, and, like virtually everything Koontz writes, read by millions." *New York Times Book Review* contributor Jay E. Rosen observed that Koontz had succeeded in leaving the supernatural behind; "he has switched gears ... and written a believable high-tech thriller."

From serial killers to out-of-control technology, Koontz has surveyed the darker regions of life. His novels not only address modern times but, in their depiction of violence, are mirrors of them as well. "I strongly believe that, in addition to entertaining, it is the function of fiction to explore the way we live, reinforce our noble traits, and suggest ways to improve the world where we can," Koontz once stated. Yet as reviewer Paul Wilner noted in *Los Angeles Times Book Review,* the very popularity of Koontz's novels "indicates something disturbing about our fascination with military violence and violence in our own souls.... This broader fascination betokens problems that can't be resolved through wish-fulfillment fiction." Whether or not Koontz's novels are a reflection of today's social malaises, as some critics say, or are part of the solution, as Koontz contends, one thing is certain: Dean R. Koontz keeps his readers turning pages and sitting on the edges of their seats.

■ **Works Cited**

Bryant, Edward, review of *The Bad Place, Locus,* March, 1990, pp. 67-68.

Campbell, Don G., review of *The Bad Place, Los Angeles Times Book Review,* January 21, 1990, p. 12.

Review of *Dragon Tears, Kirkus Reviews,* November 1, 1992, p. 1327.

Eaglen, Audrey B., "Stunners to Stinkers: The '87 BBYA List," *School Library Journal,* April, 1988, p. 54.

Review of *Hanging On, Publishers Weekly,* September 10, 1973, p. 41.

Klett, Rex E., review of *Whispers, Library Journal,* May 15, 1980, p. 1187.

Koontz, Dean, interview in *Sudden Fear: The Horror and Dark Suspense Fiction of Dean R. Koontz,* edited by Bill Munster, Starmont House, 1988, p. 182.

Lochte, Dick, "The Perils of Little Laura," *Los Angeles Times Book Review,* January 31, 1988, p. 8.

Review of *Oddkins, Publishers Weekly,* September 2, 1988, pp. 87-88.

Olson, Ray, review of *Dark Rivers of the Heart, Booklist,* September 15, 1994, p. 84.

Rosen, Jay E., review of *Dark Rivers of the Heart, New York Times Book Review,* November 13, 1994, p. 58.

Tyson, Christy, review of *Dragon's Tears, Voice of Youth Advocates,* October, 1993, p. 230.

Weber, Katherine, review of *Watchers, New York Times Book Review,* March 15, 1987, p. 16.

Review of *Whispers, Publishers Weekly,* April 4, 1980, p. 61.

Wiater, Stanley, interview with Dean R. Koontz in *Writer's Digest,* November, 1989, pp. 34-38.

Wilner, Paul, review of *Watchers, Los Angeles Times Book Review,* March 8, 1987, p. 6.

Review of *Winter Moon, Publishers Weekly,* January 10, 1994, pp. 56-57.

■ **For More Information See**

BOOKS

Greenberg, Martin H., and Ed Gorman and Bill Munster, editors, *The Dean Koontz Companion,* Berkley Books, 1994.

Kotker, Joan G., *Dean Koontz: A Critical Companion,* Greenwood Press, 1996.

Munster, Bill, *Dean R. Koontz's Cold Terror,* Underwood-Miller, 1990.

Munster, Bill, editor, *Discovering Dean Koontz: Essays on America's Bestselling Writer of Suspense and Horror Fiction,* R. Reginald, 1995.

Twentieth-Century Young Adult Writers, St. James Press, 1994.

PERIODICALS

Kliatt, March, 1993, p. 8; May, 1993, p. 45; July, 1994, p. 50; November, 1994, p. 61; January, 1995, p. 9.

Library Journal, November 15, 1992, p. 120; March 1, 1993, p. 122; February 1, 1994, p. 128; May 1, 1994, p. 154; September 1, 1994, p. 215; August, 1995, p. 138; December, 1995, p. 156; March 1, 1996, p. 126.

New York Times Book Review, January 31, 1993, p. 20; October 31, 1993, p. 18.

Publishers Weekly, November 4, 1996, p. 20.

Wilson Library Bulletin, October, 1992, p. 96; March, 1993, p. 71; May, 1993, p. 102.

—*Sketch by J. Sydney Jones*

* * *

KROEGER, Mary Kay 1950-

■ **Personal**

Born February 27, 1950; daughter of William G. and Catherine M. (Brinkmeyer) Weich; married Daniel R. Kroeger (a property and facilities manager), June 16, 1973; children: Carrie Marie, Joseph Daniel. *Education:*

College of Mount Saint Joseph-on-the-Ohio, B.A., M.Ed. *Religion:* Roman Catholic.

■ Addresses

Home—8642 Wuest Road, Cincinnati, OH, 45251. *Office*—Terrace Park Elementary, 723 Elm, Terrace Park, OH 45174. *Electronic mail*— AOL DRK123.

■ Career

Terrace Park Elementary, Terrace Park, OH, fourth grade teacher, 1993—. *Member:* Society of Children's Book Writers and Illustrators, International Reading Association.

MARY KAY KROEGER

■ Writings

(With Louise Borden) *Paperboy,* illustrated by Ted Lewin, Clarion, 1996.

■ Sidelights

Mary Kay Kroeger's first book for children, *Paperboy,* was written with Louise Borden and is set in Cincinnati in 1927. Based on a true story from the childhood of Kroeger's father, the book involves a memorable event in boxing history: the Dempsey-Tunney prizefight.

The story of *Paperboy* focuses on Willie Brinkman, an enthusiastic fan of his neighborhood's hero, prizefighter Jack Dempsey, who is about to fight Tunney for the world heavyweight championship. Excited about the fight, Willie tells his boss at the newspaper that he will sell "extras" afterward. When the night of the fight arrives, Willie gathers with his tense family by the radio to listen to the fight, which takes place in Chicago. He is terribly disappointed when Dempsey loses the fight, and so are the rest of the people in his neighborhood. Although Willie is reluctant to try to sell newspapers that no one wants to read, he goes to work. As a result, his boss rewards him with a better spot to sell his papers, and Willie learns a lesson about loyalty.

Paperboy has been praised both for its narrative and for the watercolor illustrations of Caldecott honor book winner Ted Lewin, who is himself a former wrestler. According to a critic for *Publishers Weekly,* "lustrous watercolors illuminate this finely crafted period piece," which the reviewer commends for its "seamlessly told" story and "loving attention to detail." In her *Booklist* review, Hazel Rochman advises adults that *Paperboy* may be used "to start kids talking about their own family folklore."

■ Works Cited

Review of *Paperboy, Publishers Weekly,* February 26, 1996, p. 81.
Rochman, Hazel, review of *Paperboy, Booklist,* March 15, 1996, p. 1269.

L

L., Tommy
See **LORKOWSKI, Thomas V(incent)**

* * *

LANTIER-SAMPON, Patricia 1952-

■ Personal

Born July 6, 1952, in Lafayette, LA; daughter of Curtis (a banker) and Mable (a bank executive; maiden name, Delhomme) Lantier; married Glen Romero, 1972 (marriage ended); married James R. Sampon (a sales manager), October 6, 1990; children: (first marriage) Ryan M. Romero. *Education:* University of Southwestern Louisiana, B.A., 1973, M.A., 1982; Marquette University, Ph.D., 1992. *Religion:* Roman Catholic.

■ Addresses

Home—3131 West McKinley Blvd., Milwaukee, WI 53208. *Office*—Gareth Stevens Publishing, 1555 North RiverCenter Dr., Ste. 201, Milwaukee, WI 53212.

■ Career

Language arts teacher at elementary and high school levels, 1973-82; Marquette University, Milwaukee, WI, instructor in English, 1982-89; Gareth Stevens Publishing, Milwaukee, managing editor and director, creative department, 1990—. Freelance writer and editor.

■ Writings

(Adapter) *Hurricane: The Rage of Hurricane Andrew* (from text by John Dorschner and from *The Big One: Hurricane Andrew,* by the staffs of the *Miami Herald* and *El Nuevo Herald,* Miami Herald Publishing, 1992), Gareth Stevens, 1993.
(Adapter) *Guatemala Is My Home* (from Ronnie Cummins, *Children of the World: Guatemala*), Gareth Stevens, 1993.
(Adapter) *Little Lost Fox Cub* (from Louis Espinassous, *Petit Renard perdu*) Gareth Stevens, 1993.

PATRICIA LANTIER-SAMPON

Take Me Out to the Ball Game, Western Publishing (Racine, WI), 1994.

"THE ADVENTURES OF BUSTER THE PUPPY" SERIES; PICTURE BOOKS; ENGLISH TEXT

Buster Catches a Cold (published in Japan as *Ame No Hi No Korowan*), Gareth Stevens, 1991.
Buster and the Little Kitten (published in Japan as *Korowan Wa Oniichan*), Gareth Stevens, 1991.
Buster and the Dandelions (published in Japan as *Korowan To Fuwafuwa*), Gareth Stevens, 1991.
Buster's First Snow (published in Japan as *Yuki No Hi No Korowan*), Gareth Stevens, 1991.
Buster's Blustery Day (published in Japan as *Kaze No Hi No Korowan*), Gareth Stevens, 1991.
Buster's First Thunderstorm (published in Japan as *Korowan To Gorogoro*), Gareth Stevens, 1991.

"PEOPLE WHO MAKE A DIFFERENCE" SERIES;
ABRIDGER

(With James Bentley) *Albert Schweitzer: The Doctor Who Devoted His Life to Africa's Sick* (from James Bentley, *Albert Schweitzer: The Doctor Who Gave Up a Brilliant Career to Serve the People of Africa,* Exley Publications, 1988), Gareth Stevens, 1991.

(With David Winner) *Desmond Tutu: Religious Leader Devoted to Freedom* (from David Winner, *Desmond Tutu: The Courageous and Eloquent Archbishop Struggling against Apartheid in South Africa,* Exley Publications, 1989), Gareth Stevens, 1991.

(With Beverly Birch) *Louis Braille: Bringer of Hope to the Blind* (from Beverly Birch, *Louis Braille: The Inventor of a Way to Read and Write That Has Helped Millions of Blind People Communicate with the World,* Exley Publications, 1989), Gareth Stevens, 1991.

"ANIMAL WONDERS" SERIES; ADAPTER

The Wonder of Loons (from Tom Klein, *Loon Magic for Kids*), Gareth Stevens, 1992.

The Wonder of Whitetails (from Tom Wolpert, *Whitetail Magic for Kids*), Gareth Stevens, 1992.

The Wonder of Wolves (from Tom Wolpert, *Wolf Magic for Kids*), Gareth Stevens, 1992.

"WINGS" SERIES

Airplanes, illustrated by Timothy Spransy, Gareth Stevens, 1994.

Birds, illustrated by Jeff Meyer, Gareth Stevens, 1994.

Flying Animals, illustrated by Jeff Meyer, Gareth Stevens, 1994.

Flying Insects, illustrated by Timothy Spransy, Gareth Stevens, 1994.

■ Sidelights

Patricia Lantier-Sampon told *SATA:* "I have always been fascinated by language and the way it connects people and events. The written word as well as the spoken word—the collaboration affords a limitless source of personal expression. As a child, I composed lists of names and other words that caught my imagination, words that somehow exerted an influence on me and evoked specific emotions or scenes in my mind's eye—just the right name for a favorite pet or the new girl in school or the bully down the street. I refined my lists again and again and kept these treasures in a three-ring binder in a secret place in my closet. I planned to use them in stories or have them handy to use as needed in daily life.

"I still write lists, and I still collect favorite words and names for future reference. And I still have some of the original collections, although the pages are getting more than a little yellow around the edges. Words, and the way they can sing together in my mind, have always been a source of comfort and excitement to me. Finding just the right word for a given situation or character or emotion gives me tremendous satisfaction—like a singer hitting a high note, or a baseball player hitting a home run, or a chess player saying 'Checkmate!'"

LARSON, Ingrid D(ana) 1965-

■ Personal

Born September 30, 1965, in Manchester, CT; daughter of Sven Larson and Diane B. Perkins/Weinberg (counter manager of a fragrance department). *Education:* Massasoit Community College, A.S., 1987; Stonehill College, B.A., 1997. *Hobbies and other interests:* Crafts, photography, calligraphy, travel, animals.

■ Addresses

Home—486 West Union Street, East Bridgewater, MA 02333.

■ Career

Writer. Loretta Davis Promotional Agency, promotional model, 1984—; Massasoit Community College, clerk II, 1988-90; Remax Landmark Realtors, receptionist, 1994—.

■ Awards, Honors

Robin Caddell Memorial Award for creative writing, East Bridgewater High School.

INGRID D. LARSON

■ Writings

The Adventures of Herman and Hurby, Aegina, 1995.
The Adventures of Herman and Hurby and Family,
Aegina, 1997.

Poems represented in several antholagies, including *A Moment in Time,* National Library of Poetry, 1995; *A Voyage to Remember,* National Library of Poetry, 1996; *Beginnings,* Cader Publishing, 1997; and *Poetic Voices of America,* Sparrowgrass Poetry Forum, 1997.

■ Work in Progress

"I am working on another children's book about squirrels. In addition, even though I am a children's author, I am working on a love story that is set in Europe; it will be a short novel when I am finished. I will also be writing more poems and children's stories in the near future."

■ Sidelights

Ingrid D. Larson told *SATA:* "I began writing poems and short stories at the age of five. At the age of ten, my grandmother took me to Concord, Massachusetts, to visit Louisa May Alcott's home and Walden Pond, where Henry David Thoreau lived for two years. I remember that Louisa May Alcott's writing desk was in front of a window overlooking her front yard. I wrote as a child at a desk in my room overlooking my yard, too. Her view was of the yard and the road in front of her house. My view was of the cornfield and woods beyond. My grandmother gave me a copy of *Little Women* and, from that point on, I knew that I would someday be an author, too. She became my inspiration because of her life and the way she wrote. I set my goal to become an author early on and kept at my goal until it became a reality.

"As a child, I grew up surrounded by nature. Henry David Thoreau became a role model, too, because of the way he saw nature. Today one might classify him as an environmentalist, which is what I am today. I believe we should learn to appreciate nature, the ocean, and all animals because we can learn so much from observing and appreciating all of nature's magnificent wonders. We traveled to the ocean and to the hills and mountains of New Hampshire, Vermont and Maine, and took walks in the woods behind my home as well. My grandfather showed me plants, flowers, trees, and checkerberries. He also taught me how to skim rocks at a pond. During these walks into nature, I was reminded of Henry David Thoreau and Walden Woods. My pond was surrounded by tall trees, mostly pines and evergreens. It was peaceful and beautiful and I considered it to be my very own Walden Pond.

"My writing reflects the beauty of nature and my life growing up with my grandparents and my mother. I remember the simple things that made growing up so special, like my grandmother baking chocolate chip cookies for me when I came home from school and

chocolate cakes with chocolate frosting for my birthdays.... Many of the settings that I write about are actual events that took place in my life and the characters are a part of me and other people in my life. Growing up on my maternal grandparents' homestead in East Bridgewater, Massachusetts, was the perfect setting for a blossom to open and to one day make her mark in the literary world.

"*The Adventures of Herman and Hurby* was originally written at the age of thirteen sitting at my desk overlooking the cornfield. As new adventures in my life began to take form, I had to put my writing aside but my dream and my goal of becoming an author remained alive. In 1993, I found my firstborn tucked neatly in a box along with other short stories and poems and began to put it together as a book. I rewrote and expanded the stories and the characters to coincide what I had learned as a child and then as an adult with each story and character to add more depth. My firstborn was now ready to face the world.

"It is the story of grasshoppers who live in a cornfield in a town called Grasshopperville. It centers around nature and the changing of seasons. It also reflects the importance of family and friends. For example, 'Raisin Pond' is about my walks and my time with nature. The story is named after my aunt's dog Raisin. There is also a story abut getting my first bike entitled 'George's Birthday,' a story about helping a wild animal in need called 'The Tingling Noise,' and a story of a special puppy named Christmas. That story was written in memory of my dog Minga.

"My second book, *The Adventures of Herman and Hurby and Family,* is a series of short stories that also reflect the beauty of nature. There is a story about watching the Northern Lights, a story about a whale who almost rose from the ocean, a story of an old-fashioned country fair, a story of a mountaintop picnic, a story about giving abandoned baby snapping turtles a new home, and lastly a story that was inspired by my stepfather about helping a little bird tangled up in some string. My stepfather rescued the little bird and it flew up to its nest to be with its family.

"As an only child, I found writing to be an adventurous journey because I could create places and characters in my imagination and with the stroke of a pen put them into words. I used my trips to the hills, mountains, and ocean and my walks to create places where a child's imagination could travel freely. In today's society, where television and computers replace one's imagination, I hope my books will help children to know the joy in reading and how fun it can be to use your imagination to create places like Grasshopperville.

"I believe that I will always write children's books because that is where I am the most comfortable and it is the one place where my imagination can flow freely. When I hear that a child has read my book *The Adventures of Herman and Hurby* five times, I am absolutely thrilled. I know that I am on the right track, and that is exactly where I want to stay.

"The advice that I would give to aspiring writers of tomorrow is to have confidence in your writing, confidence in yourself, and determination."

* * *

LELAND, Bob 1956-
(Robert E. Leland)

■ Personal

Born March 18, 1956, in South Bend, IN; married Marie Alyce Kleinhenz (a teacher), July 1, 1995; children: (from an earlier marriage) Kacie A., Bradley E. *Education:* Texas A & M University, B.S., 1978.

■ Addresses

Home—1028 Walton Dr., College Station, TX 77840.

■ Career

Swim coach, landscape architect, and illustrator. United States Swimming, Amateur Status Olympic Development Sports, level 5 coach, 1987—; registered landscape architect. *Member:* American Swim Coaches Association, Texas Association of Landscape Contractors (president, Brazos chapter, 1986).

■ Illustrator

Donna D. Cooner, *Twelve Days in Texas,* Hendrick-Long, 1994.

■ Work in Progress

Wildlife studies; drawings.

■ Sidelights

Bob Leland told *SATA:* "I live in College Station, about one hundred miles from the nearest large city. The people orient to Texas A & M University, which is what brought my grandfather here years ago. He was in the first one hundred certified public attorneys in the state of Texas. My mother and uncle were also in education. My uncle taught chemical engineering at Rice University and my mother taught in the College Station school system.

"I draw what I see, a communication gift that many people choose not to develop. But I was encouraged as a boy, and it became a useful tool throughout my education. My athletic abilities in swimming led to a full scholarship to Texas A & M, where I achieved a B.S. in landscape architecture. I went on to run a design build business and passed requirements for architectural registration.

"While in school I was told I could not be an athlete and an architect, but I enjoyed the challenge. My swimming took me to almost every state in the country, and swimming for the United States took me to Europe, East Germany, and Russia.

"Travel, hunting, and fishing taught me to see, slowing down to let the world come into focus.

"Now I am coaching swimming and working in landscape consulting, still doing both things I was trained to do. My sketches reflect a mood or feel of places I have been, and the style is simple.

"My wife, Mia, also an athlete, respects my experiences in coaching and appreciates my artistic outlet. She and my two children are my inspiration for life."

* * *

LELAND, Robert E.
See LELAND, Bob

* * *

LEMBER, Barbara Hirsch 1941-

■ Personal

Born November 8, 1941, in Philadelphia, PA; daughter of Charles Fredrick (a salesman) and Mildred (a bookkeeper and homemaker; maiden name, Schoolman) Hirsch; married Steven Lember (a marketing executive), 1966; children: Jessica Rachel, Amanda Beth. *Education:* Philadelphia Museum College of Art (now University of the Arts), B.F.A., 1963; attended Tyler School of Art, 1987; studied under Karen Muth, Stephen Perloff, and Judith Harold-Steinhauser, 1987-90. *Hobbies and*

BARBARA HIRSCH LEMBER

other interests: Dance and music concerts, museums, cooking, English country dance, gardening, reading, Pilates, cats.

■ Addresses

Home—8225 Forest Ave., Elkins Park, PA 19027.

■ Career

Photographer; dance teacher, performer, and choreographer; writer. Hedy Tower Performing Group, child dancer, 1945-55; Terez Nelson Dance Company, performer, 1960-67; Gruppe Motion Berlin, performer, 1967-70; Bryn Mawr College, modern dance teacher and choreographer, 1968-77; teacher of adult classes, 1979—. *Exhibitions:* Work has appeared in numerous juried exhibitions and invitational shows since 1983, and in such galleries as The Works Gallery, Philadelphia PA, The Print Center, Philadelphia, Carol Schwartz Gallery, Philadelphia, DeVirgilis Gallery, North Wales, PA, Sweetheart Gallery, Woodstock, NY, and Accent Gallery, Ocean City, NJ. Pieces held in permanent collections by Vanguard Corporation, Nomura Security International, Ernst & Young, National Westminster Bank, Stanford University Medical Center, and Galfand, Berger, Lurie & March. *Member:* Philadelphia Children's Reading Round Table.

■ Awards, Honors

Abington Art Center Members' Show, Honorable Mention, 1984, third place, Schuykill Valley Nature Center, 1985; Best of Show, 1987; second place, Impressions VIII, Villanova University, 1988; first place, Mayfair Community Celebration, 1989; third place, Mayfair Arts Festival, 1992; Juror's Award, 80 Washington Square East Galleries, 1993; Merit Award, New York Book Show, 1995, for *A Book of Fruit.*

■ Writings

(Self-illustrated) *A Book of Fruit,* Ticknor and Fields, 1994.
(Self-illustrated) *The Shell Book,* Houghton, 1997.

■ Sidelights

Barbara Hirsch Lember told *SATA:* "Since early childhood I have immersed myself in art and dance. I consider myself lucky and privileged to have been able to pursue careers in both. They bring me great joy and satisfaction.

"I started dancing at the age of four, loved improvisation, modern technique and performing, and had many lead roles in my long dance career. As a child I studied and performed with the Hedy Tower Dance Company. Later I performed with both The Terez Nelson Dance Company and Gruppe Motion Berlin (newly arrived from Germany). I also studied dance at the Graham School in New York.

"A new career opened to me as a dance teacher. This was something I thought I would never enjoy doing and found, to my delight, it was wonderful 'reaching' my students. Each one was special, and many have remained in contact with me through the years. I appreciate their friendship. I've been teaching dance for thirty years. I started at art centers and a local Y, continued at Bryn Mawr College for eight years, left to spend time with my children, and returned to teaching on a limited basis.

"Even though I graduated college with a degree in photography and worked in the field, I did put it aside for fifteen years. I found being married, performing in a dance company, and teaching dance was enough to handle. I figured that a younger body was 'right' for dance and later I could return to my photography.

"I did return after my two daughters were old enough to allow me uninterrupted studio and darkroom time. I photographed my children and their friends for many years. At the same time, because I have always enjoyed the beauty of nature, I spent endless hours photographing outdoors. All my photographs are shot with black and white film.

"I entered juried photography shows, won awards, exhibited in galleries, and eventually began doing commissioned work for private clients, galleries, and art consultants. During the last ten years I've concentrated on photographing still-lifes of natural objects and fruit which I photograph with black and white infrared film and then hand-color.

"While I was raising my children, one of our absolutely greatest pleasures was reading children's books with each other. They've been an important sharing experience. Even though my daughters are grown, we still give each other children's books because we find them to be so special.

"The fact that I ended up creating a children's book is still a source of amazement to me. I was invited to create *A Book of Fruit* after a New York publisher (Norma Jean Sawicki) happened to see my fruit still-lifes. From this evolved the idea of showing fruit and where they grow. It was an interesting and illuminating experience for me. Traveling to Florida to photograph starfruit, orange groves, and banana plantations and being warned to beware of the fire ants, and going to the New Jersey pine barrens and watching them harvest cranberries are just a couple of the experiences which have become indelible in my mind.

"My new book is titled *The Shell Book.* As with other things I've photographed, working on this book gave me the opportunity to share my way of seeing with others through my photography. It's a very satisfying experience and it's a pleasure to work with something I like so much. I've always collected shells on the beaches I've visited. They are nature's works of art."

LESTER, Helen 1936-

■ Personal

Born June 12, 1936, in Evanston, IL; daughter of William Howard (a businessman) and Elizabeth (Sargent) Doughty; married Robin Lester (a historian, teacher, and author), August 26, 1967; children: Robin Debevoise, James Robinson. *Education:* Bennett Junior College, A.A.S., 1956; Wheelock College, B.S., 1959. *Religion:* Protestant. *Hobbies and other interests:* Cooking, running, drawing, hiking.

■ Addresses

Home—2230 Lincoln Park W., Chicago, IL 60614.

■ Career

Writer. Elementary school teacher in Lexington, MA, 1959-62; Francis W. Parker School, Chicago, IL, teacher of second grade, 1962-69; Hamlin School, San Francisco, CA, teacher of first grade, 1987-89; Francis W. Parker School, teacher, 1989-92. Full-time school visitor and lecturer at teachers' conferences.

■ Awards, Honors

Colorado Children's Book Award, 1990, California Young Reader Medal, 1991, Nebraska Golden Sower Award, 1992, all for *Tacky the Penguin.*

■ Writings

(And illustrator) *Cora Copycat,* Dutton, 1979.
The Wizard, the Fairy, and the Magic Chicken, illustrated by Lynn Munsinger, Houghton, 1983.
It Wasn't My Fault, illustrated by Munsinger, Houghton, 1985.
A Porcupine Named Fluffy, illustrated by Munsinger, Houghton, 1986.
Pookins Gets Her Way, illustrated by Munsinger, Houghton, 1987.
Tacky the Penguin, illustrated by Munsinger, Houghton, 1988.
The Revenge of the Magic Chicken, illustrated by Munsinger, Houghton, 1990.
Me First, illustrated by Munsinger, Houghton, 1992.
Three Cheers for Tacky, illustrated by Munsinger, Houghton, 1994.
Lin's Backpack, illustrated by Munsinger, Addison-Wesley, 1994.
Kathy's Pocket, illustrated by Paul Harvey, Newbridge Communications, 1994.
Hop to the Top, illustrated by Patrick Girouard, Newbridge Communications, 1994.
(With Robin Lester) *Wuzzy Takes Off,* illustrated by Miko Imai, Candlewick Press, 1995.
Listen, Buddy, illustrated by Lynn Munsinger, Houghton, 1995.
The Four Getters and Arf, illustrated by Brian Karas, Addison-Wesley, 1995.

HELEN LESTER

Princess Penelope's Parrot, illustrated by Lynn Munsinger, Houghton, 1996.
(And illustrator) *Author: A True Story,* Houghton, 1997.

Lester's books have been translated into Spanish, French, German, Hungarian, and Japanese, and many are available in the United Kingdom.

■ Work in Progress

Tacky in Trouble, for Houghton.

■ Sidelights

Helen Lester has published many well-received picture books for the three-to-six-year-old age group, stories which the author once typified in *Something about the Author* (*SATA*) as "humorous approaches to a message." Her stories explore themes such as cooperation, feelings of guilt, clumsiness—things that form the center of a childhood universe. "When I was a mother of young children I felt a need for more short but satisfying bedtime stories," Lester told *SATA*. "That need spurred me into writing.... Life's pretty serious sometimes, and I feel the heavier concepts are better received if given a lighter touch."

Often working with illustrator Lynn Munsinger, Lester writes of wizards, porcupines, penguins, chickens, pigs, and rabbits, as well as little boys and girls. With her first title, *Cora Copycat,* Lester presents one such little girl whose copycat antics drive her family wild until one day a Wild Woolly Wurgal freshly escaped from the zoo cures her of this habit. Lester illustrated this first book herself, and a *Kirkus Reviews* critic noted both the "funny, comix-style cartoons" as well as Lester's "snappy text." With her next book, *The Wizard, the Fairy, and the Magic Chicken,* Lester teamed with Munsinger for the first time in a story of three sorcerers who are trying to outdo one another. Creating monsters, however, soon turns the sorcerers' competition into a need for cooperation. "Little kids will be all agog when they discover what happens next," concluded a *Publishers Weekly* reviewer. "A winner for kids and the adults who'll be reading it again and again," noted *Booklist*'s Ilene Cooper. This squabbling trio earned a reprise in Lester's *Revenge of the Magic Chicken,* which Cooper found "as zany as ever."

A little boy who refuses to accept blame forms the core of *It Wasn't My Fault.* Murdley Gurdson, while out for a walk one day, has an egg land on his head. When a round-robin of animals blames one another, Murdley is finally forced to admit that it is his fault. *Kirkus Reviews* found the story "deftly contrived, and comical without overstraining," while a *Bulletin of the Center for Children's Books* reviewer commented that it was "bright, sunnily nonsensical, capably structured and told." Names are at the center of *A Porcupine Named Fluffy,* and it is only when Fluffy meets a rhino named Hippo that things look brighter for the misnamed porcupine. *Publishers Weekly* noted that Munsinger and Lester "tell a sweet story with joyful exuberance."

Ideas come to Lester from many sources: from her own career as a teacher, from her children as they were growing up, from jokes and nonsense rhymes. "I am usually moved to write a book when an idea pops into my head," Lester told *SATA.* "And an idea pops into my head usually when I'm in the middle of an unexciting task—doing such things as standing in bank lines or washing spinach . . . . Once an idea comes into my head it usually takes one or two months of misfires and charging up blind alleys until the story is completed. From then on it's in the lap of my wonderful illustrator, Lynn Munsinger. Over ten books we've become very good friends. She draws what I would if I could."

Another little girl figured in *Pookins Gets Her Way,* a cautionary tale for children who must always have their own way. Pookins has ice cream for breakfast and practices roller-skating in the living room; in fact, the threat of her tantrums gets her anything she wants until she meets her match in a gnome from whom she demands three wishes. "It's extremely satisfying to see this rotten kid get her comeuppance," noted a reviewer for *Publishers Weekly.* Lester and Munsinger turned their hands to the antics of a penguin with the award-winning *Tacky the Penguin* and its sequel, *Three Cheers for Tacky.* Tacky is not your standard penguin; in fact, dressed in Hawaiian shirts and a purple bow tie, he hardly fits in with his other black-tie cousins. Though he doesn't fit, it is Tacky who saves his friends from hunters in *Tacky the Penguin,* which Phillis Wilson in

One Saturday, Pinkerton's Pig Scout troop went on a day trip to the beach. Pinkerton was first on the bus and sat in the front row.

Always pushing his way to the front, Pinkerton the pig finally gets his comeuppance. (From *Me First,* written by Lester and illustrated by Lynn Munsinger.)

Booklist called a "perceptive text about being different." Reviewing *Three Cheers for Tacky*, Ann A. Flowers concluded in *Horn Book* that the story was "a great comfort ... to nonconformists."

A pig, a parrot, and a rabbit are protagonists in a trio of books examining the consequences of selfishness, rudeness, and inattention. Greedy Pinkerton the pig mistakes a Sandwitch for a sandwich at a beach picnic in *Me First*, and is quickly up to his snout in trouble as the witch obliges him to do chores for her. "The Sandwitch is just the corny joke to amuse most children," Carolyn Jenks noted in *Horn Book*. The birthday parrot in *Princess Penelope's Parrot* provides the comeuppance for the nasty little princess to whom it is given when it sputters all the rude remarks it has learned from her at a most inappropriate moment—when potential suitor Prince Percival comes calling. Sally R. Dow, writing in *School Library Journal*, commented on the "delightfully droll humor" in the book as well as on Munsinger's "whimsical" illustrations. "Another small funny lesson in correct behavior from a well-known pair of collaborators," concluded *Horn Book* reviewer Ann A. Flowers. In *Listen, Buddy*, the eponymous bunny has trouble concentrating on what is said to him, despite his enormous ears. An adventure with Scruffy the Varmint helps Buddy to sharpen his listening skills in this "sprightly paced tale [which] amiably nudges kids whose direction-following skills need some honing," according to *Publishers Weekly*. "Sure to bring laughs at story time," concluded Virginia Opocensky in *School Library Journal*.

Lester has also written (and illustrated) a book about the writing life in her 1997 work *Author: A True Story*. "In the past three years since I left teaching," Lester told *SATA*, "I've visited over two hundred schools, encouraging children to write. *Author: A True Story* is based on what I tell them during these visits. The enthusiasm for writing I encounter on these visits is most encouraging—both students and teachers are so much more involved than I was years ago."

■ Works Cited

Cooper, Ilene, review of *The Wizard, the Fairy, and the Magic Chicken, Booklist*, March 1, 1983, p. 907.
Cooper, Ilene, review of *The Revenge of the Magic Chicken, Booklist*, March 1, 1990, p. 1344.
Review of *Cora Copycat, Kirkus Reviews*, October 1, 1979, p. 1142.
Dow, Sally R., review of *Princess Penelope's Parrot, School Library Journal*, October, 1996, p. 101.
Flowers, Ann A., review of *Three Cheers for Tacky, Horn Book*, October, 1994, p. 578.
Flowers, Ann A., review of *Princess Penelope's Parrot, Horn Book*, November-December, 1996, p. 727.
Review of *It Wasn't My Fault, Kirkus Reviews*, March 1, 1985, p. 8.
Review of *It Wasn't My Fault, Bulletin of the Center for Children's Books*, June, 1985, p. 188.
Jenks, Carolyn K., review of *Me First, Horn Book*, November-December, 1992, p. 717.

Review of *Listen, Buddy, Publishers Weekly*, July 24, 1995, p. 64.
Opocensky, Virginia, review of *Listen, Buddy, School Library Journal*, November, 1995, p. 76.
Review of *Pookins Gets Her Way, Publishers Weekly*, February 27, 1987, p. 163.
Review of *A Porcupine Named Fluffy, Publishers Weekly*, April 25, 1986, p. 73.
Wilson, Phillis, review of *Tacky the Penguin, Booklist*, April 1, 1988, p. 1351.
Review of *The Wizard, the Fairy, and the Magic Chicken, Publishers Weekly*, May 27, 1983, p. 68.

◖ For More Information See

PERIODICALS

Booklist, March 1, 1985, p. 985; April 15, 1986, p. 1223; April 15, 1987, p. 1290; October 1, 1992, p. 336; February 15, 1994, p. 1092; October 15, 1995, p. 412.
Bulletin of the Center for Children's Books, April, 1988, p. 159; March, 1990, pp. 168-69; January, 1997, p. 179.
Horn Book, September-October, 1986, p. 582.
Junior Bookshelf, October, 1987, p. 218.
Kirkus Reviews, January 1, 1983, p. 4.
New York Times Book Review, April 6, 1986, p. 21.
Publishers Weekly, August 3, 1992, p. 71; December 20, 1993, p. 71.
School Librarian, August, 1993, p. 103.
School Library Journal, October, 1979, p. 142; August, 1983, p. 54; May, 1985, p. 78; August, 1986, p. 84; August, 1987, p. 70; April, 1988, p. 82; May, 1990, p. 88; February, 1992, p. 66; October, 1992, p. 91; May, 1994, p. 98.
Times Educational Supplement, April 2, 1993, p. 16.

—*Sketch by J. Sydney Jones*

*   *   *

LIVINGSTON, Myra Cohn 1926-1996

OBITUARY NOTICE—See index for *SATA* sketch: Born August 17, 1926, in Omaha, NE; died of cancer, August 23, 1996, in Los Angeles, CA. Musician, critic, educator, poet, anthologist, and author. Livingston was one of the foremost American children's authors of the latter twentieth-century. She wrote scores of books and compiled about forty anthologies. A noted expert on children's poetry, Livingston used a variety of techniques to express the wonders and realities of the child's everyday world. Structured as free verse and rhythmic prose as well as in more exotic forms such as haiku and cinquain, Livingston's works address such subjects as nature, routine daily activities, emotions, festivities, and social problems in clear, modern language that Livingston flavored with humor and suggestions of spontaneity. Trained from early childhood to play the French horn, she began performing professionally in 1940. Livingston also began writing book reviews in 1948 for newspapers such as the *Los Angeles Daily News* and the *Los Angeles Mirror*. In 1950 she accepted a position as a personal secretary for entertainer Dinah Shore; she also held a similar post with musician Jascha Heifetz, and was working on a biography of the violinist before her death. In 1958 she began a series of jobs as an instructor at such institutions as the Dallas Public Library and Dallas Public School System and the University of California-Los Angeles. From 1966 until 1984, she was poet-in-residence at the Beverly Hills United School District. Beginning in 1975, Livingston worked as a poetry consultant to various publishers. She also taught classes for the International Reading Association, the National Council of Teachers of English, and other organizations. A prolific poet for children, she wrote volumes such as *Whispers and Other Poems, A Lollygag of Limericks,* and *My Head Is Red and Other Riddle Rhymes.* Her most recent books include *Light and Shadow, Let Freedom Ring: A Ballad of Martin Luther King, Jr., Flights and Fancy and Other Poems,* and *Abraham Lincoln: A Man for All People.* Among her many honors are the Kerlan Award from the University of Minnesota and a 1980 award from the National Council of Teachers of English for Excellence in Poetry for Children.

OBITUARIES AND OTHER SOURCES:

BOOKS

Children's Books and Their Creators, edited by Anita Silvey, Houghton Mifflin, 1995, p. 413.
Something about the Author Autobiography Series, Vol. 1, Gale, 1986, pp. 169-84.
Twentieth-Century Children's Writers, Fourth Edition, Gale, 1995, pp. 592-94.

PERIODICALS

Los Angeles Times, August 27, 1996, p. A19.
New York Times, August 27, 1996, p. B13.
Publishers Weekly, September 23, 1996, p. 31.
Teaching and Learning Literature, January-February, 1997, pp. 57-60.
Washington Post, August 26, 1996, p. B5.

* * *

LORKOWSKI, Thomas V(incent) 1950-
(Tommy L., Tom Lorkowski; Mr. Tivil, a pseudonym)

■ **Personal**

Born November 5, 1950, in Akron, OH; son of Vincent V. (a tinner) and Bessie (a homemaker) Lorkowski; married Candace Lee Keck, November 5, 1976; children: Tracy, John, Chris. *Education:* Kent State University, B.F.A. *Politics:* "Registered Democrat, vote independent." *Religion:* Catholic. *Hobbies and other interests:* "Touring the U.S. on my Honda Gold Wing motorcycle."

■ **Addresses**

Home—1739 Northeast Ave., Tallmadge, OH 44278.

THOMAS V. LORKOWSKI

■ **Career**

Goodyear Tire and Rubber, Akron, OH, molder and tire tread sculptor, 1973—; freelance artist for Record Publishing (includes *Tallmadge Express, Hudson Hub Times,* and *Falls News*). Freelance designer for businesses and organizations, including Goodyear Tire and Rubber, Inventure Place Science Museum, and Kent Toys; also designer of toys and games. Visiting author and illustrator at local schools, 1994—. *Member:* Honda Red Riders Club.

■ **Writings**

SELF-ILLUSTRATED; UNDER NAME TOMMY L.

Dr. Nim and the Nombex, University Classics (Athens, OH), 1994.
Dr. Nim and the Strange Quest, University Classics, 1995.
The Snoofle Hound Blues, University Classics, 1997.
Flight of the Smidgeon, University Classics, in press.

OTHER

Also author of *How I Write Stories,* self-published, 1995. Author and illustrator, under pseudonym Mr. Tivil, of *Bunn D. Baker and the Anything Maker, The Voice in the Stone, Bunn D. Baker and the Blue Bamboozle Berries,* and *Caring for Calvin Caboodle;* illustrator of story "Toodle D. Poodle," by Katherine Oana, University Classics, 1993; illustrator of "EnviroLearn" series by Carolyn Modugno and Rosalie McDermott, ECS Learning Systems (San Antonio, TX), 1996, and creator of cartoon, "Here 'Bouts," for *Tallmadge Express,* 1980s, both under name Tom Lorkowski.

Dr. Nim and the Nombex was chosen for inclusion in the DeGrummond Children's Literature Collection housed in the McCain Library Archives at the University of Southern Mississippi, 1995.

■ Sidelights

Thomas V. Lorkowski told *SATA:* "I began illustrating and writing twenty-five years ago after graduating from college. I sent my first drafts of *Dr. Nim* to publishers and was roundly rejected by them. (I sent *Dr. Nim* to about six of the larger publishing houses; they accepted only solicited works.)

"I soon got married and began the process of raising three children, leaving *Dr. Nim* by the wayside. Eventually the kids grew older, establishing lives of their own, so I dusted off my *Nim* manuscript and found a publisher in 1994. I polished my skills by cartooning for local newspapers and illustrating for local companies.

"Each book is a fable containing a moral. Hopefully, this will fill a niche in today's marketplace. My work is very influenced by Dr. Seuss and Richard Scarry. These are my all-time favorites. Using promotion, good writing, and good marketing tactics, University Classics and I think my books will do well. More later!"

■ For More Information See

PERIODICALS

Akron Beacon Journal, December 25, 1994, p. H4;
    September 17, 1995, p. G5.
Children's Room, November, 1994.
Record-Courier (Ravenna-Kent, OH) October 14, 1994,
    p. 5.
Tallmadge Express (OH), September 4, 1994, p. 18;
    December 11, 1994, p. 12; December 24, 1995, p. 7.

* * *

LORKOWSKI, Tom
See LORKOWSKI, Thomas V(incent)

* * *

LOVE, Douglas 1967-

■ Personal

Born August 3, 1967, in Milwaukee, WI; son of Martin (an attorney) and Beverly (a teacher; maiden name, Bernstein) Love.

■ Addresses

Agent—Renee Cho, McIntosh & Otis, 310 Madison Ave., New York, NY 10017.

DOUGLAS LOVE

■ Career

Writer, dramatist, educator. *Member:* Dramatists Guild.

■ Writings

Be Kind to Your Mother (Earth), illustrated by Robert Zimmerman, HarperCollins, 1993.
Blame It on the Wolf, illustrated by Robert Zimmerman, HarperCollins, 1993.
So You Want to Be a Star [play production kit including *Blame It on the Wolf* and *Be Kind to Your Mother (Earth)*], illustrated by Robert Zimmerman, HarperCollins, 1993.
Blame It on the Wolf and *Be Kind to Your Mother (Earth): Two Original Plays,* illustrated by Robert Zimmerman, HarperFestival, 1993.
Holiday in the Rain Forest, illustrated by Robert Zimmerman, HarperCollins, 1994.
Kabuki Gift, illustrated by Robert Zimmerman, HarperCollins, 1994.
Holiday in the Rain Forest and *Kabuki Gift: Two Plays,* illustrated by Robert Zimmerman, HarperCollins, 1994.
Imagination Station: 99 Games to Spark Your Imagination, HarperCollins, 1995.
The Little House Christmas Theater Kit, illustrated by Holly Jones, HarperCollins, 1995.

Great American Kids Slumber Party Book, Morrow, 1997.

Great American Kids Backyard Campout Book, Morrow, 1997.

Disney Do-It-Yourself Costume & Face Painting Kit, Disney Press, 1997.

ADAPTER

Marlo Thomas and others, *Free to Be ... You and Me,* Rodgers and Hammerstein Theatre Library, 1989.

■ Sidelights

Author, playwright, producer/director, lecturer, and teacher, Douglas Love has been involved with the theater professionally since he was a child actor. He told *SATA,* "From the very first moment I stepped foot inside a theater, I came to realize that it was the most magical place in the world. My life would never be the same." Love appeared in more than 50 productions as a child, ranging from *The Skin of Our Teeth* and Moliere's *The Miser* to Shakespeare's *Macbeth.*

Using his early acting experience, Love has learned to create plays that introduce children to the performing arts not only as something that is fun to participate in, but also as a way of opening doors to new knowledge and a higher quality of life. His plays *Blame It on the Wolf* and *Be Kind to Your Mother (Earth)* take familiar children's stories or historical events and add a contemporary twist that induces young readers and actors to think about these narratives in a new way. Thus in *Blame It on the Wolf,* the wolf is put on trial for eating Little Red Riding Hood's grandmother, and the reader sees things from the wolf's point of view. Similarly, in *Be Kind to Your Mother (Earth),* three young time-travelers journey to eighteenth-century America to explain the environmental evils of chopping down cherry trees to George Washington and to stop the Patriots in Boston from polluting their harbor with tea.

These two plays have been published to critical praise not only as separate trade books but as parts of a "theater kit" that includes a Director's Guide, a marquis, playbills, and dressing room stickers. "Students will enjoy reading and presenting these two original plays.... They're filled with offbeat, slapstick humor and lots of opportunities for young actors to ham it up," commented Chris Sherman in *Booklist.* Writing in *School Library Journal,* Judie Porter praised Love's introduction for its "valuable instructions for young would-be actors and directors."

Using a theatrical approach to science, Love also created *Imagination Station,* a spiral-bound book of 99 activities to encourage children to think creatively or act out ideas about scientific questions, such as how two disparate objects can go together, how to create a new product, or how a butterfly might talk. The activities were described by Cathy Collison in the *Detroit Free Press* as "great right-brain exercises to spark that creative fire."

Love has also been active as a creator of children's theater productions and as an adapter of children's stories for the theater. Indeed, many of his published plays have also received student workshop productions at the Children's Theater School of Milwaukee, Wisconsin, and Vail, Colorado, of which Love is a founding board member and guest artist. In the six years of its existence as a nonprofit institution, the Children's Theater School has brought extracurricular theater arts instruction to over 3,000 children and adults. Love's adaptation of Marlo Thomas's *Free to Be ... You and Me* was published by the Rodgers and Hammerstein Theatre Library in 1989.

Currently Love is the Producing/Artistic Director of the Broadway Children's Theater. He is also developing a new television series for the Disney channel and has multiproject contracts with HarperCollins, Morrow, and Hyperion publishers. He is a popular keynote speaker and workshop leader. As a speaker, he has appeared at conventions of the American Booksellers Association, California Reading Association, Dramatists Guild, and Asilomar Reading Conference. He has led workshops at the Children's Museum in Manhattan, the League of American Theatres and Producers, Walker Arts Center in Minneapolis, Vail Valley Arts Council, and the Milwaukee Ballet, among other venues.

Love's understanding of his field can perhaps best be summed up in his observation that "in the world of children performing plays, there are no small parts—just some small actors."

■ Works Cited

Collison, Cathy, review of *Imagination Station, Detroit Free Press,* November 8, 1995.

Porter, Judie, review of *Be Kind to Your Mother (Earth)* and *Blame It on the Wolf, School Library Journal,* May, 1993, p. 117.

Sherman, Chris, review of *Be Kind to Your Mother (Earth)* and *Blame It on the Wolf, Booklist,* March 1, 1993, p. 1228.

■ For More Information See

PERIODICALS

Los Angeles Times Book Review, May 2, 1993, p. 72.
Publishers Weekly, September 25, 1995, p. 58.
Voice of Youth Advocates, June, 1993, p. 118.

M

MAGORIAN, James 1942-

■ Personal

Born April 24, 1942, in Palisade, NE; son of Jack and Dorothy (Gorthey) Magorian. *Education:* University of Nebraska, B.S., 1965; Illinois State University, M.S., 1969; attended Oxford University, 1972, and Harvard University, 1973. *Hobbies and other interests:* "Projects on behalf of wildlife and a cleaner environment."

■ Addresses

Home—Helena, MT. *Office*—1225 North 46th St., Lincoln, NE 68503.

■ Career

Writer.

■ Writings

FOR CHILDREN

School Daze, Peradam Publishing House, 1978.
Seventeen Percent, Black Oak Press, 1978.
The Magic Pretzel, Black Oak Press, 1979.
Ketchup Bottles, Peradam Publishing House, 1979.
Imaginary Radishes, Black Oak Press, 1979.
Plucked Chickens, Black Oak Press, 1980.
Fimperings and Torples, Black Oak Press, 1981.
Floyd, Black Oak Press, 1982.
The Three Diminutive Pigs, Black Oak Press, 1982.
Kumquats, Black Oak Press, 1983.
Fouled Spark Plugs, Black Oak Press, 1983.
Griddlemort and the Questionists, Black Oak Press, 1983.
The Witches' Olympics, Black Oak Press, 1983.
Piffle, Black Oak Press, 1983.
Cucumber Cake, Black Oak Press, 1984.
The Lion and the Mouse, Black Oak Press, 1984.
Keeper of Fire, Council for Indian Education, 1984.
Bad Report Cards, Black Oak Press, 1985.
Ground Hog Day, Black Oak Press, 1987.
Magic Spell # 207, Centaur Books, 1988.

JAMES MAGORIAN

The Beautiful Music, Black Oak Press, 1988.
The Bad Eggs, Centaur Books, 1989.
Spoonproof Jello, Black Oak Press, 1990.
Mud Pies, Black Oak Press, 1991.
The Tooth Fairy, Black Oak Press, 1993.
All the Wild Witches, Those Most Noble Ladies, Black Oak Press, 1995.
Aardvarks on a Holiday, Black Oak Press, 1996.

POETRY

Hitchhiker in Hall Country, Ibis Press, 1968.

Almost Noon, Ibis Press, 1969.
Ambushes and Apologies, Ibis Press, 1970.
The Garden of Epicurus, Ibis Press, 1971.
The Last Reel of the Late Movie, Third Eye Press, 1972.
Distances, Ibis Press, 1972.
Mandrake Root Beer, Cosmic Wheelbarrow Chapbooks, 1973.
The Red, White and Blue Bus, Samisdat Press, 1975.
Bosnia and Herzegovina, Third Eye Press, 1976.
Alphabetical Order, Amphion Press, 1976.
Two Hundred Push-Ups at the Y.M.C.A., Specific Gravity Publications, 1977.
The Ghost of Hamlet's Father, Peradam Publishing House, 1977.
Safe Passage, Stone Country Press, 1977.
Notes to the Milkman, Black Oak Press, 1978.
Phases of the Moon, Black Oak Press, 1978.
Piano Tuning at Midnight, Laughing Bear Press, 1979.
Revenge, Samisdat Press, 1979.
The Night Shift at the Poetry Factory, Broken Whisker Studio Press, 1979.
Spiritual Rodeo, Toothpaste Press, 1980.
Ideas for a Bridal Shower, Black Oak Press, 1980.
Tap Dancing on a Tightrope, Laughing Bear Press, 1981.
Training at Home to Be a Locksmith, Black Oak Press, 1981.
The Great Injun Carnival, Black Oak Press, 1982.
Taxidermy Lessons, Black Oak Press, 1982.
The Walden Pond Caper, Black Oak Press, 1983.
Travel Expenses, Laughing Bear Press, 1984.
The Emily Dickinson Jogging Book, Black Oak Press, 1984.
Weighing the Sun's Light, Centaur, 1985.
Charles Darwin and the Theory of Evolution, Black Oak Press, 1985.
Summer Snow, Black Oak Press, 1985.
The Magician's Handbook, Centaur, 1986.
Karl Marx and International Communism, Black Oak Press, 1986.
Squall Line, Black Oak Press, 1986.
The Hideout of the Sigmund Freud Gang, Black Oak Press, 1987.
Mountain Man, Black Oak Press, 1989.
Amelia Earhart Playing Video Games, Centaur Books, 1990.
Saudi Arabia, Centaur Books, 1991.
Borderlands, Black Oak Press, 1992.
Catalpa Blossoms, Black Oak Press, 1994.
The Yellowstone Meditations, Poetry Forum Press, 1996.

OTHER

America First, Black Oak Press, 1992.
The Man Who Wore Layers of Clothing in the Winter, Black Oak Press, 1994.
Hearts of Gold, Acme Press, 1996.

Contributor of poems to more than 150 literary magazines, including *American Poet, Ararat, Bitterroot, Haiku Journal, Kansas Quarterly, New Earth Review, Spoon River Review, Black River Review, Bogg, Calypso, Different Drummer, Gulf Stream, Huron Review, Illinois Quarterly, Laughing Bear, Montana Gothic, Nebraska Review, Oxford Magazine, Plastic Tower, Rolling Stone, Slant, Stone Country*, and *Whole Notes*.

■ Work in Progress

"A young adult novel set in a small Nebraska town during World War II."

■ Sidelights

James Magorian once told *SATA:* "I deal in whimsy. Eccentric characters and dadaistic characters are bread and butter to me. I like to concoct gently bizarre stories. If I don't have fun writing a story, I throw it away and start another one. I seldom start a children's book with a clear goal or moral in mind. I write mostly nonsense stories in which I let situations and crazy creatures move in a manner and at a pace that they would move if they really existed. I am tolerant of those creatures and their obsessions, and I don't mind losing control of them and allowing things to happen that I never thought until the moment I write them. Nonsense has a progression, but it is according to its own weird logic. If a reader can anticipate what's coming on the next page, then I've failed as a writer. My stories for young people are purely for enjoyment. I reserve social ills, politics, violence, etc., as topics for my poetry and leave them out of my children's stories. My children's-story creatures are usually guilty of nothing more than simple foolishness."

Recently Magorian added, "When I write poetry I seldom begin with a blueprint, logical foreordained goals. Some word or image or connection sets off the flow. I seem to be kin to the Native American view of the land and flow of life, of images, a usable, sentimental past, letting things drift into their own order rather than trying to pound them into place, accepting the welling up, the mystical flashes and transcendences of the ordinary day."

■ For More Information See

PERIODICALS

Publishers Weekly, April 4, 1996, p. 52.
Small Press Review, February, 1995, pp. 8-9.

*   *   *

MANIATTY, Taramesha 1978-

■ Personal

Born May 25, 1978, in Newport, VT; daughter of John Soteros (a minister) and Deborah Jean (an administrative assistant; maiden name, Willemain) Maniatty. *Politics:* "Generally Republican." *Religion:* "Born-again Christian." *Hobbies and other interests:* Horseback riding, playing guitars, writing songs.

TARAMESHA MANIATTY

■ Addresses

Home and office—RR 1, Box 680, Morrisville, VT 05661. *Electronic mail*—Taramesha@AOL.com (America Online).

■ Career

Author and illustrator. *Member:* Absolutely Free (a local food bank for the poor).

■ Awards, Honors

First place, Landmark Editions National Written and Illustrated By ... Awards Contest, 1994, for *Glory Trail.*

■ Writings

(Self-illustrated) *Glory Trail,* Landmark Editions, 1995.

■ Work in Progress

First book of a historical novel series "Sovereign Soul," which takes place during the Third Crusade from the years 1187-1191 A.D.

■ Sidelights

Taramesha Maniatty told *SATA:* "In 1994 I composed the book *Glory Trail* to enter in Landmark's national contest. By the fall I received a call that I had won the awards contest. Soon I had signed the contract and was on my way to having my very first book published. After much time and devotion *Glory Trail* was published. This past year I have traveled to schools throughout Vermont and other states to speak about my book, Landmark Edition's Contest, and how students may create and enter a book of their very own, always with the possibility of having it published!

"For the first couple of years of high school I had struggled with the option of college. Did I want to go? What would I go for? I loved writing, yet I loved painting as well. I loved children, yet I loved to work alone as well. Was there any occupation in which I could do all of it while still fulfilling my deepest desire to marry and have a family of my own? It seemed impossible but as I trusted my Lord Jesus and sought His direction, He revealed His will for my life. Those desires were God-given, and if I returned them to the very One who gave them, I knew He would show me where and what to do.

"Putting together *Glory Trail* was the very first time I had put writing and illustrating together. After *Glory Trail* was published I knew the Lord had answered my prayers. My gifts could be used together after all! As I traveled to speak to kids about my book and enjoyed working with the young children, I realized the Lord had answered yet another desire.... I can see the direction, though all the bends and turns may not be visible yet as my eyes stay on the One lighting the path I shall see them when they come.

"I am now working on my next project: a historical novel series based around King Richard the Lionhearted and the Third Crusade. Though this next book is definitely aimed at a higher reading level than *Glory Trail,* it should still be understood and entertaining for students in the intermediate and advanced levels of schooling. When I am not researching or writing, my time is spent painting, drawing, and sketching. My inventory of art work is ever increasing.

"Being a self-employed writer and artist can be difficult sometimes, that is sure, but being at home with my very supportive family—including both parents and five sisters—makes the tough times easier. By learning my artistic skills now, when I get married it will be less work to be able to sit down for two hours and produce a piece of work.

"Looking back I recall the longing to know what to do and where to go in life. There was a point, however, where it just didn't matter anymore, and *that* is when my Lord was able to start showing me *His way,* and *His way* is so much better than mine could ever be!"

*   *   *

MARKLE, Sandra L(ee) 1946-

■ Personal

Born November 10, 1946, in Fostoria, OH; daughter of Robert (a general foreman) and Dorothy (a secretary;

maiden name, Sauler) Haldeman; married William Markle (a programmer/analyst), August 10, 1968; children: Scott, Holly. *Education:* Bowling Green State University, B.S. (magna cum laude), 1968; graduate study at Ohio University, 1970-71, and University of North Carolina, 1973-74.

■ Addresses

Home and office—2416 Magnolia Springs Court, Atlanta, GA 30345. *Agent*—Carolyn Krupp IMG-Bach, 22 E. 71st St., New York, NY 10021. *Electronic mail*—markle@compuquill.com.

■ Career

Full-time writer, 1980—. Teacher at elementary schools in Woodville, OH, 1968-69, Athens, OH, 1969-71, and Asheville, NC, 1971-79; Chapel Hill Middle School, Douglasville, GA, science teacher, 1979-80. Presents teacher workshops and science assembly programs for students; science consultant for *Instructor* and Corporation for Public Broadcasting; planning committee consultant for *Peanut* (Harcourt Brace Jovanovich); consultant on computer book projects for Learning Works and Lothrop, Lee & Shepard; consultant and writer of teacher's guides and worksheets for *Class Works!* (Scholastic); science education consultant for *Big Science* (Scholastic).

Writer and presenter of *Science Shop,* a series on WLOS-TV, Asheville, NC, 1978, and *Ms. Whiz,* a series on WANX-TV, Atlanta, GA, 1979-80; consultant, designer, and planner of elementary science textbook

SANDRA L. MARKLE

series for Addison-Wesley, 1988-89; researcher and planner for "A Hole in the Sky," a CNN special, 1992; planner for "Young and Dangerous: The Problem of Teen Violence," a CNN special, 1994; consultant for *Featherby's Fables,* a science series for K-3 grade children for Children's Television for the Corporation for Public Broadcasting; technical consultant for "Dr. Fad," a nationally syndicated television program.

■ Awards, Honors

Outstanding Book selection, National Science Teachers Association, for *Exploring Winter;* "Pick of the List," American Booksellers Association, 1991, for *Outside and Inside You,* and 1995, for *Outside and Inside Snakes;* Young Adults choice book, International Reading Association, 1994, for *The Fledglings;* Outstanding Science Trade Books for Children, National Science Teachers Association/Children's Book Council, 1995, for *Outside and Inside Spiders, Outside and Inside Birds,* and *Science to the Rescue;* Notable Books selection, American Library Association, 1995, for *Outside and Inside Birds;* selected participant, Authors and Artist Program in Antarctica, National Science Foundation, 1996.

■ Writings

NONFICTION

Kids' Computer Capers: Investigations for Beginners, illustrated by Stella Ormai, Lothrop, 1983.
The Programmer's Guide to the Galaxy, illustrated by Ormai, Lothrop, 1984.
(And illustrator; with husband, William Markle) *In Search of Graphics: Adventures in Computer Art,* Lothrop, 1984.
(And illustrator) *Digging Deeper: Investigations into Rocks, Shocks, Quakes, and Other Earthy Matters,* Lothrop, 1987.
(And illustrator) *Science Mini-Mysteries,* Atheneum, 1988.
(And illustrator) *Power Up: Experiments, Puzzles, and Games Exploring Electricity,* Atheneum, 1989.
A Young Scientists' Guide to Successful Science Projects, Lothrop, 1990.
Discovering Science Secrets, Scholastic/Lucky, 1991.
Earth Alive!, Lothrop, 1991.
(And illustrator) *The Kids' Earth Handbook,* Atheneum Children's, 1991.
Discovering More Science Secrets, Scholastic, 1992.
Science in a Bag, Scholastic/Lucky, 1993.
(And illustrator) *Math Mini-Mysteries,* Atheneum, 1993.
A Rainy Day, illustrated by Cathy Johnson, Orchard Books, 1993.
Science: Just Add Salt, Scholastic, 1994.
Science to the Rescue, Atheneum, 1994.
Science in a Bottle, Scholastic/Lucky, 1995.
Measuring Up: Experiments, Puzzles & Games Exploring Measurement, Atheneum, 1995.
What Happens Next?, Longstreet Press, 1995.
Discovering Graph Secrets, Atheneum, 1996.
What Happens Next? Two, Longstreet Press, 1996.

Creepy, Crawly Baby Bugs, Walker, 1996.
Creepy, Spooky Science, illustrated by Cecile Schoberle, Hyperion, 1996.
Icky Squishy Science, Hyperion, 1996.
Science Surprises, Scholastic/Lucky, 1996.
Still More What Happens Next?, Longstreet Press, 1996.
A Hole in the Sky: Investigating the Ozone Problem, Sierra Club, 1997.
All Gone! an Alphabet of Extinct Animals, illustrated by Felipe Davalos, Simon & Schuster, 1997.
Weird Science, Hyperion, 1997.
SuperCool Science: South Pole Stations Past, Present, Future, Walker, 1997.
Super Science Secrets, Longstreet, 1997.

"SEASON OF SCIENCE" SERIES; SELF-ILLUSTRATED

Exploring Winter, Atheneum, 1984.
Exploring Summer: A Season of Science Activities, Puzzlers, and Games, Atheneum, 1987.
Exploring Spring: A Season of Science Activities, Puzzlers, & Games, Atheneum, 1990.
Exploring Autumn: A Season of Science Activities, Puzzlers, & Games, Atheneum, 1991.

"OUTSIDE INSIDE" SERIES

Outside and Inside You, Simon & Schuster, 1991.
Outside and Inside Trees, Simon & Schuster, 1993.
Outside and Inside Spiders, Simon & Schuster, 1994.
Outside and Inside Birds, Simon & Schuster, 1995.
Outside and Inside Snakes, Simon & Schuster, 1995.
Outside and Inside Sharks, Atheneum, 1996.
Outside and Inside Bats, Atheneum, 1997.

"PIONEERING" SERIES

Pioneering Space, Atheneum, 1992.
Pioneering Ocean Depths, Atheneum, 1995.
Pioneering Frozen Worlds: Polar Region Exploration, Atheneum, 1996.

FICTION

The Fledglings, Bantam, 1992.

TEXTBOOKS

Primary Science Sampler, Learning Works, 1980.
Science Sampler, Learning Works, 1980.
Computer Tutor: An Introduction to Computers, illustrated by Bev Armstrong, Learning Works, 1981.
Computer Tutor Junior, illustrated by Bev Armstrong, Learning Works, 1982.
Weather/Electricity/Environmental Investigations, Learning Works, 1982.

Author of books for instructors, including *Instructor's Big Book of Health and Safety*, 1985; *Hands-On Science*, 1988; and *Creative Science Classrooms*, 1991. Also author of "Natural Wonder Notebook," a monthly column in *Instructor*, and "The Learning Center," a monthly column in *Teaching and Computers*. Contributing editor, *Teaching and Computers*, 1983—. Contributor to magazines, including *Cricket, Highlights for Children, Jack and Jill, Ranger Rick, 3-2-1 Contact, Woman's Day, The Macintosh Buyer's Guide, PC World, Early Childhood Teacher, Classworks, Big Magazine, Parenting Magazine, Family Fun*, and *Learning*.

■ Work in Progress

Outside and Inside Alligators and Crocodiles, for Simon & Schuster; *Down, Down, Down in the Sea*, for Walker; *Windy Weather Science*, for Scholastic; *Outside and Inside Pouched Animals*, for Simon & Schuster; *After the Spill: Ten Years after the Exxon Valdez*, for Walker; "Growing Up Wild" series, for Simon & Schuster; "Kit and Caboodle Curriculum: Elementary Science Curriculum on the Internet" pilot project.

■ Sidelights

Sandra L. Markle, who once worked as a science teacher, has devoted her time to the creation of science books for children. Her many books on animals, science experiments, computers, exploration, geology, and other specific topics have been well received by most critics, and Markle is a sought-after science education consultant. "Few writers have quite the handle Markle does on how kids think about science," wrote a *Kirkus Reviews* critic in a review of *Icky Squishy Science*.

An irresistible hands-on approach to science for middle graders, this collection of experiments includes how to blow up a marshmallow, build a worm farm, and see why a dead fish floats. (Cover illustration by Cecile Schoberle.)

Critics have identified more than one reason for Markle's success as a science writer for children. First, Markle carefully pairs science with fiction. *The Programmer's Guide to the Galaxy,* which frames instruction about BASIC programming within an adventure story, was lauded by R. Scott Grabinger in *Voice of Youth Advocates* as "fun," "instructional," and an "excellent book for beginning and intermediate BASIC programmers." Second, as many critics have noted, Markle writes about science in a lucid manner. This is exemplified in *Digging Deeper: Investigations into Rocks, Shocks, Quakes, and Other Earthy Matters,* a book which educates children about geography while showing them how to construct volcanoes and conduct other projects. Beth Ames Herbert commented in *Booklist* that "Markle's lighthanded touch makes even technical jargon unintimidating." As *Power Up: Experiments, Puzzles, and Games Exploring Electricity* demonstrates, Markle makes it easy to learn about science without spending a lot of money or working in a lab. *A Rainy Day* is meant to be read by a child who enjoys walking in the rain and explains such things as how a cloud forms and why umbrellas are shaped the way they are. Janice Del Negro remarked in *Booklist* that *A Rainy Day* uses "a picture book format with strong visual narrative." Finally, in books like *Icky Squishy Science* and *Creepy, Spooky Science,* Markle encourages children to learn about science as they do something they love: get their hands dirty.

Another reason for Markle's success as a science writer is, perhaps, based on her own enthusiasm for exploration and her eagerness to share this with children. She told *SATA,* "I can't believe the opportunities writing provides me! I've just returned from spending a month exploring New Zealand, and before that I was in Antarctica for six weeks. I was able to travel to the South Pole—something I'd always dreamed of doing—and was transported by helicopter to spend a few hours as the only human in the midst of a penguin rookery. I've also spent a few days behind the scenes with the Ringling Brothers Barnum & Bailey Circus, been up in the Good Year Blimp, and lots more. Each new project brings new adventures. I always think of myself as the eyes and ears and fingers of all the young readers that will eventually be sharing my experiences through my books and magazine articles."

Many of Markle's books are published in series or thematically related groups. The "Outside and Inside" books provide children with a scientific understanding of some of their favorite plants and creatures. *Outside and Inside Sharks,* for example, explains how a shark's body works to make it a good hunter. *School Library Journal* contributor Melissa Hudak remarked that young shark lovers would be "thrilled" with *Outside and Inside Sharks. Outside and Inside Snakes,* which, according to Karey Wehner in *School Library Journal,* is a "remarkably perceptive introduction to the ever-fascinating slitherer," discusses the anatomy, bodily functions, habits, and life cycle of the snake. *Outside and Inside Spiders,* noted a *Kirkus Reviews* critic, tells how spiders "move, eat, molt, build webs and raise young."

"Succinctly written," Karey Wehner explained in *School Library Journal, Outside and Inside Spiders* "offers more detail on body functions than is currently available in other books." *Booklist* critic Chris Sherman described *Outside and Inside Birds* as an "introduction to avian anatomy" that "will fascinate browsers."

One of the "Outside and Inside" books takes a look at a familiar creature: the healthy human child. *Outside and Inside You* includes questions, suggestions, answers, and comparisons illustrated with close-up photos, X-rays, and computer pictures to provide children with the opportunity to understand their bodies. Markle covers skin, muscles, bones, major organs, and other parts of the body. Stephanie Zvirin of *Booklist* described Markle's text as "accessible," commenting that her "clear explanations are rooted in children's everyday experience." The "Outside and Inside" books, with color photos, also include glossaries, indexes, and pronunciation guides.

Markle's "Pioneering" books allow children to witness the scientific exploration of far away worlds and encourage them to use their own scientific skills. In *Pioneering Frozen Worlds: Polar Region Exploration,* Markle follows scientists working in the North and South Poles and explains how they live and work. She describes the experiments the scientists are conducting, and includes notes and suggestions for minor experiments that can help children understand. *Pioneering Space* tells about space travel, space equipment, and future space colonization. It provides instructions for two experiments (one on rocket power and another on hydroponics systems). "This timely, attractively illustrated treatment of space exploration will excite young readers," Margaret M. Hagel commented in *School Library Journal.*

Markle's books in the "Season of Science" series, which she illustrated herself with line drawings, explain seasonal changes as well as traditional seasonal activities. The books provide a variety of lessons, science experiments, crafts, and games for children. A number of historical facts, mythical stories, riddles, and jokes are also included. *Exploring Spring,* for example, shows readers how to identify flowers and teaches them about egg development. Gayle Berge explained in *School Library Journal* that *Exploring Summer* could "provide an entire summer of ... growing in scientific knowledge." "The number of winter tidbits assembled here is amazing," *School Library Journal* contributor Jeffrey A. French wrote in a review of *Exploring Winter.* These seasonal books are designed to make learning fun, and Markle's style reflects this. As Hazel Rochman pointed out in a review of *Exploring Autumn* for *Booklist,* "Markle isn't afraid to be lyrical ... or silly."

Although most of Markle's books are nonfiction, she is also the author of a novel, *The Fledglings.* In this story, Kate's mother is killed by a drunk driver, leaving the fourteen-year-old protagonist an orphan. She is faced with the prospect of living with the family of her disagreeable uncle and aunt when she learns that her paternal grandfather is still alive. Although this grandfa-

A Rainy Day
by SANDRA MARKLE
illustrated by CATHY JOHNSON

Markle invites very young children to observe, enjoy, and learn simple scientific concepts from raindrops with the help of Cathy Johnson's apt illustrations.

ther has refused to care for her, Kate runs away to Cherokee, North Carolina, to find him. At first, her grandfather does not welcome her. Gradually, however, Kate earns his trust, and comes to learn about her Cherokee heritage and life in the forest. In addition, Kate helps fight illegal poaching and cares for a fledgling eagle, prompting a *Publishers Weekly* reviewer to praise her "pluck and resourcefulness in daunting surroundings" while concluding Markle's story "fun to read."

Markle hasn't kept her talents reserved for the realm of text. She has worked on television programs for many years and is making her work accessible in cyberspace. "I've been communicating via the Internet and my special project called Online Expeditions," she told *SATA*. "The Internet is perfect for me because now I'm able to share what's happening in real time—including digitized pictures—even from places as remote as an icebreaker in the middle of the Ross Sea off the coast of Antarctica."

■ Works Cited

Berge, Gayle, review of *Exploring Summer, School Library Journal,* April, 1987, p. 100.

Del Negro, Janice, review of *A Rainy Day, Booklist,* March 1, 1993, p. 1233.

Review of *The Fledglings, Publishers Weekly,* June 8, 1992, p. 64.

French, Jeffrey A., review of *Exploring Winter, School Library Journal,* November, 1984, p. 126.

Grabinger, R. Scott, review of *The Programmer's Guide to the Galaxy, Voice of Youth Advocates,* April, 1985, p. 66.

Hagel, Margaret M., review of *Pioneering Space, School Library Journal,* February, 1993, p. 101.

Herbert, Beth Ames, review of *Digging Deeper, Booklist,* December 15, 1987, pp. 710-11.

Hudak, Melissa, review of *Outside and Inside Sharks, School Library Journal,* March, 1996, p. 212.

Review of *Icky Squishy Science, Kirkus Reviews,* April 18, 1996, p. 230.

Review of *Outside and Inside Spiders, Kirkus Reviews,*
     March 15, 1994, p. 399.
Rochman, Hazel, review of *Exploring Autumn, Booklist,*
     November 1, 1991, p. 514.
Sherman, Chris, review of *Outside and Inside Birds,
     Booklist,* November 1, 1994, p. 504.
Wehner, Karey, review of *Outside and Inside Snakes,
     School Library Journal,* June, 1995, p. 122.
Wehner, Karey, review of *Outside and Inside Spiders,
     School Library Journal,* June, 1994, p. 141.
Zvirin, Stephanie, review of *Outside and Inside You,
     Booklist,* March 15, 1991, p. 1494.

■ For More Information See

PERIODICALS

Booklist, July, 1990, p. 2091; January 1, 1992, p. 827;
     May 1, 1996, p. 1501.
Bulletin of the Center for Children's Books, September,
     1992, pp. 18-19; February, 1996, p. 196.
Horn Book, March-April, 1991, pp. 216-17.
Kirkus Reviews, April 1, 1987, p. 555; July 1, 1989, p.
     994; August 15, 1992, p. 1064; March 15, 1994, p.
     399; January 15, 1996, p. 136.
Publishers Weekly, March 8, 1993, p. 77.
School Library Journal, January, 1988, p. 82; October,
     1988, p. 157; June, 1995, p. 122; May, 1996, p. 124;
     October, 1996, p. 136.
Voice of Youth Advocates, December, 1993, p. 324.

*   *   *

MASTERS, William
See COUSINS, Margaret

*   *   *

McGILL, Ormond 1913-

■ Personal

Born June 15, 1913, in Palo Alto, CA; son of Harry A.
and Julia Battele; married Delight Olmstead, 1943
(deceased, 1976). *Education:* Attended San Jose State
College.

■ Addresses

Home and office—455 E. Charleston Rd., Palo Alto, CA
94306. *Agent*—Henry Rossoff Literary Agency, 4800
Osage Dr., Boulder, CO 80303.

■ Career

Magician, hypnotist, and author. Performed in western
resorts, 1930s; launched original Spook Show under title
"The Great London Hypnotic Seance," touring throughout American west and midwest and Canada, beginning
1942; has performed in numerous countries. Instructor
in hypnotism and hypnotherapy, beginning 1980s; has
served on the faculty of the Hypnotherapy Training

Institute (H.T.I.) of Northern California. Former member of Advisory Board of National Guild of Hypnotists.

■ Awards, Honors

Children's Choice Award, International Reading Associ-
ation/Children's Book Council (IRA/CBC), 1993, for
Paper Magic; recipient of Dr. Rexford L. North Award
from National Guild of Hypnotists. Honorary Ph.D. in
hypnotherapy from St. John's University (Louisiana);
Ormond McGill Day declared by New Hampshire state
legislature; Ormond McGill Chair awarded annually by
National Guild of Hypnotists.

■ Writings

FOR CHILDREN

Science Magic: 101 Experiments You Can Do, Arco,
     1984.
Balancing Magic and Other Tricks, illustrated by Anne
     Canevari Green, Franklin Watts, 1986.
*Paper Magic: Creating Fantasies & Performing Tricks
     with Paper,* illustrated by Anne Canevari Green,
     Millbrook, 1992.
*Voice Magic: Secrets of Ventriloquism & Voice Conjur-
     ing,* illustrated by Anne Canevari Green, Millbrook,
     1992.
Chalk Talks!: The Magical Art of Drawing with Chalk,
     illustrated by Anne Canevari Green, Millbrook,
     1995.
Mind Magic: Tricks for Reading Minds, illustrated by
     Anne Canevari Green, Millbrook, 1995.

ORMOND McGILL

Author of columns "The Psychic Circle" and "Hypnotic Comments" in the original *TOPS* magazine.

FOR ADULTS

The Encyclopedia of Genuine Stage Hypnotism, Abbott's Magic Company, 1947; revised and expanded as *Professional Stage Hypnotism,* Westwood (Los Angeles, CA), 1994; volume 2: *The Art of Stage Hypnotism,* Magic Limited (Oakland, CA), 1975.

The Secret World Of Witchcraft, A. S. Barnes (South Brunswick, NJ), 1973.

How to Produce Miracles, A. S. Barnes, 1976.

(With Ron Ormond) *Into the Strange Unknown: Religious Mysteries of the Orient,* A. S. Barnes, 1976; revised, expanded, and published as *Hypnotism and Mysticism of India,* Westwood, 1979.

Entertaining with Magic, A. S. Barnes., 1977.

The Mysticism and Magic of India, A. S. Barnes, 1977.

Hypnotism and Meditation, Westwood, 1981.

Grieve No More, Beloved: The Book of Delight, Anglo-American Book Co., 1995.

The New Encyclopedia of Stage Hypnotism, Anglo-American Book Co., 1996.

Seeing the Unseen, Anglo-American Book Co., 1997.

Contributor to *The Journal of Hypnotism,* beginning 1951.

■ Sidelights

After a full career as a professional magician and hypnotist and author of books on those subjects for adults, Ormond McGill took up writing for children in his seventies in 1984, and by 1995 had published six books on magic for young people.

His first such book, *Science Magic,* presents scientific principles and then describes magic tricks based on them. Lists of materials needed to present each trick and methods of presentation, including diagrams, are also included. Writing in *Kliatt,* a reviewer praised *Science Magic* for the "rather clever and captivating" ways in which the author "tickles the thought processes." Two years later, McGill published *Balancing Magic and Other Tricks,* with chapters divided according to the item employed—matches, balls, coins, eggs, and glasses. The book includes a ten-point list of hints for beginning magicians, diagrams, and directions, as well as a section with more complicated tricks that combine balancing and juggling. Writing in *Voice of Youth Advocates,* Kim Sands praised *Balancing Magic*'s "clear instructions and illustrations" and called it a "fun book."

Paper Magic, published in 1992, includes descriptions of six magic tricks and six fantasies. Explanations of the tricks show how each actually works as well as how it should appear to the audience. The fantasies show how to make such items as a tree and ladder from newspaper and the stories to tell to accompany them. The importance of practice is emphasized. Kay Weisman, writing in *Booklist,* found the book "a good introduction for novice tricksters as well as a source for rainy-day fun." Also published in 1992 was *Voice Magic,* which includes

instructions on how to make sounds in various parts of the mouth, and how to simulate voices coming from dummies or distant places. *School Library Journal* contributor Marilyn Long Graham described the book as a "clear introduction to a skill that demands much practice."

McGill also wrote two books that appeared in 1995. The first, *Chalk Talks!,* describes twelve "transformation pictures" drawn with chalk on black paper that are then manipulated to create different shapes. *Mind Magic* focuses on tricks that use such skills as organizing, memorizing, attending to detail, and acting to fool audiences into believing that the magician can, for example, know what question will be asked from the audience before it is asked. The tricks require much practice, but according to *Booklist* reviewer Ilene Cooper, "those who persevere will find lots that's fun."

■ Works Cited

Cooper, Ilene, review of *Mind Magic, Booklist,* March 1, 1995, p. 1238.

Graham, Marilyn Long, review of *Voice Magic: Secrets of Ventriloquism and Voice Conjuring, School Library Journal,* May, 1992, p. 124.

Sands, Kim, review of *Balancing Magic, Voice of Youth Advocates,* February, 1987, p. 300.

Review of *Science Magic, Kliatt,* winter, 1985, p. 60.

Weisman, Kay, review of *Paper Magic: Creating Fantasies and Performing Tricks with Paper, Booklist,* March 1, 1992, p. 1275.

■ For More Information See

PERIODICALS

Booklist, February 1, 1978, p. 888; December 1, 1986, p. 580; April 1, 1992, p. 1442.

Kirkus Reviews, January 1, 1992, p. 60; January 15, 1992, p. 117.

School Library Journal, March, 1985, p. 179; February, 1987, p. 81; October, 1995, p. 149; January, 1996, p. 120.

*   *   *

McKAY, Hilary 1959-

■ Personal

Born June 12, 1959, in England; daughter of Ronald (an engineer) and Mary (a nurse) Damms; married Kevin McKay (a teacher), August 13, 1992; children: Jim, Bella. *Education:* University of St. Andrew, B.S., 1981.

■ Addresses

Agent—Jennifer Luthlen, 88 Holmfield Road, Leicester, England.

■ Career

Writer. Laboratory technician.

■ Writings

The Exiles, Victor Gollancz (London, England), 1991, McElderry, 1992.
The Exiles at Home, Gollancz, 1993, McElderry, 1994.
Dog Friday, Gollancz, 1994, McElderry, 1995.
The Amber Cat, Gollancz, 1995.
Happy and Glorious, illustrated by Hilda Offen, Hodder & Stoughton, 1996.
Practically Perfect, illustrated by Hilda Offen, Hodder Children's, 1996.
Why Didn't You Tell Me?, illustrated by John Eastwood, Piccadilly, 1996.
The Exiles in Love, Gollancz, 1996.

"PARADISE HOUSE" SERIES; ILLUSTRATED BY TONY KENYON

The Zoo in the Attic, Gollancz, 1995.
The Treasure in the Garden, Gollancz, 1995.
The Echo in the Chimney, Gollancz, 1996.
The Magic in the Mirror, Gollancz, 1996.

■ Sidelights

Although she writes, as she told *SATA,* "primarily for myself," Hilary McKay has charmed young readers with books like *The Exiles* and *Dog Friday.* Such books, critics have noted, present realistic plots, likable characters, and many humorous moments. Furthermore, McKay's books aren't condescending or preachy. She noted, "I don't believe in writing down to children and am not conceited enough to desire to inflict my own opinions on other people. Can't stand Good Cause books!"

McKay, who has a bachelor's degree in science and worked as a laboratory technician, was surprised that her career as a writer "took off so quickly." She explained to *SATA* that she began to write "as an extension of reading.... I have read thousands of books. They influence my writing in the same way as the weather and as people I trust do. They are part of my landscape."

McKay's developed a love of books when she was very young. Her parents refused to bring a television into the home. Each member of the family was expected to read, and each did so eagerly. "In my family we read like starving dogs eat, huge, indiscriminate, barely chewed gulps," she wrote in an essay for *Something about the Author Autobiography Series* (*SAAS*). "Anything, ancient damp relics from the six-penny secondhand bookstall on the market, books scrounged from neighbors, books from the town library (blessed place), books that belonged to bookshops ... we raced through whole paperbacks at a time." As a child, McKay's favorite authors included Enid Blyton, E. Nesbit, Arthur Ransome, L.M. Montgomery, Marjorie Kinnan Rawlings, Mark Twain, Eleanor Farjeon, and Louisa May Alcott.

McKay shared her books with her three sisters Bridget, Robin, and Lorna. Together, the four lived much like the girls in McKay's "Exiles" books. When they weren't

HILARY McKAY

in school, they spent a great deal of time reading. They quarreled and kidded one another. They earned pocket money by harvesting produce and working on a farm. McKay told about her work on the farm in her *SAAS* sketch: "It was a lovely place. We would never have gone home given half a chance. I had never been so happy, or so dirty, or so exhausted."

McKay studied zoology and botany at the University of St. Andrew in Scotland. She explained in *SAAS* that, after earning a science degree, she "married an old St. Andrew's friend," and lived in Cumbria, England. "In Cumbria we lived in great poverty and cheerfulness in a haunted seventeenth-cottage. Kevin taught maths, and I worked in the local pub and cleaned holiday cottages and painted pictures to sell to tourists, and all our St. Andrew's friends came to stay, especially Isabel, who said, 'I don't see why you don't write a book. You know what books are and you can write letters. Sometimes they are quite amusing. And you might get some money.'"

It was then that McKay wrote the book that, after revision, would be published as *The Exiles.* After it was completed, McKay and her husband moved to Derbyshire. She began to work as a chemist during the day, and to write books at night. With the birth of her first child, she decided to give up chemistry and become a full-time writer.

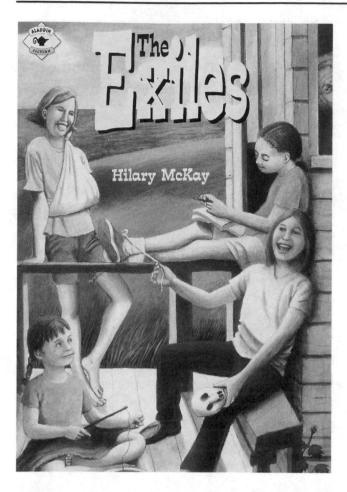

Big Grandma has her hands full one summer, trying to lure her four granddaughters away from books to enjoy hard work and the out-of-doors in this first of McKay's popular "Exiles" titles.

The Exiles begins when four sisters learn that their father has inherited money. At first, the sisters—Ruth, Naomi, Rachel, and Phoebe Conroy—are excited about the money. But when they hear that their parents plan to use the money to remodel their house and that they are to stay with their grandmother for the summer, they are upset. To make matters worse, when they arrive at their grandmother's house in Cumbria, they find that she has few books to read. "Big Grandma," as they call her, expects the girls to exercise, explore nature in the Lake District, seek adventure, and help out around the house. So the "exiled" girls read cookbooks and the works of Shakespeare (the only books they can find) and begin to enjoy the activities Grandma forces upon them. They even begin to appreciate and understand their grandmother. Although they accidentally set the house on fire, the story ends happily. "Like the writings of Beverly Cleary and Lois Lowry, this warm-hearted first novel provides an ample supply of chuckles," commented a *Publishers Weekly* reviewer. A critic for *Kirkus Reviews* described the work as "delightful," and concluded: "McKay has a real gift for amusing dialogue and descriptions."

In *The Exiles at Home*, McKay's sequel to her first book, readers find the four sisters back with their parents. They get into trouble when Ruth secretly pledges ten pounds each month to help educate a boy in Africa. Gradually, all of the sisters find work to help her pay the ten pounds, because she can't make enough money baby-sitting. Naomi gardens for an elderly couple, and Rachel and Phoebe sell food to their classmates. While the girls get into all kinds of trouble, they enjoy writing to their new African friend. Big Grandma finds out about the pledge and the girls' determination to meet it; at the end of the story, an elderly neighbor bequeaths enough money for both the African boy's education and a trip to Africa for the girls and Big Grandma. Patricia J. Morrow of *Voice of Youth Advocates* noted that, while in *The Exiles* "some of the girls' actions were dangerous," in *The Exiles at Home* "they are more entrepreneurial though still short-sighted." The book's conclusion, wrote A. R. Williams of *The Junior Bookshelf*, "should awake a glow of satisfaction in readers." Carolyn Phelan of *Booklist* found *The Exiles at Home* refreshing "for its wit and emotional candor."

The Exiles in Love continues McKay's popular series. In this story, older sisters Ruth and Naomi brood over new romantic interests, while younger siblings Rachel and Phoebe occupy themselves in other ways—Rachel in gaining recognition as May Queen, and Phoebe in preparing herself for a future career as an international spy. The girls' subsequent eager attention to a French visitor named Philippe causes Big Grandma to offer to take all four to France to get them out of their parents' hair for awhile. "Part of the appeal of these books is the light, amusing style, the warmth and accuracy (exaggerated but believable) of the portrayal of the girls' feelings, and the way such basically good-hearted characters never become dull," commented a *Junior Bookshelf* contributor.

Dog Friday is the story of Robin, a ten-year-old boy who has been afraid of dogs since one attacked him at the beach. He must also contend with his father's death and with the fact that his mother's bed-and-breakfast business is not faring well. When he meets the dog next door (named Old Blanket) and the children who own him (Ant, Perry, Beany, and Sun Dance), Robin begins to recover. He makes a canine friend of his own when he encounters a stray dog on the beach and saves him. Robin names the dog Friday, and tries to persuade his mother to let him keep the dog. She favors turning the dog in to the authorities. Robin's friendship with the dog is also threatened when he reads a note that has been posted about a lost dog and thinks the dog must be Friday. Although he is tempted to ignore the note for fear of losing his new companion, he finally does contact the owners, and finds that Friday is not the lost dog after all. Describing the novel as "poignant," *School Library Journal* contributor Ann M. Burlingame explained that it is about "honesty and the complexities of friendship." Carolyn Phelan of *Booklist* concluded that this "distinctive and refreshing" novel possesses "sharply realized characters, [a] fast-paced story, and witty dialogue."

"Children will be greatly entertained by this rollicking story," remarked a critic for *The Junior Bookshelf*.

One of McKay's most recent efforts has been likened to a fairy tale—but with the author's own trademark stamp of humor. "Hilary McKay has set no limits to her love of the absurd as a foundation for humour," wrote *Junior Bookshelf* contributor D. A. Young in a review of *Practically Perfect*. In this story, McKay features a ten-year-old Queen who alleviates her boredom by creating her own royal racecourse, riding the Royal Donkey to victory. As the story progresses and years pass, the Queen's Ladies-in-Waiting grow more anxious to marry the restive adolescent, who dismisses a host of suitors to marry, at the age of eighteen, her childhood friend—the gardener's boy.

"Most of my books have sold foreign language rights," McKay told *SATA*. "Some have also been put onto audio tape, but I am thinking of the British editions. The U.S. ones are adaptations of the British ones and the changes are not done by me. Good adaptations, I am sure, but they do not feel exactly the books I wrote. That is probably ridiculous of me!" McKay plans to continue writing books for children. "Children's minds grow just as their bodies do; it seems very important to me that there should be books worth reading for them right from the start," she wrote in her *SAAS* piece. "To be at home with books is to have a whole world of doorways open to you. Adults who know this already can open or shut the doors at will; what they make of what they find on the other side is up to them. Children have first to discover that the doors are there. That seems to me to be the thing that matters most; to get them wanting to open the doors. That is why I think children's books are so important ... and why it seems such a privilege, such an enormous stroke of luck, that I have slipped into this job. I am helping to make the worlds behind the doors."

■ **Works Cited**

Burlingame, Ann M., review of *Dog Friday, School Library Journal*, October, 1995, p. 136.
Review of *Dog Friday, The Junior Bookshelf*, April, 1995, p. 72.
Review of *The Exiles, Kirkus Reviews*, November 1, 1992, p. 1381.
Review of *The Exiles, Publishers Weekly*, October 19, 1992, p. 79.
Review of *The Exiles in Love, The Junior Bookshelf*, December, 1996, p. 271.
McKay, Hilary, essay in *Something about the Author Autobiography Series*, Volume 23, Gale, 1997, pp. 147-159.
Morrow, Patricia J., review of *The Exiles at Home, Voice of Youth Advocates*, April, 1995, p. 24.
Phelan, Carolyn, review of *Dog Friday, Booklist*, November 15, 1995, p. 560.
Phelan, Carolyn, review of *The Exiles at Home, Booklist*, January 15, 1995, p. 925.
Williams, A. R., review of *The Exiles at Home, The Junior Bookshelf*, April, 1994, p. 72.

Young, D. A., review of *Practically Perfect, The Junior Bookshelf*, December, 1996, p. 256.

■ **For More Information See**

PERIODICALS

Bulletin of the Center for Children's Books, October, 1995, pp. 62.
Horn Book Magazine, January-February, 1993, p. 86.
The Junior Bookshelf, August, 1995, p. 146.
Publishers Weekly, October 23, 1995, p. 69.
School Library Journal, October, 1992, p. 118.

*   *   *

McNAUGHTON, Colin 1951-

■ **Personal**

Born May 18, 1951, in Wallsend-upon-Tyne, England; son of Thomas (a pattern maker) and May (Dixon) McNaughton; married Francoise (Julie), June 27, 1970; children: Ben, Timothy. *Education:* Central School of Art and Design, B.A., 1973; Royal College of Art, M.A., 1976.

■ **Addresses**

Home—C 29 Odhams Walk, Covent Garden, London, WC2H 9SA, England.

■ **Career**

Taught at Cambridge School of Art; freelance author and illustrator, 1976—. *Member:* Society of Authors.

■ **Awards, Honors**

First Prize for Didactic Literature from the Cultural Activities Board of the city of Trento in association with the Children's Literature Department of the University of Padua, Italy, 1978, for *C'era una volta* (Italian edition of combined volumes *Colin McNaughton ABC and Things* and *Colin McNaughton's 1, 2, 3 and Things*); British Book Design and Production Award, 1989, for *Jolly Roger and the Pirates of Abdul the Skinhead*, 1993, for *Who's That Banging on the Ceiling? A Multistory Story*, and 1994, for *Making Friends with Frankenstein*; *Jolly Roger and the Pirates of Abdul the Skinhead*, 1988, was shortlisted for the Kurt Maschler Award; *Jolly Roger and the Pirates of Abdul the Skinhead*, 1988, and *Suddenly!*, 1994, were both shortlisted for the Smarties Prize for Children's Books; Kurt Maschler Award, Book Trust, 1991, for *Have You Seen Who's Just Moved Next Door to Us?*; *Watch Out for the Giant-Killers!*, 1991, was shortlisted for the Earthworm Award; Book Award, United Kingdom Reading Association, 1995, and Nottinghamshire Children's Acorn Award, 1995, both for *Suddenly!*; *Here Come the Aliens!*, 1995, was shortlisted for the Kate Greenaway Medal; Smarties Prize for Children's Books, Book Trust, for *Oops!*, 1996.

COLIN McNAUGHTON

■ Writings

SELF-ILLUSTRATED

Colin McNaughton's ABC and 1, 2, 3: A Book for All Ages for Reading Alone or Together, Doubleday, 1976, published in England in two volumes as *Colin McNaughton's ABC and Things* and *Colin McNaughton's 1, 2, 3 and Things,* Benn, 1976, also published in England as *ABC and Things* and *1, 2, 3 and Things,* Macmillan, 1989.

(With Elizabeth Attenborough) *Walk, Rabbit, Walk,* Viking, 1977.

The Great Zoo Escape, Heinemann, 1978, Viking, 1979.

The Rat Race: The Amazing Adventures of Anton B. Stanton, Doubleday, 1978, Walker, 1988.

Anton B. Stanton and the Pirats, Doubleday, 1979, published in England as *The Pirats: The Amazing Adventures of Anton B. Stanton,* Benn, 1979.

Football Crazy, Heinemann, 1980, published in the U.S. as *Soccer Crazy,* Atheneum, 1981.

King Nonn the Wiser, Heinemann, 1981.

If Dinosaurs Were Cats and Dogs, verses adapted by Alice Low, Four Winds Press, 1981, revised edition with verses by McNaughton, 1991.

Fat Pig, Benn, 1981, Puffin, 1987.

Crazy Bear, Holt, 1983.

"There's an Awful Lot of Weirdos in Our Neighborhood" and Other Wickedly Funny Verse, Simon & Schuster, 1987, published in England as *There's an Awful Lot of Weirdos in Our Neighbourhood: A Book of Rather Silly Verse and Pictures,* Walker, 1987.

Santa Clause Is Superman, Walker, 1988.

Jolly Roger and the Pirates of Abdul the Skinhead, Simon & Schuster, 1988, Walker, 1988.

Who's Been Sleeping in My Porridge? A Book of Silly Poems and Pictures, Ideals Children's Books, 1990, Walker, 1990.

Watch Out for the Giant-Killers!, Walker, 1991.

Guess Who's Just Moved in Next Door?, Random House, 1991, published in England as *Have You Seen Who's Just Moved in Next Door to Us?,* Walker, 1991.

Who's That Banging on the Ceiling? A Multistory Story, Walker, 1992, Candlewick Press, 1994.

Making Friends with Frankenstein, Walker, 1993, Candlewick Press, 1994.

Captain Abdul's Pirate School, Candlewick Press, 1994, Walker, 1994.

Merry Christmas, Sainsbury/Walker, 1994.

Suddenly!, Andersen Press, 1994, Harcourt Brace, 1995.

Here Come the Aliens, Candlewick Press, 1995, Walker, 1995.

Boo!, Andersen Press, 1995, Harcourt Brace, 1996.

Oops!, Andersen Press, 1996.

"BOOKS OF OPPOSITES" SERIES; SELF-ILLUSTRATED

At Home, Philomel Books, 1982, published in England as *Long-Short: At Home,* Methuen/Walker, 1982.

At Playschool, Philomel Books, 1982, published in England as *Over-Under: At Playschool,* Methuen/Walker, 1982.

At the Party, Philomel Books, 1982, published in England as *Hide-Seek: At the Party,* Methuen/Walker, 1982.

At the Park, Philomel Books, 1982, published in England as *In-Out: At the Park,* Methuen/Walker, 1982.

At the Stores, Philomel Books, 1982, published in England as *Fat-Thin: At the Shops,* Methuen/Walker, 1982.

"VERY FIRST BOOKS" SERIES; SELF-ILLUSTRATED

Spring, Methuen/Walker, 1983, Dial, 1984.
Summer, Methuen/Walker, 1983, Dial, 1984.
Autumn, Methuen/Walker, 1983, Dial, 1984.
Winter, Methuen/Walker, 1983, Dial, 1984.

ILLUSTRATOR

James Reeves, compiler, *The Springtime Book: A Collection of Prose and Poetry,* Heinemann, 1976.

James Reeves, compiler, *The Autumn Book: A Collection of Prose and Poetry,* Heinemann, 1977.

Hester Burton, *A Grenville Goes to Sea,* Heinemann, 1977.

James Reeves, *Eggtime Stories,* Blackie & Son, 1978.

Mary McCaffrey, *The Mighty Muddle,* Eel Pie Publishing, 1979.

Jenny Hawkesworth, *A Handbook of Family Monsters,* Dent, 1980.

Wendy Wood, *The Silver Chanter: Traditional Scottish Tales and Legends,* Chatto & Windus, 1980.

Emil Pacholek, *A Ship to Sail the Seven Seas,* Kestrel, 1980.

Allan Ahlberg, *Miss Brick the Builder's Baby,* Kestrel, 1981, Golden Press, 1982.

Allan Ahlberg, *Mr. and Mrs. Hay the Horse,* Kestrel, 1981.

Russell Hoban, *The Great Fruit Gum Robbery,* Methuen/Walker, 1981, published as *The Great Gum Drop Robbery,* Philomel, 1982.

Russell Hoban, *They Came from Aargh,* Philomel, 1981.

Russell Hoban, *The Flight of Bembel Rudzuk,* Philomel, 1982.

Russell Hoban, *The Battle of Zormla,* Philomel, 1982.

Andrew Lang, compiler, *The Pink Fairy Book* (fairy tales), edited by Brian Alderson, revised edition (McNaughton was not associated with the previous edition), Viking, 1982.

Allan Ahlberg, *Mrs. Jolly's Joke Shop,* Kestrel, 1988.

Robert Louis Stevenson, *Treasure Island,* Holt, 1993.

Adrian Henry and others, *One of Your Legs Is Both the Same,* Macmillan, 1994.

Roger McGough and others, *Another Day on Your Foot and I Would Have Died,* Macmillan, 1996.

James Berry and others, *We Couldn't Provide Fish Thumbs,* Macmillan, 1997.

ILLUSTRATOR; "RED NOSE READERS" SERIES BY ALLAN AHLBERG

Help!, Random House, 1985, Walker, 1985.
Jumping, Random House, 1985, Walker, 1985.
Make a Face, Random House, 1985, Walker, 1985.
Big Bad Pig, Random House, 1985.
Fee Fi Fo Fum, Random House, 1985, Walker, 1985.
Happy Worm, Random House, 1985, Walker, 1985.
Bear's Birthday, Random House, 1985, Walker, 1986.
So Can I, Random House, 1985, Walker, 1985.
Shirley's Shops, Random House, 1986, Walker, 1986.
Push the Dog, Random House, 1986, Walker, 1986.
Crash, Bang, Wallop!, Random House, 1986, Walker, 1986.
Me and My Friend, Random House, 1986, Walker, 1986.
Blow Me Down, Random House, 1986, Walker, 1986.
Look Out for the Seals, Random House, 1986, Walker, 1986.
One Two Flea, Random House, 1986, Walker, 1986.
Tell Us a Story, Random House, 1986, Walker, 1986.
Put on a Show, Walker, 1995.
Who Stole the Pie, Walker, 1995.

ILLUSTRATOR; "FOLDAWAY" SERIES BY ALLAN AHLBERG

Circus, Granada/Collins, 1984, Derrydale, 1988.
Zoo, Granada/Collins, 1984, Derrydale, 1988.
Families, Granada/Collins, 1984, Derrydale, 1988.
Monsters, Granada/Collins, 1984, Derrydale, 1988.

■ Adaptations

Fat Pig was adapted for the stage as a rock musical in 1983 and has been produced in France, Germany, Austria, Great Britain, the United States, Finland, and Norway.

■ Work in Progress

"Writing and illustrating *Goal!,* another adventure of Preston the Pig."

■ Sidelights

Award-winning children's author and illustrator Colin McNaughton has delighted countless children on both sides of the Atlantic with his lighthearted stories and cartoon-like drawings for young readers. Reflecting on his artistic style, McNaughton once told *SATA* that "the only picture books I knew as a child were the comic annuals I was given at Christmas: *Beano, Dandy, Topper, Eagle,* and *Lion.* Looking back it is not difficult to say that these comics were the main influence on my work. These and the films I saw every Saturday morning ... pirate films, knights in shining armour, cowboys and Indians." This childhood love of comedy, excitement, and make-believe continues to provide McNaughton with a unique ability to make children laugh; the author notes that "although I am married, with two sons and a lovely French wife, I still like the same things—the escapism of the adventure film and the crazy madness of the comic. I guess I never grew up."

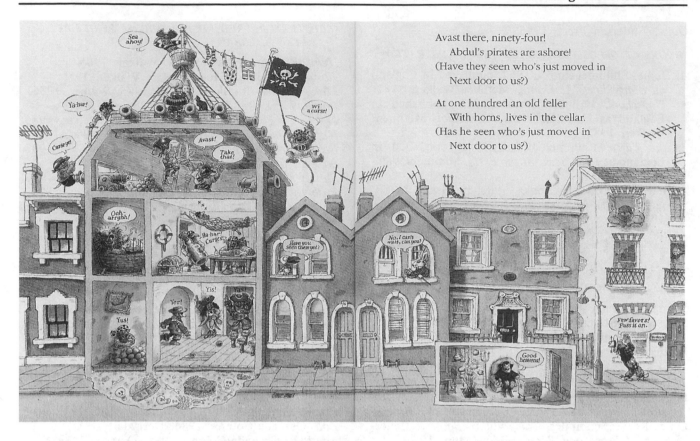

A odd assortment of characters—including a houseful of pirates, Frankenstein, and the devil himself—dread the prospect of "strange" new neighbors in McNaughton's hilarious self-illustrated _Guess Who's Just Moved in Next Door._

Early in McNaughton's career, he began illustrating the works of other authors before concentrating on his own stories. His 1977 collaboration with Elizabeth Attenborough, _Walk, Rabbit, Walk,_ received much praise from critics. In this easy-to-read book, a young rabbit on his way to a friend's house eschews modern methods of transport, including sports cars, helicopters, and even a hot air balloon ride, in favor of enjoying a pleasant walk with his own two feet. A critic in _Junior Bookshelf_ said McNaughton's illustrations "compliment the story perfectly," while Merrie Lou Cohen writing in _School Library Journal_ praised _Walk, Rabbit, Walk_'s "refreshing text and nice homey illustrations," going on to call the story "funny, imaginative, and full of rollicking action."

Another of McNaughton's successful partnerships is with children's author Allan Ahlberg. Together the two have created many books for young people, including the popular "Red Nose Reader" series. The books in this series help readers understand concepts; for example, in _Big Bad Pig_ McNaughton and Ahlberg explain the difference between "big and little," while _Help!_ tries to teach children to overcome their fears. In _Help!_, a small boy is frightened by the monsters, burglars, and other hideous creatures who invade his bedroom. Gathering his courage, the lad devises a clever plan to scare away all the uninvited guests. In a _School Library Journal_ review of _Help!_ and other books in the series, Louise L. Sherman applauded the "simple use of words and the clear comic illustrations," exclaiming that they

"will tickle the funny bones of children." A critic in _Publishers Weekly_ deemed these early reader books "absurd and amusing."

McNaughton's off-beat sense of humor also surfaces in his self-illustrated award-winning work _Guess Who's Just Moved in Next Door?_ News of a new family joining the neighborhood spreads quickly from house to house. As readers follow the message being passed through the street, they cannot help but notice the odd characters that fill the town, including an apartment full of pirates, a clan of space creatures, and a group of pigs shopping for wigs. When the mystery neighbors finally arrive, the entire neighborhood of strange inhabitants appear horrified by the family's ordinariness. Describing the humor in the book as "both cheeky and camp," a critic in _Publishers Weekly_ believed that McNaughton's "rollicking verse will make reading aloud a zany treat." A reviewer in _Junior Bookshelf_ also praised the author's creative verse and noticed McNaughton's "repetitions, detail, and ... sure feel of what children enjoy."

In 1992 McNaughton published another well received picture book about neighbors spying on their neighbors in _Who's That Banging on the Ceiling._ Sharing space in a twelve-story apartment building, each resident takes ridiculous guesses about what the neighbors above them are doing to make such a racket. As readers turn the page, McNaughton reveals how the crazy apartment dwellers create so much noise—children bouncing on the bed, young men gorging themselves at the table, and even King Kong tap-dancing on the roof. Describing *Who's That Banging on the Ceiling* as a "clever novelty book," *School Library Journal* contributor Kathy Piehl commented that the tale will "amuse young audiences." *Booklist* reviewer Emily Melton suggested that the page design may be challenging for some readers, but admitted that "the silly humor, the repetitive text, and giant fold-out will probably appeal to children."

Continuing to focus on self-illustrated books of witty poems for young readers, McNaughton created *Making Friends with Frankenstein: A Book of Monstrous Poems and Pictures* in 1993. In this volume of children's verse, a mad scientist actually "makes a friend" in his laboratory, ghosts act out a "phantomime," and witches who play in the sand become "sandwitches." Describing the poems as "deliciously outrageous," a *Publishers Weekly* reviewer commended McNaughton's "wacky cartoon characters, nimble puns, and clever spoofs." While noting that the book is filled with "disgusting bodily functions that children will find hilarious," Marjorie Lewis wrote in *School Library Journal* that the poems are well suited to reading aloud. Calling *Making Friends with Frankenstein* "a must for Halloween," *Booklist* contributor Hazel Rochman asserted that McNaughton's "nonsense verse and comic illustrations" will entertain children throughout the entire year.

Adding to his works featuring horrible monsters, creepy characters, and juicy illustrations, McNaughton has also published stories about softer, more lovable creatures.

For example, in his 1994 picture book *Suddenly!*, the artist introduces a cute, innocent little animal named Preston the Pig. Completely unaware that a ferocious wolf is stalking him, Preston goes about his daily business without a care in the world. As he returns home from school, the young piglet suddenly remembers he must stop at the store for his mother and quickly changes his course. Walking home from the store, Preston indulges a sudden urge to go to the playground, deviating from his plans once again. Oblivious to him, upon each change of direction, Preston narrowly misses the sharp teeth of the wolf. By the end of the story, he reaches his house safely, while the frustrated wolf ends up at the hospital. Writing in *Booklist*, Annie Ayres claimed that children will be entertained by this "deftly executed and designed" picture book. In a *School Library Journal* review, Lisa S. Murphy applauded *Suddenly!* for providing "zany fun that's perfect for young audiences," while a critic in *Junior Bookshelf* declared that the book "will be a big hit with small children."

■ Works Cited

Ayres, Annie, review of *Suddenly!*, *Booklist*, May 5, 1995, p. 1652.

Cohen, Merrie Lou, review of *Walk, Rabbit, Walk*, *School Library Journal*, April, 1978, p. 73.

Review of *Guess Who's Just Moved in Next Door?*, *Publishers Weekly*, August 9, 1991, p. 56.

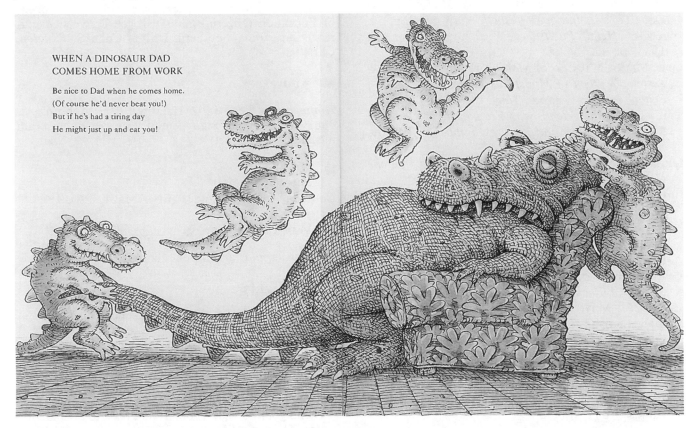

WHEN A DINOSAUR DAD
COMES HOME FROM WORK

Be nice to Dad when he comes home.
(Of course he'd never beat you!)
But if he's had a tiring day
He might just up and eat you!

Making Friends with Frankenstein **is a collection of comic verse and wacky illustrations, both by McNaughton, abounding with puns and parodies for Halloween.**

Preston Pig is the humorous hero of McNaughton's engaging, self-illustrated *Suddenly!*

Review of *Have You Seen Who's Just Moved in Next Door To Us?*, *Junior Bookshelf*, April, 1992, p. 56.

Review of *Help!*, *Publishers Weekly*, December 20, 1985, p. 66.

Lewis, Marjorie, review of *Making Friends with Frankenstein: A Book of Monstrous Poems and Pictures*, *School Library Journal*, May, 1994, p. 125.

Review of *Making Friends with Frankenstein: A Book of Monstrous Poems and Pictures*, *Publishers Weekly*, May 9, 1994, p. 73.

Melton, Emily, review of *Who's That Banging on the Ceiling?*, *Booklist*, January 15, 1993, p. 922.

Murphy, Lisa S., review of *Suddenly!*, *School Library Journal*, June, 1995, p. 92.

Piehl, Kathy, review of *Who's That Banging on the Ceiling?*, *School Library Journal*, March, 1993, p. 182.

Rochman, Hazel, review of *Making Friends with Frankenstein: A Book of Monstrous Poems and Pictures*, *Booklist*, May, 1994, p. 1678.

Sherman, Louise L., review of *Big Bad Pig, Fee Fi Fo Fum, Happy Worm*, and *Help!*, *School Library Journal*, April, 1986, p. 67.

Review of *Suddenly!*, *Junior Bookshelf*, December, 1994, p. 204.

Review of *Walk, Rabbit, Walk*, *Junior Bookshelf*, December, 1977, p. 329.

■ For More Information See

PERIODICALS

Booklist, October 1, 1982, p. 247; November 15, 1985, p. 503; February 1, 1989, p. 940.

Bulletin of the Center for Children's Books, January, 1983, p. 93; May, 1984, p. 102; January, 1989, p. 129; April, 1994, p. 1678; December, 1994, p. 138; July, 1995, p. 388.

Growing Point, May, 1985, p. 4453; July, 1991, p. 5557.

Junior Bookshelf, April, 1984, p. 61; February, 1988, p. 33; October, 1990, p. 234; June, 1991, p. 95; October, 1995, p. 171; December, 1996, p. 236.

Kirkus Reviews, September 1, 1977, p. 928; November 1, 1992, p. 1381; May 15, 1994, p. 703.

Magpies, March, 1991, p. 36; November, 1993, p. 25; July, 1994, p. 39.

Quill & Quire, January, 1995, p. 43.

School Library Journal, January, 1978, p. 80; January, 1983, p. 62; March, 1989, p. 166; February, 1991, p. 73; October, 1991, p. 101; January, 1995, p. 90.

* * *

MDURVWA, Hajara E. 1962-

■ Personal

Born September 17, 1962, in Lassa, Nigeria; daughter of Yakubu G. and Wudiki C. Gadzama; married Emmanuel Mdurvwa (a researcher), April 3, 1983; children: Deborah, Jennifer. *Education:* Attended Borno College of Education (Nigeria) and Tuskegee University; currently attending Southern Union College. *Religion:* Christian.

■ Addresses

Home and office—1402 Hampton Dr., Auburn, AL 36830. *Electronic mail*—emdurvwa @ auburn.campus.mci.net (AU net).

■ Writings

Down in Africa, Dorrance (Bryn Mawr, PA), 1995.

■ Work in Progress

Princess Jamila, a children's book.

■ Sidelights

Hajara Mdurvwa told *SATA:* "I was born and raised in Nigeria, West Africa. During my elementary years, I lived with my aunt who had never encouraged me to learn how to read and write. For that reason I did not get the opportunity to read and write stories as other children did in school.

"When I got into high school, I went back to my parents' house. There my life changed for the better, and I was able to do things like other children. During that time, I had an uncle who regularly visited us, and he loved to

HAJARA E. MDURVWA

tell stories. He was so funny, and he always made us laugh. His stories gave me the desire to read so that I could find out about other stories. This proved to be very interesting and relaxing to me so much that I began to make up my own stories. This was very easy for me because of the experiences that I went through in life.

"After high school, I got married and went to college at the same time. I had my first baby daughter, Deborah, during my college years. Following her birth my husband came to the United States for graduate studies, and we joined him the following year. That was in 1986. While in the United States, I stayed at home for four years while my husband went to school. During that time I gave birth to my second baby, Jennifer.

"As time went on, I started writing some of my stories and then read them to my children just for fun. They were thrilled by them. As they got older they encouraged me to publish the stories. I never gave it serious consideration because I thought they were not good enough. At my children's insistence, however, I decided to submit one for publication on a trial basis.

"I was glad I did because I have found it a very interesting and fulfilling experience. This is because I found a way of sharing part of my culture with the children of the world. And I hope that God will give me the opportunity to write many more nice and interesting books that children will love and learn something from."

MINAHAN, John A. 1956-

■ Personal

Born November 21, 1956, in Waterbury, CT. *Education:* Georgetown University, A.B., 1978; Rome School of Music, M.M., 1983; Brown University, A.M., 1988, Ph.D., 1990. *Politics:* "Vote early, vote often." *Religion:* "Other."

■ Addresses

Home—58 Lyndhurst Ave., Providence, RI 02908.

■ Career

University of Virginia, Charlottesville, teacher of music, 1981; Rome School of Music, teacher of music, 1982-83; Northern Virginia Community College, Alexandria, teacher of music, 1983-86; Brown University, Providence, RI, teacher of English, 1986-92; Stonehill College, North Easton, MA, teacher of English, 1992—. Worked variously as a boat builder, bartender, hardware salesperson, and bookstore clerk in the United States, Canada, and Europe, 1975-79; professional musician, 1978-81.

■ Writings

FOR CHILDREN; FICTION

Abigail's Drum, illustrated by Robert Quackenbush, Pippin Press, 1995.

FOR ADULTS; NONFICTION

Word Like a Bell: John Keats, Music, and the Romantic Poet, Kent State University Press, 1992.
Teaching Democracy: A Professor's Journal, Simon & Schuster, 1993.

■ Sidelights

Versatile writer John A. Minahan has published books in several genres: a scholarly study of John Keats's poetry, a journal based on Minahan's experience teaching at Brown University, and a work of historical fiction for primary graders. One thread that runs through most of Minahan's work, whether as a musician, writer, or teacher, is a concern for time and memory. When he was a professional musician just out of college, Minahan learned the importance of time, since music is "the most time-oriented art," as the author once stated. Minahan has also asserted that "fiction is largely driven by a need to come to terms with memory."

Minahan's study of Romantic poetry, *Word Like a Bell,* explores in depth the author's fascination with time and memory. According to Minahan, music offered John Keats and the other poets of his time an aesthetic model for the experience of time as a process of birth, growth, and decay, providing both a vocabulary and a structure for the poet's expression. Minahan finds Keats's odes, for example, to be organized by a "sonatalike musicali-

John A. Minahan recounts the daring rescue of a lighthouse keeper by his brave young daughters during the War of 1812. (From *Abigail's Drum*, illustrated by Robert Quackenbush.)

ty." Writing in *Library Journal*, Bryan Aubrey found *Word Like a Bell* an "absorbing book."

Minahan's next volume, *Teaching Democracy*, charts in journal form the progress over time of a college course on the personal essay taught by the author. The students as described in the journal are composites of those the author actually taught. With readings ranging from the Declaration of Independence to the works of E. D. Hirsch, Minahan tries to coax his students, whom he often finds bright but uninformed, to develop a sense of compassion that he considers crucial to the development of democracy both in the classroom and in the world at large. A reviewer in *Publishers Weekly* thought readers would be "invigorated by this lively confluence of reading and writing."

With *Abigail's Drum*, a work of historical fiction for younger readers, Minahan distills his concerns with time and democratic values into perhaps their simplest elements. Based on a true incident from the War of 1812, the story describes how Abigail Bates and her older sister Rebecca, daughters of the Scituate (Massachusetts) Lighthouse keeper, conspire to fool a shipload

of British soldiers who have kidnapped their father and who threaten to burn the town. Armed with only their musical instruments, the girls show both ingenuity and bravery in feigning the approach of American troops. Alarmed, the British release Mr. Bates and flee. Minahan has described his preference for "characters who dramatize basic moral dilemmas," and for novels showing that "comedy and tragedy are not far apart." *Abigail's Drum* meets both these objectives. *Bulletin of the Center for Children's Books* reviewer Elizabeth Bush found the novel "appealing to readers who are just moving into historical adventure novels," and Lee Bock, writing in *School Library Journal*, described the book as a "fine read-aloud selection for classrooms and for families."

■ Works Cited

Aubrey, Bryan, review of *Word Like a Bell: John Keats, Music, and the Romantic Poet, Library Journal*, April 1, 1992, p. 118.

Bock, Lee, review of *Abigail's Drum, School Library Journal*, February, 1996, p. 102.

Bush, Elizabeth, review of *Abigail's Drum, Bulletin of the Center for Children's Books*, February, 1996, p. 197.

Review of *Teaching Democracy: A Professor's Journal, Publishers Weekly*, July 26, 1993, p. 52.

■ For More Information See

PERIODICALS

Booklist, November 1, 1993, p. 490; February 15, 1996, p. 1022.

*   *   *

MODESITT, Jeanne 1953-

■ Personal

Born August 2, 1953, in Long Beach, CA; daughter of George Edward (a physicist) and Lorraine Helen (Stasky) Modesitt; married Robin Thomas Spowart (a children's book illustrator), September 16, 1978. *Education:* University of California—Santa Cruz, B.A. (with honors), 1981; Oregon State University, M.A. (with honors), 1986. *Politics:* Natural Law Party.

■ Addresses

Home—2066 Wilton Dr., Cambria, CA 93428. *Agent*—Barbara Kouts, P.O. Box 560, Bellport, NY 11713.

■ Career

Writer. *Member:* Society of Children's Book Writers and Illustrators.

JEANNE MODESITT

■ Writings

FOR CHILDREN; PICTURE BOOKS

Vegetable Soup, illustrated by Robin Spowart, Macmillan, 1988.

The Night Call, illustrated by Robin Spowart, Viking Kestrel, 1989.

The Story of Z, illustrated by Lonni Sue Johnson, Picture Book Studio (Saxonville, MA), 1990.

Sometimes I Feel Like a Mouse: A Book About Feelings, illustrated by Robin Spowart, Scholastic, 1992.

(Compiler) *Songs of Chanukah,* illustrated by Robin Spowart, Little, Brown, 1992.

Mama, If You Had a Wish, illustrated by Robin Spowart, Green Tiger Press (New York, NY), 1993.

Lunch with Milly, illustrated by Robin Spowart, Bridge-Water Books, 1995.

OTHER

Modesitt has also written short stories for children's periodicals, including several for *Spider Magazine.*

■ Work in Progress

A collection of humorous stories for kids ages 7-10.

■ Sidelights

Jeanne Modesitt has been writing children's stories for books and magazines since 1986; working mostly with her husband as illustrator, she has published six picture books and a Chanukah song book. Her first picture book, *Vegetable Soup,* describes the successful efforts of two rabbits to make a meal with no carrots. *Publishers*

Weekly praised the book as "good company at anyone's table." *Night Call,* which tells how two stuffed animals help return a fallen star to the sky, was recommended by Carolyn Polese in *School Library Journal* as an "appealing bedtime story." *The Story of Z,* about the letter Z's attempts to form her own alphabet after becoming tired of always being last, received a rave review from Ruth Semrau in *School Library Journal,* who described the book as a story of "unparalleled zest" in which "every page zings with zip." In *Sometimes I Feel Like a Mouse,* different animals' expressions suggest different emotions, which the children are encouraged to explore. Writing in *Booklist,* Stephanie Zvirin commended the book as "a fine way to introduce difficult concepts to young children." *Mama, If You Had a Wish* assures a worried bunny that "I love you just the way you are." A *Publishers Weekly* reviewer praised the book for achieving a "worthy purpose: promoting acceptance," and found the author's message "directly on target." A tale that complements *Vegetable Soup, Lunch with Milly* tells the story of a child who invites an adult to lunch but forgets to make dessert. *School Library Journal* contributor Carolyn Noah commented that "readers will find *Lunch with Milly* to be a quietly satisfying snack."

Describing her background and feelings about writing, Modesitt told *SATA:* "I like writing funny stories most of all. That's because when I write them, I laugh, and I love to laugh. I also love to hear others laugh when they read my stories. Laughing is definitely one of my most favorite things in the world.

"I spend about four hours a day writing. I don't use a computer; I prefer writing with pencil and paper. For

Little Bunny's questions are answered by a patient and loving mother in Modesitt's reassuring bedtime story. (From *Mama, If You Had a Wish,* illustrated by Robin Spowart.)

my final copy (the one I send to editors) I use a typewriter. Everybody tells me I will get a computer some day, but I don't think so. I like to keep my tools as simple as possible.

"I am married to one of my favorite children's book illustrators, Robin Spowart. We like working together—maybe because we like each other (and each other's work) so much!

"I took two or three writing classes in college, but I don't remember much about them. Mostly, I wrote stuff for adults in the classes and didn't have much fun. I have much more fun now.

"One of the hardest things for me as a writer is the number of rejections I get from editors. 'Your story just doesn't work,' they say, or 'This story is supposed to be funny?! What are you, a nut or something?' Rejections hurt; but I never let rejections stop me from doing what I love.

"Sometimes people tell me I should write a book about what it was like for me to grow up in a family where there was abuse. But while I greatly respect those who write such books, I don't want to write one like that. I would feel very, very sad reliving certain memories. I much prefer to spend my time writing words that cheer me, that make me laugh, that make me want to hug the whole wide world."

■ Works Cited

Review of *Mama, If You Had a Wish, Publishers Weekly,* May 31, 1993, p. 52.

Noah, Carolyn, review of *Lunch with Milly, School Library Journal,* February 2, 1995, p. 229.

Polese, Carolyn, review of *The Night Call, School Library Journal,* January, 1990, p. 86.

Semrau, Ruth, review of *The Story of Z, School Library Journal,* January, 1991, p. 78.

Review of *Vegetable Soup, Publishers Weekly,* January 29, 1988, p. 428.

Zvirin, Stephanie, review of *Sometimes I Feel Like a Mouse, Booklist,* October 1, 1992, p. 337.

■ For More Information See

PERIODICALS

Booklist, April 1, 1988, p. 1352; November 1, 1989, p. 554; September 1, 1992, p. 63; July, 1993, p. 1975.

Horn Book, November-December, 1992, p. 712.

Publishers Weekly, May 11, 1990, p. 57; November 2, 1992, p. 69.

School Library Journal, August 1993, p. 148.

Laurel Molk illustrates Jane Yolen's *Beneath the Ghost Moon* with appropriately spooky, appealing illustrations of farmyard mice in this take-off on a familiar Christmas poem.

MOLK, Laurel 1957-

■ Personal

Born May 14, 1957; married Peter Moldave (an attorney), October 22, 1989; children: Jack. *Education:* Tufts University, B.A., 1978; Rhode Island School of Design, M.A.E., 1982. *Hobbies and other interests:* Weekly open-studio life drawing.

■ Addresses

Agent—Ginger Knowlton, Curtis Brown, Ltd., 10 Astor Place, New York, NY 10003.

■ Career

Artist and illustrator.

■ Illustrator

Nancy White Carlstrom, *Grandpappy,* Little, Brown, 1990.
Lee Bennett Hopkins, compiler, *On The Farm,* Little, Brown, 1991.
Jane Yolen, *Beneath the Ghost Moon,* Little, Brown, 1994.

■ Sidelights

Illustrator Laurel Molk told *SATA:* "I've drawn pictures for as long as I can remember. In fact, I remember selling my pictures in the neighborhood as a child—one penny each or six for a nickel.

"When I graduated from Rhode Island School of Design, I did all kinds of freelance jobs, such as designing athletic shoes, setting up window displays, designing posters for state parks, illustrating for ad agencies and nature magazines, and teaching drawing.

"Illustrating children's books is what I enjoy most. There is a freedom to be whimsical and to really stretch reality.

"I have a child now and he's definitely influenced both the type of books I'd like to illustrate and my work schedule. While I used to work 8-5 with some all-nighters thrown in for good measure, now I work during pre-school hours, in the evenings, and on weekends. I listen to books on tape while I paint to keep me going late at night.

"I hope to illustrate children's books for a long, long time as the possibility to grow and experiment with each new project is seemingly endless. Also I really can't think of anything I'd prefer to do."

MORA, Pat(ricia) 1942-

■ Personal

Born January 19, 1942, in El Paso, TX; daughter of Raul Antonio (an optician) and Estella (Delgado) Mora; married William H. Burnside, Jr., July 27, 1963 (divorced, 1981); married Vernon Lee Scarborough (an archaeologist), May 25, 1984; children: (first marriage) William, Elizabeth, Cecilia. *Education:* Texas Western College, B.A., 1963; University of Texas at El Paso, M.A., 1971. *Politics:* Democrat.

■ Addresses

Home—78 Verano Loop, Sante Fe, NM 87505; and 3423 Oakview Place, Cincinnati, OH 45209.

■ Career

El Paso Independent School District, El Paso, TX, teacher, 1963-66; El Paso Community College, part-time instructor in English and communications, 1971-78; University of Texas at El Paso, part-time lecturer in English, 1979-81, assistant to vice president of academic affairs, 1981-88, director of University Museum and assistant to president, 1988-89. W. K. Kellogg Foundation, consultant, 1990-91; writer/speaker, 1991—.

PAT MORA

Member of literary advisory panel, Texas Commission on the Arts, 1987-88; poetry judge for Texas Institute of Letters, 1988. Host of radio show, *Voices: The Mexican-American in Perspective,* on National Public Radio-affiliate KTEP, 1983-84; consultant for United States-Mexico youth exchange programs; gives presentations, lectures, and poetry readings nationally and internationally. *Member:* International Reading Association, Poetry Society of America, Academy of American Poets, Society of Children's Book Writers and Illustrators, National Council of Teachers of English, National Council of La Raza, Texas Institute of Letters, United States Board on Books for Young People.

■ Awards, Honors

Poetry award, *New America: Women Artists and Writers of the Southwest,* 1982; Creative writing award, National Association for Chicano Studies, 1983; Harvey L. Johnson Book Award, Southwest Council of Latin American Studies, 1984; Southwest Book Awards, Border Regional Library, 1985, for *Chants,* 1987, for *Borders,* and 1994, for *A Birthday Basket for Tia;* Kellogg National fellowship, 1986-89; Leader in Education Award, El Paso Women's Employment and Education, 1987; Chicano/Hispanic Faculty and Professional Staff Association Award, University of Texas at El Paso, 1987, for outstanding contribution to the advancement of Hispanics; named to *El Paso Herald-Post* Writers Hall of Fame, 1988; Poetry award, Conference of Cincinnati Women, 1990; poetry fellowship, National Endowment for the Arts, 1994; *Skipping Stones* Book Award, 1995, for *The Desert Is My Mother.*

■ Writings

FOR CHILDREN

A Birthday Basket for Tia, illustrated by Cecily Lang, Macmillan, 1992.

The Desert Is My Mother/El desierto es mi madre, illustrated by Daniel Lechon, Pinata Books (Houston), 1994.

Listen to the Desert: Oye al desierto (poems), illustrated by Francisco X. Mora, Clarion, 1994.

Pablo's Tree, illustrated by Cecily Lang, Macmillan, 1994.

Agua, Agua, Agua, illustrated by Jose Ortega, Goodyear Books, 1994.

(With Charles Ramirez Berg) *The Gift of the Poinsettia/ El regalo de la flor de nochebuena,* illustrated by Daniel Lechon, Pinata Books, 1995.

The Race of the Toad and Deer, illustrated by Maya Itzna Brooks, Orchard Books, 1995.

Uno, dos, tres/One, Two, Three, illustrated by Barbara Lavallee, Clarion, 1996.

Confetti: Poems for Children (poems), illustrated by Enrique O. Sanchez, Lee & Low (New York City), 1996.

Tomas and the Library Lady, illustrated by Raul Colon, Knopf, in press.

This Big Sky, Scholastic, in press.

Delicious Hullabaloo, Pinata Books, in press.

The Rainbow Tulip, Viking, in press.

Also contributor to *Revista Chicano-Riquena: Kikiriki/ Children's Literature Anthology,* edited by Sylvia Cavazos Pena, Arte Publico (Houston), 1981, and *Tun-Ta-Ca-Tun,* edited by Sylvia Cavazos Pena, Arte Publico, 1986.

POETRY

Chants, Arte Publico, 1984.
Borders, Arte Publico, 1986.
Communion, Arte Publico, 1991.
Agua Santa/Holy Water, Beacon Press (Boston), 1995.
Divine Light, Viking, in press.

Work represented in anthologies, including *The Best American Poetry, 1996.*

OTHER

Nepantla: Essays from the Land in the Middle, University of New Mexico Press (Albuquerque), 1993.
House of Houses (family memoir), Beacon Press, 1997.

Also contributor to *New Worlds of Literature, Infinite Divisions: An Anthology of Chicana Literature,* and *Woman of Her Word: Hispanic Women Write.* Contributor of articles and stories to periodicals, including *Hispanics in the United States: An Anthology of Creative Literature, New America: Women Artists and Writers of the Southwest, Kalliope: A Journal of Women's Art,* and *Calyx.*

■ Work in Progress

Here Come the Abuelos, Twins, The Night the Moon Fell, The Bakery Lady, and *The Alphabet Aunt.*

■ Sidelights

Pat Mora has been acknowledged as a leader in the contemporary movement to recognize and express the many voices of the Hispanic population—and especially Hispanic women—in the United States. Her collections of poems for children and adults reflect her experiences as an American woman of Mexican heritage. By portraying her native traditions as well as the physical surroundings of the desert southwest, Mora gives voice both to herself and her people. As a poet and an author of children's books, she has been an important part of efforts to recognize and preserve Mexican American culture. The author herself commented in a *Horn Book* essay: "I take pride in being a Hispanic writer. I will continue to write and to struggle to say what no other writer can say in quite the same way."

Born in El Paso, Texas, Mora was raised by her parents as well as by her grandmother and her mother's half-sister. She received her bachelor's degree in 1963 from Texas Western College and married soon after graduation. Earning a master's degree from the University of Texas—El Paso in 1971, Mora held teaching positions at the secondary, post-secondary, and college levels; however, after her divorce in 1981, she began to devote herself more seriously to writing. Her first two collections of poems, *Chants* and *Borders,* are steeped in the

As the sun rose over the green jungle, parrots squawked the news. "Race today! ¡Carrera hoy! Race today!"

"Who's racing?" asked the spider monkeys swinging through the trees. "Who's racing?"

In the shade, Jaguar yawned. "Toad and Deer will race today."

"Yes, Sapo and Venado will race today!" chattered the spider monkey

A retelling of a Guatemalan folktale about arrogant Deer and clever Toad, *The Race of Toad and Deer* is fittingly illustrated by Maya Itzna Brooks, who lived in Guatemala as a teenager.

aura of the Southwest, celebrating that region's desert landscape. Throughout these works she explores the theme of identity, especially that of woman and her connection with the various forms of the "earth mother"—the *curandera,* or healer, and the *abuelita,* the nurturing grandmother. In an essay for *The Desert Is No Lady: Southwestern Landscapes in Women's Writing and Art,* Tey Diana Rebolledo noted that in Mora's poetry collections, "Nature and the land ... become allies of the woman hero. Keeping her in touch with her self, they are a kind of talisman that enables her to make her way through the alienations of male society, and also of the received female traditions of a limited society, whether represented by the history of Spain or Mexico."

In her third collection, *Communion,* Mora departs from her beloved southwest and relates impressions gained from her subsequent travels. She finds herself experiencing daily life in Cuba ("The Mystery"), overwhelmed by the aura of the big city ("New York: 2 a.m."), and washing at the Yamuna River in central India ("The Taj Mahal"). In these poems women's identities remain the prevalent concern as Mora explores the implicit questions: "Who am I? Who are we?" In doing so, however, she consciously avoids didacticism. "I try not to have a message when I start out," Mora insisted in *This Is about Vision: Interviews with Southwestern Writers.* "If I have a message then I say to myself, 'That's great, but that's not a poem.' I like to begin with an idea, a line, an image and see where it goes. But I am stubborn enough

that a lot of my deep feelings are obviously going to come in, because of the way I see the world."

Because the elements of the southwest are so prevalent in her work, Mora has been labeled a "regional" writer—even though she does not presently live in the region she writes about. Although she has expanded her view to encompass women's experience in other parts of the world, the author agrees that her "regional" emphasis is very important. As many scholars point out, the experiences of the Chicana have been virtually ignored in American society; writers such as Mora empower Hispanics—especially Hispanic women—through a celebration of the native traditions which lie at the heart of their cultural identity. "For a variety of complex reasons," Mora once stated, "anthologized American literature does not reflect the ethnic diversity of the United States. I write, in part, because Hispanic perspectives need to be part of our literary heritage; I want to be part of that validation process. I also write because I am fascinated by the pleasure and power of words."

That "validation process" has also been a strong incentive for Mora to produce children's literature and juvenile poetry for and about Hispanic Americans. Through a series of bilingual books and stories that feature Hispanic protagonists, she has sought to establish pride in heritage for young Chicanos. "There is particular pleasure for me in poetry, there's just no doubt about that, but I see children's books as very close to that," the author explained in *This Is about Vision.* "I

Puppets dance as if alive.

Two sisters, shopping in Mexican markets, incidentally teach their readers how to count in two languages. (From *Uno, Dos, Tres: One, Two, Three*, illustrated by Barbara Lavallee.)

have very strong feelings that Chicano kids need good children's books, well illustrated, from big publishing houses, and that is something I would really like to work at."

As for the muse that drives her, Mora stated in *This Is about Vision:* "I think one of my big reasons for writing poetry is to help people feel less lonely; that's what poetry did for me . . . . I was able to read women writers and feel less lonely, and so any time my poetry does that for somebody, that is probably my definition of success."

Commenting on Mora's books for children, reviewers generally point to the author's vivid presentation of family relationships and her ability to capture the nuances of Hispanic culture. For example, in a *Horn Book* review of *A Birthday Basket for Tia*, Maeve Visser Knoth described Mora's birthday story as a moving description of a joyful celebration, declaring that her text represented "the best of recent multicultural pub-

lishing." *School Library Journal* contributor Ann Welton maintained that "young readers will be engaged by the cumulative nature of the story while savoring this family's similarities to and differences from their own." Julie Corsaro of *Booklist* also praised *A Birthday Basket for Tia* as a "warm and joyful story," and commended the "energy and cadence" of Mora's text. *Pablo's Tree*, a story about a boy's visit to his grandfather's house, where a tree that had been planted for him when he was adopted is now decorated for his birthday, also received praise for its warm depiction of a family celebration. A *Kirkus Reviews* commentator described *Pablo's Tree* as "a charming story about a particularly joyful Mexican-American birthday tradition." Writing in *Booklist*, Annie Ayres commended Mora for creating a story that "rings with happiness and family love." In a *Horn Book* review of *Pablo's Tree*, Maeve Visser Knoth described Mora's text as a simple rendition of a universal story, and praised the author for presenting "a story which includes adoption and single motherhood without making them central issues."

Critics have also praised Mora's ability to celebrate nature in a direct, convincing, and accessible manner. A *Publishers Weekly* review of *The Desert Is My Mother*, a bilingual children's work, emphasized the writer's skill in invoking "the grand powers of the desert." *Booklist* reviewer Hazel Rochman admired Mora's "playful, poetic text," maintaining that *The Desert Is My Mother* "celebrates a child's connection with her desert home." In *Listen to the Desert*, Mora presents a bilingual rendering of some of the sounds common to the desert southwest. A *Kirkus Reviews* critic remarked that the poem's suggestive chant brings out the "onomatopoeic powers" of Spanish and English. *School Library Journal* contributor Graciela Italiano noted that the bilingual, repetitive text exhibits a rhythmic quality which young readers find appealing.

Mora also successfully utilizes folklore to bring a rich Hispanic heritage to her readers. In *The Race of Toad and Deer*, a Guatemalan version of the classic tortoise-and-hare fable, Mora has, as a *Publishers Weekly* reviewer declared, produced an "organically bicultural" text. *School Library Journal* contributor Martha Topol remarked that the text, while perhaps not conveying the full excitement of an adventure narrative, "works hard to make this book a cross-cultural experience." A *Kirkus Reviews* critic, however, found the story enchanting, lauding Mora's "slyly humorous text."

Mora has also teamed up with illustrator Barbara Lavallee on a bilingual counting book for preschoolers. Commenting on *Uno, Dos, Tres: One, Two, Three*, a *Kirkus Reviews* critic remarked that this one-to-ten counting book, which features two little girls in a Mexican market, conveys "a growing sense of excitement" as the numbers advance. In her *Horn Book* assessment of *Uno, Dos, Tres*, Maeve Visser Knoth deemed the "jaunty rhyme and repetition" a spirited introduction to Mexican folk art and culture. *Booklist* reviewer Annie Ayres found Mora's book "robust and radiant," declaring that *Uno, Dos, Tres* represents a true celebration of the gift of bilingualism.

Mora told *SATA*: "Am I lucky! Because I grew up in a bilingual home, I speak two languages and can write in English and Spanish. I've always enjoyed reading all kinds of books and now I get to write them too, to sit and play with words on my computer.

"I enjoy writing poems, nonfiction, and stories for children and adults. Many of my book ideas come from the desert where I grew up, the open spaces, wide sky, all that sun and all the animals that scurry across the hot sand or fly high over the mountains. I also like to write about my family, like my aunt who danced on her ninetieth birthday and my mother who wanted to be a rainbow tulip when she was in grade school."

■ Works Cited

Ayres, Annie, review of *Pablo's Tree, Booklist,* November 1, 1994, p. 507.

Ayres, Annie, review of *Uno, Dos, Tres: One, Two, Three, Booklist,* June 1, 1996, p. 1736.

Corsaro, Julie, review of *A Birthday Basket for Tia, Booklist,* September 15, 1992, p. 156.

Review of *The Desert Is My Mother/El desierto es mi madre, Publishers Weekly,* December 5, 1994, p. 76.

Italiano, Graciela, review of *Listen to the Desert/Oye al desierto, School Library Journal,* October, 1994, p. 112.

Knoth, Maeve Visser, review of *A Birthday Basket for Tia, Horn Book,* January-February, 1993, pp. 76-77.

Knoth, Maeve Visser, review of *Pablo's Tree, Horn Book,* November-December, 1994, pp. 723-24.

Knoth, Maeve Visser, review of *Uno, Dos, Tres: One, Two, Three, Horn Book,* May-June, 1996, p. 327.

Review of *Listen to the Desert/Oye al desierto, Kirkus Reviews,* May 1, 1994, p. 634.

Mora, Pat, interview in *This Is about Vision: Interviews with Southwestern Writers,* edited by William Balassi, John F. Crawford, and Annie O. Eysturoy, University of New Mexico Press, 1990, pp. 129-39.

Review of *Pablo's Tree, Kirkus Reviews,* September 15, 1994, p. 1276.

Review of *The Race of Toad and Deer, Kirkus Reviews,* September 1, 1995, p. 1285.

Review of *The Race of Toad and Deer, Publishers Weekly,* September 4, 1995, p. 68.

Rochman, Hazel, review of *The Desert Is My Mother/El desierto es mi madre, Booklist,* January 15, 1995, p. 932.

Topol, Martha, review of *The Race of Toad and Deer, School Library Journal,* December, 1995, p. 100.

Review of *Uno, Dos, Tres: One, Two, Three, Kirkus Reviews,* January 15, 1996, p. 139.

Welton, Ann, review of *A Birthday Basket for Tia, School Library Journal,* January, 1993, p. 82.

■ For More Information See

BOOKS

The Hispanic Literary Companion, Visible Ink Press, 1997.

Hispanic Literature Criticism, Volume 2, Gale, 1994, pp. 844-54.

Norwood, Vera, and Janice Monk, editors, *The Desert Is No Lady: Southwestern Landscapes in Women's Writing and Art,* Yale University Press, 1987, pp. 96-124.

Notable Hispanic American Women, Gale, 1993, pp. 280-82.

Rebolledo, Tey Diana, *Women Singing in the Snow: A Cultural Analysis of Chicana Literature,* University of Arizona Press, 1995.

PERIODICALS

Booklist, October 15, 1995, p. 407.
Horn Book, July-August, 1990, pp. 436-37.
Kirkus Reviews, September 1, 1992, p. 1132.
Publishers Weekly, August 31, 1992, p. 77.
School Library Journal, April, 1996, p. 114.

MORRIS, Jeffrey B(randon) 1941-

■ Personal

Born January 8, 1941; son of Richard Brandon (a professor of history) and Berenice (a musician and composer; maiden name, Robinson) Morris; married Dona Baron (an attorney), July 9, 1972; children: David, Deborah. *Education:* Princeton University, B.A., 1962; Columbia University School of Law, J.D., 1965, Ph.D., 1972. *Religion:* Jewish. *Hobbies and other interests:* Opera, Gilbert and Sullivan, ballet, reading.

■ Addresses

Home—234 Forest Rd., Douglaston, NY 11363. *Office*—Touro Law School, 300 Nassau Rd., Huntington, NY 11743.

■ Career

City College of the City University of New York, instructor, lecturer, assistant professor of political science, 1968-72; University of Pennsylvania, assistant professor of political science, 1981-88; Brooklyn Law School, visiting associate professor of law, 1988-90; Touro Law School, associate professor, professor of law, 1990—.

JEFFREY B. MORRIS

Part-time practice of law, New York City, 1967-74; Columbia University, special assistant to the Executive Vice President for Academic Affairs and Provost, 1974-76; Chief Justice of the United States, research assistant to administrative assistant, 1976-81. Worked variously as a teaching assistant, reader in history, and legal assistant. Admitted to the Bar of New York State, District of Columbia, Supreme Court of the United States, and United States District Court for the District of Columbia. Member of the Supreme Court of the United States Second Circuit Committee on Historical and Commemorative Events, Federal Bar Council, Association of the Bar of the City of New York, and District of Columbia Bar Association.

■ Awards, Honors

Selected as one of three Judicial Fellows in the United States, 1976-77; Christian R. and Mary F. Lindback Award for Outstanding Teaching, University of Pennsylvania, 1986; Most Outstanding Professor of the Fraternity in the Nation, Delta Theta Phi Law Fraternity, 1991-1992.

■ Writings

FOR CHILDREN; "GREAT PRESIDENTIAL DECISIONS" SERIES; PUBLISHED BY LERNER

The Washington Way, 1994.
The Jefferson Way, 1994.
The Truman Way, 1995.
The Lincoln Way, 1996.
The F.D.R. Way, 1996.
The Reagan Way, 1996.

FOR ADULTS; NONFICTION

Making Sure We Are True to Our Founders: The Association of the Bar of the City of New York in Its Second Century, 1970-1995, Fordham University Press, 1997.

OTHER

Also author of *Federal Justice in the Second Circuit: A History of the United States Courts in New York, Connecticut & Vermont, 1787 to 1987,* 1988, *To Administer Justice on Behalf of All the People: The United States District Court for the Eastern District of New York,* 1992, and (with C. Berkin, A. Brinkley, E. Foner, L. Wood and others), *American Voices: A History of the United States,* 1992. Co-editor of several reference books with Richard B. Morris, including *Great Presidential Decisions,* 7th edition, 1988, and *Encyclopedia of American History,* HarperCollins, 4th edition, 1970, 5th edition, 1976, 6th edition, 1986, 7th edition, 1996. *Yearbook, Supreme Court Historical Society,* associate editor, 1979-83; board of editors, 1983-86. Also author of a number of scholarly articles published in books, encyclopedias, and journals of law, political science, and history.

■ Work in Progress

Completing a history of the Federal Courts of the District of Columbia Circuit commissioned by the judges and the Bar of those courts.

■ Sidelights

Jeffrey B. Morris, a political scientist and law professor, told *SATA* about his work for children. "Both my father and my mother, Berenice Robinson Morris, a musician and professor of music, considered writing books for children an important undertaking and produced nine between them. During my own career, I have attempted to explain the workings of the American constitutional system to college and law students, fellow scholars and members of the general public, and so I feel very privileged to have had the opportunity to write for children and teenagers. While my academic specialty is the history of courts and legal institutions, that is not a specialty that much interests the young, so I was pleased to be able to write in an area—the Presidency of the United States—that interested me greatly as a child and has been a source of continuing interest as an adult."

Morris added, "One further influence on me in writing the six books was Chief Justice Warren E. Burger on whose staff I served for five years. Burger had a passionate love of American history and of the American constitutional system and an enormous desire to make it come alive for all Americans. That desire left an important impact upon me.

"The six books on presidents and decision-making I wrote for Lerner Publications were originally intended to be a collaboration between my father, Richard B. Morris, an eminent historian, and myself. We shared many interests, and I had worked with him on two books of particular relevance to the Lerner project—the *Encyclopedia of American History* and *Great Presidential Decisions*. Although my Dad had a grand 'old age,' writing three books (the last of over forty) in his eighties, he did not live to work on the project."

Morris's books in the "Great Presidential Decisions" series feature illustrations, photos, maps, diagrams, and indexes, while providing young people with biographical information on six great presidents and an understanding of the complex historical contexts in which they worked. The focus of the series is on the crucial issues each president was confronted with and how he arrived at and implemented his decisions. In *The FDR Way*, for example, Morris relates how President Franklin D. Roosevelt had to deal with the Great Depression, decide whether to involve the United States in World War II, and lead the formation of the United Nations. A *Kirkus Reviews* critic commended Morris for not condescending to readers or avoiding the discussion of controversies, describing *The FDR Way* as a "model of historical writing for children." Similarly, in a review of *The Truman Way, School Library Journal* contributor Mary Mueller noted that, while Morris seems to admire

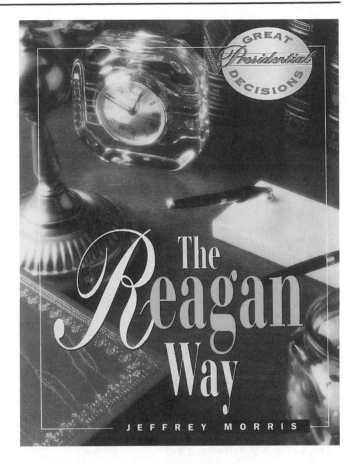

Morris's "Great Presidential Decisions" books chronicle key issues and choices confronting selected American presidents from George Washington to Ronald Reagan.

Truman, he informs readers of "the man's failings . . . . This title is in a category by itself."

The other books written by Morris in the "Great Presidential Decisions" series have also been well received by critics. Reviewing *The Jefferson Way* and *The Washington Way* in *Booklist,* Carolyn Phelan wrote that each work "provides a fuller guide to the presidency and political life of its subjects than do most children's biographies or histories of the period." Similarly, in a *School Library Journal* review of *The Reagan Way,* Mary Mueller commented favorably on Morris's "objectivity," describing the book as "an even-handed look at Reagan's strengths and weaknesses."

Morris explained to *SATA:* "It was a special pleasure to 'get to know' each of the six presidents I wrote about. Each in his own way was fascinating; perhaps Jefferson and Lincoln the most so, but Franklin D. Roosevelt and Harry Truman were also men of many parts. The more time I spent with Jefferson and Lincoln, the more remarkable I found them. F.D.R. emerges as one of the great democratic leaders in world history. My own judgment is that of the six presidents, Truman had the greatest number of truly difficult decisions to make and, if his style was not grand and his personality not elegant, most of those decisions stand up remarkably well almost a half-century later. That I found Washington a man of immense ability and remarkable character and extraordinarily difficult to make come alive should surprise no one. What did surprise me was that Ronald Reagan—such a contrast to the other five presidents in energy, diligence, mastery of detail, and thoughtfulness—should turn out to be so effective in making most of those decisions that mattered to him and that his presidential style would be so interesting to write about."

■ Works Cited

Review of *The FDR Way, Kirkus Reviews,* February 1, 1996, p. 231.
Mueller, Mary, review of *The Truman Way, School Library Journal,* April, 1995, p. 164.
Mueller, Mary, review of *The Reagan Way, School Library Journal,* February, 1996, p. 120.
Phelan, Carolyn, review of *The Jefferson Way* and *The Washington Way, Booklist,* December 15, 1994, p. 749.

■ For More Information See

PERIODICALS

School Library Journal, December, 1994, p. 137.

* * *

MUNOZ, William 1949-

■ Personal

Born January 12, 1949, in Chicago, IL; son of J. John and Margaret (Allen) Munoz; married Sandra Mulberger, November 25, 1976; children: Sean Allen. *Education:* University of Montana, B.A. *Hobbies and other interests:* skiing, gardening. *Religion:* Baha'i.

■ Addresses

Home— 11210 Kona Ranch Road, Missoula, MT 59804.

■ Career

University of Montana, Missoula, director of technical services, 1974-81; Professional photographer 1980—. *Member:* Society of Children's Book Writers and Illustrators; Outdoors Writers Association of America.

■ Awards, Honors

Children's Book of the Year, Library of Congress, 1985, and Editor's Choice, *Booklist,* 1985, both for *Where the Bald Eagles Gather;* Outstanding Science Books for Children, National Science Teachers Association, 1981, for *A Picture Book of Cows,* 1984, for *Farm Animals,* 1985, for *Quarter Horses* and *The Sheep Book,* 1986, for *Draft Horses* and *Buffalo: The American Bison Today,* 1987, for *Wheat: The Golden Harvest,* 1988, for *The Whooping Crane: A Comeback Story,* 1990, for *An Apple a Day, Flowers for Everyone,* and *Yellowstone Fires,*

1992, for *Pelicans, Nutrition,* and *Feathers,* and 1995, for *Eagles of America;* Children's Book of the Year, Bank Street Child Study Children's Book Committee, 1995, for *Why Mammals Have Fur.*

■ Illustrator

FOR CHILDREN

Roland Smith, *Snakes in the Zoo,* Millbrook, 1992.
Smith, *Primates in the Zoo,* Millbrook, 1992.
Smith, *Cats in the Zoo,* Millbrook, 1994.
Smith, *Whales, Dolphins and Porpoises in the Zoo,* Millbrook, 1994.
Ruth Berman, *Ants,* Lerner, 1995.
Gail Stewart, *The Quarter Horse,* Capstone, 1995.
Stewart, *Mustangs and Wild Horses,* Capstone, 1996.
Stewart, *The Palamino Horse,* Capstone, 1996.
Stewart, *The Pinto Horse,* Capstone, 1996.
Stewart, *The Shetland Pony,* Capstone, 1996.

FOR CHILDREN; ALL WRITTEN BY DOROTHY HINSHAW PATENT

A Picture Book of Cows, Holiday House, 1982.
A Picture Book of Ponies, Holiday House, 1983.
Farm Animals, Holiday House, 1984.
Where the Bald Eagles Gather, Clarion, 1984.

Everything you might wish to know about feathers, from their uses to their structure and type, is faithfully presented by the author Dorothy Hinshaw Patent and photographer William Munoz in their 1992 collaboration *Feathers.*

Written by Roland Smith and illustrated with Munoz's photographs, *Inside the Zoo Nursery* explains why and how some animals, including baboons, cheetah cubs, and porpoise calves, are raised in the zoo nursery.

The Sheep Book, Dodd, Mead, 1985.
Baby Horses, Dodd, Mead, 1985, revised edition, Carolrhoda, 1991.
Quarter Horses, Holiday House, 1985.
Buffalo: The American Bison Today, Clarion, 1986.
Draft Horses, Holiday House, 1986.
Maggie, a Sheep Dog, Dodd, Mead, 1986.
Wheat, the Golden Harvest, Dodd, Mead, 1987.
The Way of the Grizzly, Clarion, 1987.
Christmas Trees, Dodd, Mead, 1987.
A Horse of a Different Color, Dodd, Mead, 1988.
Appaloosa Horses, Holiday House, 1988.
The Whooping Crane: A Comeback Story, Clarion, 1988.
Where the Wild Horses Roam, Clarion, 1989.
Wild Turkey, Tame Turkey, Clarion, 1989.
Flowers for Everyone, Cobblehill, 1990.
An Apple a Day: From Orchard to You, Cobblehill, 1990.
Yellowstone Fires: Flames and Rebirth, Holiday House, 1990.
Gray Wolf, Red Wolf, Clarion, 1990.
Where Food Comes From, Holiday House, 1991.
Miniature Horses, Cobblehill, 1991.
A Family Goes Hunting, Clarion, 1991.
Pelicans, Clarion, 1992.
Places of Refuge: Our National Wildlife Refuge System, Clarion, 1992.
Feathers, Cobblehill, 1992.
Nutrition: What's in the Food We Eat, Holiday House, 1992.
Ospreys, Clarion, 1993.
Cattle, Carolrhoda, 1993.
Prairie Dogs, Clarion, 1993.
Inside the Zoo Nursery, Cobblehill, 1993.
Dogs, the Wolf Within, Carolrhoda, 1993.
Horses, Carolrhoda, 1994.
Deer and Elk, Clarion, 1994.
The American Alligator, Clarion, 1994.
Hugger to the Rescue, Cobblehill, 1994.
Looking at Bears, Holiday House, 1994.
What Good Is a Tail?, Cobblehill, 1994.
Why Mammals Have Fur, Cobblehill, 1995.
West by Covered Wagon: Retracing the Pioneer Trails, Walker, 1995.
Eagles of America, Holiday House, 1995.
Biodiversity, Clarion, 1996.
Prairies, Holiday House, 1996.
Back to the Wild, Harcourt Brace, 1997.

■ **Work in Progress**

Fire Ecology for Clarion; *Tall Grass Prairie* for Lerner Books; *Sonoran Desert* for Lerner Books.

■ **Sidelights**

William Munoz's career as a photographic illustrator began in 1980 when he met author Dorothy Hinshaw Patent. The two have since collaborated on a variety of children's informational books, garnering praise from commentators for both text and illustration. For instance, *School Library Journal* contributor Charlene Strickland, reviewing *Where the Wild Horses Roam,* maintained that Munoz's "color photos match the quality of the Patent/Munoz team's previous collaborations," while Betsy Hearne of the *Bulletin of the Center for Children's Books,* in a review of the same work, asserted: "The handsome color photographs, including stunning western landscapes, will hook horse lovers." Commenting on another of Munoz's efforts in tandem with Patent, *Voice of Youth Advocates* contributor Luvada Khun remarked of *Feathers:* "The full-color photographs are breathtaking. The superb photography includes over 50 pictures, several of which are full-page photos."

William Munoz recalled for *SATA:* "Photography has been a vehicle for me to explore the 'hidden' subtleties of nature. I view my work as a photographer in two general areas: one is editorial, the other aesthetic. In both I hope I am artistic.

"I photographically illustrate children's books. These images allow the author to eliminate words. However, while pursuing this goal, I am always aware of the need to spark a child's imagination. It is the 'wonder' of the world of nature that I feel and attempt to capture on film to share.

"Our imagination is a precious gift that allows us to soar. Through it we can conceive of things. It is our imagination that gives meaning to the beauty of a flower, the awe of the mountain, allows our hearts to fly at the sight of an eagle soaring. Our imagination allows us to find meaning in the world. It is unconditional and limitless. Life takes on meaning when we use our imagination, it is a gateway to the soul."

■ **Works Cited**

Hearne, Betsy, review of *Where the Wild Horses Roam, Bulletin of the Center for Children's Books,* June, 1989, p. 262.

Khun, Luvada, review of *Feathers, Voice of Youth Advocates,* June, 1992, p. 132.
Strickland, Charlene, review of *Where the Wild Horses Roam, School Library Journal,* August, 1989, p. 149.

■ **For More Information See**

PERIODICALS

Booklist, June 1, 1991, p. 1874.
Bulletin of the Center for Children's Books, September, 1986, p. 193; February, 1989, p. 154; June, 1989, p. 262.
Horn Book Magazine, July/August, 1995, p. 481.
Kirkus Reviews, June 1, 1992, p. 723.

N

NAPOLI, Donna Jo 1948-

■ Personal

Born February 28, 1948, in Miami, FL; daughter of Vincent Robert and Helen Gloria (Grandinetti) Napoli; married Barry Ray Furrow (a law professor), December 29, 1968; children: Elena, Michael Enzo, Nicholas Umberto, Eva, Robert Emilio. *Education:* Harvard University, B.A., 1970, Ph.D., 1973.

■ Addresses

Office—Linguistics Dept., Swarthmore College, Swarthmore, PA 19081. *Agent*—Barry Furrow, Widener University School of Law, Wilmington, DE 19803.

■ Career

Writer. Smith College, Northampton, MA, lecturer in philosophy and Italian, 1973-74; University of North Carolina, Chapel Hill, NC, lecturer in mathematics and Italian, 1974-75; Georgetown University, Washington, DC, assistant professor of linguistics, 1975-80; University of Michigan, Ann Arbor, MI, linguistics professor, 1980-87; Swarthmore College, Swarthmore, PA, linguistics professor, 1987—. *Member:* Society of Children's Book Writers and Illustrators, Authors Guild, Authors League of America, Linguistic Society of America, Societa linguistica italiana.

■ Awards, Honors

One Hundred Titles for Reading and Sharing selection, New York Public Library, 1992, Children's Book of the Year, Bank Street Child Study Children's Book Committee, 1993, and New Jersey Reading Association's Jerry Award, 1996, all for *The Prince of the Pond: Otherwise Known as De Fawg Pin;* Best Book selection, *Publishers Weekly,* 1993, Blue Ribbon Book designation, *Bulletin of the Center for Children's Books,* 1993, and Best Book for Young Adults selection, Young Adult Library Services Association (YALSA), 1994, all for *The Magic Circle;* Children's Books of the Year, Bank Street

DONNA JO NAPOLI

Child Study Children's Book Committee, 1995, for *When the Water Closes Over My Head,* and 1996, for *Jimmy, the Pickpocket of the Palace;* Leeway Foundation Prize for excellence in fiction, 1995; Pick of the List, American Booksellers Association, 1996, for *Zel* and *Song of the Magdalene;* Best Book selection, *Publishers Weekly* and *School Library Journal,* and Blue Ribbon Book designation, *Bulletin of the Center for Children's Books,* all 1996, all for *Zel;* Hall of Fame Sports Book for Kids, Free Library of Philadelphia, 1996, for *Soccer Shock.* Napoli has also held grants and fellowships in linguistics from the National Science Foundation, the National Endowment for the Humanities, the Mellon Foundation, and the Sloan Foundation.

■ Writings

JUVENILE FICTION

The Hero of Barletta, illustrated by Dana Gustafson, Carolrhoda Books, 1988.
Soccer Shock, illustrated by Meredith Johnson, Dutton Children's Books, 1991.
The Prince of the Pond: Otherwise Known as De Fawg Pin, illustrated by Judith Byron Schachner, Dutton, 1992.
The Magic Circle, Dutton, 1993.
When the Water Closes Over My Head, illustrated by Nancy Poydar, Dutton, 1994.
Shark Shock, Dutton, 1994.
Jimmy, the Pickpocket of the Palace, illustrated by Judith Byron Schachner, Dutton, 1995.
The Bravest Thing, Dutton, 1995.
Zel, Dutton, 1996.
Song of the Magdalene, Scholastic, 1996.
Trouble on the Tracks, Scholastic, 1997.
On Guard, Dutton, 1997.
Sirena, Scholastic, in press.
Albert (picture book), Harcourt, in press.
Stones in Water, Dutton, in press.

NONFICTION; FOR ADULTS

(Editor) *Elements of Tone, Stress, and Intonation,* Georgetown University Press, 1978.
(With Emily Rando) *Syntactic Argumentation,* Georgetown University Press, 1979.
(Editor with William Cressey) *Linguistic Symposium on Romance Languages: 9,* Georgetown University Press, 1981.
Predication Theory: A Case Study for Indexing Theory, Cambridge University Press, 1989.
(Editor with Judy Anne Kegl) *Bridges between Psychology and Linguistics: A Swarthmore Festschrift for Lila Gleitman,* L. Erlbaum, 1991.
Syntax: Theory and Problems, Oxford University Press, 1993.
(With Stuart Davis) *Phonological Factors in Historical Change: The Passage of the Latin Second Conjugation into Romance,* Rosenberg and Sellier, 1994.
Linguistics: Theory and Problems, Oxford University Press, 1996.

Also contributor to and editor of poetry books, including *The Linguistic Muse, Meliglossa, Lingua Franca,* and *Speaking in Tongues.* Author of numerous professional articles on linguistics. Also author of two short stories, "Sweet Giongio" and "Little Lella," both in collections compiled and illustrated by Diane Goode and published by Dutton in 1992 and 1997.

■ Work in Progress

Changing Tunes, a children's book for Dutton; *For the Love of Venice* (tentative title), for Bantam, Doubleday, Dell.

■ Sidelights

A professor of linguistics at Swarthmore College, Donna Jo Napoli cares ardently about language, as can be seen in her novels for young adults and middle-grade readers. Exploring topics ranging from sports and sharks to dark fairy tales, Napoli employs both humor and skillful prose to craft stories of hope and inspiration. "A gifted author," is how a *Kirkus Reviews* commentator has described her, yet Napoli herself told *SATA* that she had not expected to be a writer. "It just happened to me, when I found that writing helped me through difficult times in my life. I'm happy when I write. Very."

The youngest of four children, Napoli was born in Miami, Florida. Her early years were ones of continual moving—by age thirteen she had lived in thirteen different houses that her father, a contractor, built on speculation and subsequently sold. Though she remained in the same school, her neighborhood kept shifting and friends were lost. Napoli grew up feeling like an "outsider," as she wrote in an essay for *Something about the Author Autobiography Series* (*SAAS*). She was a slow learner when it came to reading, but when the words finally clicked together for her in the second grade, she found new friends in the school library. "We had no books in our house," Napoli explained in *SAAS*. "None whatsoever. We had no magazines. My father read the newspaper. I'm not sure I ever saw my mother read at all. My older siblings had school books. And I had the never-ending library." For Napoli, school was a "haven—where no one shouted and there were so many books." A good student once her problems with poor eyesight were handled properly, Napoli blossomed in high school in such subjects as French, Latin, and math.

Graduating from high school, Napoli attended Radcliffe, then the name of the women's college of Harvard University. "The world of ideas that I had yearned for in the books I read and gotten a hint of in my high school honors classes opened up to me at last," she recalled in *SAAS*. She took her undergraduate degree in mathematics, but switched to Romance linguistics for her doctorate, which was the perfect blend of her interests both in math and in languages. During her junior year in college she also married, though graduate studies and teaching positions kept her domestic life a challenge for many years. Writing as a career was the farthest thing from Napoli's mind at the time. Although she took a course in composition and was encouraged by her instructor to pursue a career in writing, she had no desire "to be a poor writer," as she wrote in *SAAS*. "I wanted to earn money and never have to make my family move and never have to make my children worry about whether there would be food on the table. I was practical."

After earning her doctorate, Napoli held lecturer and assistant professor positions at Smith College, University of North Carolina, and Georgetown University. The birth of her first child made her and her husband, Barry Furrow, seek more stable situations. Furrow quit legal practice and became a professor of law, while Napoli

A frog-prince, a/k/a De Fawg Pin, manages to cope with his bewitched status, thanks to a compassionate little female frog who in turn learns about the strange world of humans in Napoli's *The Prince of the Pond.* **(Illustration by Judith Byron Schachner.)**

worked toward becoming a full professor in linguistics. In addition to her numerous professional publications of both books and articles, Napoli was also writing poetry. A miscarriage between her first and second children sent her into an emotional tailspin, and to find her center, she began writing daily letters to a friend. "I wrote my heart out," Napoli recalled in *SAAS*. "Eventually, I came to terms with the loss of that baby." Her correspondent saved the letters and later gave them to her in a big box. "As I looked at those letters," Napoli explained, "I realized it allowed me to be whoever I wanted to be, for some of those letters didn't sound like me—they sounded at once much stronger and wiser and much more vulnerable and lost than I really was. That was the start of my writing career."

From Georgetown Napoli went to the University of Michigan, and then on to Swarthmore College in Pennsylvania. Finally, her first children's book was published by Carolrhoda Press in Minnesota. *The Hero of Barletta* was a retelling of an Italian folk tale—Napoli and her family had spent many summers in Italy—in which a clever giant saves his town from an advancing army. "I felt happy to sell that first story," she explained in *SAAS*, "but I also felt rather strange: the message seemed to be that I could tell traditional stories, but not stories I made up from scratch. It was a mixed message." A linguist, Napoli decided to make the message a little less mixed, and wrote from scratch about something close to the family—soccer, a sport which her son Michael played. Adam, the ten-year-old protagonist of the novel, discovers that he has magic freckles—they can both see and talk. He decides to use this secret to help him earn a place on the school soccer team. Napoli first sent the book to an agent who recommended cutting the freckles as they were too "dopey," but advice from her children and other writers prevailed. Napoli submitted the book unchanged to Dutton in 1990 and it was accepted. "The freckles really steal the show here," commented a *Kirkus Reviews* critic, who also described *Soccer Shock* as "a well-written story with an affectionate, tolerant cast." Denise Krell, writing in *School Library Journal,* however, referred to the "far-fetched" freckles, but decided that even with such a "fantastic twist," this "lighthearted novel succeeds with genuine characters in a believable setting." Napoli wrote a sequel to the book with *Shark Shock,* in which Adam, a year older and having lost and then regained communication with his freckles, strikes up a friendship with a blind boy during his summer vacation at the beach. While commenting that Napoli's idea of talking freckles "stretches credibility to the breaking point," Maggie McEwen concluded in *School Library Journal* that "this light read will appeal to children who have an appreciation for the absurd."

Napoli's next book for middle-grade readers, *The Prince of the Pond,* was a result of family storytelling nights and employs the fairy tale frog-prince motif, but with a unique twist. A prince is turned into a frog by a hag, and is then taken under the protective arm of Jade, a female frog who teaches him the ropes in the pond. Blessed with a prodigious number of spawn, the sensitive frog-prince determines to raise some of them personally. Yet when a princess passes by, the frog-prince leaps to the cheek, kisses her, and becomes a prince once again, leaving Jade and their offspring behind. "The frog prince motif has inspired many books," noted *Booklist* reviewer Carolyn Phelan, "but few as original as this novel." Betsy Hearne of the *Bulletin of the Center for Children's Books* commented both on the point of view—the story is told by Jade, the female frog—and the book's willingness to deal with loss, and concluded that *The Prince of the Pond* is "an animal fantasy that fairy tale readers will relish." A *Kirkus Reviews* critic felt that the author had done her research well: "[This is] a book with an astonishing amount of in-depth natural history cleverly embedded in its endearing, screwball charm." In fact, Napoli spent a great deal of time reading about amphibians and observing pond life. "When I write for children," Napoli explained in *SAAS,* "I am dead serious. If you sit back and think seriously about the frog prince story even just for a moment, you will realize that without a frog to help this prince through the ordeal, he would have been snake meat fast." To please her fans, who were curious to know what became of the frog family, Napoli wrote a sequel, *Jimmy, the Pickpocket of the Palace.* Attempting to save his pond from the miserable hag, young Jimmy, a frog offspring of the prince, is transformed into a human and does not care much for the change. He inevitably ends up working in the palace where he encounters his father. "This successful successor is certain to satisfy old fans and win new friends to the frog prince and his brood," commented a *Kirkus Reviews* critic.

Napoli's first young adult novel, *The Magic Circle,* was inspired by an innocent question posed by the author's daughter, Eva, as to the preponderance of wicked witches and stepmothers in fairy tales, and the dearth of equally evil warlocks and stepfathers. "My little feminist heart beat hard," Napoli recalled in *SAAS,* "and I flipped the pages of my mind through all the fairy tales I knew, looking for the worst woman character I could find. There she was: the witch in Hansel and Gretel." Napoli's subsequent book was an attempt to give a history and motivation to the witch in a prequel to the Hansel and Gretel fairy tale. In Napoli's rendition, the witch was a good-hearted woman at one time who learned sorcery to become a healer, but evil spirits have turned her into a bad witch, with a hunger for children. She takes herself off to the woods where she will not be tempted, until one day two succulent children appear on her doorstep. "Napoli flexes her proven talent for unexpected viewpoints, builds strong pace with compressed vigor, and evokes powerful sensory images," noted Betsy Hearne of the *Bulletin of the Center for Children's Books.* Lisa Dennis, writing in *School Library Journal,* observed "a strongly medieval flavor" in the setting, characterization, and tone, and concluded that "Napoli's writing and the clarity of her vision make this story fresh and absorbing. A brilliantly conceived and beautifully executed novel that is sure to be appreciated by thoughtful readers." A *Publishers Weekly* reviewer summed up the feeling of many commentators for this unique book, dubbing *The Magic Circle* a young adult novel of "genuine magic and suspense" that would "captivate adults as well." In 1996 Napoli published a second in a series of planned revisionings of dark fairy tales, this one based on the Rapunzel story and titled *Zel*. Told alternately from the point of view of Zel held in the tower, the prince who wants to save her, and Zel's witch mother who put the girl in the tower, the book plunges into the psychology of the characters. "The genius of the novel lies not just in the details but in its breadth of vision," noted *Publishers Weekly*. "Its shiveringly romantic conclusion will leave readers spellbound." In a *Horn Book* review of *Zel*, Roger Sutton commented that the early chapters of the book are a bit of a "wander," but concluded that the novel ultimately "transforms myth without flippancy, honoring the power of its roots."

Napoli turned to realistic novels with *When the Water Closes Over My Head* and *The Bravest Thing*. Both stories had a little help from Napoli's children; the first was inspired by her son Michael's fear of drowning, and the second by her daughter Eva's desire to become a veterinarian. On vacation with grandparents in Iowa, nine-year-old Mikey is continually confronted with his fear of drowning in *When the Water Closes Over My Head*, and eventually surmounts this phobia. The book is "a funny, easily read story that boys and girls should take to like ducks to water," enthused a *Kirkus Reviews* commentator. Hazel Rochman, writing in *Booklist*, drew attention to Napoli's technique of "tightly structured, cinematic episodes," and use of dialogue that captured the "daily tangle of close relationships," and concluded that "kids will want more stories about this family." In *The Bravest Thing*, ten-year-old Laurel has to face the death of her newborn bunnies, an aunt with cancer, and her own diagnosis of scoliosis. "Despite the multitude of hard knocks, this is not a problem novel," noted *Publishers Weekly*. "Napoli ... inspires the reader to believe that obstacles, no matter how daunting, can be made smaller through courage."

Having overcome his fear of drowning, fourth-grader Mikey returns in Napoli's *On Guard*, this time to confront anxieties of another sort. The second of four children, Mikey fears that he will not be special enough in any one way to distinguish himself among his siblings. Mikey discovers the sport of fencing, and determines to win the medal his teacher awards weekly to a student who has impressed her with a particular skill, accomplishment, or quality. "Napoli is excellent at depicting Mikey's general tendency towards uncertainty, his frustration at his lack of family stardom, and his passionate attachment to his new field," wrote *Bulletin of the Center for Children's Books* reviewer Deborah Stevenson. "Especially with its lure of an offbeat and glamorous sport, this will please many young readers."

Napoli has also written historical fiction for young people. *Song of the Magdalene*, set in ancient Israel, constructs an account of the life of biblical figure Mary Magdalene from a troubled youth as the daughter of a wealthy Jewish widower in the town of Magdala to her experiences as a helper of Jesus. A *Publishers Weekly* reviewer faulted the work as uneven in many respects, noting, for instance, that "the pacing seems clotted around climactic moments," but nevertheless conceded that "readers may come away with new thoughts about a different era." *Voice of Youth Advocates* contributor Libby Bergstrom offered a more favorable assessment of *Song of the Magdalene*, asserting that "the power of Napoli's investigation into the human psyche will draw YA readers into this book; Miriam [Mary] is a character they will not soon forget." *Trouble on the Tracks*, set in Australia, and *Sirena*, set in ancient Greece, are two further works of fiction penned by Napoli, the first a realistic contemporary adventure and the second a fantasy set in ancient Greece. "People often ask me where the ideas for my stories come from," Napoli noted in *SAAS*. "While I'm not sure that I always know where a story comes from, I can say that I never have trouble coming up with ideas and I have difficulty understanding how anyone could have that trouble.... I believe that if you keep your eyes and ears and mind and heart open, you will find plenty to write about—more than anyone could ever write in a lifetime.... I write from my heart and gut. So it's not surprising that a lot of my views on life are discernible in my books. But I never set out to convince people of a particular moral. And I deeply resent children's books that do." While finding material is never a problem for Napoli—who has also written picture books and adult mysteries—finding the time in her busy life for writing *is* a problem. An organized professional, Napoli even writes in her laundry room so that she can do two tasks at once. Her advice to young writers is simple: write what you know about; write about something that is important; and use good language. A conscientious re-writer, Napoli gets feedback from her editor, family, school children, and even strangers on the street.

If Napoli tries not to shove a certain theme down the throats of her readers, still she does have a message. "When I write for children," Napoli concluded in *SAAS*, "I do not hesitate to present them with the sadness of mortality and the horrors of wickedness—but I always try to leave them with a sense that whether or not they can change the problems in life, they can find a way to live decently and joyfully. Hope is an internal matter. I strive to cultivate it in my readers. Children offer fertile ground."

■ Works Cited

Bergstrom, Libby, review of *Song of the Magdalene*, *Voice of Youth Advocates*, February, 1997, p. 331.

Review of *The Bravest Thing*, *Publishers Weekly*, October 30, 1995, p. 62.

Dennis, Lisa, review of *The Magic Circle*, *School Library Journal*, August, 1993, p. 186.

Hearne, Betsy, review of *The Prince of the Pond: Otherwise Known as De Fawg Pin*, *Bulletin of the Center for Children's Books*, January, 1993, p. 153.

Hearne, Betsy, review of *The Magic Circle*, *Bulletin of the Center for Children's Books*, April, 1993, p. 260.

Review of *Jimmy, the Pickpocket of the Palace*, *Kirkus Reviews*, May 1, 1995.

Krell, Denise, review of *Soccer Shock, School Library Journal,* April, 1992, p. 118.

Review of *The Magic Circle, Publishers Weekly,* June 14, 1993, p. 73.

McEwen, Maggie, review of *Shark Shock, School Library Journal,* January, 1995, p. 109.

Napoli, Donna Jo, essay in *Something about the Author Autobiography Series,* Volume 23, Gale, 1997, pp. 161-78.

Phelan, Carolyn, review of *The Prince of the Pond: Otherwise Known as De Fawg Pin, Booklist,* January 15, 1993, p. 909.

Review of *The Prince of the Pond: Otherwise Known as De Fawg Pin, Kirkus Reviews,* October 1, 1992, p. 1259.

Rochman, Hazel, review of *When the Water Closes Over My Head, Booklist,* January 1, 1994, p. 827.

Review of *Soccer Shock, Kirkus Reviews,* September 15, 1991, p. 1225.

Review of *Song of the Magdalene, Publishers Weekly,* November 4, 1996, p. 77.

Stevenson, Deborah, review of *On Guard, Bulletin of the Center for Children's Books,* February, 1997, p. 217.

Sutton, Roger, review of *Zel, Horn Book,* September-October, 1996, p. 603.

Review of *When the Water Closes Over My Head, Kirkus Reviews,* January 1, 1994, p. 72.

Review of *Zel, Publishers Weekly,* June 17, 1996, p. 66.

■ For More Information See

PERIODICALS

Booklist, July, 1993, p. 1957; October 15, 1994, p. 427; March 15, 1995, p. 1331; October 1, 1995, p. 317.

Bulletin of the Center for Children's Books, September, 1994, p. 21; June, 1995, p. 355; October, 1995, p. 64; January, 1997, p. 182; March, 1997, p. 253.

Kirkus Reviews, June 15, 1993, p. 789; January 15, 1997, p. 144.

Publishers Weekly, January 27, 1992, p. 98; November 16, 1992, p. 64 ; June 14, 1993, p. 73; February 21, 1994, p. 255; June 12, 1995, p. 61; July 3, 1995, p. 62.

School Library Journal, August, 1988, p. 84; October, 1992, p. 118; March, 1994, p. 223; June, 1995, p. 112; October, 1995, p. 138.

Voice of Youth Advocates, August, 1993, p. 169.

—*Sketch by J. Sydney Jones*

*   *   *

NEWSOM, Carol 1948-

■ Personal

Born August 15, 1948, in Fort Worth, TX; daughter of Elvin (an engineer) and Beth (Bicknell) Bobo; married Tom Newsom (an illustrator), April 4, 1969; children: Andy, Philip. *Education:* Art Center College of Design, Los Angeles, CA, B.F.A., 1972. *Religion:* Church of Christ. *Hobbies and other interests:* Skiing in the winter, camping and hiking in the summer.

■ Addresses

Home and office—7713 Red Rock Cir., Larkspur, CO 80118. *Agent*—Mendola Ltd., 420 Lexington Ave., New York, NY 10170.

■ Career

Freelance illustrator, 1972—.

■ Illustrator

Joan Carris, *When the Boys Ran the House,* Lippincott, 1982.

Edward Lear, *An Edward Lear Alphabet,* Lothrop, 1983.

Stephen Roos, *The Terrible Truth: Secrets of a Sixth Grader,* Delacorte, 1983.

Carol Farley, *The Mystery of the Fiery Message,* Avon, 1983.

Stephen Roos, *My Horrible Secret,* Delacorte, 1983.

Eve Bunting, *Karen Kepplewhite Is the World's Best Kisser,* Clarion, 1983.

Marcia Leonard, *Little Owl Leaves the Nest,* Bantam, 1984.

Joan Carris, *Pets, Vets, and Marty Howard,* Harper, 1984.

Barbara Douglas, *The Great Town and Country Bicycle Balloon Chase,* Lothrop, 1984.

Stephen Roos, *My Secret Admirer,* Delacorte, 1984.

Berniece Freschet, *Owl in the Garden,* Lothrop, 1985.

Doris Orgel, *My War with Mrs. Galloway,* Viking Kestrel, 1985.

Patricia Hermes, *Kevin Corbett Eats Flies,* Harcourt, 1986.

CAROL NEWSOM

Barbara Lucas, compiler, *Cats by Mother Goose,* Lothrop, 1986.

Doris Orgel, *Whiskers, Once and Always,* Viking Kestrel, 1986.

Doris Orgel, *Midnight Soup and a Witch's Hat,* Viking Kestrel, 1987.

Patricia Hermes, *Heads, I Win* (sequel to *Kevin Corbett Eats Flies*), Harcourt, 1988.

Joan Davenport Carris, *Hedgehogs in the Closet,* Lippincott, 1988.

Leo F. Buscaglia, *A Memory for Tino,* SLACK, Inc., 1988.

Jackie French Koller, *Impy for Always,* Little, Brown, 1989.

Doris Orgel, *Starring Becky Suslow,* Viking, 1989.

Joan Davenport Carris, *The Greatest Idea Ever,* Lippincott, 1990.

(With Tom Newsom) Lael Littke, *Olympia Odette Presents Davy Crockett's Bearly Believable Sneeze,* Thinking Well, 1990.

(With Tom Newsom) Lael Littke, *Olympia Odette Presents Nellie Bly's in a Jam Telegram,* Thinking Well, 1990.

(With Tom Newsom) Lael Littke, *Olympia Odette Presents Paul Bunyan's Blue Ox Blues,* Thinking Well, 1990.

Stephen Roos, *Twelve-Year-Old Vows Revenge!: After Being Dumped by Extraterrestrial on First Date,* Delacorte, 1990.

William H. Hooks, *Little Poss and Horrible Hound,* Bantam, 1992.

Debra Hess, *Alien Alert!* ("Spy from Outer Space Series" #1), Hyperion, 1993.

Debra Hess, *Too Many Spies* ("Spy from Outer Space Series" #2), Hyperion, 1993.

Joanne Oppenheim, *Do You Like Cats?,* Bantam, 1993.

Megan Stine, *The Hanukkah Miracles,* Bantam, 1993.

Debra Hess, *Escape from Earth* ("Spy from Outer Space Series" #3), Hyperion, 1994.

Debra Hess, *Spies, Incorporated* ("Spy from Outer Space Series" #4), Hyperion, 1994.

Michelle V. Dionetti, *Mice to the Rescue,* Troll Associates, 1995.

Also illustrator of a nursery rhyme book for Avon Products.

■ Sidelights

Carol Newsom has provided the pictures for some three dozen books by widely recognized authors. Her first published efforts were for Joan Carris's *When the Boys Ran the House,* a children's choice selection in several states. Over the next eight years Newsom worked with Carris on three other storybooks: *Pets, Vets, and Marty Howard* (1984), *Hedgehogs in the Closet* (1988), and *The Greatest Idea Ever* (1990).

In 1983, Newsom began another long-running connection when she teamed with Stephen Roos on two titles. *My Horrible Secret* concerns the summer camp adventures of two brothers, one of them afraid to catch or hit a baseball. In that book's companion, *The Terrible*

Escape from Earth, **written by Debra Hess, combines science fiction with mystery in an easy-to-read format, humorously illustrated by Newsom.**

Truth, the conflict is between two girls who must settle their differences when both arrive at a Halloween party dressed as George and Martha Washington. Kate M. Flanagan of *Horn Book* singled out Newsom's "realistic pencil drawings" in *The Terrible Truth* for doing an "excellent job of interpreting the various personalities" of the story. In 1984 Newsom and Roos created *My Secret Admirer,* and in 1990 they teamed again in *Twelve-Year-Old Vows Revenge!* to continue this series on the "Life and Times of the Kids from New Eden."

Newsom began her third book series in 1986 when she joined Doris Orgel to create *My War with Mrs. Galloway.* The team also produced *Midnight Soup and a Witch's Hat,* the penultimate book in this series of four, which deals with the interactions of the various members of a family affected by divorce.

Newsom has illustrated other series books with Lael Littke ("Olympia Odette Presents" series), Patricia Hermes (*Kevin Corbett Eats Flies* and *Heads, I Win*); and, most recently, with Debra Hess (the "Spy from Outer Space" series). Newsom's illustrations for *An Edward Lear Alphabet* (1983) were recognized as "skilled" and "imaginative" by *Parents' Choice* in 1988. Reviewing Jackie French Koller's *Impy for Always,* Phyllis Wilson wrote in *Booklist,* "Newsom's upbeat line drawings reflect the action of this warmly appealing story."

■ Works Cited

Review of *An Edward Lear Alphabet, Parents' Choice,* spring 1988.

Flanagan, Kate M., review of *The Terrible Truth, Horn Book,* February, 1984, pp. 55-56.

Wilson, Phyllis, review of *Impy for Always, Booklist,* June 15, 1989.

■ For More Information See

PERIODICALS

Booklist, November 15, 1987, p. 572; August 1993, p. 2062.

Bulletin of the Center for Children's Books, December 1983, p. 76.

Kirkus Reviews, March 15, 1983, p. 307.

Publishers Weekly, June 8, 1990, p. 55; July 12, 1993, p. 80.

School Library Journal, February, 1987, p. 62; March, 1988, pp. 187-88; September, 1989, p. 299; July, 1990, p. 78; September, 1993, p. 232.

* * *

NICHOLS, Leigh
See KOONTZ, Dean R(ay)

* * *

NOLAN, Dennis 1945-

■ Personal

Born October 19, 1945, in San Francisco, CA; son of Arthur Thomas (an opera singer) and Helen (Fortier) Nolan; married Susan Christine Ericksen, January 28, 1967; married Lauren Ainsworth Mills, June 1, 1987; children: (first marriage) Andrew William. *Education:* Attended College of San Mateo, 1963-65; San Jose State College (now University), B.A., 1967, M.A., 1968.

■ Addresses

Home and office—Westhampton, MA 01027.

■ Career

San Mateo County Library, Belmont, CA, graphic artist, 1970-77; Canada Junior College, Redwood City, CA, art instructor, 1979-86; University of Hartford, West Hartford, CT, coordinator of illustration program in Hartford Art School, 1986—. Art instructor at College of San Mateo, 1982-86, and at San Jose State University, 1983-86. Work has been exhibited in one-man shows and in group shows.

■ Awards, Honors

Outstanding Science Book Award, National Science Teachers Association, 1981, for *The Joy of Chickens,* and 1987, for *Step into the Night;* Pick of the List, American Booksellers, 1987, Top Twelve Books, *Christian Science Monitor,* 1987, and Prix de Zephyr, French Librarian Award, 1988, all for *The Castle Builder; Parents Choice* Magazine Top 15 Books, 1988, and Commonwealth Club of California award, 1988, both for *Step into the Night;* Notable Social Studies Books selection, 1988, for *Legend of the White Doe;* Golden Kite Picture Book Honor, 1990, for *Dinosaur Dream. Monster Bubbles: A Counting Book* was a Junior Literary Guild selection.

■ Writings

FOR CHILDREN; SELF-ILLUSTRATED

Big Pig (picture book), Prentice-Hall, 1976.
Monster Bubbles: A Counting Book (picture book), Prentice-Hall, 1976.
Alphabrutes (picture book), Prentice-Hall, 1977.
Wizard McBean and His Flying Machine (picture book), Prentice-Hall, 1977.
Witch Bazooza (picture book), Prentice-Hall, 1979.
The Joy of Chickens (nonfiction), Prentice-Hall, 1981.
The Castle Builder (picture book), Macmillan, 1987.
Wolf Child (picture book), Macmillan, 1989.
Dinosaur Dream (picture book), Macmillan, 1990.
(Reteller) *Androcles and the Lion,* Harcourt, 1997.

ILLUSTRATOR

Charles Keller (compiler), *Llama Beans,* Prentice Hall, 1979.
Bill Nygren, *Gnomes Color and Story Album,* Troubador Press, 1980.
Karen Schiller, *Bears Color and Story Album,* Troubador Press, 1982.
William Hooks, *The Legend of the White Doe,* Macmillan, 1988.
Joanne Ryder, *Step into the Night,* Four Winds, 1988.
Joanne Ryder, *Mockingbird Morning,* Four Winds, 1989.
Jane Yolen, *Dove Isabeau,* Harcourt, 1989.
Nancy Carlstrom, *Heather Hiding,* Macmillan, 1990.
Joanne Ryder, *Under Your Feet,* Four Winds, 1990.
Jane Yolen, *Wings,* Harcourt, 1991.
Nancy Carlstrom, *No Nap for Benjamin Badger,* Macmillan, 1991.
Ann Tompert, *Savina, the Gypsy Dancer,* Macmillan, 1991.
Maxinne Rhea Leighton, *An Ellis Island Christmas,* Viking, 1992.
T. H. White, *The Sword in the Stone,* Philomel Books, 1993.
Diane Stanley, *The Gentleman and the Kitchen Maid,* Dial Books for Young Readers, 1994.
Bruce Coville, reteller, *William Shakespeare's A Midsummer Night's Dream,* Dial Books, 1995.
Lauren A. Mills, *Fairy Wings: A Story,* Little, Brown, 1995.
Lauren A. Mills, *The Dog Prince,* Little, Brown, 1996.

FOR ADULTS; ILLUSTRATOR

Jim Barrett and others, editors, *"Sunset" Homeowner's Guide to Wood Stoves,* Lane, 1979.
David E. Clark and others, editors, *Gardeners Answer Book,* Lane, 1983.

■ Sidelights

Award-winning author and illustrator Dennis Nolan is known for his highly realistic acrylic paintings, though he has also used soft watercolors, such as those seen in Nancy Carlstrom's *No Nap for Benjamin Badger,* and experimented with a more fanciful, Arthur Rackham-like style in *Fairy Wings,* on which Nolan collaborated with Lauren Mills. While still working as a graphic artist for several years for the San Mateo County Library in Belmont, California, Nolan published his first self-illustrated picture book, *Big Pig,* in 1976. A silly poetic romp in which preschool readers can find all sorts of obese animals (like stout trouts, blimpy chimpies, and, on every page, a fat pig), *Big Pig* "is an ingenious but incongruous little book," according to one *Booklist* reviewer. Although the critic felt young readers would enjoy the book, he felt the intended audience would require help from an adult to understand all the words used in the text. Nolan achieved better success with his next work, *Monster Bubbles: A Counting Book,* which was a Junior Literary Guild selection, but other early

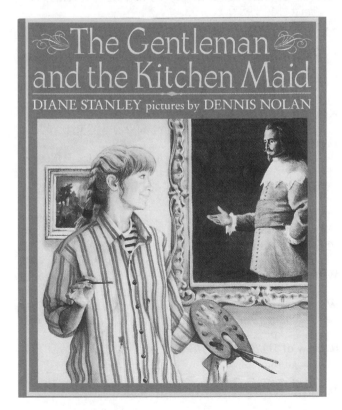

For this clever fantasy relating the love between two figures in different paintings in an art museum, Nolan not only illustrates Stanley's original story but captures the great masters from Chagall to Picasso to Vermeer with style.

works, such as *Alphabrutes* and *Wizard McBean and the Flying Machine,* received mixed reviews.

After spending much of the early 1980s as an art instructor at a California junior college, during which he worked on only a few children's books, Nolan actively began to pursue illustrating and writing again in the latter half of the decade. *The Castle Builder,* published in 1987, enters the world of childhood imagination as it tells of one young boy's day at the beach. The boy builds a sand castle and imagines himself to be its lord, Sir Christopher, a brave hero who defends his home against dragons and evil knights. When the tide comes in, however, the waves become a foe the boy can't defeat. His castle is washed away, but, undaunted, he vows to return to the beach and build a new one. A number of critics praised Nolan's picture book, including *School Library Journal* reviewer Shirley Wilton, who called it "a charming evocation of a child's world." Nolan's artwork was praised as well. For example, a *Publishers Weekly* critic wrote that the "photograph-like pictures in halftones ... exhibit startling clarity." And Betsy Hearne of the *Bulletin of the Center for Children's Books* commented, "The duality of trompe l'oeil screened by a surface of dots serves the fantasy theme well."

The Castle Builder was followed by the somewhat less successful *Wolf Child,* a story set in prehistoric times about a little boy who befriends a wolf cub that later saves him from a charging mammoth. Some critics felt the story and characters were uninspired, though Nolan still received praise for his illustrations. For instance, one *Kirkus Reviews* writer called *Wolf Child* an "unexceptional story," while lauding the "well-crafted paintings ... [that are] in a formal style that recalls N. C. Wyeth."

In 1990 Nolan won a Golden Kite Picture Book Honor for his *Dinosaur Dream.* Returning to the world of childhood imagination that worked so well for him in *The Castle Builder,* Nolan once again brought dreams to life in this story about a modern boy who helps a baby apatosaurus find its way home. Wilbur is awakened one night when Gideon the dinosaur taps at his window. The boy, knowing immediately what must be done, resolves to return Gideon to the Jurassic Era. He manages to do this by simply walking back through time, with Gideon following him obediently like a puppy, past the Ice Age and back into the world of dinosaurs, while braving hazards like volcanoes and saber-tooth cats. When they at last arrive at their destination, Wilbur hugs Gideon and bids him a fond farewell. Throughout the story, Nolan leaves it up to the reader to decide whether this adventure is reality or merely a dream Wilbur is having after reading a book about dinosaurs before falling asleep. Although Cathryn A. Camper, a *School Library Journal* contributor, called the premise a "trite plot gimmick" and the conclusion "cloying," *Booklist* reviewer Leone McDermott called *Dinosaur Dream* "a dinosaur lover's delight." A *Publishers Weekly* commentator felt the story was clever, especially the role reversal between Wilbur and Gideon that depicts the boy to be unexpectedly braver than his

The wingless fairy Fia braves the ugly troll to rescue other fairies in this fantasy written by Lauren Mills and co-illustrated with her husband, Nolan.

rather sheepish and cowardly dinosaur friend. She also considered the ending genuinely moving, adding that Gideon "ranks with the best of animal creations."

Since about the time he published *Dinosaur Dream,* Nolan has concentrated more on illustrating the books of other children's authors than on his own original stories, teaming with such notable writers as William Hooks, Joanne Ryder, Jane Yolen, Nancy Carlstrom, and Ann Tompert. In 1994, Nolan provided the illustrations for Diane Stanley's *The Gentleman and the Kitchen Maid,* a very unique and well-received fantasy about the love between two figures in separate portraits hanging in a city art museum. A young art student who has come to copy the work of the Dutch masters becomes attuned to the plight of these unrequited lovers, and joins the two in a painting of her own making. "Hats off to Nolan for his thorough research and credible renderings of paintings in the style of artists ranging from Rembrandt to Picasso," commented a *Publishers Weekly* reviewer. Carolyn Phelan of *Booklist* called *The Gentleman and the Kitchen Maid* "an original," adding: "Nolan's sensitive watercolor illustrations make each portrait in the museum a definite character in the story." *School Library Journal* contributor Shirley Wilton also commented favorably on Stanley's and Nolan's effort in this work, asserting that "this lighthearted story is deftly told and handsomely illustrated." More recently, Nolan has collaborated with his wife Lauren Mills on the illustrations for Mills's *Fairy Wings,* a tale about a wingless, ridiculed

fairy who saves her fellow fairies from a wicked troll. Many commentators praised the artwork for this book. "Delicate, detailed watercolors add greatly to the book's appeal," noted *Booklist* reviewer Susan Dove Lempke. *School Library Journal* contributor Lisa Dennis similarly praised the "lovely illustrations, reminiscent of Arthur Rackham's ethereal style."

Nolan once told *SATA:* "My grandparents were artists, as were my parents (my father was an operatic tenor). Art was not only encouraged but always around. Books have always been a large part of my life so the blending of two loves—art and books—seemed natural. As an illustrator I approach most of my projects with the visual problems foremost in my mind. The story generally moves along after the pictures have been visualized, at least in my mind if not on paper. Planning the illustrations for the lead-in, the climax, and the ending across a thirty-two page format is also a major concern. Most of my books are humorous, and I plan them in storyboard form somewhat like an animated film. In this way I can control the timing of the punch lines, surprises, and build-ups. I have found that varying my style and technical approach has kept me fresh for each new project."

■ Works Cited

Review of *Big Pig, Booklist,* April 15, 1976, p. 1192.

Review of *The Castle Builder, Publishers Weekly,* August 14, 1987, p. 103.

Camper, Cathryn A., review of *Dinosaur Dream, School Library Journal,* November, 1990, p. 96.

Dennis, Lisa, review of *Fairy Wings, School Library Journal,* January, 1996, p. 90.

Review of *Dinosaur Dream, Publishers Weekly,* October 26, 1990, p. 67.

Review of *The Gentleman and the Kitchen Maid, Publishers Weekly,* November 22, 1993, p. 63.

Hearne, Betsy, review of *The Castle Builder, Bulletin of the Center for Children's Books,* January, 1988, p. 96.

Lempke, Susan Dove, review of *Fairy Wings, Booklist,* November 1, 1995, p. 478.

McDermott, Leone, review of *Dinosaur Dream, Booklist,* October 15, 1990, p. 439.

Phelan, Carolyn, review of *The Gentleman and the Kitchen Maid, Booklist,* January 15, 1994, p. 939.

Wilton, Shirley, review of *The Castle Builder, School Library Journal,* January, 1988, p. 68.

Wilton, Shirley, review of *The Gentleman and the Kitchen Maid, School Library Journal,* August, 1994, p. 146.

Review of *Wolf Child, Kirkus Reviews,* August 15, 1989, p. 1248.

■ For More Information See

PERIODICALS

Booklist, February 15, 1978, p. 1010; December 1, 1989, p. 750; December 15, 1989, p. 834; March 15, 1990, p. 1443; October 15, 1990, p. 439; November 1, 1991, p. 330; January 15, 1994, p. 939.

Bulletin of the Center for Children's Books, July, 1977, p. 178; February, 1988, p. 110.

Kirkus Reviews, March 1, 1976, p. 253; January 15, 1977, p. 43; January 1, 1978, p. 1; October 1, 1989, p. 1483; February 15, 1990, p. 273; October 1, 1991, p. 1293.

Los Angeles Times Book Review, November 25, 1990, p. 18; December 16, 1990, p. 9.

Newsweek, December 3, 1990, p. 64.

Publishers Weekly, March 15, 1976, p. 57; January 17, 1977, p. 82; December 19, 1980, p. 52; January 20, 1989, p. 147; July 28, 1989, p. 221; February 9, 1990, p. 60; September 20, 1991, p. 132; November 6, 1995, p. 94.

School Library Journal, April, 1976, p. 62; May, 1977, p. 54; February, 1978, p. 49; January, 1980, p. 60; July, 1989, p. 75; December, 1989, p. 102; April, 1990, p. 110; July, 1990, p. 79.*

*   *   *

NORMAN, Charles 1904-1996

OBITUARY NOTICE—See index for *SATA* sketch: Born May 9, 1904, in Russia; immigrated to the United States, 1910; naturalized U.S. citizen, 1924; died September 10, 1996, in Newport, RI. Journalist, biographer, poet, author. Norman gained recognition as a biographer and prolific author of children's books; most notably, the *Mr. Upstairs and Mr. Downstairs* series, chronicling the exploits of the Jonquil family. In 1924 Norman's first compilation of poetry was published; *The Far Harbor: A Sea Narrative* was based on his experiences aboard a freighter bound for South America. During the 1920s, he became a reporter for the *Paris Times* and later worked for the North American Newspaper Alliance, United Press International, Associated Press, and newspaper *P.M.* During World War II he produced two books of poetry, *A Soldier's Diary* and *The Savage Century,* both based on his wartime experiences in the U.S. Army. Norman also wrote many biographies, including *The Magic Maker: E. E. Cummings, So Worthy a Friend: William Shakespeare,* and *Ezra Pound. A Study in Mauve, To a Different Drum: The Story of Henry David Thoreau,* and *The Hornbeam Tree and Other Poems* are among his other works.

OBITUARIES AND OTHER SOURCES

BOOKS

Dictionary of Literary Biography, Volume 111: American Literary Biographers, Gale, 1991.

PERIODICALS

New York Times, September 14, 1996, p. 10.
Washington Post, September 17, 1996, p. D5.

*   *   *

NORTH, Anthony
See KOONTZ, Dean R(ay)

P

PAIGE, Richard
See KOONTZ, Dean R(ay)

*   *   *

PARKER, Julie F. 1961-

■ Personal

Born April 20, 1961, in Glen Ridge, NJ; daughter of David L. (a Methodist minister) and Merolyn (a massage therapist; maiden name, Graham) Parker; married Bill Crawford (a Presbyterian minister), August 19, 1989; children: Graham, Mari. *Education:* Hamilton College, Clinton, NY, B.A., 1983; Union Theological Seminary, New York, NY, M.Div., 1988. *Politics:* Democrat. *Religion:* United Methodist. *Hobbies and other interests:* Marathon running, karate, theater, choral singing.

■ Addresses

Home—150 Stokes Ave., Freeport, NY 11520. *Office*—Hofstra Protestant Chaplaincy, 213 Student Center, 200 Hofstra University, Hempstead, NY 11550. *Electronic mail*—JulieFaith@aol.com.

■ Career

United Methodist Minister, 1987—; Hofstra Protestant Chaplaincy, Hempstead, NY, chaplain, 1991—; writer. Preacher and lecturer, New York metropolitan area; active in a variety of philanthropical pursuits. *Member:* Methodist Federal for Social Action, Planned Parenthood, Democratic National Committee, American Civil Liberties Union, Phi Beta Kappa, Pi Delta Phi.

■ Awards, Honors

Books for the Teen Age selection, New York Public Library, 1993, for *Careers for Women as Clergy.*

JULIE F. PARKER

■ Writings

Careers for Women as Clergy, Rosen, 1993.
Everything You Need to Know about Living in a Shelter, Rosen, 1995.
Everything You Need to Know about Decision-Making, Rosen, 1996.
High Performance Through Leadership, Rosen, 1996.

■ Work in Progress

A revised edition of *Careers for Women as Clergy.*

■ Sidelights

The Reverend Julie F. Parker has dedicated herself to a life of teaching and learning. An ordained Methodist minister since 1987, Parker has recently added writing to her long list of accomplishments. Her first book, *Careers for Women as Clergy,* was selected by the New York Public Library as a Book for the Teen Age. In this work, Parker offers a detailed exploration of all aspects of her vocation, including information on the various positions available within the church/synagogue and in a variety of other institutional settings, education, training, salary and benefits as well as the challenges and rewards that await women entering this traditionally male profession. "This is important reading for women entering the clergy," noted *Booklist* reviewer Kathy Bonnar. *Voice of Youth Advocates* contributor Joanne Johnson praised *Careers for Women as Clergy* as "a balanced and unique look at the increasing role women are playing in religion," adding that "this will be a valuable and interesting addition to many career collections." Parker's subsequent efforts, including the books *Everything You Need to Know about Living in a Shelter* and *Everything You Need to Know about Decision-Making,* have also been aimed at teenage readers. The former specifically targets young readers who are confronted with the challenge of life in a homeless shelter, but "should be read by *all* teens," according to *Voice of Youth Advocates* contributor Terri Evans.

Parker cites discipline as the key to her success. She recently told *SATA,* "I run marathons and have practiced karate. For me these activities are a lot like writing: they require discipline. I enjoy training on my morning run, executing katas, and typing at my laptop, but what I really love is the accomplishment at the end.

"As both a mother of two small children and a Methodist minister, I often find it a real challenge to make the time to write. But the words and phrases come to me and stick in my mind until I discipline myself to transfer them to a disk. The word discipline comes from the Greek (the language of the New Testament) and means 'to learn.' One of the greatest joys of writing is the learning it requires. So as I write, I learn, and I am grateful for the chance to do both."

■ Works Cited

Bonnar, Kathy, review of *Careers for Women as Clergy, Booklist,* October 1, 1993, p. 329.

Evans, Terri, review of *Everything You Need to Know about Living in a Shelter, Voice of Youth Advocates,* February, 1996, p. 398.

Johnson, Joanne, review of *Careers for Women as Clergy, Voice of Youth Advocates,* August, 1993, p. 200.

■ For More Information See

PERIODICALS

School Library Journal, August, 1993, p. 200; December, 1995, pp. 138-39.

*   *   *

PARRISH, Mary
See COUSINS, Margaret

*   *   *

PARSONS, Alexandra 1947-

■ Personal

Born January 10, 1947, in London, England; daughter of Frederic H. (a head teacher) and Margaret (a homemaker) Towle; married Iain R. D. Parsons (a publisher), 1981; children: Chloe. *Education:* "Life." *Politics:* Liberal. *Religion:* "None." *Hobbies and other interests:* Sculpture, travel.

■ Addresses

Home and office—17 St. Peters Rd., St. Margarets, Twickenham, Middlesex, TWI IQY, United Kingdom.

ALEXANDRA PARSONS

■ Career

Mitchell Beazley, England, senior executive editor, 1978-83; The Watermark Press, Australia, co-founder, 1983-88; writer, 1988—.

■ Awards, Honors

Best nonfiction book, Yorkshire Post, 1983, for editing *Music in Time;* award for best jacket design, American Book Publishers Association, 1987, for *Tony Bilson's Recipe Book;* Science Writing Award, American Institute of Physics, 1994, for "Make It Work Science" series.

■ Writings

Araminta Goes Shopping (children's fiction), Heinemann, 1991.

(With husband, Iain Parsons) *Making It from 12 to 20: How to Survive Your Teens* (nonfiction for teenagers), Piatkus, 1991.

"EYEWITNESS JUNIORS" SERIES (APPEARED IN ENGLAND AS "AMAZING WORLDS" SERIES); PHOTOGRAPHS BY JERRY YOUNG

Amazing Birds, Knopf, 1990, Dorling Kindersley, 1990.

Amazing Mammals, Knopf, 1990, Dorling Kindersley, 1990.

Amazing Snakes, Knopf, 1990, Dorling Kindersley, 1990.

Amazing Spiders, Knopf, 1990, Dorling Kindersley, 1990.

Amazing Cats, Knopf, 1990, Dorling Kindersley, 1990.

Amazing Poisonous Animals, Knopf, 1990, Dorling Kindersley, 1990.

"WHAT'S INSIDE?" SERIES; PUBLISHED BY DORLING KINDERSLEY

Toys, illustrated by Richard Manning, 1991.

Shells, illustrated by Manning, 1991.

Small Animals, illustrated by Manning, 1991.

Baby, illustrated by Manning, 1992.

Boats, illustrated by Manning, 1992.

Everyday Things, illustrated by Paul Cooper and Jon Sayer, 1992.

Trucks, illustrated by Richard Manning and Ed Stuart, 1992.

Plants, illustrated by Manning, 1992.

Insects, illustrated by Manning, 1992.

Spacecraft, illustrated by Richard Ward, 1992.

Great Inventions, illustrated by Ray Hutchens, Barry Robson, and Steve Weston, 1993.

Sea Creatures, illustrated by Stuart Lafford, Barry Robson, and Steve Weston, 1993.

Cars, illustrated by Ron Ballard, Ray Hutchens, Icon Design, Barry Robson, and Pete Sarjeant, 1993.

Animal Homes, illustrated by Stuart Lafford and Michelle Ross, 1993.

"MAKE-IT-WORK SCIENCE" SERIES

Earth, photographs by Jon Barnes, Two-Can, 1992, reprinted as *Earth: A Creative Hands-on Approach to Science,* Aladdin, 1993.

Electricity, photographs by Jon Barnes, Two-Can, 1992, reprinted as *Electricity: A Creative Hands-on Approach to Science,* Aladdin, 1993.

Sound, photographs by Jon Barnes, Two-Can, 1992, reprinted as *Sound: A Creative Hands-on Approach to Science,* Aladdin, 1993.

(With Claire Watts) *Plants: A Creative Hands-on Approach to Science,* Aladdin, 1993.

"MAKE-IT-WORK HISTORY" SERIES; WITH ANDREW HASLAM

Ancient Egypt, Thomson Learning, 1995, Two-Can, 1995.

Arctic Peoples, Thomson Learning, 1995, Two-Can, 1995.

North American Indians, Thomson Learning, 1995, Two-Can, 1995.

"MICKEY WONDERS WHY?" SERIES; ILLUSTRATED BY THE ALVIN WHITE STUDIOS AND RICHARD MANNING

Can You Really Fry an Egg on a Stone?, Disney Books by Mail, 1992.

How Far Is It to the Moon?, Disney, 1992.

How Do Birds Fly?, Disney, 1992.

Were Dinosaurs Smart?, Disney, 1992.

What is Toothpaste Made Of?, Disney, 1992.

Where Do Rainbows End?, Disney, 1992.

Why Do Boomerangs Come Back?, Disney, 1992.

Why Do Camels Have Humps?, Disney, 1992.

Why Do Puppies Chew Slippers?, Disney, 1992.

Why Do Some Kids Have Freckles?, Disney, 1992.

Why Do Tigers Have Stripes?, Disney, 1992.

Why Do Whales Sing?, Disney, 1992.

Why Is the Grass Green?, Disney, 1992.

Are Jellyfish Made of Jelly?, Disney, 1993.

"LIFE EDUCATION" SERIES

An Amazing Machine, illustrated by John Shackell, Stuart Harrison, and Paul Banville, F. Watts, 1996.

Being Me, illustrated by Teri Gower and Stuart Harrison, F. Watts, 1996.

Fit for Life, F. Watts, 1996.

Me and My World, illustrated by Teri Gower and Stuart Harrison, F. Watts, 1996.

I'm Happy, I'm Healthy, F. Watts, 1997.

I Am Special, F. Watts, 1997.

My Wonderful Body, F. Watts, 1997.

You're Special, Too, F. Watts, 1997.

OTHER

Facts and Phalluses: A Collection of Bizarre and Intriguing Truths, Legends, and Measurements (adult nonfiction), illustrated by Jennifer Black, Souvenir Press, 1989, St. Martin's Press, 1990.

A Proper Breakfast (cookbook), illustrated by Evie Safarewicz, St. Martin's Press, 1991.

Author of *Mothers* and *Fathers,* both literary anthologies, published in the United States by Simon and Schuster. Also author of screenplays and TV scripts, including "Maggie Goes to Hollywood" and "Working the Tweedle." Editor of *Music in Time.* Some of the author's books in the "Eyewitness Juniors" series have been translated into Spanish.

■ Work in Progress

A novelization of the television film *Mountain of Adventure,* based on Enid Blyton's story for children; books and television scripts for a children's television series called *The Movie Brats.*

■ Sidelights

Writer and editor Alexandra Parsons has a long list of published children's books and an award from the American Institute of Physics for a science series to her credit. If Parsons's works of nonfiction help children understand complicated subjects and make learning fun, it is due to her own efforts to understand the subjects she explores in her books. She explained to *SATA* that she was "particularly happy to win the American Institute of Physics [Science Writing] Award.... This was a very sweet success, as I never studied science seriously at school and never passed a science exam. I started with about as much knowledge as my potential audience, and what helped me explain basic physics to children was first explaining it to myself."

Parsons began her career as an editor at Mitchell Beazley in England. She told *SATA* that there, she "conceived and managed publishing projects in the cookery and design fields." In 1983, Parsons moved to Australia and co-founded a publishing company, The Watermark Press. During this time in Australia, Parsons noted a dearth of "life education" books for her teenage stepsons and "became seriously interested in writing for children." Parsons and her husband wrote such a book themselves, *Making It from 12 to 20.* According to Parsons, the book is "still bringing in the royalty cheques after ten years."

In 1988, Parsons returned to England, and she began to write for a number of series, including "What's Inside?," "Mickey Wonders Why?," "Make-It-Work Science," "Make-It-Work History," and "Life Education." This latter series, said Parsons, is "designed to give children the necessary knowledge of the way the body works to help them understand how drugs affect the body, to give them the self-esteem to help them avoid the pitfalls of peer pressure, and to help them distinguish between right and wrong."

Another nonfiction series to which Parsons has contributed, the Alfred A. Knopf "Eyewitness Juniors" series, has garnered attention from critics. The books in this series introduce animals and insects to young readers. Each book begins by explaining what each animal is before moving on to discuss various species. As critics have noted, readers of these books are both entertained and informed. A "variety of trivia, folklore, and world-record type information" is presented in the books, explained Kay Weisman in a *Booklist* review of *Amazing Birds* and other books in the series. A critic in *Publishers Weekly* reviewing *Amazing Birds* and other series books called attention to the "absolute clarity of text" and the absence of "potentially intimidating blocks of text." In a *School Library Journal* review of *Amazing Poisonous Animals* and *Amazing Lizards,* Ruth M. McConnell commented that the books make "terrific choices for reluctant and even remedial readers."

■ Works Cited

Review of *Amazing Birds, Amazing Mammals, Amazing Snakes,* and *Amazing Spiders, Publishers Weekly,* June 8, 1990, p. 57.

McConnell, Ruth M., review of *Amazing Frogs and Toads, Amazing Cats, Amazing Poisonous Animals,* and *Amazing Lizards, School Library Journal,* February, 1991, p. 86.

Weisman, Kay, review of *Amazing Birds, Amazing Mammals, Amazing Snakes,* and *Amazing Spiders, Booklist,* August, 1990, p. 2178.

■ For More Information See

PERIODICALS

Booklist, October 1, 1991, p. 230.

Bulletin of the Center for Children's Books, November, 1995, p. 2.

School Library Journal, August, 1992, p. 153.

*   *   *

PATERSON, Katherine (Womeldorf) 1932-

■ Personal

Born October 31, 1932, in Qing Jiang, China; daughter of George Raymond (a clergyman) and Mary (Goetchius) Womeldorf; married John Barstow Paterson (a clergyman), July 14, 1962; children: Elizabeth Po Lin, John Barstow, Jr., David Lord, Mary Katherine. *Education:* King College, A.B. (summa cum laude), 1954; Presbyterian School of Christian Education, M.A., 1957; postgraduate study at Kobe School of Japanese Language, 1957-60; Union Theological Seminary, New York City, M.R.E., 1962. *Politics:* Democrat. *Religion:* "Presbyterian Church in the United States." *Hobbies and other interests:* Reading, swimming, tennis, sailing.

■ Addresses

Home—Barre, VT. *Office*—c/o E. P. Dutton, 2 Park Ave., New York, NY 10016.

■ Career

Writer, 1966—. Public school teacher in Lovettsville, VA, 1954-55; Presbyterian Church in the United States, Board of World Missions, Nashville, TN, missionary in Japan, 1957-62; Pennington School for Boys, Pennington, NJ, master of sacred studies and English, 1963-65. *Member:* Authors Guild, Authors League of America, PEN, Children's Book Guild of Washington.

KATHERINE PATERSON

■ Awards, Honors

American Library Association (ALA) Notable Children's Book, 1974, and Phoenix Award, Children's Literature Association, 1994, for *Of Nightingales That Weep;* ALA Notable Children's Book, 1976, National Book Award for Children's Literature, 1977, runner-up for Edgar Allan Poe Award (juvenile division), Mystery Writers of America, 1977, and American Book Award nomination (children's fiction paperback), 1982, all for *The Master Puppeteer;* ALA Notable Children's Book, 1977, John Newbery Medal, 1978, Lewis Carroll Shelf Award, 1978, and Michigan Young Reader's Award Division II runner-up, 1980, all for *Bridge to Terabithia;* ALA Notable Children's Book, 1978, National Book Award for Children's Literature, 1979, Christopher Award (ages 9-12), 1979, Newbery Honor Book, 1979, CRABbery (Children Raving About Books) Honor Book, 1979, American Book Award nominee (children's paperback), 1980, William Allen White Children's Book Award, 1981, Garden State Children's Book Award (younger division), New Jersey Library Association, 1981, Georgia Children's Book Award, 1981, Iowa Children's Choice Award, 1981, Massachusetts Children's Book Award (elementary), 1981, all for *The Great Gilly Hopkins;* Hans Christian Andersen Award U.S. nominee, 1980, *New York Times* Outstanding Book List, 1980, Newbery Medal, 1981, CRABbery Honor Book, 1981, American Book Award nominee (children's hardcover), 1981, children's paperback, 1982, all for

Jacob Have I Loved; Outstanding Books and Best Illustrated Books selection, *New York Times,* 1981, for *The Crane Wife,* illustrated by Suekichi Akaba and translated by Paterson from a retelling by Sumiko Yagawea; Parent's Choice Award, Parent's Choice Foundation, 1983, for *Rebels of the Heavenly Kingdom;* Irvin Kerlan Award "in recognition of singular attainments in the creation of children's literature," 1983; University of Southern Mississippi School of Library Service Silver Medallion, 1983, for outstanding contributions to the field of children's literature; Parent's Choice Award, Parent's Choice Foundation, and Notable Books list, *New York Times,* both 1985, both for *Come Sing, Jimmy Jo;* Laura Ingalls Wilder Award nominee, 1986; ALAN Award, 1987; Keene State College Award, 1987; Regina Medal Award, Catholic Library Association, 1988, for demonstrating "the timeless standards and ideals for the writing of good literature for children"; Best Illustrated list, *New York Times,* 1990, and Best Picture Books selection, *Boston Globe-Horn Book,* 1991, both for *The Tale of the Mandarin Ducks;* Irma S. and James H. Black Award, 1992, for *The King's Equal;* Scott O'Dell Award for Historical Fiction, Scott O'Dell Foundation, 1997, for *Jip: His Story.* Litt.D., King College, 1978; D.H.L., Otterbein College (Westerville, OH), 1980; Litt. D., St. Mary's of the Woods, 1981; Litt. D., University of Maryland, 1982; Litt. D., Shenandoah College, 1982; D.H.L., Washington and Lee University, 1982; D.H.L., Norwich University and Mount St. Vincent University, both 1990.

■ Writings

The Sign of the Chrysanthemum, illustrated by Peter Landa, Crowell Junior Books, 1973.
Of Nightingales That Weep, illustrated by Haru Wells, Crowell Junior Books, 1974.
The Master Puppeteer, illustrated by Haru Wells, Crowell Junior Books, 1976.
Bridge to Terabithia, illustrated by Donna Diamond, Crowell Junior Books, 1977.
The Great Gilly Hopkins, Crowell Junior Books, 1978.
Angels and Other Strangers: Family Christmas Stories, Crowell Junior Books, 1979 (published in England as *Star of Night: Stories for Christmas,* Gollancz, 1980).
Jacob Have I Loved, Crowell Junior Books, 1980.
Rebels of the Heavenly Kingdom, Lodestar, 1983.
Come Sing, Jimmy Jo, Lodestar, 1985.
Park's Quest, Lodestar, 1988.
The Smallest Cow in the World, illustrated by Jane Clark Brown, Vermont Migrant Education Program, 1988.
The Tale of the Mandarin Ducks, illustrated by Leo and Diane Dillon, Lodestar, 1990.
Lyddie, Lodestar, 1991.
The King's Equal, illustrated by Vladimir Vagin, HarperCollins, 1992.
Flip-Flop Girl, Lodestar, 1994.
A Midnight Clear: Stories for the Christmas Season, Lodestar, 1995.

The Angel and the Donkey (retelling), illustrated by Alexander Koshkin, Clarion Books, 1996.

Jip: His Story, Lodestar, 1996.

Celia and the Sweet, Sweet Water, illustrated by Vladimir Vagin, Lodestar, in press.

Marvin's Best Christmas Present Ever, illustrated by Jane Clark Brown, HarperCollins, in press.

(With John Paterson) *Images of God,* illustrated by Alexander Koshkin, Clarion Books, in press.

Contributor of articles and reviews to periodicals; anthologized in *On the Wings of Peace;* co-editor of *The Big Book of Our Planet* and *The World in 1492.* Reviewer, *Washington Post Book World,* 1975—; member of editorial board, *Writer,* 1987—.

NONFICTION

Who Am I? (curriculum unit), CLC Press, 1966.

To Make Men Free (curriculum unit; includes books, records, pamphlets, and filmstrip), John Knox, 1973.

Justice for All People, Friendship, 1973.

Gates of Excellence: On Reading and Writing Books for Children, Lodestar, 1981.

(With husband, John Paterson) *Consider the Lilies: Flowers of the Bible,* Crowell Junior Books, 1986.

The Spying Heart: More Thoughts on Reading and Writing Books for Children, Lodestar, 1989.

A Sense of Wonder: On Reading and Writing Books for Children (includes *Gates of Excellence* and *The Spying Heart*), Plume, 1995.

TRANSLATOR

Sumiko Yagawa, *The Crane Wife,* Morrow, 1981.

Momoko Ishii, *Tongue-Cut Sparrow,* Lodestar, 1987.

Also translator of Hans Christian Andersen's *The Tongue Cut Sparrow,* for Lodestar.

■ Adaptations

The Great Gilly Hopkins was filmed by Hanna-Barbera, 1980; *Bridge to Terabithia* was filmed for PBS television, 1985, and adapted as a play with music, libretto by Paterson and Stephanie Tolan and music by Steve Liebman, French, 1992; *Jacob Have I Loved* was filmed for PBS, 1990. Several of Paterson's books, including *Bridge to Terabithia, The Great Gilly Hopkins, Angels and Other Strangers,* and *Jacob Have I Loved,* have also been adapted for audio cassette by Random House.

■ Sidelights

Two-time Newbery Medal winner Katherine Paterson writes of children in crisis, at the crossroads of major decisions in their lives. Her youthful protagonists turn "tragedy to triumph by bravely choosing a way that is not selfishly determined," according to M. Sarah Smedman in *Dictionary of Literary Biography.* "They embody the theme of redemption through sacrifice of oneself and one's ambitions," Smedman noted, "a theme that resounds convincingly, never cliched, never preached, always with the force of fresh discovery." Paterson's

delicate touch with emotionally heavy topics such as death and familial jealousy sets her apart from other problem book authors. "The distinctive quality of Paterson's art," commented Smedman, "is her colorful concision. Whether she is narrating or describing, her mode is understatement, her style pithy. She dramatizes, never exhorts.... [She is] a major artist, skilled, discerning, and compassionate."

Smedman might also have added humorous. Paterson's wry understatement saves her work from sentimentality. In books such as *Bridge to Terabithia* and *Jacob Have I Loved,* she tackles serious themes head on, but always with compassion and strong storytelling skills. In others, such as *The Great Gilly Hopkins,* her humor and wit are showcased. Paterson establishes a powerful identification with the reader because she so strongly believes what she writes. "Why do I keep writing stories about children and young people who are orphaned or otherwise isolated or estranged?" Paterson asked in *Theory into Practice.* "It's because I have within myself a lonely, frightened child who keeps demanding my comfort. I have a rejected child, a jealous and jilted adolescent inside who demands, if not revenge, a certain degree of satisfaction. I am sure it is she, or should I say they, who keep demanding that I write for them."

The Tale of the Mandarin Ducks, **Paterson's retelling of a Japanese folktale, is illustrated in authentic Japanese ukiyoe style by Leo and Diane Dillon.**

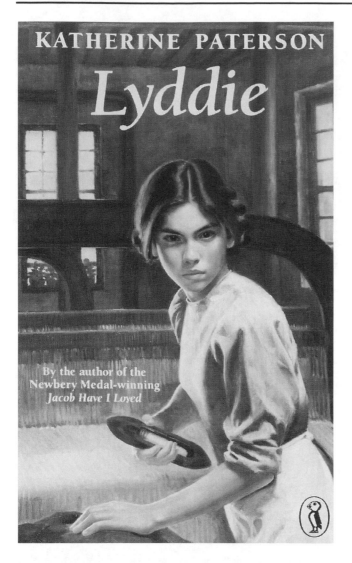

KATHERINE PATERSON

Lyddie

By the author of the Newbery Medal-winning *Jacob Have I Loved*

Lyddie, a young nineteenth-century mill laborer, must determine whether to risk losing her job—and the money she needs to reunite her dispersed siblings—by joining with co-workers in protesting their working conditions.

Paterson often writes about children who are orphaned or estranged from their parents, teens who isolate themselves or who associate only with one or two close friends. These recurring situations reflect the instability of the author's childhood. "If I tell you that I was born in China of Southern Presbyterian missionary parents, I have already given away three chief clues to my tribal memory," Paterson once wrote in *Horn Book.* The third of five children, Paterson spent her early years in China, repatriating to the United States by the onset of World War II. Chinese being her first language, Paterson learned English with a distinct British accent, and dressed in missionary hand-me-downs—a sure recipe for ridicule from her classmates in North Carolina where the family resettled. Paterson, bereft of friends, found consolation in the school library and in books. Perennially the new kid in school—the family moved fifteen times in thirteen years—Paterson learned survival skills on the playground and delved even further into

her private world of books and began writing her own stories. She was a self-confessed outsider and "weird" kid. "I'm sure there are plenty of fine writers who have overcome the disadvantage of a normal childhood and gone on to do great things," Paterson wrote in *Gates of Excellence: On Reading and Writing Books for Children.* "It's just that we weird little kids do seem to have a head start."

After high school, Paterson attended King College in Bristol, Tennessee, majoring in English literature. A year of teaching in a rural Virginia school followed, then a master's degree in education, and finally missionary work in Japan. Until that time her only contact with the Japanese had been with conquering soldiers when she was a child in war-torn China. But the four years she spent in Japan were a revelation for her, and she grew to love the country and its people. Paterson's experiences in Japan figured prominently in her first books, written several years later. In 1961 she returned to the United States, married, and began raising a family of four children, two of whom were adopted. Slowly she turned to writing as a private solace at the end of long and hectic days. Her literary career officially began with works for church school curricula. When finished with the project, she turned her hand to fiction, her first love. Seven years later, she had what she considered publishable material.

Paterson's first three books are historical fiction, set in Japan. The twelfth century and its civil wars are the setting for *The Sign of the Chrysanthemum* and *Of Nightingales That Weep,* while her third novel, *The Master Puppeteer,* is a mystery set in eighteenth-century Osaka during a great famine. All three books deal with teenagers who are either orphaned or have lost one parent and who must make it on their own in exceptionally difficult times. In *The Sign of the Chrysanthemum,* young Muna experiences the loss of his mother and tries without success to find his samurai father, whom he would know by the tatoo of a chrysanthemum on his shoulder. Although he does not find his father, in searching for him Muna travels a road of self-discovery that is not without its own rewards. Reviewing this first novel in *Horn Book,* Virginia Haviland noted that "the storytelling holds the reader by the quick pace of the lively episodes, the colorful detail, and the superb development of three important characters." Graham Hammond, writing in *Times Literary Supplement,* commented that "the book is about pain, wisdom, choosing, and growing up, but it is far from didactic." *Of Nightingales That Weep,* Paterson's second novel, deals with the fortunes of a young girl during the same period in Japan, and could, according to Margery Fisher of *Growing Point,* "satisfy adolescents and adults alike with its exotic flavour and mature handling of characters." Marcus Crouch, writing in *Junior Bookshelf,* noted his own initial reluctance to read a book dealing with twelfth-century Japan, but concluded that once started, the book was "hypnotically dominating."

Paterson's third novel, *The Master Puppeteer,* was her break-out book for which she won a National Book

Award in 1977. Using the world of traditional Japanese puppet drama as a backdrop, Paterson wove a mystery around young Jiro and his best friend Kinshi, the son of a puppet master. Both boys are alienated from their fathers and find stability in their relationship with one another. Diana L. Spirt in her *Introducing More Books: A Guide for the Middle Grades,* described the book as "engrossing," and noted that "the author has blended a literate mix of adventure and Japanese history with a subtle knowledge of young people." Zena Sutherland, reviewing the novel in *Bulletin of the Center for Children's Books,* compared *The Master Puppeteer* to "intricate embroidery," and concluded with a terse, telling description: "good style, good story." The interplay of technique and content was also noted by Dora Jean Young in *School Library Journal.* "This novel ... should be very popular for its combination of excellent writing and irresistible intrigue," Young declared.

Paterson turned to a contemporary rural American setting for her fourth novel, inspired by the death of her son David's favorite friend, who was struck by lightning. In *Bridge to Terabithia,* Jess and Leslie are fifth-graders whose loneliness brings them together as fast friends. They build a secret hideout and call it the magical kingdom of Terabithia. Heavy rains make it impossible to go there for a time, but after returning from a trip, Jess learns that Leslie has drowned trying to get to their hideout. Thereafter, he builds his own monument to the young girl. A Newbery Award winning novel, *Bridge to Terabithia* is "an unromantic, realistic, and moving reaction to personal tragedy," according to Jack Forman in *School Library Journal.* Jill Paton Walsh, reviewing the work in the *Christian Science Monitor,* commends it as "tender and poetic without ever being sentimental, written in simple language which never fails to carry the emotional charge." A novel with a lighter touch is *The Great Gilly Hopkins,* a somewhat comic view of a spunky foster child and the foster mother who ultimately wins the girl's affection. The novel was the result of Paterson's own experiences as a foster mother for two months. "This is quite a book!" proclaimed Ellen M. Davidson in *Children's Book Review Service.* "It confronts racism, sexism, ageism, I.Q.ism and just about all the other prejudices of our society." However, Bryna J. Fireside in *New York Times Book Review* took Paterson to task for this very plenitude of issues. Fireside commented that the novel would have been better "without mixing up race relations, learning disabilities, the important relationships between young and old, *and* a terrific young girl who gamely comes to terms with her status as a foster child." Yet most reviewers—and awards committees—responded more favorably. Natalie Babbitt, reviewing the book in *Washington Post Book World,* concluded that *The Great Gilly Hopkins* "is a finely written story. Its characters linger long in the reader's thoughts after it is finished."

Smedman, writing in *Dictionary of Literary Biography,* described Paterson's next novel, *Jacob Have I Loved,* as the author's "most complex." A second Newbery Award winner, this novel examines the feelings of a twin for her tremendously talented sibling. Set on a Chesapeake

island at the outset of World War II, the story is about Sara Louise—known as Wheeze—and her delicate and musically talented sister Caroline, as related from the adult Wheeze's retrospective point of view. Paul Heins, writing in *Horn Book,* commented that Paterson had again "written a story that courageously sounds emotional depths." *Christian Science Monitor* contributor Betty Levin dubbed the book "a breathtaking novel for older children and adults ... a book full of humor and compassion and sharpness."

Paterson returned to Far Eastern settings for *Rebels of the Heavenly Kingdom,* set in nineteenth-century China. The story of a young peasant boy, Wang Lee, kidnapped by bandits, and his friendship with and growing love for Mei Lin, who helps to rescue him, the book is "on the epic scale" and is "skillfully crafted," according to *Publishers Weekly.* Mary Hobbs, writing in *Junior Bookshelf,* noted that the story "is beautifully told," and painlessly teaches the reader about details of "the traditional Chinese ways of life and thought."

Although nine-year-old Vinnie and her young brother Mason find it difficult to accept their father's death, they receive help from the "flip-flop" girl Lupe, who has problems of her own in this well-received Paterson tale.

Paterson retells the Biblical tale of how a donkey and an angel save the Israelites from the King of Moab. (From *The Angel and the Donkey,* illustrated by Alexander Koshkin.)

Biblical and universal themes are at the heart of Paterson's books. Never preachy in tone, her stories nonetheless teach lessons—of humility, responsibility, and hope. As the author once wrote in *Horn Book,* "I have learned, for all my failings and limitations, that when I am willing to give myself away in a book, readers will respond by giving themselves away as well, and the book I labored over so long becomes in our mutual giving something far richer and more powerful than I could have ever imagined." Paterson elaborated on her artistic philosophy in an article for *The Writer,* where she explains: "I keep learning that if I am willing to go deep into my own heart, I am able miraculously to touch

other people at the core. But that is because I do have a reader I must try to satisfy—that is the reader I am and the reader I was as a child. I know this reader in a way that I can never know a generic target out there somewhere. This reader demands honesty and emotional depth. She yearns for clear, rhythmically pleasing language . . . . And above all she wants characters who will make her laugh and cry and bind her to themselves in a fierce friendship."

Come Sing, Jimmy Jo and *Park's Quest* are two of Paterson's works that have been praised for the honesty, emotional depth, and character recognition that the author seeks to impart. The former relates the story of eleven-year-old James Johnson, a small, timid child taken from his grandmother and their quiet Appalachian mountain home to join his musician family on stage and on television. The family's agent, who has recognized the child's gifted voice, changes James's name to Jimmy Jo and propels him toward stardom—while James must learn to deal with all that fame offers, including difficulties among jealous family members and with schoolmates. "Paterson captures the subtleties of childhood friendships in James's relationships with his classmates and records family interaction with a sensitive ear," noted *School Library Journal* contributor Cathryn A. Camper. A *Bulletin of the Center for Children's Books* reviewer similarly maintained that "Paterson creates strong characters and convincing dialogue, so that her story is effective even to those to whom the heavy emphasis on country music strikes no sympathetic chord." Denise M. Wilms of *Booklist* concluded that *Come Sing, Jimmy Jo* is "a rich, sensitive portrayal of growing up." *Park's Quest* is Paterson's tale of a boy's efforts to learn more about his father, who was killed in the Vietnam War. "In a multilayered novel filled with themes of reconciliation and renewal," wrote a *Kirkus Reviews* commentator, "[Paterson] draws parallels between a boy's quest for the family of his father, killed in Vietnam, and the Arthurian legends.... Park's quest is a fine journey of discovery, and the characters he meets are uniquely memorable." Many critics commented favorably on the author's skillful interweaving of Park's favorite reading matter—tales of Arthur and his knights—with the boy's own determination to solve the "mystery" of his father's life. The story is "a quest," according to Ethel L. Heins of *Horn Book*, "that will ultimately be fraught with emotional peril and stunning revelations." Heins added that *Park's Quest* "realistically presents a heroic response to a contemporary condition."

In addition to her longer juvenile and young adult novels, Paterson has written short stories for Christmas, gathered in *Angels and Other Strangers* and *A Midnight Clear*, and picture books, including the award winning *Tale of the Mandarin Ducks* along with *The Smallest Cow in the World*, *The King's Equal*, and *The Angel and the Donkey*. Two companion novels written in the 1990s are *Lyddie* and *Jip: His Story*, both set in New England in the middle to late nineteenth century. In the first of the novels, thirteen-year-old Lyddie is hired out as a servant after the failure of the family farm. She soon flees this situation for the mills of Lowell, Massachusetts, only to discover an even more grueling life in this new labor. She finds refuge in books and determines to get a college degree and pull herself out of her degrading existence. *Voice of Youth Advocates* contributor Mary L. Adams commented: "While the setting is interesting and authentic, the story and characterizations are Paterson at her best. Readers will carry the image of Lyddie with them for many years." Zena Sutherland, writing in *Bulletin of the Center for Children's Books*, noted that Paterson maintained her "usual fine job" in blending narrative with history in this book of "industrial oppression, workers' and women's rights, and prejudice."

Elizabeth S. Watson of *Horn Book* concluded that this was "a superb story of grit, determination, and personal growth." Lyddie makes another appearance in *Jip: His Story*, when as a teacher she helps young Jip, the son of a runaway slave, to escape his impoverished life and the miserable conditions of a poor farm for a new start in Canada. *School Library Journal* contributor Ellen Fader noted that readers of *Jip* would be rewarded "with memorable characters and a gripping plot," adding that "Paterson's story resonates with respect for the Vermont landscape and its mid-19th-century residents, with the drama of life during a dark period in our nation's history, and with the human quest for freedom." Mary M. Burns of *Horn Book* praised Paterson's work as "an intense, third-person novel that maintains its riveting pace from the opening chapter to the final moment when the protagonist triumphs over adversity."

A tale with a more contemporary setting, *Flip-Flop Girl* is Paterson's story of distraught nine-year-old Vinnie, grieving for the death of her father. Forced to move to her grandmother's house, Vinnie is an outsider at school, her only friend the mysterious "Flip-Flop Girl" Lupe, whose own father is in jail for having killed her mother. The positive attention of Vinnie's male teacher helps matters for a time, though his simultaneous concern for Lupe and his later engagement to be married both come as a betrayal to Vinnie. A *Publishers Weekly* commentator noted that Paterson is "a master of rendering the intensity of childhood emotions," adding that in *Flip-Flop Girl* she explores "the impact of grief and the slow process of healing." Similarly, *Junior Bookshelf* reviewer Marcus Crouch maintained that "Paterson is always particularly good at exploring relationships and probing the minds of troubled children," noting that *Flip-Flop Girl* "is a beautifully planned and developed narrative which treats the minor pains and embarrassments of childhood with due seriousness." Ellen Fader, in *Horn Book*, concluded that "all children will discover parts of themselves in Vinnie, and, like Vinnie, will know more about themselves when they get to the conclusion of this powerful story."

For all the prizes and critical acclaim she has received, Paterson remains typically understated about her achievements. As she once commented in *Theory into Practice*, her aim, "like that of most writers of fiction, is to tell a story. My gift seems to be that I am one of those fortunate people who can, if she works hard at it, uncover a story that children will enjoy."

■ Works Cited

Adams, Mary L., review of *Lyddie*, *Voice of Youth Advocates*, April, 1991, p. 34.

Babbitt, Natalie, "A Home for Nobody's Child," *Washington Post Book World*, May 14, 1978, pp. 1-2.

Burns, Mary M., review of *Jip: His Story*, *Horn Book*, November-December, 1996, pp. 739-40.

Camper, Cathryn A., review of *Come Sing, Jimmy Jo*, *School Library Journal*, April, 1985, p. 91.

Review of *Come Sing, Jimmy Jo*, *Bulletin of the Center for Children's Books*, June, 1985, pp. 191-92.

Crouch, Marcus, review of *Of Nightingales That Weep, Junior Bookshelf,* August, 1977, pp. 239-40.

Crouch, Marcus, review of *Flip-Flop Girl, Junior Bookshelf,* August, 1994, pp. 146-47.

Davidson, Ellen M., review of *The Great Gilly Hopkins, Children's Book Review Service,* April, 1978, p. 89.

Fader, Ellen, review of *Flip-Flop Girl, Horn Book,* March-April, 1994, pp. 200-201.

Fader, Ellen, review of *Jip: His Story, School Library Journal,* October, 1996, p. 124.

Fireside, Bryna J., "Two Orphans without Mothers," *New York Times Book Review,* April 30, 1978, p. 54.

Fisher, Margery, review of *Of Nightingales That Weep, Growing Point,* March, 1977, p. 3060.

Review of *Flip-Flop Girl, Publishers Weekly,* November 22, 1993, p. 64.

Forman, Jack, review of *Bridge to Terabithia, School Library Journal,* November, 1977, p. 61.

Hammond, Graham, "Feminine Insight," *Times Literary Supplement,* September 19, 1975, p. 1056.

Haviland, Virginia, review of *The Sign of the Chrysanthemum, Horn Book,* October, 1975, p. 468.

Heins, Ethel L., review of *Park's Quest, Horn Book,* July-August, 1988, pp. 496-97.

Heins, Paul, review of *Jacob Have I Loved, Horn Book,* September, 1980, pp. 622-23.

Hobbs, Mary, review of *Rebels of the Heavenly Kingdom, Junior Bookshelf,* December, 1983, pp. 254-55.

Levin, Betty, "A Funny, Sad, Sharp Look Back at Growing Up," *Christian Science Monitor,* January 21, 1981, p. 17.

Review of *Park's Quest, Kirkus Reviews,* March 1, 1988, p. 358.

Paterson, Katherine, "Newbery Medal Acceptance," *Horn Book,* August, 1981.

Paterson, Katherine, "Sounds in the Heart," *Horn Book,* December, 1981.

Paterson, Katherine, *Gates of Excellence: On Reading and Writing Books for Children,* Elsevier/Nelson, 1981.

Paterson, Katherine, "The Aim of the Writer Who Writes for Children," *Theory into Practice,* Autumn, 1982, pp. 325-31.

Paterson, Katherine, "What Writing Has Taught Me: Three Lessons," *The Writer,* August, 1990, pp. 9-10.

Review of *Rebels of the Heavenly Kingdom, Publishers Weekly,* May 6, 1983, p. 98.

Smedman, M. Sarah, "Katherine Paterson," *Dictionary of Literary Biography, Volume 52: American Writers for Children Since 1960,* Gale, 1986, pp. 296-314.

Spirt, Diana L., "Forming a View of the World: 'The Master Puppeteer'," *Introducing More Books: A Guide for the Middle Grades,* R. R. Bowker, 1977, pp. 114-17.

Sutherland, Zena, review of *The Master Puppeteer, Bulletin of the Center for Children's Books,* July-August, 1976, p. 181.

Sutherland, Zena, review of *Lyddie, Bulletin of the Center for Children's Books,* February, 1991, p. 151.

Walsh, Jill Paton, "Novels for Teens: Delicate Themes of Friendship, Fantasy," *Christian Science Monitor,* May 3, 1978, p. B2.

Watson, Elizabeth S., review of *Lyddie, Horn Book,* May-June, 1991, pp. 338-39.

Wilms, Denise M., review of *Come Sing, Jimmy Jo, Booklist,* May 1, 1985, p. 1257.

Young, Dora Jean, review of *The Master Puppeteer, School Library Journal,* March, 1976, p. 117.

■ For More Information See

BOOKS

Children's Literature Review, Volume 7, Gale, 1984.

Cullinan, Mary, with Mary K. Karrer and Arlene M. Pillar, *Literature and the Child,* Harcourt, 1981.

Peterson, Linda, and Marilyn Solt, *Newbery and Caldecott Medal and Honor Books: An Annotated Bibliography,* Twayne, 1982.

Schmidt, Gary D., *Katherine Paterson,* Twayne, 1994.

Twentieth-Century Children's Writers, 4th edition, St. James Press, 1995.

PERIODICALS

Booklist, September 1, 1990, p. 59; September 15, 1991, p. 169; December 15, 1993, p. 755; September 15, 1995, p. 171; March 1, 1996, p. 1189.

Books for Keeps, November, 1996, p. 11.

Bulletin of the Center for Children's Books, April, 1988, pp. 164-65; September, 1990, pp. 14-15; November, 1995, pp. 102-103; December, 1996, p. 147.

Children's Literature in Education, autumn, 1983.

Horn Book, July-August, 1985, p. 456; November-December, 1990, pp. 753-54; November-December, 1995, pp. 729-30.

Junior Bookshelf, October, 1996, p. 205.

Kirkus Reviews, May 15, 1985, p. J53; July 15, 1991, p. 933; December 15, 1993, p. 1596; October 1, 1995, p. 1435; January 1, 1996, p. 72.

New Advocate, fall, 1997, pp. 5-14.

Publishers Weekly, July 27, 1990, p. 233; July 12, 1991, p. 65; February 12, 1996, p. 71.

School Library Journal, May, 1988, p. 111; October, 1990, p. 111; January, 1992, p. 96; May, 1994, p. 117; March, 1996, p. 213.

—*Sketch by J. Sydney Jones*

*   *   *

PECK, Marshall III 1951-

■ Personal

Born April 11, 1951, in Paris, France; son of Marshall II (a news publisher) and Hugguette (a teacher and writer; maiden name, Vitu) Peck; married Beth Dunbar (a registered nurse), 1980; children: Mira, Aimee, Benjamin. *Education:* St. Luke's School, New Cannaan, CT; California College of Arts and Crafts, Oakland, CA, B.F.A.

■ Addresses

Home—10 Larch Lane, Londonderry, NH, 03053.
Agent—Publishers' Graphics, 251 Greenwood Ave., Bethel, CT. *Electronic mail*—Peck@aol.com.

■ Career

Illustrator. Principal activities include children's book illustration, t-shirt design, wildlife paintings, advertising, and visiting and speaking at schools.

■ Illustrator

FOR CHILDREN

George Shea, *Amazing Rescues,* Random House, 1992.
Alexandra Wright, *At Home in the Tide Pool,* Charlesbridge (Watertown, MA), 1992.
Heavy-Duty Trucks, Random House, 1992.
Dick King-Smith, *Pretty Polly,* Crown Publishers, 1992.
Alexandra Wright, *Will We Miss Them? Endangered Species,* Charlesbridge, 1992.
Caroline Arnold, *Sea Turtles,* Scholastic, 1994.
Norma Cole, *Blast-Off: A Space Counting Book,* Charlesbridge, 1994.
Alexandra Wright, *Can We Be Friends? Nature's Partners,* Charlesbridge, 1994.
Mallory, Kenneth, *Families of the Deep Blue Sea,* Charlesbridge, 1995.

OTHER

Peck has also illustrated a privately printed family memoir entitled *France, 1939,* written by his mother, Hugguette Vitu Peck.

■ Work in Progress

Historic Maps for Connecticut Towns, a book for children featuring text and full page paintings by Peck.

■ Sidelights

Illustrator Marshall Peck III recalled for *SATA:* "The man in jeans adjusted the lights and moved the camera a bit closer. He poured more cornflakes into our bowls. The 'old flakes' had wilted. A thick white liquid replaced the usual milk. My sister and I snickered. The lights were hot.

"'Chin up!' coaxed the main in jeans. 'Imagine you love those flakes so much you even drink up every last bit. Hold the bowl like this.' He shows us. 'But don't drink!'

"The man in jeans adjusts our clothes and assumes a pose of great joy as a flurry of flashes and clicks and windings sprinkle around us. 'Okay! Perfect! Thank you Ann and Marshall.'

"That was in the early 60's. My sister and I would find ourselves on some cereal box in an idyllic scene illustrated by the man in jeans. He was an illustrator, although I had little understanding of what that was at

MARSHALL PECK, III

the time. I *did* instantly love what he was doing, however, and whatever it was, I was going to do it.

"The studio of the man in jeans was a wonderful world of paintings in various stages of finish, portraits, all manner of interesting objects, miles of photo negatives drying everywhere, and best of all, a world totally controlled and created by the man in jeans. What a glorious way to live, I thought.

"Today, of course, that world of the illustrator has the added dimension of dealing with deadlines, bills, getting paid, promoting oneself, and the nameless, numerous tasks that any career depends on. I always think of that wondrous early experience.

"My work has mainly focused on children's books as well as special projects along the way. Many children's books from Europe such as Herge's *Tintin* and Franquin's *Spirov and Fantasio* are responsible for inducing the desire to form pictures myself and tell stories. I still have all my early books and am thrilled to see my children enjoying them too! My most energizing experience these days is spending a day talking to children in schools about the language of art and how one should learn to speak and write in shapes as well as words.

"A recent book about my mother's experience during World War II as a young schoolgirl, written by my mother and illustrated by me, is a wonderful project which brings together history, storytelling, drawing, and the overarching feeling of family bonds over more than a half century."

■ For More Information See

PERIODICALS

Booklist, March 1, 1993, p. 1240.

Bulletin of the Center for Children's Books, November, 1992, p. 88.
School Library Journal, April, 1993, p. 114; March, 1995, p. 200.

* * *

PENN, Ruth Bonn
See CLIFFORD, Eth

* * *

PIKE, R. William 1956-

■ Personal

Born March 7, 1956, in Bay Shore, New York; son of Robert and Alice Pike; married Ann (a teacher), August, 1984; children: Christopher. *Education:* Attended University of Bath in England, 1976; Skidmore College, teaching certificate, 1977; Union College, B.A. (with honors), 1978; State University of New York at Stony Brook, M.A. (with honors), 1981.

■ Addresses

Home—32 Trout Brook Lane, Riverhead, NY 11901.

■ Career

Author, playwright, journalist, and educator. Ticonderoga Central School District, Ticonderoga, NY, secondary English teacher, 1978-80; Sachem Central School District, Ronkonkoma, NY, secondary English teacher, 1980-81; Holt, Rinehart and Winston, School Division, New York City, freelance writer, 1981-82; William Floyd Central School District, Mastic Beach, NY, secondary English teacher, 1981—; *Family Life Journal,* book reviewer, 1992—.

■ Writings

Act for Health: Using Theater to Teach Tough Teen Topics, ETR Associates, 1991.
Stop, Look, Listen Up! And Other Dramas for Confronting Social Issues in Elementary School, music by Flora E. Metrick, Resource Publications, 1993.
Facing Violence: Discussion-Starting Skits for Teenagers, Resource Publications, 1995.
Facing Substance Abuse: Discussion-Starting Skits for Teenagers, Resource Publications, 1996.

Also author of educational pamphlets for young adults, including *Abstinence and Self-Esteem* and *Abstinence and Relationships,* ETR Associates, 1996.

■ Work in Progress

A Song for Okeanos, a story book about a modern-day seal myth.

R. WILLIAM PIKE

■ Sidelights

R. William Pike told *SATA:* "I have been writing about tough social issues for children and adolescents since the mid-eighties; that's when we all realized that teenagers were soon to be the number one target population for HIV and the AIDS virus. Back then, words like 'condoms' and 'safe sex' were taboo. Today, along with 'abstinence,' they are considered the mainstay of one aspect of a young adult's education.

"Over the years, I have written about sexual abuse, physical abuse, date rape, alcoholism, drug addiction, homosexuality ... the list goes on. I have found that the underlying theme of all my writing (from abstinence to gay marriages) is tolerance. My writing has attempted to encourage acceptance of all people and to celebrate diversity.

"In recent years, I have turned to younger children as my audience. Through storybooks, rhyme, and whimsy, I have tried to introduce children to these same ideas.

"In a world that is growing more challenging to children and young people every day, I hope, through my writing, to reveal the rich diversity of our society and to empower children through the strength of their imaginations."

■ For More Information See

PERIODICALS

Children's Bookwatch, November, 1993, p. 8.
Science Books and Films, June, 1992, p. 142.
Voice of Youth Advocates, December, 1992, p. 316.

R

Kristen D. Randle with her family.

RANDLE, Kristen D(owney) 1952-

■ Personal

Born May 8, 1952, in Kansas City, MO; daughter of Jack Delmont (an engineer) and Jackie (maiden name, Sneed) Downey; married Guy Lawrence Randle (a music producer), April 17, 1978; children: Virginia, Cammon, Charlotte, Jackson. *Education:* Brigham Young University, B.A., 1973, additional study, 1975-76. *Politics:* "Moderately Conservative." *Religion:* Latter Day Saint ("Mormon").

■ Career

Teacher at Brigham Young University and at high schools in Utah; secretary and treasurer of Rosewood Recording Company; partner in Moonstone Media (music production company); has recorded several albums of children's songs. Has also worked as a studio manager, bookkeeper, singer, genealogist, dental assistant, and photographer.

■ Awards, Honors

Best Books, American Library Association (ALA), 1995, New York City Public Libraries, 1996, Dorothy Canfield Fischer (Vermont), 1996, Utah Association of Literature, 1996, and Book of the Year for Young Adults, Michigan Library Association, 1996, all for *The Only Alien on the Planet*.

■ Writings

Home Again (novel), Embryo, 1981.
One Song for Two (novel), Bookcraft, 1984.
The Morning Comes Singing (novel), Bookcraft, 1986.
Why Did Grandma Have to Die?, illustrated by Shauna Mooney, Bookcraft, 1988.
On the Side of the Angels, Bookcraft, 1989.
The Only Alien on the Planet, Scholastic, 1995.

■ Work in Progress

Young adult, science fiction, and fantasy books.

■ Sidelights

Kristen D. Randle told *SATA* that she isn't a "career writer." She just writes when she feels a story coming to her that needs to be told. "I don't believe that 'writers' make books," she explained. "I believe that some people, in the course of living their lives, find that there is a story in them that insists on being told; if these people keep their mouths closed, teeth clenched, over the story, it will come leaking out of their fingers. Thus stories make writers."

Randle's novel, *The Only Alien on the Planet*, has won praise from critics. It begins as the story of Ginny Christianson, whose happy life is disrupted by her family's move to the east coast and her brother's departure for college. Gradually, Ginny begins to make friends, but she is troubled by the behavior of Smitty Tibbs, a handsome, smart, silent boy the other kids call "the Alien." Ginny and her neighbor, Caulder Pretiger, attempt to get to know the Alien, but his desire for isolation makes their work difficult. After causing Smitty a great deal of pain with their attempts to help him, Ginny and Caulder learn that he has been abused by an older brother. Smitty emerges from a breakdown and seeks professional help, and Ginny and Smitty begin a romance.

According to Anne O'Malley of *Booklist*, the "overall impact of this psychological novel is ... powerful." A *Kirkus Reviews* critic asserted that readers of *The Only Alien on the Planet* "will be left with a better appreciation for the richness of their own social and emotional landscapes." *School Library Journal* contributor Susan L. Rogers wrote that Randle's book "becomes utterly

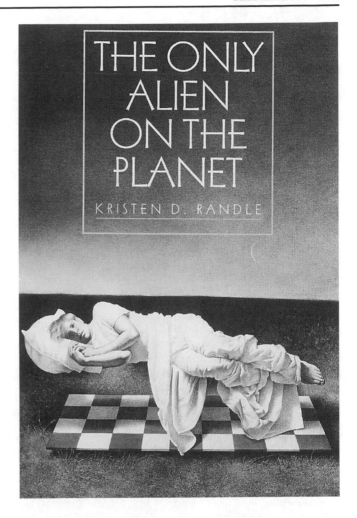

When high school senior Ginny befriends the painfully introverted boy everyone calls "The Alien," she learns about the distressing consequences of abuse. (Cover illustration by John Jude Palencar.)

compelling" when Smitty breaks his silence, and concludes that the novel is "a fast-moving, unusual contemporary romance that should have great appeal." *Voice of Youth Advocates* critic Judy Sasges recommends the novel to "budding psychologists and optimistic romantics."

Randle told *SATA* that, as much as some stories beg to be told, she believes artists should not tell all stories. "The arts we share should strengthen, enlarge heart and mind, give hope, have at *least* a suggestion of meaning.... Art should comfort us, bring us hope, ennoble us, shore up our courage, put higher prices on us, allow us to see ourselves as people with choices, even in the midst of seemingly impossible circumstances. Selling a book means nothing. Offering a gift of self means everything.... You search for light—you head for it and you take as many as you can along. You give your best."

■ Works Cited

O'Malley, Anne, review of *The Only Alien on the Planet*, *Booklist*, January 15, 1995, p. 913.

Review of *The Only Alien on the Planet, Kirkus Reviews,* March 15, 1995, p. 392.

Rogers, Susan L., review of *The Only Alien on the Planet, School Library Journal,* March, 1995, p. 225.

Sasges, Judy, review of *The Only Alien on the Planet, Voice of Youth Advocates,* April, 1995, p. 26.

■ **For More Information See**

PERIODICALS

Kliatt, January, 1997, p. 10.
Publishers Weekly, January 23, 1995, p. 71.

*   *   *

RICE, Earle, Jr. 1928-

■ **Personal**

Born October 21, 1928, in Lynn, MA; son of Earle, Sr. (a musician and employee of General Electric) and Grace (a homemaker; maiden name, Nottingham) Rice; married Georgia Joy Blackwood (a weaver and homemaker), November 1, 1958; children: Ellen Jean Rice, Earle Rice III. *Education:* Attended San Jose City College, 1958-60, and Foothill College, 1970-71. *Politics:* Republican. *Religion:* Protestant. *Hobbies and other interests:* Reading, TV sports.

■ **Addresses**

Home and office—P.O. Box 2131, Julian, CA 92036-2131.

■ **Career**

Worked as a designer, technical writer, and senior design engineer in the aerospace, electronics, and nuclear industries, 1960-93; freelance writer, 1993—. *Military service:* U.S. Marine Corps, 1948-57, received Purple Heart.

■ **Writings**

FICTION

Tiger, Lion, Hawk, Fearon Pitman, 1977.
The Animals, Fearon Pitman, 1979.
Death Angel, Davis S. Lake, 1981.
The Gringo Dies at Dawn, Fearon/Janus/Quercus, 1993.

RETELLER; ALL PUBLISHED BY GLOBE FEARON

Dracula, 1995.
All Quiet on the Western Front, 1995.
The Grapes of Wrath, 1996.

NONFICTION

"BATTLE" SERIES; ALL PUBLISHED BY LUCENT

The Battle of Belleau Wood: Battles of World War I, 1996.
The Battle of Britain: Battles of World War II, 1996.
The Battle of Midway: Battles of World War II, 1996.

EARLE RICE, JR.

The Inchon Invasion: Battles of the Twentieth Century, 1996.
The Attack on Pearl Harbor, 1997.
The Tet Offensive, 1997.

"FAMOUS TRIALS" SERIES; ALL PUBLISHED BY LUCENT

The Nuremberg Trials, 1997.
The Salem Witch Trials, 1997.
The O. J. Simpson Trial, 1997.

"WORLD HISTORY" SERIES; PUBLISHED BY LUCENT

The Cuban Revolution, 1995.
The Battle of the Little Big Horn, 1997.

SPORTS FICTION

Fear on Ice, Davis S. Lake, 1981.
More Than Macho, Davis S. Lake, 1981.

"HOLOCAUST" SERIES; PUBLISHED BY LUCENT

The Final Solution, 1997.
Nazi War Criminals, 1997.

■ **Work in Progress**

Researching eight more books for Lucent: two titles in the "World History" series, and five titles in "The Way People Live" series; and one title in "The Importance of" series; a novel, a history of soldiers of fortune; several multimedia concepts.

■ Sidelights

Earle Rice, Jr. told *SATA:* "I guess I decided to become a writer while still a child, swinging on a swing and daydreaming the hours away. After spending the next thirty-five or forty years preparing myself—nine years in the Marine Corps, the remainder as a dishwasher, letter carrier, draftsman, designer, technical writer, electromechanical design checker, and senior design engineer—I began to write.

"I now write six to eight hours a day, seven days a week, about subjects I find fascinating and irresistible, hoping to share some of my enthusiasm for my topics with readers. If my work both entertains and informs, and I hope it does, I can ask for little more.

"Advice for new writers and illustrators? Milton Caniff, the late, incredibly talented creator of "Terry and the Pirates," "Male Call," and "Steve Canyon" comic strips once said, 'You can't ink-in with a swizzle stick,' meaning that you can't sit at some country club bar and get any work done. To learn the craft and get published, only one word comes to mind: *WRITE!* There's no other way."

■ For More Information See

PERIODICALS

Publishers Weekly, November 27, 1995, p. 63.
School Library Journal, March, 1995, p. 233; February, 1996, p. 119.

*   *   *

RINDER, Lenore 1949-

■ Personal

Born November 20, 1949, in Chicago, IL; daughter of Irwin Daniel (a professor) and Ruth (a physician; maiden name, Schnapper) Rinder. *Education:* Macalester College, B.A. (with honors), 1972; University of Wisconsin-Milwaukee, M.A, 1986.

■ Addresses

1652 South 36th St., Milwaukee, WI 53215.

■ Career

Educator, filmmaker. University of Wisconsin, Milwaukee, WI, taught film, painting, and animation, 1981-88; Warner Cable/Community Television, Milwaukee, video production and public access training, 1992—.

■ Awards, Honors

Film in the Cities grant, Jerome Foundation, 1983, for animated film *Yoni's Line;* Arts Midwest grant, Billboard "Home Street Home," 1992, for "Jobs with Peace," an artist/organization collaboration.

■ Writings

A Big Mistake, illustrated by Susan Horn, Gareth Stevens, 1994.

Also contributed photos to *Viva La Company,* 1979.

■ Work in Progress

Two children's books, *Tiger Tail* and *Fat & Thin,* and a science fiction novel.

■ Sidelights

Lenore Rinder told *SATA:* "As a child, the oldest of five, I was given the duty of entertaining my four younger siblings while my parents went out. I created a 'Kitty Club' at about seven years of age. This baby-sitting was structured and consisted of original songwriting, the creation of coloring books, and other activities. Ever since then, I have been involved in multimedia and fine arts.

"During the past four years at Warner Cable, my interests have been nurtured as I teach and produce video programs for children. This is a stimulating job, which helps my writing (I am starting to write scripts) and enables me to be in an exciting audiovisual atmosphere.

"Childhood really is where we develop our values; therefore, it is of the utmost importance that we reach this population with our teachings. Subjects that are vital to me are the conservation and appreciation of the earth and respect for all creatures and living beings. I like the low-tech of human warmth and simplicity. There is too much emphasis on making things easy at the expense of losing touch with what is important."

■ For More Information See

PERIODICALS

School Library Journal, February, 1995, p. 81.

*   *   *

ROBINSON, Glen(dal P.) 1953-

■ Personal

Born November 11, 1953, in San Jose, CA; son of Glen A. Robinson (a mechanic) and Mildred M. Haynes Pipkins (a nurse); married Michaela L. (Shelly) Scheffer (a registered nurse), August 24, 1975; children: Matthew, Melissa. *Education:* Pacific Union College, B.A., 1975; California State University, Chico, M.A., 1988. *Politics:* "Non-partisan (registered Democrat)." *Religion:* Seventh-day Adventist. *Hobbies and other interests:* Canoeing, sailing, genealogy, writing and performing music.

■ Addresses

Home—2706 Polk St., Caldwell, ID 83605. *Office*—Pacific Press, 1350 North Kings Road, Nampa, ID 83687. *Electronic mail*—74617,3163 @ compuserve.com (Compuserve); and gleRob @ Pacific-Press.com (internet).

■ Career

Worked as a newspaper editor, 1975-80, and in hospital public relations, 1980-88; Pacific Press, Nampa, ID, editor, 1988—.

■ Writings

52 Things to Do on Sabbath, Review & Herald, 1983.
(Editor) Paul A. Gordon, *Herald of the Midnight Cry,* Pacific Press, 1990.
The Mysterious Treasure Map, Pacific Press, 1994.
The Broken Dozen Mystery, Pacific Press, 1995.
The Case of the Secret Code, illustrated by Mark Ford, Pacific Press, 1995.
The Clue in the Secret Passage, Pacific Press, 1997.

■ Sidelights

Glen Robinson told *SATA:* "I decided in high school that I wanted a career as a writer. My teachers discouraged me from doing so; because 'I had not read the classics,' they said I would never be successful. Over the years I read everything I could about writing; when the advice I read started repeating itself I stopped. I learned the only true way to measure a writer was whether he or she got words on paper—many people can talk writing, but few are willing to do the work of writing.

"I want to convey a strong sense of adventure in my writing. I hope to encourage readers to discover the innate adventure in life—especially in the Christian life.

"I would classify myself as a 'binge' writer—obsessive-compulsive. I've never been very good at writing a little bit every day. I'm much better at taking a week of vacation or a long weekend to write. I plan my plots carefully at the beginning, with the outline becoming more general as the book goes on. I leave room for the story to write itself. Then I write very fast. It can take me as little as two full days to write a children's mystery. It really depends how much research is involved.

"My favorite authors are J. R. R. Tolkien, C. S. Lewis, Steven Lawhead, Frank Peretti, and Jerry Pournelle. I am continually looking for authors whose style will captivate and inspire me. Once I find one, I read everything he/she has written. The best advice I can give a would-be writer is this: (1) Get it on paper; (2) be willing to pay the price; and (3) never, *never* give up on yourself."

ROSENBERG, Ethel (Clifford)
See CLIFFORD, Eth

* * *

ROSS, Stewart 1947-

■ Personal

Born April 4, 1947, in Aylesbury, England; son of Graham and Marjorie (a physiotherapist) Ross; married wife, Lucy (a manager), August 8, 1978; children: James, Kate, Alex, Eleanor. *Education:* Exeter University, B.A., 1969, M.A., 1972; Bristol University, certificate in education, 1970; Rollins College, M.A.T., 1979. *Politics:* Liberal. *Religion:* "Vaguely Christian." *Hobbies and other interests:* Drama, opera, sport.

■ Addresses

Home—3 Westfield, Blean, Canterbury, Kent CT2 9ER England.

■ Career

Trinity College, Sri Lanka, teacher, 1965-66; Exeter University, England, assistant tutor, 1970-72; University of Riyadh, Saudi Arabia, lecturer, 1972-74; King's School, Canterbury, England, master/housemaster, 1974-78; Rollins College, Florida, lecturer, 1979-89; full-time writer, 1989—. I.C.E.S. La Roche-sur-Yon, France, lecturer, 1995-97; frequent lecturer and broadcaster. *Member:* Canterbury Arts Council (vice-chairman), Society of Authors.

■ Awards, Honors

Best Books, American Library Association, 1995, for *Shakespeare and Macbeth;* Pick of the List, American Booksellers Association, 1996, for *Witches.*

■ Writings

NONFICTION; FOR CHILDREN

Columbus and the Age of Exploration, illustrated by Ken Stott, Bookwright, 1985.
Chaucer and the Middle Ages, illustrated by John James, Wayland, 1985.
A Medieval Serf, illustrated by Alan Langford, Wayland, 1985.
Pepys and the Stuarts, illustrated by Gerry Wood, Wayland, 1985.
A Saxon Farmer, illustrated by Mark Bergin, Wayland, 1985.
A Victorian Factory Worker, illustrated by Alan Langford, Wayland, 1985.
Dickens and the Victorians, illustrated by Gerry Wood, Wayland, 1986.
Spotlight on Medieval Europe, Wayland, 1986.
The Ancient Britons, illustrated by Mark Bergin, Wayland, 1987.

STEWART ROSS

Lloyd George and the First World War, illustrated by Martin Salisbury, Wayland, 1987.
Spotlight on the Stuarts, Wayland, 1987.
Spotlight on the Victorians, Wayland, 1987.
Winston Churchill and the Second World War, illustrated by Richard Scollins, Wayland, 1987.
The Ancient World, Watts, 1990.
Britain between the Wars, Wayland, 1990.
The Home Front, Wayland, 1990.
Elizabethan Life, Batsford, 1991.
The Nineteen Eighties, Trafalgar Square, 1991.
Europe, Franklin Watts, 1992.
Racism in the Third Reich, Batsford, 1992.
Battle of Little Bighorn, D. Bennett, 1993.
Britain at War 1914-1918, Batsford, 1993.
Gunfight at O.K. Corral, D. Bennett, 1993.
Propaganda, Thomson Learning, 1993.
Wild Bill Hickok and Calamity Jane, D. Bennett, 1993.
World Leaders, Thomson Learning, 1993.
Wounded Knee, D. Bennett, 1993.
Cavaliers and Roundheads, Batsford, 1994.
Shakespeare and Macbeth: The Story behind the Play, illustrated by Tony Karpinski and Victor Ambrus, Viking, 1994.
Britain since 1930, Evans, 1995.
Ancient Greece: Greek Theatre, Wayland, 1996.
Ancient Greece: The Original Olympics, Thomson Learning, 1996.
And Then—: A History of the World in 128 Pages, illustrated by John Lobban, Copper Beech, 1996.

Beware the King! The Story of Anne Boleyn and King Henry VIII, Evans, 1996.
Down with the Romans: The Tragic Tale of Queen Boudicca, Evans, 1996.

"HOW THEY LIVED" SERIES; FOR CHILDREN

A Family in World War II, illustrated by Alan Langford, Wayland, 1985.
An Edwardian Household, illustrated by John James, Wayland, 1986.
A Crusading Knight, illustrated by Mark Bergin, Rourke Enterprises, 1986.
A Roman Centurion, illustrated by Alan Langford, Wayland, 1985, Rourke Enterprises, 1987.
A Soldier in World War I, illustrated by John Haysom, Wayland, 1987.

"POLITICS TODAY" SERIES; FOR CHILDREN

The Alliance Parties, Wayland, 1986.
The Conservative Party, Wayland, 1986.
The House of Commons, Wayland, 1986.
The House of Lords, Wayland, 1986.
The Labour Party, Wayland, 1986.
The Prime Minister, Wayland, 1986.
The Cabinet and Government, Wayland, 1987.
Elections, Wayland, 1987.
The European Parliament and the European Community, Wayland, 1987.
Local Government, Wayland, 1987.
The Monarchy, Wayland, 1987.
Trade Unions and Pressure Groups, Wayland, 1987.

"WITNESS HISTORY" SERIES; FOR CHILDREN

Toward European Unity, Wayland, 1989.
China since 1945, Wayland, 1988, Bookwright, 1989.
The Origins of World War I, Bookwright, 1989.
The Russian Revolution, Bookwright, 1989.
The United Nations, Wayland, 1989, Bookwright, 1990.
The USSR under Stalin, Bookwright, 1991.
War in the Trenches, Wayland, 1990, Bookwright, 1990.

"STARTING HISTORY" SERIES; FOR CHILDREN

Food We Ate, Wayland, 1991.
How We Travelled, Wayland, 1991.
What We Wore, Wayland, 1991.
Where We Lived, Wayland, 1991.
Our Environment, Wayland, 1992.
Our Family, Wayland, 1992.
Our Health, Wayland, 1992.
Our Holidays, Wayland, 1992.
Our Schools, Wayland, 1992.
Shopping, Wayland, 1992.

"FACT OR FICTION" SERIES; FOR CHILDREN

Spies and Traitors, Copper Beech, 1995.
Pirates: The Story of Buccaneers, Brigands, Corsairs, and Their Piracy on the High Seas from the Spanish Main to the China Sea, Copper Beech, 1995.
Cowboys: A Journey down the Long, Lonely Cattle Trail in Search of the Hard-Riding, Gun-Slinging Cowhands of the Old West, Copper Beech, 1995.
Bandits and Outlaws: The Truth about Outlaws, Highwaymen, Smugglers, and Robbers from the Bandit

Gangs of Ancient China to the Desperados of Today,
Copper Beech, 1995.
Conquerors and Explorers, Copper Beech, 1996.
Secret Societies, Copper Beech, 1996.
Knights, Copper Beech, 1996.
Witches, Copper Beech, 1996.

*"CAUSES AND CONSEQUENCES" SERIES; FOR
CHILDREN*

Causes and Consequences of the Arab-Israeli Conflict,
Raintree Steck-Vaughn, 1996.
*Causes and Consequences of the Rise of Japan and the
Pacific Rim,* Raintree Steck-Vaughn, 1996.
Causes and Consequences of World War II, Raintree
Steck-Vaughn, 1996.

NONFICTION; FOR ADULTS

Monarchs of Scotland, Facts on File, 1990.
Scottish Castles, illustrated by David Simon, Lochar,
1990.
Ancient Scotland, Lochar, 1991.
*History in Hiding: The Story of Britain's Secret Passages
and Hiding Places,* R. Hale, 1991.
The Stewart Dynasty, Nairn, Thomas and Lochar, 1993.

FICTION; FOR ADULTS

One Crowded Hour, Warner (London), 1994.
Beneath Another Sun, Warner, 1994.

OTHER

(Editor) *The First World War,* Wayland, 1989.
(Editor) *The Second World War,* Wayland, 1989.
The Last Clarinet (a libretto), with music by Paul
Englishby, Oxford University Press, 1995.

Also author of numerous articles and a play that was
performed in 1992.

■ Work in Progress

*Charlotte Bronte and Jane Eyre; Mark Twain and
Huckleberry Finn; Monsters of the Deep; Beasts; Long
Live Mary, Queen of Scots!; Find King Arthur!.*

■ Sidelights

In eight years as a full-time writer, Stewart Ross has
published eighty books of nonfiction for young readers,
as well as two novels and several other books for adults.
In an essay for *Something about the Author Autobiography Series (SAAS)*, Ross traced his productive career as
an author directly back to his childhood love of reading.
"I read voraciously. The more I read, the more I wanted
to read," he recalled. "This love of books and the words
within them made me determined to be a writer." One
particular book influenced him toward writing nonfiction in order to provide young readers with interesting
glimpses into the past. "My passion for history grew
from the seeds planted by an attractive book of stories
from the past, brightly colored pictures on one side and
the text on the other, most of it myth. That didn't
matter at the time: inspiration first, analysis later," he
commented in *SAAS*.

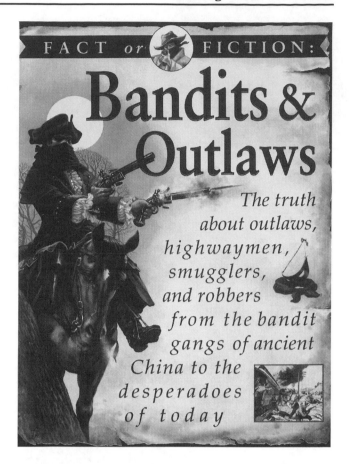

Ross debunks the myths surrounding Robin Hood, Rob
Roy, Jesse James, and others in this factual account of
their lives and adventures. (Illustrated by McRae
Books, Italy.)

Born in Aylesbury, England, in 1947, Ross grew up in
the English countryside. When he was not reading, he
spent many hours creating daring, imaginative adventures with his brother in the woods and fields near their
home. These experiences, too, fueled his desire to
become a writer. "My early childhood furnished me
with the two things essential to all writers: a love for
words and a turbulent imagination. Neither is a gift
from on high. We are probably all born with an equal
capacity to imagine, but we are not given an equal
chance to set it free. My upbringing released my
imagination, trained it, and encouraged it to develop,"
he explained in his autobiography. "Nothing feeds the
young imagination like a potent cocktail of books, time,
and space."

From the age of eight, Ross attended private boarding
schools in England. Though he appreciated the high
academic standards set forth at the schools and the self-
reliance he gained there, he resented being forced to
wear a uniform and being subjected to corporal punish-
ment. Only in his last two years was he allowed to
concentrate in the subjects he loved: literature and
history. Through the work of two enthusiastic teachers,
he developed a special fondness for the books of
William Shakespeare and Charles Dickens. "My mother
says that at the age of seventeen I sat on an Italian beach

more engrossed in [Dickens's novel] *Nicholas Nickleby* than the surrounding bikinis," Ross wrote in *SAAS.* "It's a good story, but I don't believe her."

After graduating in 1965, Ross traveled to Sri Lanka as part of the British Voluntary Service Overseas, an organization similar to the American Peace Corps. He spent the next year teaching English "exuberantly and no doubt rather badly," as he admitted in his autobiography, before returning to England by way of India, Ethiopia, Egypt, and Greece. Ross attended college for the next six years, earning bachelor's and master's degrees in history from Exeter University and a teaching certificate from Bristol University. Over the next dozen years, he took teaching positions in Saudi Arabia, England, and Florida. "I discovered early on that you never really know your subject until you have to teach it. To give a course of study you not only have to know the facts, but you have to be able to present them in a memorable and digestible form," Ross noted in *SAAS.* "The hours and hours of reading and research stood me in good stead as a teacher and, later, as a writer. Many of my early books were little more than extensions of my teaching notes."

Ross's writing career got its start in 1984, when he was given the opportunity to write a book for young readers about Christopher Columbus. When the book, *Columbus and the Age of Exploration*, was published the following year, it led to contracts for several more books

This book from Ross's "Fact or Fiction" series relates true-life narratives of warriors from the ancient world, through the age of chivalry, and into the present. (Illustrated by McRae Books, Italy.)

that explained historical events to students. Before long, Ross, who by this time was married with four children, felt overwhelmed by the demands of teaching, writing, and family. He quit teaching in 1989 in order to become a full-time writer and spend more time with his family, though he continued to work occasionally as a lecturer and broadcaster.

Since then, Ross has produced as many as a dozen books per year about famous people, world events, and historical time periods. In his "superb" *Shakespeare and Macbeth: The Story behind the Play,* for instance, Ross did "a terrific job of making the vitality of Shakespeare accessible" to young readers, according to a writer for *Kirkus Reviews.* The 1994 book describes what London was like during Shakespeare's time, takes readers behind the scenes at the famous Globe Theatre, and explains the pressures the Bard faced while writing his play. Ross contends that Shakespeare wrote and rewrote *Macbeth* in order to please the recently crowned King James—all the while keeping the script secret even from the actors to prevent competing theaters from stealing his ideas. A reviewer for *Publishers Weekly* called the book "intelligent and informative," adding that it "excels at introducing theater as a living art form." Sally Margolis, in a review for *School Library Journal,* stated that "the perpetual grouse by Shakespeare buffs that a book can't give young people the true sense of a stage production is at least partly countered by this dynamic gem."

Ross composes his books in a small, insulated hut in the garden of his family's home. Calling himself "the most fortunate of men" in his *SAAS* essay, he explained that he could hardly wait to make his ten-yard commute each morning and begin writing. "I have no magic formula for those who wish to write. But if you don't love words, stop now and set your sights on something more conventional. Writing is primarily about playing with words, not ideas: expression first, content second," Ross wrote in his autobiography. "If you have a passion for words and wish to write, read, read, and read again. Read critically, omnivorously, all day, every day. Old books, new books—any books: poetry, manuals, novels, essays, newspapers. And as you read, write. Write as much as you can. Get others to read what you have written and listen to what they say. In this way, gradually, you will develop a style of your own, a unique voice."

■ Works Cited

Margolis, Sally, review of *Shakespeare and Macbeth, School Library Journal,* January, 1995, p. 142.

Review of *Shakespeare and Macbeth, Kirkus Reviews,* November 15, 1994, p. 1542.

Review of *Shakespeare and Macbeth, Publishers Weekly,* October 31, 1994, p. 63.

Ross, Stewart, "Wordsong," *Something about the Author Autobiography Series,* Vol. 23, Gale, 1996.

■ For More Information See

PERIODICALS

Booklist, June 1, 1989, p. 1726; March 15, 1995, p. 1324; July 1, 1995, p. 1877; December 15, 1995, p. 694.

School Library Journal, August, 1989, p. 158; July, 1990, p. 93; May, 1995, p. 115; January, 1996, p. 136; February, 1996, p. 120; March, 1996, p. 214; June, 1996, pp. 141, 147.

Voice of Youth Advocates, October, 1990, p. 250.

* * *

RUBINETTI, Donald 1947-

■ Personal

Born January 10, 1947, in Jersey City, NJ; son of Mark Anthony (a business executive) and Anna (a medical secretary; maiden name, DeTore) Rubinetti; married wife Jacqueline (a homemaker/bank manager), June, 1987; children: Amanda, Amy. *Education:* Trenton State College, B.A., 1971; Montclair State University, M.A., 1981; attended Montclair State College and William Paterson College. *Hobbies and other interests:* Reading, golf, fishing, cooking, and baking.

■ Addresses

Office—Franklin Lakes Public Schools, Pulis Avenue, Franklin Lakes, NJ 07417.

■ Career

South Junior High School, Bloomfield, NJ, teacher, 1974; North Junior High School, Bloomfield, NJ, teacher, 1976, 1977-79, 1980-83; North Arlington High School, North Arlington, NJ, teacher, 1979-80; Bloomfield High School, Bloomfield, NJ, teacher, 1980-83; Whippany Park High School, Whippany, NJ, teacher, 1983-86; New Jersey Commission for the Blind and Visually Impaired, Newark, NJ, teacher, summers, 1985—; Franklin Avenue Middle School, Franklin Lakes, NJ, teacher, 1986—; Montclair State College, Upper Montclair, NJ, adjunct instructor, 1986—. Has worked in corporate sales, office supervision, and automobile repairs. Conducts summer storytime for young children at the local public library. *Member:* International Reading Association (IRA), Children's Literature and Reading Special Interest Group of the IRA, Society of Children's Book Writers and Illustrators, National Council of Teachers of English, National Education Association, New Jersey Education Association, North Jersey Reading Council.

■ Writings

Cappy the Lonely Camel, illustrated by Liisa Chauncy Guida, Silver Burdett, 1996.

DONALD RUBINETTI

■ Work in Progress

Several children's and young adult manuscripts.

■ Sidelights

Donald Rubinetti told *SATA:* "I have been teaching for over twenty years, and my experience has been diverse. I have taught both English and reading in grades seven through twelve, and I have been an adjunct instructor in the Reading and Educational Media Department at Montclair State University for ten years. Additionally, I have spent the past eleven summers in the employ of the New Jersey Commission for the Blind and Visually Impaired, teaching research and writing skills to blind and visually impaired college aspirants from all over the state. This program is held on the Drew University campus in Madison, New Jersey. Further, I have conducted teacher workshops in writing instruction and Registered Holistic Scoring Method, and in techniques for development of flexible reading rates.

"In my community, I am active in school affairs, working with the Board of Education in an effort to provide the highest possible quality of education in our public school system. Additionally, I conduct a summer storytime program at the local public library.

"Of course, considering my background, my interest in literature is not new. Even as a young child, I loved reading. As a teacher of adolescents and adults, I have long been reading and enjoying young adult literature. My interest in children's literature was launched when I began reading to my own children. I have found a great deal of quality literature for young children, and we enjoy many of these stories in our family.

"The first manuscript which I submitted to a publisher was a work of young adult fiction about a fourteen-year-old boy who moves after graduating from eighth grade. Although it is fiction, I drew upon my own experience with moving in order to capture and relate the boy's emotions as he adjusts to his new environment. I have received some serious encouragement with *Say Good-bye; Say Hello,* but as of this writing, I have not yet placed it, although I have recently sent out copies of a new rewrite. I am a firm believer in the idea that a manuscript is never in its final draft until it is bound. If a writer refuses to rewrite, he or she is closed to the possibility of improving a manuscript and to personal growth as a writer.

"In writing *Cappy the Lonely Camel,* it was my intention to write a children's book that would teach, without preaching, about the foolishness and hurtfulness inher-ent in lack of tolerance. *Cappy* is a story of prejudice (something to combat), heroism (something to admire), and forgiveness (something to practice). It is my belief that if we are to succeed in eradicating many of the ills of society, we must start by teaching the children. It is my great hope that *Cappy* will make a contribution in this area.

"As a writer, I am working on other ideas for children's books and young adult books. As a teacher, I continue to encourage students to enjoy reading and writing. As a parent, I will always share good literature with my children."

■ For More Information See

PERIODICALS

Kirkus Reviews, June 1, 1996, p. 829.
Parade Magazine, June 16, 1996, p. 11.
Publishers Weekly, June 10, 1996, p. 100.

S

SALEM, Kay 1952-

■ Personal

Born March 5, 1952, in McKinney, TX; daughter of Cecil Ray (an evangelist and undertaker) and Juanita (an office clerk; maiden name, Hunter) McGarrah; married Lonnie Earl Henderson, March 7, 1969 (divorced, 1971); married Nicholas Peter Salem III (a firefighter); children: (first marriage) Lonna Berlyn Henderson. *Education:* Attended Art Institute of Houston and Glassel Museum School; studied watercolor painting with Janet Hassinger. *Politics:* Conservative. *Religion:* "Spirit-filled Christian."

■ Addresses

Home—13418 Splintered Oak, Houston, TX 77065.

■ Career

Muralist for Lifemark Hospital Group, 1980-84; freelance illustrator, 1984—. Member of board, Houston Society of Illustrators.

■ Illustrator

Jackie Hopkins, *Tumbleweed Tom on the Texas Trail,* Charlesbridge, 1994.
Pam M. Ryan, *Along the California Trail,* Charlesbridge, 1997.

Along the California Trail has been published in Spanish.

■ Sidelights

Kay Salem told *SATA:* "I've always enjoyed painting people. My first experience was coloring Barbie Bride coloring books in the '50s. I've illustrated over twenty juvenile chapter book covers, more than fifty Christian romance novel covers, and one storybook for toddlers." Salem added that she has done work for numerous publishers, including Concordia, Tyndale House, Standard, Barbour, and Victor Books.

* * *

SCHRAFF, Anne E(laine) 1939-

■ Personal

Born September 21, 1939, in Cleveland, OH; daughter of Frank C. (a post office accountant) and Helen (a teacher; maiden name, Benninger) Schraff. *Education:* Pierce Junior College, A.A., 1964; San Fernando Valley State College (now California State University, North-

ANNE E. SCHRAFF

ridge), B.A., 1966, M.A., 1967. *Politics:* Independent. *Religion:* Roman Catholic. *Hobbies and other interests:* Music, walking, travel, parish work.

■ **Addresses**

Home—P.O. Box 1345, Spring Valley, CA 91979.

■ **Career**

Academy of Our Lady of Peace, San Diego, CA, teacher, 1967-77; writer, 1977—. *Member:* California Social Studies Council, Society of Children's Book Writers and Illustrators, International Reading Association.

■ **Writings**

(With brother, Francis N. Schraff) *Jesus Our Brother,* Liguori Publications, 1968.

Black Courage: Sagas of Pioneers, Sailors, Explorers, Miners, Cowboys—Twenty-One Heros of the American West, Macrae, 1969.

North Star, Macrae, 1972.

The Day the World Went Away, Doubleday, 1973.

(With Francis N. Schraff) *The Adventures of Peter and Paul: Acts of the Apostles for the Young,* Liguori Publications, 1978.

Faith of the Presidents, Concordia, 1978.

Tecumseh: The Story of an American Indian, Dillon, 1979.

Christians Courageous, illustrated by Ned Ostendorf, Concordia, 1980.

(With Francis N. Schraff and Suzanne Hockel) *Learning about Jesus: Stories, Plays, Activities for Children,* illustrated by Jim Corbett, Liguori Publications, 1980.

You Can't Stop Me, So Don't Even Try, Perfection Form, 1980.

Caught in the Middle, Baker Book, 1981.

Who Do You Think You Are, Sam West?, Perfection Learning (Logan, IA), 1986.

Fifty Great Americans, J. Weston Walch, 1986.

The Sorceress and the Book of Spells, Berkley, 1988.

When a Hero Dies (with workbook), Perfection Learning, 1989.

Sparrow's Treasure (with workbook), Perfection Learning, 1989.

Maitland's Kid (with workbook), Perfection Learning, 1989.

A Song to Sing (with workbook), Perfection Learning, 1989.

The Great Depression and the New Deal: America's Economic Collapse and Recovery, foreword by Elliot Roosevelt, consulting editor, Barbara Silberdick Feinberg, Franklin Watts, 1990.

Summer of Shame, Perfection Learning, 1992.

The Darkest Secret, Perfection Learning, 1993.

The Shadow Man, Perfection Learning, 1993.

Women of Peace: Nobel Peace Prize Winners, Enslow Publishing, 1994.

To Slay the Dragon, Perfection Learning, 1995.

Shining Mark, Perfection Learning, 1995.

Bridge to the Moon, Perfection Learning, 1995.

Power of the Rose, Perfection Learning, 1995.

American Heroes of Exploration and Flight, Enslow Publishing, 1996.

Beyond the Cherry Tree, J. Weston Walch, 1996.

Colin Powell: Soldier & Patriot, Enslow Publishers, 1997.

Are We Moving to Mars?, John Muir Publications, 1996.

"PASSAGES READING PROGRAM" SERIES

Don't Blame the Children (with workbook), Perfection Form, 1978.

Please Don't Ask Me to Love You (with workbook), Perfection Form, 1978.

An Alien Spring (with workbook), Perfection Form, 1978.

The Vandal (with workbook), Perfection Form, 1978.

The Ghost Boy (with workbook), Perfection Form, 1978.

The Haunting of Hawthorne (with workbook), Perfection Form, 1978.

"RACEWAY DOUBLES READING PROGRAM" SERIES

That's What Friends Are For (with workbook and cassette), Perfection Form, 1981.

The Crook at Cleveland High (with workbook and cassette), Perfection Form, 1981.

The Coward (with workbook and cassette), Perfection Form, 1981.

Escape (with workbook and cassette), Perfection Form, 1981.

The Ghost of Sulphur Ridge (with workbook and cassette), Perfection Form, 1981.

Stranger at Windbreak Mountain (with workbook and cassette), Perfection Form, 1981.

Julia (with workbook and cassette), Perfection Form, 1981.

Jeremy (with workbook and cassette), Perfection Form, 1981.

You'll Never Get Out Alive (with workbook and cassette), Perfection Form, 1981.

The Journey (with workbook and cassette), Perfection Form, 1981.

Time of Terror (with workbook and cassette), Perfection Form, 1981.

Shearwaters (with workbook and cassette), Perfection Form, 1981.

"TALETWISTERS READING PROGRAM" SERIES

Fantastic Fortune, Perfection Form, 1982.

The Storm, Perfection Form, 1982.

The Most Amazing Amusement Park in the World, Perfection Form, 1982.

The Pirate House, Perfection Form, 1982.

Lost in the Wilds, Perfection Form, 1982.

The Wizard's Web, Perfection Form, 1982.

Mystery of Bat Cave, Perfection Form, 1982.

"CHOOSING YOUR WAY" SERIES

Choosing Your Way Through America's Past, illustrated by Steven Meyers, J. Weston Walch (Portland, ME), 1990.

Choosing Your Way Through Ancient History, J. Weston Walch, 1991.

Choosing Your Way Through Medieval History, J. Weston Walch, 1991.

Choosing Your Way Through World's Modern Past, J. Weston Walch, 1991.

"SILVER LEAF" SERIES

The Vampire Bat Girls Club, Perfection Learning, 1991.

El Zorrero and Son, illustrated by Helen Kunze, Perfection Learning, 1991.

In the Web of the Spider, Perfection Learning, 1991.

The Whispering Shell, Perfection Learning, 1991.

The Witch of Banneker School, Perfection Learning, 1991.

Mister Fudge and Missy Moran, Perfection Learning, 1991.

"TAKE TEN BOOKS" SERIES; EDITED BY LIZ PARKER

Nobody Lives Long in Apartment N-2, illustrated by Marjorie Taylor, Saddleback Publishing, 1992.

The Phantom Falcon, illustrated by Marjorie Taylor and Fujiko Miller, Saddleback Publishing, 1992.

Swamp Furies, edited by Liz Parker, illustrated by Marjorie Taylor, Saddleback Publishing, 1992.

"STANDING TALL" MYSTERY SERIES; EDITED BY CAROL NEWELL

As the Eagle Goes, Saddleback Publishing, 1995.

Beyond Glory, Saddleback Publishing, 1995.

Ghost Biker, Saddleback Publishing, 1995.

The Haunted Hound, Saddleback Publishing, 1995.

The Howling House, Saddleback Publishing, 1995.

Shadow on the Snow, Saddleback Publishing, 1995.

Terror on Tulip Lane, Saddleback Publishing, 1995.

The Twin, Saddleback Publishing, 1995.

The Vanished One, Saddleback Publishing, 1995.

Don't Look Now or Ever, Saddleback Publishing, 1995.

"PASSAGES TO SUSPENSE" SERIES

A Deadly Obsession (with workbook and software), Perfection Learning, 1996.

The Frozen Face (with workbook and software), Perfection Learning, 1996.

Like Father, Like Son (with workbook and software), Perfection Learning, 1996.

New Kid in Class (with workbook and software), Perfection Learning, 1996.

Rage of the Tiger (with workbook and software), Perfection Learning, 1996.

OTHER

Also author of interactive fiction for Homecomputer, 1984. Contributor of reviews to *Scholastic Teacher.*

■ Work in Progress

Biographies on Coretta Scott King and Presidents Carter and Wilson, language arts and social science workbooks, a picture book about a sombrero, and several stories for CD-ROMs.

■ Sidelights

Anne E. Schraff has written a number of fiction and nonfiction works for young adults, especially reluctant readers. Filled with mystery and suspense, many of her novels address common adolescent themes, such as divorce, friendship, death, and self-perception. Her nonfiction work covers major historical eras and events, along with the lives of both famous and obscure figures from the American west, science, religion, the military, and politics. Schraff once commented, "I've been motivated by a powerful desire to write that made it impossible to do otherwise."

Schraff's novels for reluctant readers include the "Passages Reading Program" series, the "Silver Leaf" series, and the "Taletwisters Reading Program" series. Most of the stories revolve around mysteries or science fiction involving young adult protagonists, such as the *Mystery of Bat Cave* and *Time of Terror.* Other stories focus on common situations or problems young adults face while growing up. For example, *Mister Fudge and Missy*

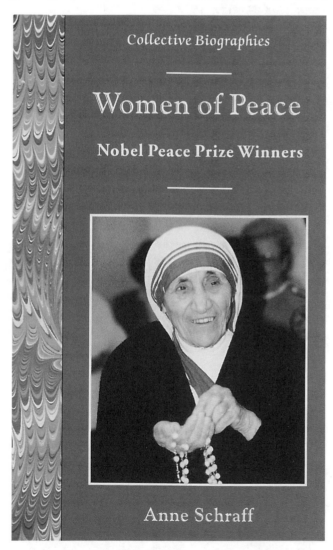

Schraff recounts the struggles of the nine women who have been awarded the Nobel Peace Prize since it was first bestowed in 1901.

Moran from the "Silver Leaf" series features eleven-year-old Missy who must decide with which divorced parent she wants to live. Schraff once explained that she began the "Passages Reading Program" series "to create exciting stories to interest reluctant teenaged readers who usually didn't read. Some letters from kids have told me my books were the first they ever read straight through. That pleased me greatly."

As a former high school teacher, Schraff has had a lot of experience in working with young adults. She once revealed to *SATA* that "the hopes and dreams of hundreds of kids have been the stuff of which my books are made. My characters are composites of people I have known, a bit from one person, a piece from another." Typical of her writing process is *The Haunting of Hawthorne.* "One morning on my way to school," Schraff informed *SATA,* "I saw a statue on a pedestal in an antique shop. The statue was of an intense young man in old-fashioned clothes. From that sight I told the story of a courageous high school principal who died rescuing his students in a long ago fire, only to return a hundred years later to save his beloved school and its modern students from the ravages of apathy and violence."

Schraff imparts the same enthusiasm for researching and writing nonfiction as she does fiction. "I love doing research and for me it's like detective work," Schraff once explained to *SATA.* "When I come across a historic person who fascinates me, I cannot rest until I've told his or her story." Individual biographies penned by Schraff include *Tecumseh: The Story of an American Indian,* George Washington in *Beyond the Cherry Tree,* and *Colin Powell: Soldier & Patriot.* Inspiration to write *Tecumseh: The Story of an American Indian* came from the author's childhood travels around the country and "the pleasure of meeting many Indians and the special courage of these early Americans," Schraff commented.

Schraff's collective biographies include *Christians Courageous, Women of Peace: Nobel Peace Prize Winners,* and *American Heroes of Exploration and Flight. Women of Peace* tells the stories of nine women from around the world who were awarded the prestigious Nobel Peace Prize for their individual contributions toward social change. Jane Addams, Mother Teresa, and Daw Aung San Suu Kyi are among the prominent women covered. Julie Corsaro, writing for *Booklist,* appreciated Schraff's "clear, accessible [writing] style" and the way she "frankly discusses the tremendous sacrifices made by these women in their pursuit." *American Heroes of Exploration and Flight* features ten men and women, such as the Wright brothers, Sally Ride, and Jacqueline Cochran, who have made significant contributions in their respective fields. "Each bio ... provides the most engaging highlights of the person's life, beginning with an exciting event to capture the readers' interest," noted Sandra L. Doggett in her review for *School Library Journal.*

In addition to biographies, Schraff has written about American and world history in her "Choosing Your Way" series. She has also written *The Great Depression and the New Deal: America's Economic Collapse and Recovery,* "a readable and objective look at a decade in which 'America would be changed forever,'" as reviewer David A. Lindsey noted in *School Library Journal.* Concerned that today's students don't know about or fully comprehend the Depression, Tom Pearson declared in the *Voice of Youth Advocates* that this work "is an interesting and well-written book which will help make the Great Depression easier for the average junior and senior high school student to understand."

Schraff has two objectives for her work, as she once explained to *SATA:* "In my books, I hope to enable my readers to share the magic and adventure of life that I enjoyed in the books I devoured as a child. I also hope to convey the powerful beliefs that life is worth living and goodness is worth achieving."

■ Works Cited

Corsaro, Julie, review of *Women of Peace: Nobel Peace Prize Winners, Booklist,* January 1, 1995, p. 813.

Doggett, Sandra L. review of *American Heroes of Exploration and Flight, School Library Journal,* May, 1996, p. 136.

Lindsey, David A., *The Great Depression and the New Deal: America's Economic Collapse and Recovery, School Library Journal,* January, 1991, p. 120.

Pearson, Tom, review of *The Great Depression and the New Deal: America's Economic Collapse and Recovery, Voice of Youth Advocates,* October, 1990, p. 251-52.

■ For More Information See

PERIODICALS

School Library Journal, September, 1994, p. 235.
Voice of Youth Advocates, June, 1996.

* * *

SCOPPETTONE, Sandra 1936-
(Jack Early)

■ Personal

Born June 1, 1936, in Morristown, NJ; daughter of Casimiro Radames and Helen Katherine (Greis) Scoppettone; companion of Linda Crawford (a writer) since 1972. *Hobbies and other interests:* Old movies, reading, gambling (in moderation), the internet, tennis.

■ Addresses

Home—P.O. Box 1814, Southold, NY 11971. *Agent*—Charlotte Sheedy, Charlotte Sheedy Literary Agency, 65 Bleecker St., New York, NY 10012.

■ Career

Writer.

SANDRA SCOPPETTONE

■ Awards, Honors

Eugene O'Neill Memorial Theatre Award, 1972, for *Stuck;* Ludwig Vogelstein Foundation grant, 1974; American Library Association best young adult book citation, 1975, and New Jersey Institute of Technology's New Jersey Authors Award, 1976, both for *Trying Hard to Hear You;* California Young Readers Medal (high school), California Reading Association, 1979, for *The Late Great Me;* Book for the Teen Age, New York Public Library, 1979, for *Happy Endings Are All Alike;* (as Jack Early) Shamus Award, Private Eye Writers of America, and Edgar Allan Poe Award nomination, Mystery Writers of America, both 1985, both for *A Creative Kind of Killer;* Edgar Allan Poe Award runner-up, 1986, for *Playing Murder.*

■ Writings

PICTURE BOOKS; ILLUSTRATED BY LOUISE FITZHUGH

Suzuki Beane, Doubleday, 1961.
Bang Bang You're Dead, Harper, 1968.

YOUNG ADULT NOVELS

Trying Hard to Hear You, Harper, 1974.
The Late Great Me, Putnam, 1976.
Happy Endings Are All Alike, Harper, 1978.
Long Time between Kisses, Harper, 1982.
Playing Murder, Harper, 1985.

NOVELS; FOR ADULTS

Some Unknown Person, Putnam, 1977.
Such Nice People, Putnam, 1980.
Innocent Bystanders, New American Library (New York City), 1983.
Everything You Have Is Mine, Little, Brown, 1991.
I'll Be Leaving You Always, Little, Brown, 1993.
My Sweet Untraceable You, Little, Brown, 1994.

Let's Face the Music and Die, Little, Brown, 1996.

NOVELS; UNDER PSEUDONYM JACK EARLY

A Creative Kind of Killer, F. Watts (New York City), 1984, republished under name Scoppettone by Carroll & Graf, 1995.
Razzamatazz, F. Watts, 1985.
Donato and Daughter, Dutton, 1988.

PLAYS

Home Again, Home Again Jiggity Jig, produced at Cubiculo Theatre, 1969.
Something for Kitty Genovese (one-act), performed by Valerie Bettis Repertory Company, 1971.
Scarecrow in a Garden of Cucumbers (screenplay), Maron-New Line, 1972.
Love of Life (teleplay), Columbia Broadcasting System (CBS-TV), 1972.
Stuck, produced at Eugene O'Neill Memorial Theatre, Waterford, CT, 1972, produced at Open Space Theatre, New York City, 1976.
A Little Bit Like Murder (teleplay), American Broadcasting Companies (ABC-TV), 1973.

OTHER

Scoppettone's manuscripts are housed in the Kerlan Collection at the University of Minnesota.

■ Adaptations

The Late Great Me was adapted as a film by Daniel Wilson Productions, 1982; *Donato and Daughter* was adapted as a television movie, CBS-TV, 1993.

■ Sidelights

Noted for her upfront treatment of controversial subjects, Sandra Scoppettone is the author of several young adult novels that deal with homosexuality, alcoholism, and rape. While some critics contend that she has chosen to focus on attention-getting topics to sell books, Scoppettone begs to differ. "The books I've written have been about important issues in my own life or in the lives of people I've known," she noted in an essay published in *Speaking for Ourselves.* From her popular novels for young adults, which include the 1976 work *The Late Great Me* and the 1985 publication *Playing Murder,* Scoppettone has gone on to write a series of adult mystery novels featuring lesbian detective Lauren Laurano, as well as several crime novels under the pseudonym Jack Early.

Born in 1936 and raised in South Orange, New Jersey, Scoppettone knew she was destined to be a writer from an early age. Encouraged by her parents to pursue her dream, she traveled to New York City at the age of eighteen. Her first published work was a picture book called *Suzuki Beane,* illustrated by the well-known children's author Louise Fitzhugh. The two collaborated on another children's book before Scoppettone began to branch out into writing for television, film, and the theater. After several frustrating years working within an environment that she considered highly biased against women writers, Scoppettone went back to writing books—"where I get satisfaction plus publication plus money," she once quipped to *SATA*.

Scoppettone's first novel was a story for young adults dealing with homosexuality. "I wrote *Trying Hard to Hear You* because during the summer of 1973 I directed a production of *Anything Goes* with about sixty teenagers," Scoppettone once told *SATA*. "The kids and an incident and the fact that I am a lesbian led me to write this book." Published the year following the events that inspired it, Scoppettone's novel is set on Long Island, where a group of teens are working on a production of *Anything Goes*. Camilla Crawford, the novel's narrator, is attracted to one of the other actors, but when they spend time together he keeps pumping her for information about a friend of hers, her next-door neighbor Jeff. As a close relationship begins to develop between her two male friends, Camilla realizes that they are gay. The other teens do as well, and their reaction is sarcastic and condemning. The novel closes with the tragic death of one of the young men in a car accident after a night of heavy drinking provoked by the intolerance of the others. "This goes farther than other books in explaining the homosexual relationship," noted Zena Sutherland of the *Bulletin of the Center for Children's Books,* "since Jeff is willing to talk about his love for Phil, about the fact that it is not merely physical, and since Camilla can discuss it with her mother, a psychiatrist." *Trying Hard to Hear You* was praised by a *Publishers Weekly* reviewer as an "unblemished" work that should serve as "a model to those authors who serve up fakery and flimsiness under the label of realism." A *Kirkus Reviews* critic similarly maintained that Scoppettone's "approach to homosexuality is honest and substantial enough to justify the discussion it will no doubt generate."

Scoppettone's *Happy Endings Are All Alike* also deals with gay issues, although this time the topic is lesbianism, which author Scoppettone understands first-hand, having come out publically as a lesbian at a relatively early age. *Happy Endings* depicts the strong emotional and sexual bond between two young women who know they must separate in September to attend colleges in different parts of the country. When one of the young women is raped and beaten by a resident of their small town, prejudice and intolerance come to a head. Because of Scoppettone's inclusion of graphic violence in the book's rape scene, the novel was banned by several school libraries. In addition, critical reception was mixed: while *School Library Journal* contributor Linda Silver charged that the novel "is irrelevant to any understanding of lesbianism or rape," Zena Sutherland of the *Bulletin of the Center for Children's Books* deemed Scoppettone's work "candid and honest."

The Late Great Me, published in 1976, confronts another social problem faced by many teens: alcohol abuse. The protagonist of Scoppettone's second YA novel—which the author admits was inspired by her own problems with alcohol—is Geri Peters, a shy seventeen-year-old who is introduced to alcohol by a

Shortly after taking on the case of a rape victim, lesbian private investigator Lauren Laurano finds out her client has been murdered and begins to fear for her own life as she uncovers more evidence.

young man she begins to date during her junior year of high school. Relying on drinking to cover her feelings of insecurity, Geri is soon hiding bottles in her school locker and in her room at home, but her problem continues unabated until one of her teachers—a recovering alcoholic—convinces the young woman to join Alcoholics Anonymous and come to terms with the problem that threatens to ruin her life.

Long Time between Kisses goes to the heart of being a teen in its examination of one young woman's search for personal identity. Sixteen-year-old Billie lives in New York City, where her divorced—and very unconventional—parents are enmeshed in their own lives. In an effort to find her way, Billie symbolically shears off her long brown hair and dyes the remaining stubble bright purple. While her new look causes a rift between Billie and her boyfriend, she couldn't care less; she's fallen in love with twenty-one-year-old Mitch, who has multiple sclerosis. Billie's compassionate nature begins to surface when she unselfishly helps Mitch cope with his situation by reuniting him with his family and ex-fiance; she also befriends other lonely people in her urban neighborhood. "Wit and humor, and finely drawn characters . . . work together to flesh out this bittersweet identity crisis and first love," maintained reviewer Jorja Davis in *Voice of Youth Advocates*. Ann A. Flowers of *Horn Book* described *Long Time Between Kisses* as a "street-wise novel of New York City [that] presents a hard-boiled—but fundamentally soft-hearted—heroine," and concluded that "the book generates a warm and friendly feeling."

Scoppettone explores the world of crime in 1977's *Some Unknown Person*, a crime novel for adult readers that combines fact with fiction in recounting the life and violent death of twenty-five-year-old Manhattan socialite Starr Faithfull. Popular with readers, the book marked its author's shift from YA writer to crime writer. Although Scoppettone would produce another novel for teens—*Playing Murder*—in 1985, she has found increasing critical and popular success through her detective novels. In addition to those that she has written under the pseudonym Jack Early—including *A Creative Kind of Killer, Razzamatazz,* and *Donato and Daughter*—Scoppettone's books featuring lesbian sleuth Lauren Laurano have gained a large readership. In her 1991 book *Everything You Have Is Mine*, Scoppettone first introduced the savvy, short-of-stature, chocaholic P.I. who has since sleuthed her way through a series of Big Apple-based mysteries. *My Sweet Untraceable You*, the third of Scoppettone's Lauren Laurano stories, prompted *Booklist* reviewer Marie Kuda to call Scoppettone "a highly entertaining writer with her fingers on current political and commercial pulses."

Scoppettone's "Lauren Laurano" mystery novels have been groundbreaking as the first mainstream detective books to feature a lesbian P.I. Equally groundbreaking were her earlier works for younger readers, which were motivated by a desire to help adolescents deal with the kinds of problems that she had to cope with during her own teen years.

■ Works Cited

Davis, Jorja, review of *Long Time between Kisses, Voice of Youth Advocates*, August, 1982, pp. 36-37.
Flowers, Ann A., review of *Long Time between Kisses, Horn Book*, August, 1982, pp. 417-18.
Kuda, Marie, review of *My Sweet Untraceable You, Booklist*, May 15, 1994, p. 1668.
Scoppettone, Sandra, essay in *Speaking for Ourselves*, edited by Donald R. Gallo, National Council of Teachers of English, 1990, pp. 186-87.
Silver, Linda, review of *Happy Endings Are All Alike, School Library Journal*, February, 1979, p. 65.
Sutherland, Zena, review of *Trying Hard to Hear You, Bulletin of the Center for Children's Books*, February, 1975, p. 99.
Sutherland, Zena, review of *Happy Endings Are All Alike, Bulletin of the Center for Children's Books*, January, 1979, p. 86.

Review of *Trying Hard to Hear You, Kirkus Reviews*, October 15, 1974, p. 1110.
Review of *Trying Hard to Hear You, Publishers Weekly*, August 19, 1974, p. 83.

■ For More Information See

BOOKS

Contemporary Literary Criticism, Vol. 26, Gale, 1983.

PERIODICALS

Bulletin of the Center for Children's Books, July, 1982, p. 214.
Kirkus Reviews, May 15, 1985, p. 44; March 15, 1991, pp. 363-64; November 15, 1992, p. 1410.
Lion and the Unicorn, winter, 1979-80, pp. 125-48.
Publishers Weekly, November 10, 1975, p. 47; July 24, 1978, p. 100; June 20, 1987, p. 66; February 22, 1991, p. 213.
School Library Journal, May, 1980, p. 92.
Voice of Youth Advocates, June, 1985, p. 135.

* * *

SELSAM, Millicent E(llis) 1912-1996

OBITUARY NOTICE—See index for *SATA* sketch: Born May 30, 1912, in Brooklyn, NY; died October 12, 1996, in New York, NY. Author and teacher. The writer of scores of science books for young people, Selsam helped many children and teenagers understand how the physical world works. Born and raised in New York City, she developed an interest in nature and science from school field trips. A graduate of Brooklyn College with a bachelor's degree in biology, Selsam earned her master's degree in botany from Columbia University and became a science teacher in New York City public schools. Her first book, *Egg to Chick*, was published in 1946. Though primarily known for her science books, Selsam also published some learning books for teenagers and adults. She started the *I Can Read* series for Harper and in 1977 co-edited the *First Look* series of children's science books. Her other publications include *Microbes at Work, Plants that Heal, The Language of Animals, The Apple and Other Fruits, Animals of the Sea, Sea Monsters of Long Ago, Tyrannosaurus Rex,* and *Night Animals*. Selsam's 1965 book, *Biography of an Atom*, earned her a Thomas A. Edison Award for best juvenile science book. She also received the Nonfiction Award from the Washington Post/Children's Book Guild in 1977 for her body of work.

OBITUARIES AND OTHER SOURCES:

BOOKS

Children's Books and Their Creators, edited by Anita Silvey, Houghton Mifflin, 1995, p. 584.
Something about the Author Autobiography Series, Volume 19, Gale, 1995.

PERIODICALS

New York Times, October 15, 1996, p. B10.
Publishers Weekly, October 28, 1996, p. 34.

Washington Post, October 19, 1996, p. D6.

* * *

SHAHAN, Sherry 1949-

■ Personal

Born August 14, 1949, in Los Angeles, CA; daughter of Frank Webb and Sylvia Brunner Benedict; married Ed Shahan (a rancher); children: Kristina O'Connor, Kyle Beal. *Education:* California Polytechnic State University, B.S.

■ Addresses

Home and office—3280 Hidden Valley Rd., Templeton, CA 93465.

■ Career

Freelance travel journalist and children's book author. *Member:* Society of Children's Book Writers and Illustrators, Professional Photographers of America, Inc., International Food, Wine and Travel Writers Association.

■ Writings

FICTION

One Sister Too Many, Willowisp, 1988.
Wanted: A Date for Mom, Willowisp, 1988.
Fifth-Grade Crush, Willowisp, 1993.
Sixth-Grade Crush, Willowisp, 1993.
Telephone Tag, Bantam Doubleday Dell, 1996.
Wait Until Dark: Seven Scary Sleepover Stories, Bantam Doubleday Dell, 1996.
Love Stories, Willowisp, 1996.

NONFICTION

(And illustrator) *Barnacles Eat with Their Feet: Delicious Facts about the Tide Pool Food Chain,* Millbrook, 1995.
(Illustrator) Cherie Winner, *The Sunflower Family,* Lerner Group, 1996.
(And illustrator) *Dashing through the Snow: The Story of Alaska's Jr. Iditarod,* Millbrook, 1997.

Also author of *There's Something in There.* Has published hundreds of articles and images in national and international periodicals.

■ Sidelights

Sherry Shahan told *SATA:* "As a travel writer and photographer my assignments for international and national magazines have taken me on horseback into Africa's Maasailand, hiking a leech-infested rain forest in Australia, paddling a kayak in Alaska, riding horseback with gauchos in Argentina, and hiking Ayer's Rock in Australia. And those are just the A's.

SHERRY SHAHAN

"While traveling the world with my camera I'm able to gather information for children's books, both fiction and nonfiction. Several years ago I participated in the first annual Iditarod Trail Sled Dog Race Auction, in which non-mushers bid to ride with a musher for the ceremonial start of the famed 1049-mile race.

"While in Anchorage I learned about the Jr. Iditarod Trail Sled Dog Race, an event for mushers between fourteen and seventeen years of age. The result? A forty-eight page photo-essay, *Dashing through the Snow: The Story of Alaska's Jr. Iditarod.*

"This summer I'm hiking Mt. Whitney, the highest mountain in the contiguous United States. Who knows what type of book will come from that experience?"

■ For More Information See

PERIODICALS

School Library Journal, April, 1996.

SHOWERS, Paul C. 1910-

■ Personal

Born April 12, 1910, in Sunnyside, WA; son of Frank L. (a music teacher) and M. Ethelyn (a singer; maiden name, Walker) Showers; married Kay M. Sperry (a psychologist), August 5, 1946 (divorced, 1973); children: Paul Walker, Kate Barger (twins). *Education:* University of Michigan, A.B., 1931; New York University, post-graduate study, 1952-53. *Hobbies and other interests:* Music, social history.

■ Addresses

Home—101 Alma St., Apt. 408, Palo Alto, CA 94301-1049.

■ Career

Detroit Free Press, Detroit, MI, copyreader, 1937-40; *New York Herald Tribune,* New York City, copy desk staff member, 1940-41; *Sunday Mirror,* New York City, writer and copy editor, 1946; *New York Times,* New York City, member of Sunday department, 1946-76, assistant travel editor, 1949-61, copy editor of Sunday magazine, 1961-76; freelance writer, 1976—. *Military service:* U.S. Army, 1942-45; served on staff of *Yank* (army weekly), editor of Okinawa edition; became staff sergeant.

■ Awards, Honors

Science award, New Jersey Institute of Technology, 1961, for *Find Out by Touching, The Listening Walk,* and *In the Night,* 1967, for *How You Talk,* and 1968, for *A Drop of Blood, Before You Were a Baby,* and *Hear Your Heart.*

■ Writings

NONFICTION; "LET'S READ AND FIND OUT" SCIENCE SERIES

Find Out by Touching, illustrated by Robert Galster, Crowell (New York City), 1961.

In the Night, illustrated by Ezra Jack Keats, Crowell, 1961.

The Listening Walk, illustrated by Aliki, Crowell, 1961, new edition, HarperCollins, 1991.

How Many Teeth?, illustrated by Paul Galdone, Crowell, 1962, revised edition illustrated by True Kelley, HarperCollins (New York City), 1991.

Look at Your Eyes, illustrated by Galdone, Crowell, 1962, revised edition, illustrated by Kelley, HarperCollins, 1993.

Follow Your Nose, illustrated by Galdone, Crowell, 1963.

Your Skin and Mine, illustrated by Galdone, Crowell, 1965, revised edition illustrated by Kathleen Kuchera, HarperCollins, 1991.

A Drop of Blood, illustrated by Don Madden, Crowell, 1967, revised edition, 1989.

PAUL C. SHOWERS

How You Talk, illustrated by Galster, Crowell, 1967, revised edition illustrated by Megan Lloyd, HarperCollins, 1992.

(With wife, Kay M. Showers) *Before You Were a Baby,* illustrated by Ingrid Fetz, Crowell, 1968.

Hear Your Heart, illustrated by Joseph Low, Crowell, 1968.

A Baby Starts to Grow, illustrated by Rosalind Fry, Crowell, 1969.

What Happens to a Hamburger?, illustrated by Anne Rockwell, Crowell, 1970, revised edition, Harper (New York City), 1985.

Use Your Brain, illustrated by Rosalind Fry, Crowell, 1971.

Sleep Is for Everyone, illustrated by Wendy Watson, Crowell, 1974.

Where Does the Garbage Go?, illustrated by Loretta Lustig, Crowell, 1974, revised edition, illustrated by Randy Chewning, HarperCollins, 1994.

Me and My Family Tree, illustrated by Don Madden, Crowell, 1978.

No Measles, No Mumps for Me, illustrated by Harriet Barton, Crowell, 1980.

You Can't Make a Move without Your Muscles, illustrated by Barton, Crowell, 1982.

Ears Are for Hearing, illustrated by Holly Keller, Crowell, 1990.

Showers's works have been translated into Spanish, French, Dutch, Portuguese, and Japanese.

NONFICTION

Columbus Day, illustrated by Ed Emberly, Crowell, 1965.

Indian Festivals, illustrated by Lorence Bjorklund, Crowell, 1969.

The Bird and the Stars, illustrated by Mila Lazarevich, Doubleday, 1975.

The Moon Walker, illustrated by Susan Perl, Doubleday, 1975.

A Book of Scary Things, illustrated by Perl, Doubleday, 1977.

OTHER

Fortune Telling for Fun and Popularity, New Home Library (New York City), 1942, published as *Fortune Telling for Fun,* Newcastle (San Bernardino, CA), 1971, and *Fortune Telling for Fun and Profit,* Bell (New York City), 1985.

Contributor of articles and book reviews to *New York Times Book Review;* contributor of humorous verse and short articles to *Life, Judge,* and *Ballyhoo* (national humor magazine).

Showers's manuscripts are included in the Kerlan Collection, University of Minnesota.

■ Adaptations

Many of Showers's "Let's Find Out" books were adapted by Crowell into filmstrips or educational videos.

■ Sidelights

Paul C. Showers worked for many years as a newspaperman—his career in journalism spanned thirty-nine years and encompassed newspapers in Detroit and New York City—before becoming an author of children's nonfiction. It was while he was on staff at the *New York Times* that Showers would first try his hand at writing a book for young readers. The year was 1960 and the American Museum of Natural History was preparing to launch a series of science-related books designed for the early grades. Showers's first title for the "Let's Read and Find Out" series, as it came to be called, was *Find Out by Touching;* the book's success encouraged him to continue writing juvenile nonfiction. Showers has since authored numerous other books on science-related topics in the direct and informal style that has won him praise from critics, teachers, and readers alike.

Graduating from the University of Michigan with the dream of becoming an actor and playwright, Showers found only bit parts and short-term work in "summer stock" theater. Discouraged by the lack of significant roles open to him, as well as by his inability to land a producer for his plays, the practical young man eventually realized that a career change was in order. During his years as an actor, he had supplemented his meager earnings by doing freelance writing for several national humor magazines, one of which was *Life.* In 1932 *Life* attempted to expand its circulation by including a novelty crossword feature, a gigantic "cockeyed" puzzle

that covered an entire two-page spread. Showers recalled his transition to the field of publishing in an autobiographical essay in *Something about the Author Autobiography Series* (*SAAS*): "I had just sold a standard-size puzzle to *Life* when the decision was made to give the readers the biggest puzzle then on the market, and I was offered the job at fifty dollars a puzzle. At a time when T-bone steak was selling for twenty-eight cents a pound, an income of fifty dollars a month held definite potential, and I accepted." Constructing puzzles quickly became Showers's main occupation. "*Life* called its puzzle 'cockeyed' because the definitions were to be outrageously misleading and, whenever possible, funny.... All words had to be in the average reader's vocabulary; none could be used that required a hunt through the dictionary." Filling in the diagram was the easy part: "In a way it was fun. Thinking up the definitions was the dismaying part. Each month I had to rack my brains for suitably cockeyed definitions for a list of between 250 and 300 words. The only one I can now recall was for a four-letter word meaning 'A bender you can take the children on.' The answer was KNEE."

Showers's puzzlemaking career ended in 1936, after *Life* was bought by *Time* magazine. Wishing to remain in the publishing field, he took a job on the copy desk of the *Detroit Free Press* and learned how to edit reporters'

You do not even have to take a walk to hear sounds.
There are sounds everywhere all the time.
All you have to do is keep still and listen to them.

In this updated edition of *The Listening Walk,* Showers invites his readers to experience more fully the many ways in which they benefit from their sense of hearing. (Illustrated by Aliki Brandenberg.)

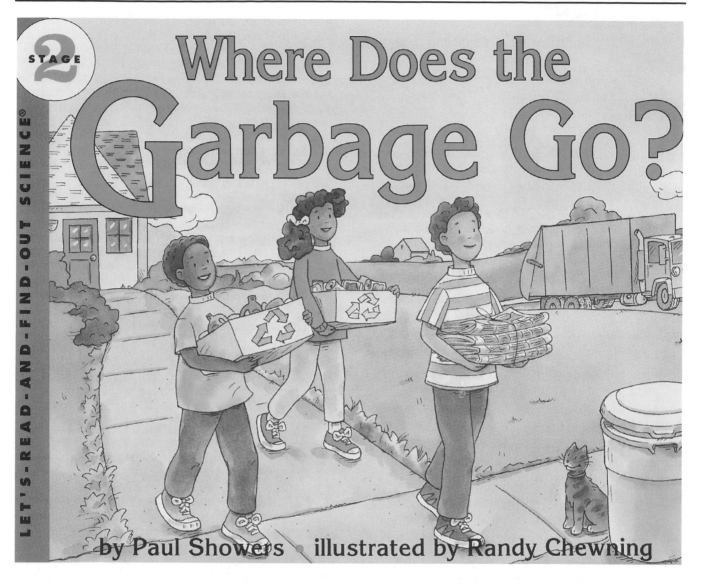

STAGE 2

LET'S-READ-AND-FIND-OUT SCIENCE®

Where Does the Garbage Go?

by Paul Showers · illustrated by Randy Chewning

Primary grade readers are given an explanation of the various methods of trash disposal, along with ideas for becoming part of the solution to waste management in this revised edition of one of Showers's well-received nonfictions. (Illustrated by Randy Chewning.)

written copy and compose headlines. Three years later he left the Midwest and headed to New York City, where a job with the *New York Herald-Tribune* awaited him. After the United States entered World War II, Showers served three years in the Army, returning home in 1945 to get married, raise a family, and work as an editor for the *New York Times.* He would remain at that prestigious newspaper for three decades, finally submitting his resignation on July 4, 1976. The date was not only of significance as the bicentennial anniversary of the signing of the Declaration of Independence; for Showers, it was "a once-in-a-lifetime opportunity to make my personal declaration of independence from the newspaper business to work at my own pace as a freelance writer. That night the occasion was celebrated with a spectacular fireworks display over the Statue of Liberty in New York Harbor!"

Since his *Find Out by Touching* was published in 1961, Showers has made steady contributions to the efforts of

parents and teachers to increase scientific literacy in young children. Through such entertaining books as *How Many Teeth?, Ears Are for Hearing, Follow Your Nose,* and *A Drop of Blood,* he has encouraged children's natural curiosity about the world around them, particularly about how their own body works. *Ears Are for Hearing,* for example, describes the way in which sound waves are translated into signals that the brain can interpret, while *How Many Teeth?* answers youngsters concerns about why their teeth keep falling out. In *The Listening Walk,* first published in 1961 and revised in 1991, Showers frames a discussion of the sense of hearing within the story of a girl and her father going for a walk. 1975's *The Bird and the Stars* uses a folk-rhyme format to introduce children to map reading, while *What Happens to a Hamburger?* explains how the food youngsters eat translates into strong bones, muscles to run fast, and energy enough to play all day. Society's concern with the ecosystem is addressed by Showers in the updated edition of his 1974 book *Where Does the*

Garbage Go? A discussion of how garbage is sent on a path to a recycling plant, an incinerator, or to a local landfill site, the book was praised by *School Library Journal* reviewer Judith V. Lechner as "an enjoyable and useful introduction to the subject."

Each of Showers's "Let's Read and Find Out" titles—first published by Crowell—are based on topics suggested by the series' editorial staff. But once he has been given a topic, Showers has always had the freedom to compose his texts in an original manner, particularly taking into account the reading level of his audience. "I am less interested in writing about science than in putting together books that will appeal to kids who are still learning to read a new language (as kids in kindergarten and the first three grades are doing)," he once explained to *SATA*.

Although they are elementary-level introductions to science, each of the "Let's Read and Find Out" books actually involves a great deal of work for their author. After thoroughly researching the subject at hand, Showers organizes all the information he has gathered in a way that he believes kids can best understand. "When I finally get down to the typewriter, I work out all sorts of sentence sequences, trying to be clear and specific and, when possible, amusing. It takes a lot of tries to work out a simple text that develops a new idea in [everyday] terms ... and also repeats word combinations and groupings to give the struggling reader occasional patches of familiar ground," the author explains. He makes it a special point to include basic words and simple sentence structures; otherwise, the "inevitable [scientific] terminology" might discourage curious-minded young readers. Despite the use of elementary vocabulary and grammar, Showers also tries to present the subject matter with some degree of complexity; although a child might be a beginning-level reader, his questions usually involve more advanced concepts than a primary-grade reading vocabulary can express. For Showers, the task of bridging this gap between language and concept while keeping his texts interesting and engaging has been the greatest challenge in writing juvenile nonfiction.

In addition to the actual nuts and bolts of writing, being an author has its clandestine side as well: "When working on a book, I try, whenever possible, to eavesdrop on the conversation of kids, paying attention to the kinds of sentences they use when talking among themselves," Showers readily admitted to *SATA*. The way four-to-eight year olds talk among themselves was a good measure for Showers in testing the readability of many of his books. "We lived in the suburbs and had a house and a garden with a swing in it," he explained in *SAAS*. "The swing was a magnet for the kindergarten set in our neighborhood, and when I was preparing to write a book, I would spend time on weekends working in the garden and eavesdropping on the swing crowd.... Later, when I sat at my typewriter, I would test each sentence I wrote against my recollection of those conversations. Is this how the kids would have phrased it? If I

were talking to them instead of writing it down, is this the way I would say it?"

While repetition and simple sentence construction help in keeping beginning readers on track, they can often result in boring, simplistic texts, according to Showers. His success as a children's author can partially be explained by his efforts to add a little humor to his writing. "To relieve the monotony of the endless simplicities, I try mixing in jingles and phonic devices of one sort or another and, whenever possible, attempt to make a little joke," he noted.

Showers's success in writing for young readers has been demonstrated by the enduring popularity of many of his titles; whether his subject has been heredity, sleep, digestion, hearing, preventative medicine, sight, or blood and its function, his texts have remained popular with readers, sometimes running through several editions. Critics have been as enthusiastic about the author's nonfiction titles as have readers; in *Booklist* Denise Wilms commends Showers's *Ears Are for Hearing,* calling it "a fine introduction to a common curriculum topic," while *School Library Journal* contributor Denise L. Moll praises the 1989 revision of *A Drop of Blood* as "lively and highly readable, peppered with rhymes that reinforce the text."

Showers's ability to connect with young readers while answering basic questions about science makes his books notable in their field. In sparking the enthusiasm of young children to find out more about the world, he is also reminded of his own "early attempts to get sensible explanations about the world and its mysteries." While he recalled in *SAAS* that "As a small boy, I very soon learned never to expect intelligent answers from the grownups," Showers has made it his business as a children's author to point curious minds in the right direction on the pathway to scientific understanding.

■ Works Cited

Lechner, Judith V., review of *Where Does the Garbage Go?, School Library Journal,* April, 1994, p. 122.

Moll, Denise L., review of *A Drop of Blood, School Library Journal,* February, 1990, p. 85.

Showers, Paul C., essay in *Something about the Author Autobiography Series,* Volume 7, Gale, 1989, pp. 285-98.

Wilms, Denise, review of *Ears Are for Hearing, Booklist,* March 15, 1990, p. 1459.

■ For More Information See

BOOKS

Children's Literature Review, Volume 6, Gale, 1984, pp. 241-49.

PERIODICALS

Booklist, September 1, 1974, p. 47; April 15, 1980, p. 1210; March 15, 1990, p. 1459; May 1, 1991, p. 1723; January 1, 1993, p. 807; March 15, 1994, p. 1369.

Horn Book, February, 1983, p. 83; September, 1990, p. 631.
Kirkus Reviews, November 15, 1970, p. 1253.
New York Times Book Review, November 7, 1965, p. 56.
School Library Journal, April, 1967, p. 64; August, 1985, p. 57; July, 1991, p. 64; August, 1991, p. 162; March, 1992, p. 234.

* * *

SILVERSTEIN, Shel(by) 1932-
(Uncle Shelby)

■ Personal

Born in 1932, in Chicago, IL; divorced; children: one daughter.

■ Career

Cartoonist, songwriter, recording artist, and writer. *Playboy* magazine, Chicago, IL, writer and cartoonist, 1956—. Appeared in film *Who Is Harry Kellerman and Why Is He Saying Those Terrible Things about Me?,* 1971; composer of soundtracks for motion pictures. *Military service:* Served with U.S. forces in Japan and Korea during the 1950s; cartoonist for *Pacific Stars and Stripes.*

■ Awards, Honors

New York Times Notable Book designation, 1974, Michigan Young Readers award, 1981, and George G. Stone award, 1984, all for *Where the Sidewalk Ends;* Best Books, *School Library Journal,* 1981, Buckeye awards, 1983 and 1985, George G. Stone award, 1984, and William Allen White award, 1984, all for *A Light in the Attic;* International Reading Association's Children's Choice award, 1982, for *The Missing Piece Meets the Big O.*

■ Writings

FICTION; SELF-ILLUSTRATED

Uncle Shelby's Story of Lafcadio, the Lion Who Shot Back, Harper, 1963.
The Giving Tree, Harper, 1964.
Uncle Shelby's Giraffe and a Half, Harper, 1964, published as *A Giraffe and a Half,* J. Cape (London), 1988.
Uncle Shelby's Zoo: Don't Bump the Glump!, Simon & Schuster, 1964.
(Under pseudonym Uncle Shelby) *Who Wants a Cheap Rhinoceros?,* Macmillan, 1964, revised edition, 1983.
Where the Sidewalk Ends: Poems and Drawings, Harper, 1974.
The Missing Piece, Harper, 1976.
The Missing Piece Meets the Big O, Harper, 1981.
A Light in the Attic (poems), Harper, 1981.
Falling Up: Poems and Drawings, HarperCollins, 1996.

SHEL SILVERSTEIN

The Giving Tree has been translated into other languages, including Spanish.

FOR ADULTS; SELF-ILLUSTRATED

Now Here's My Plan: A Book of Futilities, foreword by Jean Shepherd, Simon & Schuster, 1960.
Uncle Shelby's ABZ Book: A Primer for Tender Minds (humor), Simon & Schuster, 1961.
A Playboy's Teevee Jeebies (cartoons), Playboy Press (Chicago), 1963.
More Playboy's Teevee Jeebies: Do-It-Yourself Dialogue for the Late Late Show, Playboy Press, 1965.

PLAYS

The Lady or the Tiger Show (one-act; based on the short story by Frank Stockwell), produced in New York City, 1981.
(And director) *Gorilla,* produced in Chicago, 1981.
Wild Life (includes one-acts *I'm Good to My Doggies, Nonstop, Chicken Suit Optional,* and *The Lady or the Tiger Show*), produced in New York City, 1983.
Remember Crazy Zelda?, produced in New York City, 1984.
The Crate, produced in New York City, 1985.

The Happy Hour, produced in New York City, 1985.
One Tennis Shoe, produced in New York City, 1985.
Little Feet, produced in New York City, 1986.
Wash and Dry, produced in New York City, 1986.
(With David Mamet) *Things Change: A Screenplay,*
Grove Press (New York City), 1988.
The Devil and Billy Markham (produced with David
Mamet's *Bobby Gould in Hell* under collective title
Oh, Hell, at Lincoln Center, New York City, 1989),
published in *Oh, Hell: Two One-Act Plays,* S. French
(New York City), 1991.

Contributor to *The Best American Short Plays, 1992-
1993: The Theatre Annual since 1937,* edited by Billy
Aronson, Applause (Diamond Bar, CA), 1993.

RECORDINGS

Dirty Feet, Hollis Music, 1968.
Shel Silverstein: Songs and Stories, Casablanca, 1978.
Where the Sidewalk Ends, Columbia, 1984.

Also recorded *Drain My Brain* and *The Great Conch
Train Robbery.*

OTHER

Different Dances (drawings), Harper, 1979.
(With David Mamet) *Things Change* (screenplay),
Grove Press, 1988.

Contributor to *I Like You, If You Like Me: Poems of
Friendship,* edited by Myra Cohn Livingston, McElderry
Books, 1987, and *Spooky Poems,* collected by Jill
Bennett, illustrated by Mary Rees, Little, Brown, 1989.
Also author of lyrics for popular songs, including "A
Boy Named Sue," "Sylvia's Mother," "Hey Loretta,"
"Boa Constrictor, "The Unicorn," and "I'm My Own
Grandpa." Albums of Silverstein's songs recorded by
other artists include *Freakin' at the Freakers Ball,*
Columbia, 1972; *Sloppy Seconds,* Columbia, 1972; *Dr.
Hook,* Columbia, 1972; and *Bobby Bare Sings Lullabies,
Legends, and Lies: The Songs of Shel Silverstein,* RCA
Victor, 1973.

■ **Adaptations**

Several of Silverstein's books have been recorded on
audiocassette.

■ **Sidelights**

His many creative outlets—as writer, illustrator, playwright, actor, performer, composer of country, pop, and
children's songs, and author of movie soundtracks—
have earned Shel Silverstein the title of "Renaissance
Man": a man of many talents. In a burst of creativity
that has spanned three decades, Silverstein has become
well known for his deftly illustrated poetry collections
Where the Sidewalk Ends and *A Light in the Attic,* as
well as for his popular story *The Giving Tree.* His large
following includes both adults and children: while his
self-illustrated volumes of prose and poetry are frequently relegated to children's literature collections,

many critics have embraced his work as speaking to
readers of all ages.

Born in Chicago, Illinois, in 1932, the young Silverstein
fell sideways into writerdom. "When I was a kid—12,
14, around there—I would much rather have been a
good baseball player or a hit with the girls," he once told
Publishers Weekly's Jean F. Mercier in a rare interview.
"But I couldn't play ball, I couldn't dance. Luckily, the
girls didn't want me; not much I could do about that. So,
I started to draw and to write.... By the time I got to
where I was attracting girls, I was already into work, and
it was more important to me."

In the 1950s Silverstein served with the U.S. armed
forces in Japan and Korea, working during that period
as a cartoonist for *Stars and Stripes,* a Pacific-based U.S.
military publication. Upon his return stateside, he took
a job with *Playboy* as a cartoonist where he has
published several collections of his humorous drawings.
Along with his drawing, Silverstein began writing songs,
which made him well-known in country music circles.
Singer Johnny Cash made a number-one hit out of the
Silverstein-penned "A Boy Named Sue" in 1969, and
Silverstein himself recorded a country music album,
The Great Conch Train Robbery, in 1980.

LITTLE PIG'S TREAT

Said the pig to his pop,
"There's the candy shop.
Oh, please let's go inside.
And I promise I won't
Make a kid of myself
If you give me a people-back ride."

Silverstein's self-illustrated *Falling Up* is a collection of
humorous poems featuring absurd characters and
situations. (Illustrated by the author.)

and

he

would

gather

her

leaves

In his classic self-illustrated fable _The Giving Tree,_ Silverstein tells of a tree which gives everything it has to a boy over the course of his lifetime.

Meanwhile, in 1963, at the suggestion of fellow illustrator Tomi Ungerer, Silverstein wrote and illustrated his first book for young readers: _Uncle Shelby's Story of Lafcadio, the Lion Who Shot Back._ The story of a lion who gets ahold of a hunter's gun, practices until he becomes a crack shot, and then joins a circus where he can exhibit his talent, _Lafcadio_ was praised by a _Publishers Weekly_ reviewer as "a wild, free-wheeling, slangy tale that most children and many parents will enjoy immensely." Silverstein's later works for young people frequently prompted similar responses from critics.

Although _Lafcadio, the Lion Who Shot Back_ was a successful debut for the newly minted children's writer, it was 1964's _The Giving Tree_ that made the name Shel Silverstein well known to children and adults across the country. A simple story that has since attained the status of a childhood classic, _The Giving Tree_ follows a young boy as he grows up. The stages of maturation into adulthood are marked by the boy's relationship with a tree, which gives the boy shade and a branch to swing from when he is young, apples to sell when he is a teenager in need of money, wood for a house when he becomes the head of a family, and a log from which to carve a boat when he wants to escape from the rat race. Finally, with its fruit, branches, and trunk now gone, the

tree continues to serve the boy; now grown to a bent old man, he uses the tree's stump as a place to rest.

The deceptive simplicity of Silverstein's poignant parable has left it open to varied interpretations. While, as Richard R. Lingeman noted in the _New York Times Book Review,_ "many readers saw a religious symbolism in the altruistic tree; ministers preached sermons on _The Giving Tree;_ it was discussed in Sunday School," other critics have maintained that the allegorical tale conceals a more sinister message. "By choosing the female pronoun for the all-giving tree and the male pronoun for the all-taking boy, it is clear that the author did have a prototypical master/slave relationship in mind," critic Barbara A. Schram argued in _Interracial Books for Children._ "How frightening," she later added, "that little boys and girls who read _The Giving Tree_ will encounter this glorification of female selflessness and male selfishness." While critics have remained divided on the true message behind the story—and Silverstein himself has refused to enter into the debate—the book continues to draw fans from each new generation that discovers it.

Equally controversial was _The Missing Piece,_ which Silverstein published in 1976. Together with its sequel, 1981's _The Missing Piece Meets the Big O,_ Silverstein relates the efforts of a partial circle, missing a pie-shaped piece, to search for that part that will make it complete. After the circle finds its missing wedge, it realizes that the process of the search was more enjoyable than reaching its goal; that the missing piece wasn't really necessary after all. In contrast, the wedge's point of view serves as the basis for *The Missing Piece Meets the Big O*. One reading of these books reveals a moral along the lines of "too much togetherness turns people into bores—that creativity is preserved by freedom to explore from one relationship to another," according to critic Anne Roiphe in her *New York Times Book Review* commentary. Roiphe also added, however, that another interpretation could be made: "no one should try to find all the answers, no one should hope to fill all the holes in themselves ... because a person without a search, loose ends, internal conflicts and external goals becomes too smooth to enjoy or know what's going on."

Where The Sidewalk Ends: Poems and Drawings, published in 1974, marked a new direction for Silverstein. Following in the footsteps of such popular writers as Dr. Seuss, Roald Dahl, and limerick-writer Edward Lear, Silverstein infused a generous dose of nonsense into his rhymes, many of which were based on song lyrics. With such gloriously titled verses as "Sarah Canthi Sylvia Stout" (who "would not take the garbage out"), "With His Mouth Full of Food," and "Band-Aids," *Where the Sidewalk Ends* was instantly popular with the younger set. "With creatures from the never-heard, Ickle Me Pickle Me, Tickle Me Too, the Mustn'ts, Hector the Collector, and Sarah Canthi Sylvia Stout ... Silverstein's funny bone seems to function wherever he goes," exclaimed reviewer Kay Winters in *Reading Teacher*. A follow-up collection of poetry, *A Light in the Attic,* would be published in 1981, to the joy of growing numbers of Silverstein devotees.

Following 1981, however, these same Silverstein devotees had to buy theatre tickets in order to keep up with new works by their favorite author. In addition to writing several plays, which have included the 1981 stage hit *The Lady or the Tiger Show,* 1984's *Remember Crazy Zelda?,* and the 1986 stage debut of *Wash and Dry,* Silverstein has collaborated with film director David Mamet on the upbeat play *Oh, Hell!* and a screenplay for the Mamet-directed film *Things Change,* released in 1988.

Finally, in 1996, a new work by Silverstein arrived in bookstores. *Falling Up: Poems and Drawings,* a collection modelled on the author's two earlier poetry works, was met by positive reviews and eager readers. Calling the one-hundred-fifty poems included in *Falling Up* an "inspired assemblage of cautionary tales, verbal hijinks, and thoughtful observations, deftly inserted," a *Kirkus Reviews* critic dubbed Silverstein's latest an irresistible read. Other reviewers have agreed; commenting on the author's interjection of social commentary about such topics as animal rights, morality, and the way some people act just plain weird, Susan Dove Lempke noted in *Booklist* that "It's been a long wait for fans of *A Light in the Attic* ... but it was worth it."

■ Works Cited

Review of *Falling Up: Poems and Drawings, Kirkus Reviews,* May 1, 1996.
Review of *Lafcadio, the Lion Who Shot Back, Publishers Weekly,* October 28, 1963, p. 52.
Lempke, Susan Dove, review of *Falling Up: Poems and Drawings, Booklist,* July, 1996, p. 1824.
Lingeman, Richard R., "The Third Mr. Silverstein," *New York Times Book Review,* April 30, 1978, p. 57.
Mercier, Jean F., "Shel Silverstein," *Publishers Weekly,* February 24, 1975, pp. 50, 52.
Roiphe, Anne, review of *The Missing Piece, New York Times Book Review,* May 2, 1976, p. 28.
Schram, Barbara A., "Misgivings about *The Giving Tree,"* *Interracial Books for Children,* Volume 5, number 5, 1974, pp. 1, 8.
Silverstein, Shel, *Where the Sidewalk Ends: Poems and Drawings,* Harper, 1974.
Winters, Kay, review of *Where the Sidewalk Ends: Poems and Drawings, Reading Teacher,* February, 1976, p. 515.

■ For More Information See

BOOKS

Children's Literature Review, Volume 5, Gale, 1983, pp. 208-13.
Legends in Their Own Time, Prentice-Hall, 1994.
Twentieth-Century Children's Writers, 4th edition, St. James Press, 1995.

PERIODICALS

Horn Book, September-October, 1996, p. 606.
Language Arts, January, 1982, p. 53.
New York Times Book Review, September 9, 1973, p. 8; November 3, 1974, pp. 24-25; October 11, 1981, p. 39; November 15, 1981, pp. 51, 60; March 9, 1986, pp. 36-37; May 19, 1996, p. 29.
People, August 18, 1980.
Publishers Weekly, December 9, 1974, p. 68; September 18, 1981, p. 155; April 29, 1996, p. 73.
School Library Journal, September, 1976, p. 125; April, 1981, p. 143; July, 1996.
Time, December 18, 1989, p. 78.
Time for Kids, May 17, 1996, p. 8.
Times Educational Supplement, November 23, 1984, p. 37.
Voice of Youth Advocates, February, 1982, p. 45.
Wilson Library Bulletin, November, 1987, p. 65.*

* * *

SPOONER, Michael (Tim) 1954-

■ Personal

Born July 2, 1954, in Milwaukee, WI; son of Robert Smith (a teacher) and Marlene (an administrator; maiden name, Wold) Spooner; married Sylvia Read (a teacher), September 10, 1988; children: Nancy, Isaac.

Education: Northern Arizona University, M.A., 1979. *Politics:* Independent. *Religion:* "Secular."

■ Addresses

Home—1241 Eastridge Dr., Logan, UT 84321. *Office*—University Press, Utah State University, Logan, UT 84322-7800. *Electronic mail*—Mspooner @ press.usu.edu (Internet).

■ Career

Worked variously as a jeweler, furniture finisher, and other jobs, 1972-84; National Council of Teachers of English, Urbana, IL, various positions, 1984-88, senior editor, 1988-93; Utah State University Press, Logan, UT, director, 1993—.

■ Writings

A Moon in Your Lunch Box (poetry), illustrated by Ib Ohlsson, Henry Holt, 1993.
(Reteller with Lolita Taylor) *Old Meshikee and the Little Crabs: An Ojibwe Story,* illustrated by John Hart, Henry Holt, 1996.

Also contributor of articles to scholarly books and journals, including *College Composition and Communication, Writing Lab Newsletter, English Education, English Journal, Mississippi Valley Review,* and *Illinois*

MICHAEL SPOONER

Writers Review. Editor of five poetry volumes published by small presses, including *Matrix Nine* and *Matrix Ten: Anthology of Red Herring Poets,* 1984 and 1985, and (with Kathryn Kerr) Debra Thomas's *Handfuls,* 1984.

■ Sidelights

Michael Spooner, who works as a publisher, is also a children's book writer. His first book for children, *A Moon in Your Lunch Box,* is a collection of forty-three poems with seasonal themes. In poems about summer dragonflies and the Fourth of July to poems about winter activities, the changing moon is featured again and again. According to a *Kirkus Reviews* critic, "Spooner has a special ability to evoke imaginative, childlike rumination and delight." The "best pieces" were described by *Booklist*'s Hazel Rochman as "strongly physical in sound and sense."

Old Meshikee and the Little Crabs, which Spooner wrote with Lolita Taylor, is a retelling of an Ojibwe tale. Old Meshikee is a drum-banging, singing turtle. His happy musical celebrations annoy the tiny sand crabs of the Great Lake shores who live across the pond. When turtle plays, the crabs (Shagizenz) cannot hear their own drums. Determined to stop the turtle's disturbing music, they catch him. Yet as the crabs get ready to burn Meshikee and boil him, the clever turtle persuades them instead to "drown" him by putting him into the pond. Of course, the turtle lives; as the crabs are in the middle of a drum ceremony celebrating his death, they hear him drumming! Martha Rosen, in *School Library Journal,* related that the book incorporates "details that are unique to the Ojibwe culture" and includes a source note. "This tale will certainly become a read-aloud favorite," wrote a critic for *Kirkus Reviews. Booklist* reviewer Carolyn Phelan observed that the book "shows the lighter side of Native American folktales."

Spooner explained his childhood, and his career as a writer, to *SATA:* "I was raised in the 1950s and 1960s in Fairbanks, Alaska. When I was ten, my parents purchased an old mining claim on a hill a few miles northeast of town and moved the family out to it. Fairbanks was a small town at that time (still is), and we were beyond the reach of city services. We had a diesel generator to give us electricity most of the time, and an oil stove was our main source of heat. But my daily life as a child included kerosene lamps, an outhouse, guns, snowshoes, chopping wood, and hauling water. We had no neighbors, so when I was not in school, I found myself alone in the woods with the moose and the rabbits much of the time. It was a *Little House in the Big Woods* sort of life.

"My family was devoutly Christian, but church and theology embarrassed me, especially as I grew older. Eventually, I took another path. But the experience of religion did a few things that were good for me. For one, it taught me the sound of English elegantly written—the language of Scripture. For another, it taught me to be

a redfeather book

A Moon in Your
Lunch Box

Poems by Michael Spooner
Illustrations by Ib Ohlsson

The various phases of the moon predominate in the seasonal imagery of Michael Spooner's collection of poems. (Illustrated by Ib Ohlsson.)

aware of the numinous in creation; some might call this a poetic sensibility.

"So there is wilderness in my background, and there is religion. These two things probably account for the melancholy, the wistful, the idealistic, and the mystical stuff in my writing. (In my writing for children, of course, not a lot of this gets past the publisher—they want it to be funny.)

"What accounts for the amusing in my work is the gift of my children. I have two children, and very often I write simply to please them, to amuse them, and to preserve some of the joy of their childhood for them and for me. This playful side shows up in the stories as well as the poems, and I think it's owing to my children's love for the intersection where reality and fantasy meet.

"I never studied under a famous writer, don't even know many, and never patterned my work as a whole after anyone else's. In my writing, I am only myself. (Or one could say I steal from everyone equally, instead of from just a few.) Writing is difficult for me, and slow. Part of this is because I've never had the luxury to be only a writer: I need to have a real job, too. Choosing to have a real job means you have far less time to write, and the time you have is far less regular, than it is for full-time writers. So it becomes a vicious circle: less time

means fewer books, which means a greater need for a real job. I hate that. Does it mean I'm not a real writer? Hmm. Probably. But I do like my job, which is in publishing. I enjoy helping authors bring their work to printed form. I'm eclectic and curious, so I can find much of interest in every book that comes my way.

"The great American poet May Swenson said 'I have never thought of myself as a poet, the way kids do nowadays.' That's how I feel, too. Sometimes I think that if you have to claim to be a poet, you aren't one."

■ Works Cited

Review of *A Moon in Your Lunch Box, Kirkus Reviews,* May 1, 1993, p. 605.
Review of *Old Meshikee and the Little Crabs, Kirkus Reviews,* March 15, 1996.
Phelan, Carolyn, review of *Old Meshikee and the Little Crabs, Booklist,* June 1, 1996, p. 1729.
Rochman, Hazel, review of *A Moon in Your Lunch Box, Booklist,* June, 1993, p. 1850.
Rosen, Martha, review of *Old Meshikee and the Little Crabs, School Library Journal,* June, 1996, p. 118.

■ For More Information See

BOOKS

Speaking of Poets: Vol 2, National Council of Teachers of English, 1994.

PERIODICALS

Bulletin of the Center for Children's Books, July, 1993, p. 358.

*　　*　　*

STEINER, K. Leslie
See DELANY, Samuel R(ay, Jr.)

*　　*　　*

STEWART, Whitney 1959-

■ Personal

Born February 3, 1959, in Boston, MA; daughter of a lawyer and a counselor; married Hans C. Andersson (September 17, 1988); children: Christoph Andersson. *Education:* Brown University, 1983. *Hobbies and other interests:* Traveling, reading, meditation, yoga, running.

■ Career

Children's book writer, freelance editor. *Member:* Society of Children's Book Writers and Illustrators, Writer's Union, PEN authors.

WHITNEY STEWART

▪ Writings

BIOGRAPHIES; FOR CHILDREN

To the Lion Throne: The Story of the Fourteenth Dalai Lama, Snow Lion, 1990.

The 14th Dalai Lama: Spiritual Leader of Tibet, Lerner, 1996.

Edmund Hillary: To Everest and Beyond, Lerner, 1996.

Aung San Suu Kyi: Fearless Voice of Burma, Lerner, 1996.

OTHER

(Editor, with Vicki Lewelling and Paula Conru) *Speaking of Language: An International Guide to Language Service Organizations* (adult linguistics text), Prentice Hall, 1993.

Also author of story "Clockwise Around the Stupa," in *Highlights.*

▪ Work in Progress

Research on the last Manchu empress of China; a middle-school novel that takes place in India.

▪ Sidelights

Whitney Stewart refers to the opportunities she has been given to write her biographies as "miracles." These fortunate events have so far included meeting the Dalai Lama four times, climbing mountains in Nepal with Sir Edmund Hillary (the first person to climb to the summit of Mount Everest), and interviewing Aung San Suu Kyi, leader of Burma's democracy movement. In an interview with Patricia Austin in *Teaching and Learning Literature,* Stewart said about her books, "I have to choose a subject I can live with for a long time. It's hard and it's involving, so I have to pick people who inspire me."

Stewart began writing in high school through a correspondence course offered by the Children's Literature Institute. While attending Brown University a few years later, she met as many authors and editors as she could. Because Brown offered no formal children's literature program, Stewart designed her own independent major and thesis. When a professor suggested that she focus on children's biographies, Stewart recalled the biographies of her youth: "awful—fictionalized and full of made-up conversation." The historical works of Jean Fritz quickly changed her opinion about biographies, though, and Stewart began a correspondence with Fritz which helped launch her own career.

Upon graduating from Brown, Stewart had a desire to travel. From her athletic and rock-climbing interests in college, she had always wanted to go to the Himalayas. After spending a year planning and reading about Tibetan history and philosophy, she made her first trip there in 1986 with her mother. While there, she was greatly inspired by the story of the Dalai Lama and his philosophy and proposed writing a book about him for Snow Lion Publishers. The publisher's acceptance resulted in letters of introduction on her behalf and eventually four interviews with the Tibetan leader.

For her next children's biography, *Edmund Hillary: To Everest and Beyond,* Stewart collaborated with photographer Anne Keiser. Lerner accepted this title, as well as another biography on the Dalai Lama. These two titles became the first in Lerner's *Newsmakers* series. Stewart was impressed by Edmund Hillary, not only for his extraordinary achievements as a mountaineer—with expeditions to the trans-Antarctic in New Zealand, travels up the Ganges River, and a search for the Himalayan yeti—but also for his humanitarian work to help the Sherpa people of the Himalayan region improve their lives and environment.

When Stewart decided to write about a woman for her next book, she bypassed the entertainer-type subjects suggested to her by teachers and librarians, and chose Aung San Suu Kyi, founder of the National League of Democracy in Burma and winner of the 1991 Nobel Peace Prize. The same week Stewart's book proposal was accepted by Lerner, Suu Kyi was released by Burma's military government after spending six years under house arrest.

Using the Internet, Stewart was able in three weeks' time to find Burmese scholars to contact for information on Suu Kyi. However, she soon found that arranging the trip to Burma and an interview with this controversial subject would not be as easy as her trips to Tibet. Since it is a punishable crime to criticize Burmese government, Stewart had to tell Burmese authorities that she was visiting Burma to meditate at Buddhist temples. In the two weeks spent in Burma, Stewart felt as if she were being followed. Her one-page letter to Suu Kyi requesting an interview cost Stewart $70.00 and had to be delivered by courier. The two finally met, but for only thirty-five minutes. When she finished writing the manuscript that would become *Aung San Suu Kyi:*

Fearless Voice of Burma, Stewart became concerned about the accuracy of details in her work and asked three Burmese scholars to read over her manuscript.

Though her interview with the Burma leader was brief, Stewart did get Suu Kyi to agree to answer questions from fourth-grade students in New Orleans about her time spent in house arrest. The children's questions ranged from "Did you cry a lot?" and "How did you get your food?" to "Are you mad at the military government?" Along with the tape recorded reply to the students, Stewart presented a slide show to the class showing pictures of Suu Kyi and the life and culture of the people of Burma.

Stewart told *SATA:* "I hope to introduce children to people and to ideas that can change my readers'

orientation to life. With global understanding comes peace. If I can contribute to that understanding, I am fulfilled."

■ Works Cited

Austin, Patricia, "Whitney Stewart, Biographer," in *Teaching and Learning Literature,* September-October, 1996, pp. 41-48.

■ For More Information See

PERIODICALS

Booklist, December 1, 1990, p. 755.
New Orleans Times-Picayune, January 25, 1996; February 25, 1996; May 12, 1996; May 23, 1996.
School Library Journal, June, 1996, p. 165.

T–U

THOMAS, Frances 1943-

■ Personal

Born October 21, 1943, in Aberdare, South Wales; daughter of David Elwyn (a teacher) and Agnes (a teacher; maiden name, Connor) Thomas; married Richard Rathbone (a university professor), 1965; children: Harriet, Lucy. *Education:* Queen Mary College, London University, B.A. (with honors), 1965. *Politics:* British Labour Party.

■ Addresses

Home—London, England. *Agent*—David Higham Associates, 5-8, Lower John St., London W1R 4HA, England.

■ Career

Writer. Former school teacher; currently teaches dyslexic children at her home.

■ Awards, Honors

Tir Na n-Og Prize, 1981, for *The Blindfold Track,* 1986, for *The Region of the Summer Stars,* and 1992, for *Who Stole a Bloater?;* Whitbread First Novel runner-up award, 1986, and Welsh Arts Council Fiction Prize, 1991, both for *Seeing Things.*

■ Writings

FOR YOUNG PEOPLE

The Blindfold Track (first novel in *Taliesin* trilogy), Macmillan (London), 1980.
Secrets (middle-grade reader), illustrated by L. Acs, Hamish Hamilton (London), 1982.
A Knot of Spells (second novel in *Taliesin* trilogy), Barn Owl Press, 1983.
Dear Comrade (for young adults), Bodley Head, 1983.
Zak (for young adults), Bodley Head, 1984.
The Region of the Summer Stars (third novel in *Taliesin* trilogy), Barn Owl Press, 1985.

Cityscape (for young adults), Heinemann, 1988.
Jam for Tea, Collins Educational, 1989.
The Prince and the Cave, Pont Books/WJEC Welsh History Project, 1991.
Who Stole a Bloater?, Seren Books, 1991.
The Bear and Mr. Bear, illustrated by Ruth Brown, Dutton's Children's Books, 1994, published in England as *Mr. Bear and the Bear,* Andersen Press, 1994.

FOR ADULTS

Seeing Things (novel), Gollancz, 1986.
The Fall of Man (novel), Gollancz, 1989.

FRANCES THOMAS

Christina Rossetti: A Biography, Self Publishing Association, 1992, Virago, 1994.

■ Adaptations

Who Stole a Bloater? was dramatized by Jackanory on BBC television in 1993.

■ Work in Progress

Supposing, a children's book, for Bloomsbury Books; *Pettifor's Angel,* a novel.

■ Sidelights

Welsh author Frances Thomas began her writing career, appropriately enough, with a historical fantasy set in her homeland. Referring to the Celtic epic, *The Mabinogion,* for inspiration, Thomas decided to write about the legend of Taliesin. *The Blindfold Track,* the first of Thomas's three books on the subject, follows the adventures of the boy Gwion, who is abandoned as a child, raised by a prince, and taught by Merlin the magician, eventually becoming the famed bard Taliesin. Margery Fisher of *Growing Point* wrote that in this retelling, Thomas depicts a "modern psychological view of a boy growing up" in a time now veiled in legend. Although *School Librarian* contributor Dennis Hamley felt that the dialogue was too "modern-sounding," *Junior Bookshelf* reviewer R. Baines called Thomas's first tale "a well-written, absorbing and enjoyable book." *The Blindfold Track* won the 1981 Tir Na n-Og Prize, and Thomas followed this success three years later with a sequel, *A Knot of Spells,* which tells how Taliesin leaves his position as the king of Powys's bard to protect the twin children of a queen who is dying in another Welsh kingdom. "The book mingles high politics and archaeology, military exploits and romantic affections," according to Fisher of *Growing Point,* who added that this time the magical elements of Taliesin's story are "subordinated" in favor of concentrating on the characters' relationships. In this complex tale, noted *Junior Bookshelf* contributor D. A. Young, an "enthusiasm for all things Welsh on the part of a reader" is helpful in maintaining interest in the involved storyline.

Thomas, who educates dyslexic children in her home, has also written other books for young readers that feature a present-day setting. *Dear Comrade* follows the written correspondences between Kate Bannister and Paul Miles as they slowly grow to love each other despite their completely opposing political views (he leans to the right, and she to the left). Kate and Paul argue about the law and other political matters, never coming to a consensus (though they do change their views a little), so that the reader must decide for himself who is in the right. Dennis Hamley, writing in *School Librarian,* found the two characters "convincing, funny and moving."

Thomas's next young adult novel is *Zak.* Told from the perspective of a teenager named Mark, *Zak* is about teens who are unhappy with who they are. Mark is bored silly by his life at school and at home, until a new kid named Zak comes to his school. Zak impresses everyone with his stories of living in Los Angeles with his father, whom he insists is a famous rock star. But when Mark visits Zak's home, he realizes the lies behind these stories. The book ends with Zak's disappearance and Mark going back to his original best friend and making amends. Young readers "will sympathise with the boredom and be entertained by Mark's contempt for adults," Margaret Campbell said in *School Librarian.*

In *Cityscape* Thomas demonstrates again her ability to write in different genres: in this case, science fiction/fantasy. Fifteen-year-old Debra Stober discovers on her route to school that an old Jacobean mansion has doors that lead to cities in other worlds. She "travels" to a world in the future ruled by the Guardians, who suppress their people by denying them the right to read books. Debra becomes attracted to Cal, a handsome man who is leading a democratic rebellion that needs Debra's help because she knows how to read and write. By teaching these people to read, Debra gains a new sense of purpose and inner pride that inspires her to accept the dangerous mission of going to the Poison Tower where the Guardians have secreted away all the books. The Guardians are overthrown, but Debra is disillusioned when she later returns to the city to discover that Cal is becoming just as corrupt as the Guardians were. Debra rejects the other world in favor of her home, to which she returns to begin a relationship with a new boyfriend. "Among the proliferation of metaphors for growing up," commented Fisher of *Growing Point,* "the image of alternative cityscapes provides valid insights into teenage personality and problems."

In addition to novels like these, Thomas has written picture books for young children, including *Secrets* and the more recent *The Bear and Mr. Bear. Secrets* is a simple story about "the social need for discretion and self-control," according to *Growing Point* reviewer Margery Fisher. It tells how two boys seek out their own secret when a friend refuses to tell them her's. *The Bear and Mr. Bear* is a sensitive tale about a man who takes pity on a dancing bear that is abused by its trainer. He buys the bear and sets him loose on the grounds of his home. The man, who is called Mr. Bear by the town's children because of his grumpy disposition, empathizes with the sad bear, and man and animal find solace and comfort in each other's company. *School Library Journal* contributor Tom S. Hurlburt deemed the book a "heartfelt, uplifting story."

Having written historical fantasy, realistic young adult novels, fantasy for teens, and picture books for small children, Thomas has proven her diversity as a writer. She told *SATA,* "For the last few years, I have divided my time between writing and teaching dyslexic children, which I do privately at home." Thomas continues to demonstrate her versatility by also writing novels for adults, and, in 1992, publishing her first biography for adults, *Christina Rossetti.*

■ Works Cited

Baines, R., review of *The Blindfold Track, Junior Bookshelf,* August, 1980, p. 201.

Campbell, Margaret, review of *Zak, School Librarian,* March, 1985, p. 63.

Fisher, Margery, review of *The Blindfold Track, Growing Point,* September, 1980, p. 3767.

Fisher, Margery, review of *Secrets, Growing Point,* January, 1983, pp. 4004-05.

Fisher, Margery, review of *A Knot of Spells, Growing Point,* May, 1984, p. 4263.

Fisher, Margery, review of *Cityscape, Growing Point,* January, 1989, pp. 5092-93.

Hamley, Dennis, review of *The Blindfold Track, School Librarian,* June, 1981, p. 157.

Hamley, Dennis, review of *Dear Comrade, School Librarian,* June, 1984, pp. 153-54.

Hurlburt, Tom S., review of *The Bear and Mr. Bear, School Library Journal,* March, 1995, p. 187.

Young, D. A., review of *A Knot of Spells, Junior Bookshelf,* June, 1984, p. 146.

■ For More Information See

PERIODICALS

Booklist, January 15, 1995, pp. 938, 940.

Books for Keeps, November, 1987.

Books for Your Children, spring, 1985, p. 18; summer, 1995, p. 21.

Publishers Weekly, December 12, 1994, p. 62.

Junior Bookshelf, February, 1983, p. 34; February, 1985, pp. 49-50; December, 1988, pp. 297-98; February, 1995, p. 12.

School Librarian, June, 1983, p. 143.

Times Literary Supplement, November 25, 1983.

*   *   *

THOMASSIE, Tynia 1959-

■ Personal

Name pronounced TAHN-ya TOM-assie; born September 1, 1959, in New Orleans, LA; daughter of Clarence Ray Thomassie (in contracting and welding) and Mireya Ponce (a nurse assistant and child care provider); married Michael Schmith, April 3, 1984 (divorced, March, 1987); married Dave Stryker (a jazz guitarist), April 20, 1991; children: Matthew Stryker, William Stryker. *Education:* Louisiana State University, B.A., 1980; attended the American Conservatory Theatre advanced acting program; attended New York University Continuing Education program (film production) and the New School (children's book illustration). *Politics:* Democrat. *Religion:* Unity. *Hobbies and other interests:* Film, theatre, cooking, wreath-making, dry flower arranging, music, gardening.

■ Addresses

Home—West Orange, New Jersey. *Office*— Home Box Office, Inc., 1100 Avenue of the Americas #13-13, New York, NY 10036. *Agent*—Edythea Selman, 14 Washington Place, New York, NY. *E-mail*— TThomassie @ homebox.com; TThomassie @ aol.com.

■ Career

Home Box Office, Inc., New York, NY, manager and program researcher, 1987—. Lecturer on children's book writing. *Member:* Society of Children's Book Writers and Illustrators.

■ Awards, Honors

Notable Trade Book selection, Joint Committee for Social Studies, 1996, for *Feliciana Feydra LeRoux.*

■ Writings

Feliciana Feydra LeRoux: A Cajun Tall Tale, illustrated by Cat Bowman Smith, Little, Brown, 1995.

Mimi's Tutu, illustrated by Jan Spivey Gilchrest, Scholastic, Inc., 1996.

■ Work in Progress

Feliciana Feydra LeRoux Meets D'Loup Garou: A Cajun Tall Tale, illustrated by Cat Bowman Smith, for Little, Brown; *Cajun Through and Through,* for Little, Brown; *Child of the Moon,* "a Chinese mother must give up her daughter for adoption and the moon directs a woman from across the ocean to go to China and adopt the child"; *Richie Brown's Christmas,* "a little boy must redefine the meaning of Christmas after a disappointing year of emotional setbacks"; a middle grade novel.

TYNIA THOMASSIE

■ Sidelights

Tynia Thomassie's first book for children, *Feliciana Feydra LeRoux: A Cajun Tall Tale,* introduces Feliciana, a Cajun girl who lives in a large family. Although her "Grampa Baby" takes this youngest child fishing, treats her, and teaches her to dance, he doesn't allow Feliciana to join her older brothers in the family alligator hunt. Grandpa Baby tells her the hunt is too dangerous for her, and her brothers tease her. Nevertheless, the daring Feliciana decides to sneak out and follow them one night. She confronts a hungry alligator, saves Grampa Baby, and even brings her family an alligator-tail feast. Next time the family goes alligator hunting, Feliciana is assured, she will surely be included. Feliciana tells the family she may not want to go along next time—Grandpa Baby is too much trouble! In addition to the story, Thomassie provides her readers with notes on Cajun history, culture, pronunciation, and vocabulary, and on the current Cajun practice of alligator hunting.

Feliciana Feydra LeRoux, with colorful illustrations by Cat Bowman Smith, won praise from critics. Janice Del Negro of *Booklist* described Feliciana as a "whiz-bang heroine," and a *Publishers Weekly* critic wrote that Thomassie's "balance of comedy and suspense is masterful." According to *School Library Journal* contributor Judy Constantinides in a starred review, the work "captures the joie de vivre of Cajun Louisiana perfectly." Deborah Stevenson of the *Bulletin of the Center for Children's Books* observed that the "lilting text begs to be read aloud," and Lauren Adams in *Horn Book* concluded that listeners, "just like the LeRoux crew, are sure to 'pass a good time.'"

Thomassie told *SATA* that she "never set out to be an author." Instead, she intended to become an actress. "I remember when I was about five, my 'Aunt Lorraine' who was a remarkable clairvoyant, was looking at the lines in my hand. I asked her, 'How many times will I be married?' She said, 'Two.' Then she smiled at me and said, 'You're going to be a really fine writer one day.' I whipped my hand back in horror—even at five—that's not what I *wanted.* But her predictions always hung on my breath—like a strong red onion.

"I attended a school in New Orleans where literature and writing were heavily stressed. We were always encouraged to keep journals, write stories, essays, plays—and I learned to express myself well through the written word. I think because I had no professional aspirations tied to writing (and still don't—even with the sale of my fourth book, I am shocked that someone deems my stories publishable), it has somehow remained 'pure' for me."

Thomassie was twenty-six years old when, as she explained to *SATA,* she "experienced one of those 'crashes' in life where you have to take spiritual inventory and reassess whether your choices have been personally enriching ones. I was in a failed marriage, my aunt and my grandmother—both my guardians since I was fourteen—died in the same year, and I was miserable

pursuing a career that dealt daily rejections on a very personal level. Long story short—I decided to 'follow my joy' and took a class in children's book writing and illustration at the New School in New York City. I realized that no matter how dark and sarcastic I felt about things going on around me, if I was in the children's book section of a store, I became uplifted with hope and the awe of a child."

Thomassie concluded, "The children's books I find most inspiring, and the kind of stories I like to write are ones that empower the child to conquer her/his world. I really enjoy the control I feel as a writer. If I want to put a light switch on the sun and have my characters turn it on and off at will—I can do that. If I want my characters to fly, to have gills, to save the day—I can *let* them. I'm not bound by the constraints of the adult world. How freeing! How wonderful!"

■ Works Cited

Adams, Lauren, review of *Feliciana Feydra LeRoux: A Cajun Tall Tale, Horn Book,* September-October, 1995, p. 592.

Constantinides, Judy, review of *Feliciana Feydra LeRoux: A Cajun Tall Tale, School Library Journal,* April, 1995, p. 118.

Del Negro, Janice, review of *Feliciana Feydra LeRoux: A Cajun Tall Tale, Booklist,* April 1, 1995, p. 1429.

Review of *Feliciana Feydra LeRoux: A Cajun Tall Tale, Publishers Weekly,* May 1, 1995, p. 58.

Stevenson, Deborah, review of *Feliciana Feydra LeRoux: A Cajun Tall Tale, Bulletin of the Center for Children's Books,* May, 1995, p. 324.

* * *

TIVIL, Mr.
See LORKOWSKI, Thomas V(incent)

* * *

TWINEM, Neecy 1958-

■ Personal

Born May 1, 1958, in Kansas City, MO; daughter of J. R. (a medical doctor) and Charlene (a nurse; maiden name, Beverage) Twinem; married Barry Herrero (a restaurant manager), May 23, 1981; children: Tonia Naleen. *Education:* Attended University of Minnesota, 1978; San Francisco Art Institute, B.F.A., 1980.

■ Addresses

Home and office—13 Carolina Dr., New City, NY 10956. *Agent*—Melissa Turk, 9 Babbling Brook Lane, Suffern, NY 10901.

■ Career

Freelance art teacher, 1991—; freelance illustrator, 1992—; children's book author and artist, 1993—. *Exhibitions:* Solo exhibitions include Tappan Library, Tappan, NY, 1991; "Animals Under Siege," Finkelstein Memorial Library, Spring Valley, NY, 1991; "Recent Works," New City Library, New City, NY, 1991; and "Aye-Ayes, Bears, and Condors," Suffern Library, Suffern, NY, 1994. Group exhibitions include Galaxy Gallery, Miami Beach, FL, 1989; Michigan Gallery, Detroit, MI, 1990; "Kaleidoscope," Suffern Town Hall, Suffern, NY, 1991; and "Through Youthful Eyes," Colleen Greco Gallery, Montebello Park Mansion, Suffern, NY, 1992. *Member:* Sierra Club, International Wildlife Conservation Society.

■ Writings

SELF-ILLUSTRATED

Aye-Ayes, Bears, and Condors: An ABC of Endangered Animals and Their Babies, W. H. Freeman, 1994.
The Seasons at My House, American Editions Publishers, 1996.

"ANIMAL CLUES" SERIES; SELF-ILLUSTRATED

Changing Colors, Charlesbridge Publishing, 1996.
High in the Trees, Charlesbridge Publishing, 1996.
In the Air, Charlesbridge Publishing, 1997.
In the Ocean, Charlesbridge Publishing, in press.

ILLUSTRATOR

Jocelyn Little, *World's Strangest Animal Facts,* Sterling Publishing, 1994.
Welcome to Gullah Gullah Island Paper Doll Book, Simon & Schuster, 1996.
Kulling, Monica, *Edgar Badger's Fix-it Day,* Mondo Publishing, 1997.

Also illustrator of puzzles, T-shirts, posters, and greeting cards.

■ Work in Progress

A toddler book series on nature topics; research on science and nature picture books.

■ Sidelights

Neecy Twinem told *SATA:* "It does not come as a surprise to my family and friends that I have focused my career on writing and illustrating children's books. All of my life I have considered children's books as a wonderful expression of thought and imagination. I have always loved toys, animated feature films, cartoons, puppets, and anything created for a childlike imagination. No wonder I have found that I almost feel more comfortable with kids than with adults.

NEECY TWINEM

"Through my childhood and into my adult life, I have extensively collected picture books. Drawn in by their lush pictures, innovative words, and vibrant ideas, I have always thought of children's books as a perfect artistic medium. During high school I started to dream of expressing my art in this form. I loved to paint and to sculpt, but illustrating seemed to be a natural means of expression. I drifted away from illustration as my college education concentrated on a fine arts degree and I discovered other avant-garde methods of visage. Looking back I see how this background gives my work a painterly feel and less of a commercial look.

"I worked for many years in the New York visual display and fashion world while creating my fine art in various forms. It wasn't until I had a child of my own that I started to focus heavily on a children's book career.

"My deep passion for animals and nature became a perfect starting point for my writing as it had been for my painting. I feel very strongly about environmental issues, and children's books are a wonderful education tool. Children also feel passionate about environmental issues and are drawn to animals and nature. I love the research that goes into my writing and my artwork. A tremendous amount of my time is spent doing research on the subjects for my books, but I feel most work is stronger if you write about what you know and love. Hopefully children (and adults) can learn that even in the smallest ways, they *can* make a difference."

■ **For More Information See**

PERIODICALS

Publishers Weekly, March 7, 1994, p. 68; June 24, 1996,
    p. 58.
School Library Journal, October, 1994, p. 116.

*   *   *

UNCLE SHELBY
    See SILVERSTEIN, Shel(by)

V–W

VANSANT, Rhonda Joy Edwards 1950-

■ Personal

Born September 16, 1950, in Fayetteville, NC; married Johnathan Paul Vansant (a professor of medicine); children: Melanie Noel, Joanna Joy. *Education:* University of Georgia, B.S., 1971, M.A., 1972; Peabody College for Teachers, Ed.S, 1975; Vanderbilt University, Ed.D, 1991.

■ Addresses

Home—1419 Waterford Green Drive, Marietta, GA 30068.

■ Career

Elementary school teacher, educational consultant, children's science book author. Sue Reynolds Elementary School, Augusta, GA, second grade teacher, 1972-78; Hornsby Elementary School, Augusta, GA, third grade teacher, 1973-74; Ashland City Elementary School, Ashland City, TN, reading specialist, 1975-77; Reese Road Elementary School, Columbus, GA, taught second and third grades, 1977-83; Clubview Elementary School, Columbus, GA, kindergarten teacher, 1985-88; A. L. Burruss Elementary School, Marietta, GA, taught first grade, 1993-94, kindergarten, 1994-95, first grade, 1995-96. Supervisor of student teachers, 1988-89, supervisor of practicum students in math, science, and social studies, 1989-90, teacher/planner of National Science Foundation videotaped lessons, 1989-90, consultant to Abintra Montessori Preschool, 1989, curriculum developer, 1989-90; Kennesaw State College, Marietta, GA, assistant professor of early childhood and elementary education, 1991-93. Has spoken at numerous professional conferences; conducted workshops for certified teachers and for the community; and served on various educational committees. *Member:* National Association for the Education of Young Children, National Science Teachers Association, Association for Supervision and Curriculum Development, Association for Childhood

RHONDA JOY EDWARDS VANSANT

Education International, Phi Kappa Phi Honor Society, Kappa Delta Pi Honor Society.

■ Awards, Honors

Outstanding Teacher award, Muscogee County School District, 1978-79; Outstanding Professional Promise award, Dept. of Teaching and Learning, Peabody College (Vanderbilt University), 1991; Outstanding New Certified Employee, Marietta City Schools, 1993-94.

■ Writings

WITH CO-AUTHOR BARBARA DONDIEGO, ILLUSTRATED BY CLAIRE KALISH

Cats, Dogs, and Classroom Pets: Science in Art, Song, and Play, TAB Books, 1995.
Moths, Butterflies, Insects and Spiders: Science in Art, Song, and Play, TAB Books, 1995.
Seeds, Flowers, and Trees: Science in Art, Song, and Play, McGraw-Hill, 1996.
Shells, Whales, and Fishtails: Science in Art, Song, and Play, McGraw-Hill, 1996.

Also co-author of an article published in *Reaching through Teaching* (Kennesaw State College Press); music and lyrics for "Lullaby of Love," 1993; contributed a science lesson to *The Giant Encyclopedia of Theme Activities for Children 2 to 5,* Gryphon House, 1993.

■ Work in Progress

Nocturnal Animals and Classroom Nights, co-authored by Barbara Dondiego, illustrated by Claire Kalish, for McGraw-Hill.

■ Sidelights

Rhonda Vansant told *SATA:* "Throughout my years of teaching I have always enjoyed science. I was thrilled to be able to write a series of science books. I love learning about nature and sharing my knowledge with other people.

"I truly hope that this generation of children will come to love and want to care for the earth."

*   *   *

WEINBERG, Lawrence (E.) (Larry Weinberg)

■ Addresses

Home—Woodstock, NY.

■ Career

Author, playwright, and attorney.

■ Writings

FOR CHILDREN

The Forgetful Bears, illustrated by Paula Winter, Scholastic, 1981.
What Is This For?, illustrated by Jody Wheeler, Little Simon, 1982.
The ABCs, illustrated by Jody Wheeler, Little Simon, 1982.
The Forgetfuls Give a Wedding, Scholastic, 1984.

FOR CHILDREN; AS LARRY WEINBERG

The Legend of the Lone Ranger Storybook, Random House, 1981.
Guess a Rhyme: Poems to Complete! Riddles to Solve!, illustrated by Roy McKie, Random House, 1982.
(Author of story) *Phil Mendez's Kissyfur and the Birthday Hugs* (created by Phil Mendez), illustrated by Tom Knowles, Scholastic, 1986.
The Forgetful Bears Meet Mr. Memory, illustrated by Bruce Degen, Scholastic, 1987.
The Forgetful Bears Help Santa, illustrated by Bruce Degen, Scholastic, 1988.
Shivers and Shakes, illustrated by Mia Tavonatti, Troll, 1994.

FOR YOUNG ADULTS

(Adapter) *Tron: The Storybook* (based on the motion picture from Walt Disney Productions), Little Simon, 1982.
(Adapter) *Star Trek III, the Search for Spock: Storybook* (based on the screenplay by Harve Bennett), Little Simon, 1984.

FOR YOUNG ADULTS; AS LARRY WEINBERG

Star Wars: The Making of the Movie, Random House, 1980.
(Adapter) *Dragonslayer: The Storybook Based on the Movie,* Random House, 1981.
Dangerous Run, photographs by Bill Cadge, Bantam, 1982.
Shooting for the Stars, photographs by Bill Cadge, Bantam, 1982.
(Author of novelization) *Father Murphy's Promise,* Random House, 1982.
(Adapter) Mary Shelley, *Frankenstein,* illustrated by Ken Barr, Random House, 1982.
The Hooded Avengers, Bantam, 1983.
The Curse, Bantam, 1984.
The Cry of the Seals, Bantam, 1984.
War Zone, Bantam, 1985.
(Adapter) *Star Wars* (based on screenplay by George Lucas), Random House, 1985.
(Adapter) *The Empire Strikes Back: From the Screen Play by Leigh Brackett and Lawrence Kasdan,* Random House, 1985.
Wicket and the Dandelion Warriors: An Ewok Adventure (based on a story by Bob Carrau), illustrated by Deborah Colvin Borgo, Random House, 1985.
Spoils of Success, illustrated by Tom Tierney, Golden Book, 1986.
How Movies Are Made: Featuring the Films of George Lucas, Random House, 1988.
The Story of Abraham Lincoln: President for the People (biography), illustrated by Tom LaPadula, Dell, 1991.
Ghost Hotel, Troll, 1994.
The Hostage, Grosset & Dunlap, 1994.
Return to Ghost Hotel, Troll, 1996.
The Drummer Boy, Avon, 1996.

■ Sidelights

Lawrence Weinberg's writing for young people comprises several different genres. His works range from picture books for the early elementary years to young adult novels and even to novelizations of movie filmscripts and other books about the movie industry, including examinations of the filmmaking process. His 1980 publication *Star Wars: The Making of the Movie* offers a "mature" format to appeal to older as well as younger readers, according to Judith Goldberger in *Booklist*.

Weinberg's most popular works are his four picture books about the Forgetful Bears, a family of four whose absent-mindedness often lands them in humorous predicaments. *The Forgetful Bears,* the first book in the series, introduces the family as they prepare for a picnic. Unfortunately, the Bears cannot remember anything, not the food, where they live, or even each other. Luckily, Grandpa Forgetful, the only member of the clan able to keep his wits about him, gathers everything and saves the picnic.

In *The Forgetful Bears Meet Mr. Memory,* the family encounters an elephant, Mr. Memory, who attempts—with much frustration—to help them plan a family holiday. As the Forgetful family tries to pack for their vacation, they stumble over everything. Instead of airplane tickets, they bring tickets to a basketball game; instead of luggage bags, the family remembers garbage bags. Even poor Mr. Memory is reduced to tears trying to help the Bears organize their trip. But in the end the gentle elephant finds the lost airplane tickets and makes sure the Forgetfuls arrive at the airport for an unpredictable holiday. Ilene Cooper described the story in *Booklist* as "vastly amusing," adding that "this silliness has all the elements kids adore: mistakes, mishaps, and nonsensical situation," while a critic in *Publishers Weekly* labeled the book "nonstop fun." *School Library Journal* contributor Luann Toth commented that the combined "humorous details ... and nonsensical antics" are "guaranteed to produce storyhour howls."

Weinberg's fourth book in the series, *The Forgetful Bears Help Santa,* begins with Santa getting stuck in the Bears' chimney. Not remembering that it is Christmas Eve, Mr. Forgetful thinks the man in the chimney is a burglar. Eventually, the family rescues the soot covered Santa and insists on washing his sooty red suit before allowing him to return to his Christmas Eve activities. Unfortunately, when the Bears decide to help Santa deliver his Christmas gifts, they forget to bring Santa and all the presents go to the wrong children. "Children are sure to chuckle at the Bears' density," claimed Susan Hepler in a *School Library Journal* review. *Booklist* critic Phillis Wilson observed that the fourth Forgetful book "is a pleasant addition for readers who enjoy slapstick humor."

Also writing for the older reader, Weinberg creates novels, mysteries, and screenplay adaptations of popular movies. The young adult novel *Shooting for the Stars* traces the paths of friends Julia and Nona; although different in temperament, both girls dream of becoming professional performers. When a rock musician and his band come to town, their arrival prompts unexpected events. Attending a party thrown by the rock group, Julia and Nona are confronted with difficult choices, like whether to accept the free alcohol and drugs offered to them. A reviewer in *Kliatt* called the book's conflicts "realistic." In *Voice of Youth Advocates,* Patricia Tomillo observed that the author conveys his message "without didacticism," saying that the book's presentation "will guarantee popularity with YAs."

1982's *Dangerous Run* explores a teenage son's readjustment to his father's return from prison, where he spent seven years for robbery. Throughout the homecoming process, Bruce struggles with feelings of ambivalence for his father, particularly as new issues arise concerning his dad's safety from criminal retribution. Carmen Oyenque remarked in *Voice of Youth Advocates* that the book provides "lots of action," while *School Library Journal* contributor Richard Luzer described the novel as "well-conceived, thoughtfully designed, skillfully executed."

In *The Hooded Avengers,* Weinberg examines racial tension and bigotry through the eyes of a troubled teen. After graduating from high school, protagonist Ben moves away from his small town to live with his cousin Willis, a tough and rowdy young man with a penchant for violent behavior. Through Willis and his criminal-element friends, Ben becomes involved with the Hooded Avengers, a group advocating white supremacy, similar in nature to the Ku Klux Klan. When Ben realizes the murderous intentions of this group, he attempts to warn the authorities and his family, placing his own safety in jeopardy. A reviewer writing in *Kliatt* described the character of Ben as "excellent," further commenting that the book's "quick pace and action will appeal to many readers." A *School Library Journal* contributor observed that "Weinberg has placed realistic characters in a rough setting" to illustrate the speed with which hate can corrupt and lead to violence.

Weinberg chooses the Vietnam era as the setting for his young adult novel *War Zone.* Sixteen-year-old Woody Glover and his family have been feuding with the Griggs family for years. In fact, the Griggs family is suspected of killing Woody's older brother. To avenge his son's death, Woody's father orders him to kill the eldest Griggs son, Del. When Del enlists in the army and is sent to Vietnam, Woody assumes his older brother's identity to enlist also; in Vietnam, Woody intends to carry out his father's wishes. However, amidst jungle warfare and the reality of the war, he soon realizes that death and murder do not solve any problems. Both Woody and Del acknowledge that the hate and conflict plaguing their upbringing have been completely wrong and misguided. Del eventually dies saving Woody's life, and Woody returns home to the hills of Tennessee determined to end the long-lasting feud. After his father disowns him, Woody leaves to begin life anew on his own. Lorelei B. Neal asserted in *Voice of Youth Advo-*

cates that *War Zone* is "first of all an exciting story." *School Library Journal* contributor Richard Luzer maintained that "Weinberg does a fine job" of illustrating how easily a young man can be dissuaded from trusting his instincts. Luzer concluded that the dialogue "rings true," particularly in the army sequences, "with a minimum of profanity."

■ Works Cited

Cooper, Ilene, review of *The Forgetful Bears Meet Mr. Memory, Booklist,* February 1, 1987, p. 846.

Review of *The Forgetful Bears Meet Mr. Memory, Publishers Weekly,* January 23, 1987, p. 68.

Goldberger, Judith, review of *Star Wars: The Making of the Movie, Booklist,* November 15, 1980, p. 464.

Hepler, Susan, review of *The Forgetful Bears Help Santa, School Library Journal,* October, 1988, p. 38.

Review of *The Hooded Avengers, Kliatt,* spring, 1983, pp. 13-14.

Review of *The Hooded Avengers, School Library Journal,* May, 1983, p. 94.

Luzer, Richard, review of *Dangerous Run, School Library Journal,* May, 1982, p. 76.

Luzer, Richard, review of *War Zone, School Library Journal,* November, 1985, p. 102.

Neal, Lorelei B., review of *War Zone, Voice of Youth Advocates,* October, 1985, p. 261.

Oyenque, Carmen, review of *Dangerous Run, Voice of Youth Advocates,* August, 1982, p. 38.

Review of *Shooting for the Stars, Kliatt,* spring, 1982, p. 6.

Tomillo, Patricia, review of *Shooting for the Stars, Voice of Youth Advocates,* August, 1982, p. 38.

Toth, Luann, review of *The Forgetful Bears Meet Mr. Memory, School Library Journal,* April, 1987, p. 91.

Wilson, Phillis, review of *The Forgetful Bears Help Santa, Booklist,* September 15, 1988, p. 168.

■ For More Information See

PERIODICALS

Bulletin of the Center for Children's Books, September, 1984.

Children's Book Watch, July, 1994, p. 6.

Kirkus Reviews, April 15, 1982, p. 488.

School Library Journal, December, 1980, p. 62; May, 1982, p. 58; September, 1982, pp. 130-31; December, 1984, p. 100; December, 1992, p. 59.

Voice of Youth Advocates, October, 1983, p. 209; December, 1984, p. 260.*

*   *   *

WEINBERG, Larry
 See WEINBERG, Lawrence (E.)

WEIS, Margaret (Edith) 1948-
 (Margaret Baldwin)

■ Personal

Born March 16, 1948, in Independence, MO; daughter of George Edward (an engineer) and Frances Irene (Reed) Weis; married Robert William Baldwin, August 22, 1970 (divorced, 1982); married Donald Bayne Stewart Perrin (an author), May 5, 1996; children: (first marriage) David William, Elizabeth Lynn. *Education:* University of Missouri, B.A., 1970. *Politics:* Independent. *Religion:* "No formal."

■ Addresses

Office—P.O. Box 1106, Williams Bay, WI 53191. *Agent*—Jonathon Lazear, Lazear Agency, 430 First Ave. N., Suite 416, Minneapolis, MN 55401. *Electronic mail*—mweis@mag7.com.

■ Career

Author and editor. Herald Publishing House, Independence, MO, advertising director, 1972-81, director of Independence Press trade division, 1981-83; TSR Hobbies, Inc., Lake Geneva, WI, editor of juvenile romances and other special product lines, 1983-86; freelance writer, 1987—. Former president and owner of Mag Force 7, Inc. (producer of trading card games). *Member:* Great Alkali Plainsmen (Kansas City, MO).

MARGARET WEIS

■ Writings

Fortune-Telling (nonfiction), Messner, 1984.

My First Book of Robots (nonfiction), F. Watts, 1984.

My First Book of Computer Graphics (nonfiction), F. Watts, 1984.

The Endless Catacombs (fantasy), illustrated by Jeff Easley, TSR (Lake Geneva, WI), 1984.

(Editor) *The Art of the Dungeons and Dragons Fantasy Game,* TSR, 1985.

(With Janet Pack) *Lost Childhood: Children of World War II* (nonfiction), Messner, 1986.

(Editor with Tracy Hickman) *Leaves from the Inn of the Last Home: The Complete Krynn Source Book,* TSR, 1987.

(Editor with Tracy Hickman) *Love and War,* TSR, 1987.

(With Tracy Hickman) *DragonLance Adventures* (game source book), TSR, 1987.

(Editor) *A Dragon Lovers Treasury of the Fantastic,* Warner, 1994.

(With Tracy Hickman) *The Second Generation,* poetry by Michael Williams, illustrated by Ned Dameron, TSR, 1994.

(Editor and author of introduction) *Fantastic Alice* (short stories loosely based on Lewis Carroll's *Alice's Adventures in Wonderland*), Ace Books, 1995.

(Editor with Tracy Hickman) *The History of Dragon-Lance: Being the Notes, Journals, and Memorabilia of Krynn,* compiled by Maryls Heeszel, TSR, 1995.

(With husband, Don Perrin) *Knights of the Black Earth* (a Mag Force 7 novel), ROC, 1995.

(With Don Perrin) *Doom Brigade* (a DragonLance novel), TSR, 1996.

(With Tracy Hickman) *Star Shield,* Del Rey, 1996.

"DRAGONLANCE CHRONICLES"; WITH TRACY HICKMAN; POETRY BY MICHAEL WILLIAMS

Dragons of Autumn Twilight, illustrated by Denis Beauvais, TSR, 1984.

Dragons of Winter Night, TSR, 1984.

Dragons of Spring Dawning, illustrated by Jeffrey Butler, TSR, 1984.

Dragons of Summer Flame, illustrated by Larry Elmore, TSR, 1995.

"DRAGONLANCE LEGENDS" FANTASY NOVELS; WITH TRACY HICKMAN; POETRY BY MICHAEL WILLIAMS

Time of the Twins, TSR, 1985.

War of the Twins, TSR, 1985.

Test of the Twins, TSR, 1985.

"DARKSWORD TRILOGY"; WITH TRACY HICKMAN; PUBLISHED BY BANTAM

Forging the Darksword, 1988.

Doom of the Darksword, 1988.

Triumph of the Darksword, 1988.

"THE ROSE OF THE PROPHET TRILOGY"; WITH TRACY HICKMAN; PUBLISHED BY BANTAM

The Will of the Wanderer, 1989.

The Paladin of the Night, 1989.

The Prophet of Akran, 1989.

"STAR OF THE GUARDIAN" SCIENCE FICTION SERIES; PUBLISHED BY BANTAM

The Lost King, 1990.

King's Test, 1990.

King's Sacrifice, 1991.

Ghost Legion, 1993.

"DEATH'S GATE CYCLE" FANTASY SERIES; WITH TRACY HICKMAN; PUBLISHED BY BANTAM

Dragon Wing, 1990.

Elven Star, 1990.

Fire Sea, 1990.

Serpent Mage, 1990.

The Hand of Chaos, 1990.

Into the Labyrinth, 1993.

The Seventh Gate, 1994.

NONFICTION; AS MARGARET BALDWIN

The Boy Who Saved the Children (remedial reader for young adults; based on autobiography *Growing up in the Holocaust* by Ben Edelbaum), Messner, 1981.

(With Pat O'Brien) *Wanted! Frank and Jesse James: The Real Story* (young adult biography), Messner, 1981.

Kisses of Death: A Great Escape Story of World War II (remedial reader for young adults), illustrated by Norma Welliver, Messner, 1983.

My First Book: Thanksgiving (juvenile), F. Watts, 1983.

OTHER

Contributor to *The DragonLance Saga* by Roy Thomas (includes adaptations of *Dragons of Autumn Twilight* and *Dragons of Winter Night*), illustrated by Thomas Yeates with Mark Johnson, TSR, 1987. Also author of *Lasers,* F. Watts; author, with Gary Pack, of *Computer Graphics* and *Robots and Robotics,* both F. Watts. Author of graphic novels *A Fable of the Serra Angel,* Acclaim Comics, and (with David Baldwin) *Testament of the Dragon,* Teckno Books.

Creator of trading card games, including *Star of the Guardians* and *Wing Commander.* Weis's books have been translated into many languages, including French, Spanish, Japanese, German, Portuguese, Italian, Russian, Czech, Rumanian, Hebrew, Danish, and Finnish.
MED

■ Adaptations

An audio recording was made of *Elven Star,* Bantam Audio, 1991.

■ Work in Progress

The Soul Forge, for TSR; *Murder at the Exile Cafe,* a mystery set in the "Star of the Guardians" universe; *Robot Blues,* a Mag Force 7 action-adventure science fiction novel with Don Perrin; two anthologies of stories, *Dragons of War* and *Dragons of Chaos;* editing the anthology, *The New Amazons,* for ROC.

■ Sidelights

A prolific and popular author, Margaret Weis is best known as the coauthor, with Tracy Hickman, of the many "DragonLance" fantasy adventures set in the imaginary world of Krynn. She began her career, however, by writing juvenile books, remedial readers, and nonfiction. Weis once commented, "I have always enjoyed writing—mainly, I believe, because I enjoy reading. But I did not seriously consider writing as a vocation during school; I wanted to be an artist. Several incidents caused me to change my mind, and they point out, I believe, how strong an effect good teachers can have on our lives. First, my high school English teacher, D. R. Smith, taught me how to write. Mr. Smith began by tossing out the curriculum intended for high school juniors. (He was forever in trouble with the school administrators. Aside from teaching me to write, the most important thing he taught me was to be my own person and stand up for my ideals.) Our class spent the first semester writing sentences. That's all. Just one sentence every day. We started out with simple sentences—a subject and verb. Then we were allowed to add an adjective. I remember the thrill, weeks later, when we could proudly put in an adverb. After sixteen weeks, Mr. Smith decided we were ready to move on. We wrote paragraphs—five sentences each. We did that for the next sixteen weeks. I came to respect words in his class. I came to realize how critical every word—no matter how insignificant—is in writing. I saw how sentences joined together to form paragraphs. When we read books, in his class, we studied not only the literary content but how the writer created the effect he wanted by use of words and sentence structure. Mr. Smith showed me the door, but it still remained closed.

"I went to college, intending to make art my career. One day, however, my teacher for freshman English—a student teacher; I can't even remember her name—kept me after class, took me to the student union, and asked if I had considered studying writing. She told me about the University of Missouri's English program. (The university was one of the few in the 1960s to offer a creative writing program separate from journalism.) I have often thought this young woman should have been an army recruiter. If she had, I would no doubt have joined on the spot. I investigated the writing program, liked it, and switched my major. She gave me the key to the door.

"Finally, I met Dr. Donald Drummond, poet and professor. He showed me how the key opened the door. I entered and knew that I had come home. We wrote poetry in Dr. Drummond's class. They were grueling class sessions. The poet was required to read his work aloud, while his fellow poets sat, knives out, waiting to draw blood. Classes met at night, often for several hours. We came out battle-scarred, but we could write. Dr. Drummond was another unusual teacher. He began by giving us a long list of subjects we were under no circumstances to write about. These included: Love (with a capital 'L'), truth, beauty, death, and the Vietnam War. 'And,' he growled, 'if I get one poem

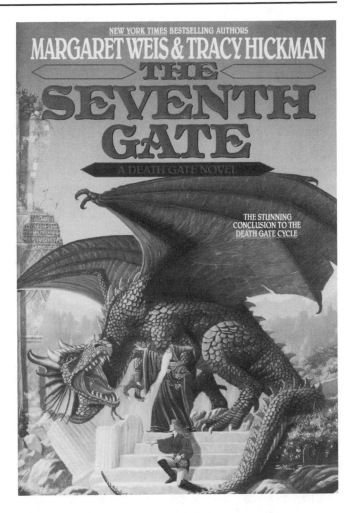

In this fantasy, which Weis co-wrote with Tracy Hickman, the valiant protagonists fear their use of the Seventh Gate will reveal its destructive powers to the forces of evil. (Cover illustration by Stephen Youll.)

about a daffodil you will flunk the semester!' Needless to say, I never have, and I never will, write about a daffodil."

What Weis has done, however, is become an internationally recognized author of fantasy and science fiction. The "DragonLance" books she wrote with Tracy Hickman have become even more popular with spin-off products like art books, trading cards, and role-playing games. In addition to these works, Weis has also written other well-known series, including the "Death's Gate Cycle" fantasy books.

The "Death Gate" books, which Weis also wrote with Hickman, perhaps represent Weis's most complex works. The premise of the series is that two godlike races, the Sartan and the Patryns, have, through mutual enmity, caused the world to divide into four distinctive worlds separated by a magical labyrinth. The first four books in the series, *Dragon Wing, Elven Star, Fire Sea,* and *Serpent Mage,* describe the four different worlds. Evil serpents have come to threaten the existence of all four realms; by the last installment, *The Seventh Gate,* it becomes clear that the only way to defeat this threat is for the Sartan and Patryns to set aside their differences, cooperate, and combine their magic against a common enemy. In his *Booklist* review of the final volume, Roland Green noted that Weis and Hickman have demonstrated "complete mastery of the art of turning classic fantasy elements into equally classic well-told tales." A critic in *Voice of Youth Advocates* added that in the six previous books the coauthors had been "creating unique worlds, characters to believe in, and giving them dire circumstances to work through." With the seventh volume, the critic continued, "the message is what the reader wanted the characters to embrace all along. They all but say, 'there is that of God in all of us.'"

Most commentators and many loyal young readers appreciate Weis's fantasy epics and science fiction adventures; as *Voice of Youth Advocates* contributor Jennifer A. Fakolt noted in her review of *Ghost Legion,* "In much the same way as the Star Wars trilogy did, [Weis] captures our hearts and imaginations."

■ Works Cited

Fakolt, Jennifer A., review of *Ghost Legion, Voice of Youth Advocates,* December, 1993, p. 315.
Green, Roland, review of *The Seventh Gate, Booklist,* August, 1994, p. 2030.
Review of *The Seventh Gate, Voice of Youth Advocates,* February, 1995, p. 352.

■ For More Information See

PERIODICALS

Booklist, September 1, 1990, p. 32; November 1, 1993, p. 505; April 15, 1995, p. 1484.
Kirkus Reviews, January 1, 1993, p. 30; October 1, 1993, p. 1234; June 15, 1994, p. 812; March 15, 1995, p. 530.
Library Journal, February 15, 1993, p. 196; April 15, 1995, p. 119.
Publishers Weekly, October 18, 1993, p. 67; January 17, 1994, p. 420; July 25, 1994, p. 38; April 24, 1995, p. 64; November 6, 1995, p. 88.

*　　*　　*

WEST, Owen
See KOONTZ, Dean R(ay)

*　　*　　*

WOOLDRIDGE, Connie Nordhielm 1950-

■ Personal

Born June 16, 1950, in Asheville, NC; daughter of Berndt Evald (an executive with Coca-Cola) and Naomi (a homemaker; maiden name, Harris) Nordhielm; married Carl Wooldridge (an orthopedic surgeon), July 23, 1977; children: Christina, Scott, Sean, Eric. *Education:* Mount Holyoke College, B.A., 1972; University of Chicago, M.L.S. and M.A. (education), 1977. *Politics:* Republican. *Religion:* Lutheran.

■ Addresses

Home—1831 South B St., Richmond, IN 47374.

■ Career

American Airlines, flight attendant, 1972-73; Seoul Foreign School, Seoul, Korea, first grade teacher, 1973-75; Sieden Prairie Elementary School, Matteson, IL, school librarian, 1977-78; freelance writer, 1978—.

■ Awards, Honors

Blue Ribbon Book designation, *Bulletin of the Center for Children's Books,* and *School Library Journal* Best Books selection, both 1995, and Irma S. and James H. Black Award, Bank Street College of Education, 1996, all for *Wicked Jack.*

■ Writings

Wicked Jack, illustrated by Will Hillenbrand, Holiday House, 1995.
Thank You Very Much, Captain Ericsson, Holiday House, in press.

Contributor to periodicals, including *Cricket* and *Highlights for Children.*

CONNIE NORDHIELM WOOLDRIDGE

■ Work in Progress

Picture-book renditions of two historic events.

■ Sidelights

"There are certain characters who flat out demand to have their stories told," author Connie Nordhielm Wooldridge told *SATA.* "Wicked Jack was one of them." After working as a school teacher and librarian for several years, Wooldridge finally brought this folk character to life. With his roots in the Southern folk tales anthologized by such writers as Richard Chase and Zora Neale Hurston, Wicked Jack became the title character of Wooldridge's first picture book, published in 1995. A contributor to several children's magazines, Wooldridge has since gone on to write and research other stories for young children.

Wooldridge was first introduced to the story of Wicked Jack while she was attending college classes. A black-smith so full of spite that he even teaches the Devil a thing or two, Wicked Jack spends his time finding ways to make other people miserable. He finally gets his comeuppance after he slips up and is accidentally nice to a crippled old man who turns out to be Saint Peter. Jack is granted three wishes; they cause so much trouble that the evil-doer ends up getting kicked out of both Heaven *and* Hell, and Wicked Jack is forced to wander through the swamps for the rest of eternity. "Somebody should write that down," Wooldridge remembered thinking when she first heard this humorous tale. But it would be years later—after she had written several stories for magazines like *Cricket* and *Highlights for Children*—that she began to imagine the voice of the folk character Jack insisting, "Why don't *you* write my story?"

"'Because I'm a good Lutheran,'" Wooldridge would always answer the twangy Southern voice inside her head, "'and I make it a point to avoid characters like you.'" That wasn't the end of it, though. "I'd underestimated his persistence," the author explained. "Every time I came upon a collection of Southern folktales, I'd look to see if Jack was in it. Phrases started to come to mind that would be perfect for this or that part of the story … *if* I wrote it down, which I wouldn't."

The summer of 1989 found Wooldridge and her family on vacation in the beautiful Smoky Mountains of North Carolina. "When we wandered into a tourist shop, I walked straight over to the book section and picked up one of Richard Chase's folktale collections as if I knew it was there." The story of Wicked Jack was featured in the book, and Wooldridge bought the collection "on the spot."

"He was wearing me down—I recognized that—but I wasn't giving in yet. 'I'll give your story words,' I conceded when I got back home, 'but then you're going straight into my file drawer. I'm not … turning you

loose on the world.'" She wrote the first half of *Wicked Jack* in a few hours: "I laughed out loud as I typed," Wooldridge remembers. The second half of the story went less quickly. "Even though it was a made-up folktale, I was uncomfortable with Saint Peter as the sole proprietor of heaven. I made some small changes that left the distinct impression Saint Peter got his list of approved entrants from a Higher Power: someone even Jack didn't dare to argue with." *Wicked Jack* was soon in the mail to its future publisher. "I didn't even consider putting it in the file drawer," the author notes. "I think it would have leaped out if I'd tried."

The day *Wicked Jack* arrived in the mail was a special one for Wooldridge—she finally held in her hands her first published book. "On the day I received the brown package that held the finished copies of my book, I felt a moment of panic before I tore it open," she admits. "What would the illustrator (someone I didn't know and who didn't know Jack) have done to my crusty old friend? When I saw the cover, all I could do was smile. That old coot Jack! When he'd finished bugging me about writing, he must have trucked on over to Ohio and gotten acquainted with his illustrator. I knew from the pictures in the book that his manners had definitely not improved; he had shown [illustrator] Will Hillenbrand his true colors."

Wicked Jack has received much praise from reviewers; Lauralyn Persson noted in *School Library Journal* that *Wicked Jack* is "one of those great spooky-funny books where [readers are] laughing too hard to ever be really scared." And, calling it a "pleasingly tart tale," a *Publishers Weekly* reviewer praised *Wicked Jack* as "intelligent and fun, with a moral thrown in for good measure." A *Kirkus Reviews* critic described Wooldridge's picture book as "stunning," going on to say that she "narrates the story in the voice of a toothless storyteller." Wooldridge has found her first picture book as satisfying as have her readers: "Putting ideas into words can make all sorts of things come out right," she remarked. "Jack got his story told, God was just and in His heaven, and a good Lutheran had made peace with a scoundrel from the swamp. I suppose that's why I'm a writer."

■ Works Cited

Persson, Lauralyn, review of *Wicked Jack, School Library Journal,* December, 1995, p. 101.
Review of *Wicked Jack, Kirkus Reviews,* September 1, 1995, p. 1290.
Review of *Wicked Jack, Publishers Weekly,* October 2, 1995, p. 73.

■ For More Information See

PERIODICALS

Bulletin of the Center for Children's Books, December, 1995, p. 145.
Booklist, November 1, 1995, p. 475.

Y–Z

SARA YAMAKA

YAMAKA, Sara 1978-

■ Personal

Born March 6, 1978, in Columbia, MD; daughter of Matthew Wesley (a retail manager) and Jo Anne (a teacher; maiden name, Belle) Yamaka. *Education:* Peabody Preparatory, Johns Hopkins University, diploma (dance); student at Goucher College. *Hobbies and other interests:* Dance.

■ Career

Writer and waitress, 1995—.

■ Writings

The Gift of Driscoll Lipscomb, illustrated by Joung Un Kim, Simon & Schuster, 1995.

■ Sidelights

Sara Yamaka was only fourteen when she wrote *The Gift of Driscoll Lipscomb;* she had the rare distinction of being a "published author" by the time she graduated from high school. Inspired by Yamaka's own love for young children, the picture book *Driscoll Lipscomb* paints a sensitive portrait of the development of the artistic consciousness of a young child. Befriended by her neighbor, the painter Driscoll Lipscomb, young Molly is given the gift of a pot of paint and a brush each year on her birthday; every year the pot contains a different pigment. The creative Molly—who also narrates the story—receives a pot of bright red paint the day she turns four: a world of red, which includes tomatoes, apples, and roses, emerges from her imagination and comes to life in the wake of her paintbrush. Other colors follow in the coming years—orange, yellow, blue, and green—until her twelfth year, when Molly is given a special gift. "Now you have a rainbow," the painter explains to the girl. "Do with it what you want. Paint your dreams."

Shirley Wilton praised Yamaka's "gentle story" in *School Library Journal,* calling *The Gift of Driscoll Lipscomb* "a poetic story meant to celebrate the ways in which art adds enjoyment to life." And while noting that the moral of the story may be lost on younger readers, *Booklist* reviewer Mary Harris Veeder described the work as "an appealing tale."

While her career aspirations lie outside of the world of children's literature, Yamaka plans to follow the success of her first book. "I hope to find a career in foreign service that allows me to continue to write," the young author told *SATA*. "I must give credit to my extraordinary teachers for encouraging my writing and my parents for unending support."

Works Cited

Veeder, Mary Harris, review of *The Gift of Driscoll Lipscomb, Booklist,* June 1, 1995, p. 1789.
Wilton, Shirley, review of *The Gift of Driscoll Lipscomb, School Library Journal,* August, 1995, p. 131.

For More Information See

PERIODICALS

Kirkus Reviews, May 15, 1995, p. 718.
Publishers Weekly, May 15, 1995, p. 72.

*   *   *

YATES, Philip 1956-

Personal

Born September 6, 1956, in Darby, PA; son of Edward J. (former director of *American Bandstand*) and Teresa Yates; married Maria Beach, June 9, 1996. *Education:* Widener University, B.A. (with honors), 1989; Villanova University, M.A., 1994.

Addresses

Home—1300 South Pleasant Valley #267, Austin, TX 78741.

Career

Villanova University, telecommunications assistant, 1980-85; Widener University, instructional media specialist, 1990-96; stand-up comedian and performer with comedy troupe, the Laugh-A-Roni Institute, 1991-93; teacher of elementary and middle school workshops on writing and performing jokes, 1993—; children's book author, 1993—. *Member:* Society of Children's Book Writers and Illustrators, Authors League.

Awards, Honors

Pennsylvania Council on the Arts Grant for one-act play.

Writings

(With Matt Rissinger) *Great Book of Zany Jokes,* illustrated by Lucy Corvino, Sterling Publishing, 1994.
(With Rissinger) *Biggest Joke Book in the World,* illustrated by Jeff Sinclair, Sterling Publishing, 1995.

PHILIP YATES

(With Rissinger) *World's Silliest Joke Book,* illustrated by Jeff Sinclair, Sterling Publishing, 1997.
(With Rissinger) *Best School Jokes Ever,* Sterling Publishing, in press.

Also author of plays, including *Splitting Image* (radio play), performed in Philadelphia, PA, on Radio Cabaret at Temple University Stage Three, 1988; and *REM,* first produced at Villanova University, 1993.

■ Work in Progress

Hush! T-Rex Is Sleeping!, a book of dinosaur poems and lullabies for children; *There's a Human under My Bed,* a collection of poems for children.

■ Sidelights

Philip Yates told *SATA:* "I stumbled into writing humor books for children quite by accident. My friend (and eventual coauthor) Matt Rissinger and I met in a comedy writing group. Several of us got together once or twice a week to write and perform jokes for each other. Eventually, we stopped performing for each other and hit the comedy club circuit, to mixed success. There was a mixture of comedy types in the group—some of us did straight stand-up, some did song parodies, others did improvisational bits . . . . Matt and I hit it off right away, eventually becoming known as the 'writers' of the group. We started writing and performing in our own sketches. We also took a class taught by Joe Medeiros, Jay Leno's head writer.

"Eventually, our comedy-writing group broke up, but Matt Rissinger and I kept in touch . . . . Since Matt and I were kind of tired of the whole adult comedy performing scene, we tossed around the idea of writing a children's joke cookbook. Lots of food jokes and funny recipes. We had lots of rejections until Sheila Barry at

Sterling Publishing sensed our potential and offered us a contract for a joke book. We wrote over two thousand jokes for the first book, although only about six hundred were really required. Our second book, *Biggest Joke Book in the World,* required us not only to come up with more original jokes, but to collect and rewrite some old ones, giving them a new twist.

"We try to approach each joke as if it's a story with a beginning, middle, and end. That's the impossible goal of joke writing: you have to create a setting, evoke a character, and deliver a socko punch line all in the context of a few sentences. Picture books are great, but with humor sometimes the only picture available is the one the hearers will create in their heads when they hear a joke. Matt and I both love words—love experimenting with words and twisting them inside out until a joke comes squirming into the world.

"Believe it or not, some of our best jokes were written while driving in the car—long distances, of course. Matt always drives while I write the jokes. Sometimes it's very random writing, other times we have specific subjects in mind. You're very relaxed in the car and your mind is free to roam over all kinds of subjects. We once wrote a hundred or so jokes in the car on our way to a book signing at a library. Sometimes we write our jokes separately, then get together and help fix each other's one-liners, riddles, and knock-knocks. We're very honest with each other. You have to be when you write humor for children, because when you end up telling them out loud, you either sink or swim.

"We think it's important for children to learn that words can be the magic ingredient in the joke, especially in their alternative meanings. Like when you hear the word 'order': The judge slams the gavel and shouts, 'Order, order in the court.' Naturally, everyone understands the judge is talking decorum. But when some smart aleck shouts, 'I'll have a cheeseburger with fries,' suddenly 'order' takes on a new meaning. It's so important to select the proper word for best effect. The right word means the difference between laughter and silence.

"Matt and I perform at schools, libraries, bookstores, and once even at a firehouse. We do a forty-five-minute set of knock-knocks, riddles, and other sketches. The highlight is when we ask the kids to come up at the end and deliver their own jokes. This gives us a chance to see what appeals to them. Sometimes we hear new ones, and, when we do, we never hesitate to write them down for inspiration. These shows allow us to keep in touch with what types of humor children today are really into. We also explain to them that jokes, like other books, have to be written and rewritten until they are perfect.

"Victor Borge, I think, once said, 'Laughter is the shortest distance between two people,' and I think he hit the nail on the head."

ZONDERMAN, Jon 1957-

■ Personal

Born February 4, 1957, in Boston, MA; son of Louis (an attorney) and Irene (a bookkeeper; maiden name, Harris) Zonderman; married Laurel Shader (a pediatrician), September 4, 1983; children: Anna, Jacob. *Education:* Trinity College, A.B., 1979; Columbia University, M.S, 1980. *Religion:* Jewish. *Hobbies and other interests:* Community work, golf.

■ Addresses

Home and office—535 Howellton Rd., Orange, CT 06477.

■ Career

Writer and editor, 1981—. Temple Emanuel, Orange, CT, vice-president, 1993-95, president, 1995—; Trinity Class of 1979, president, 1994—; Union of American Hebrew Congregations, Northeast Council director, 1996. *Member:* Amnesty International, National Association of Science Writers, American Medical Writers Association, Society of Professional Journalists, Habitat for Humanity (New Haven director, 1997).

JON ZONDERMAN

■ Awards, Honors

Scharfman Fellowship, Brandeis University, 1994.

■ Writings

NONFICTION; FOR YOUNG PEOPLE

(With Laurel Shader, M.D.) *Drugs and Disease,* Chelsea House, 1987.

(With Shader) *Mononucleosis and Other Infectious Diseases,* Chelsea House, 1989.

(With Shader) *Environmental Diseases,* Twenty-First Century Books, 1993.

(With Shader) *Nutritional Diseases,* Twenty-First Century Books, 1993.

A Colonial Printer, illustrated by Richard Smolinski, Rourke, 1994.

A Whaling Captain, illustrated by Richard Smolinski, Rourke, 1994.

Helen Keller and Annie Sullivan: Working Miracles Together, illustrated by Jerry Harston, Blackbirch, 1994.

NONFICTION; FOR ADULTS

(With Ralph Alterowitz) *New Corporate Ventures: How to Make Them Work,* Wiley, 1988.

Beyond the Crime Lab: The New Science of Investigation, Wiley, 1990.

Has also ghostwritten more than twenty books on business and management topics.

■ Work in Progress

More ghostwriting projects; research on violence as a medical and scientific issue; entries for Web-based medical encyclopedia.

■ Sidelights

Jon Zonderman told *SATA:* "On the first day of graduate school, my writing and reporting instructor asked us all to tell each other what kind of journalistic work we hoped to do after earning our degrees. We had undergraduate majors in social work, engineering, history, English, and a host of other disciplines. I told my classmates I wanted to be a police and courts reporter for a city newspaper. In the second semester I found that I loved science writing, explaining to people 'how things work,' while my colleagues who specialized in urban reporting, political reporting, and the like told people 'what's wrong.'

"After a year of newspaper work and four years of freelance magazine writing, and after meeting four editors at two different publishing companies through my 'ghostwriting' projects for management consultants, I finally got the chance to put my two real writing desires together. I sold an idea to an editor about a book on how science and technology are used to solve crimes. That idea became *Beyond the Crime Lab: The New Science of Investigation.* The book discusses topics from fingerprinting to DNA technology to creating psychological profiles of serial killers. It was fascinating to report and research, and fun to write.

"Although the seven books I've written for young readers, either alone or with my wife, who is a pediatrician, were all fun to do, and although I've written at least twenty other books as a ghostwriter, nothing can match the thrill of seeing your first book published with your name on it.

"I continue to be fascinated by breakthroughs in science and by the increasing knowledge we have about the complexity of human beings. There is still a great debate about whether criminals are made or born, whether they are genetically predestined to criminal behavior or whether their environment is the cause. I hope to add to my library of science/crime books with a book about the scientific and medical research being done in relation to crime, especially violent crime."

■ For More Information See

PERIODICALS

Booklist, July, 1994, p. 1935.

Popular Mechanics, December, 1991, p. 29.

School Library Journal, November, 1989, p. 132; April, 1994, p. 167.